The Strategic Digital
Media Entrepreneur

The Strategic Digital Media Entrepreneur

Penelope Muse Abernathy
JoAnn Sciarrino

WILEY Blackwell

Registered Office(s)
John Wiley & Sons, Inc., 111 River Street, Hoboken, NJ 07030, USA

Editorial Office
101 Station Landing, Medford, MA 02155, USA

For details of our global editorial offices, customer services, and more information about Wiley products visit us at www.wiley.com.

Wiley also publishes its books in a variety of electronic formats and by print-on-demand. Some content that appears in standard print versions of this book may not be available in other formats.

Library of Congress Cataloging-in-Publication Data applied for

Hardback [9781119218036]
Paperback [9781119218043]

Cover image: © JohnDWilliams/iStock/Getty Images Plus
Cover design by Wiley

Set in 10/12pt Warnock by SPi Global, Pondicherry, India
Printed in Singapore by C.O.S. Printers Pte Ltd

10 9 8 7 6 5 4 3 2 1

Contents

Preface

Sometimes innovation comes in an almost blinding flash of creative insight. More often those ideas result from a disciplined, strategic process of exploration and testing. Regardless of how innovation is born, the hard part is transforming that insight into a profitable business proposition. The most innovative and creative minds often fail as entrepreneurs.

The media industry is experiencing what the economist Joseph Schumpeter famously termed "creative destruction." A new technology has rendered business models obsolete that until recently sustained century-old media enterprises—from books and newspapers to television. Customers and investors are moving away from an aging industry, shifting their focus and resources to the new entrants. From the experience of other industries that have weathered "the gales of creative destruction," we know that those who thrive in this new environment will need to adapt quickly.

New business models are beginning to emerge as leaders in both the academy and the industry explore ways to tap into the potential unleashed by this interactive, always-on technology that connects media enterprises with their readers, viewers, and online visitors in revolutionary ways. Colleges and universities have established innovation and entrepreneurial centers that give students hands-on experience with "ideation" and prototyping, and that, maybe—just maybe—will inspire one or more of them to come up with the next Facebook. Leaders of established, century-old media empires commission innovation reports and encourage their employees to "think out of the box" about new ways to connect with current and potential customers. All of this occurs as the pace of change in the industry has increased significantly in recent years and shows no sign of slowing down. Indeed, many prognosticators predict it will increase.

As former executives of media companies, and now as college professors, we have our feet firmly planted in both worlds. Whether we are teaching tomorrow's media leaders or conducting workshops for today's leaders in the industry, we have noticed there are three significant hurdles that both students and professionals face. First, many of them lack the financial and strategic background to assess whether their great idea will be a profitable and sustainable business enterprise. Second, they need a new way of thinking about strategy and business models, a new framework for the digital space. Third, they cannot do it alone; they need to nurture entrepreneurial leadership at all levels and in all functions in their organizations. Therefore, we have designed a book that attempts to address those three missing links.

Acknowledgements

Inspiration for *The Strategic Digital Media Entrepreneur* comes from the many media innovators and entrepreneurs we've met in the profession and the classroom. During a time of immense uncertainty in the industry, they have focused their sights and energies on developing strategies that will allow their enterprises to thrive in the digital age.

A book is always a collaborative effort with many participants, who have generously shared insights and provided feedback that helped us refine concepts and ideas, and then communicate them in multiple venues—in print, in person and through online outlets.

We are indebted to our colleagues in the School of Media and Journalism at the University of North Carolina at Chapel Hill, especially Dean Susan King and UNC Provost James Dean, who have been strong advocates for our research and for the Center for Innovation and Sustainability in Local Media. The Center is funded by generous grants from the Knight Foundation and the University. The mission of the Center is to support both start-up and existing news organizations by researching and developing sustainable business models, as well as innovative digital tools, and then disseminating that information widely. We have received invaluable support from both faculty and staff associated with the Center. We thank senior researcher Erinn Whitaker for her extensive and committed editing and research effort, Lorraine Ahearn for her editing advice, as well as John Prudente and Jill Fontaine for their research assistance. Craig Anderson, Madeline Brown and Pamela Evans provided timely administrative support.

Finally, our thanks to the editors at Wiley Blackwell. We are grateful to acquisitions editor Elizabeth Swayze, who saw the need for a book on this topic and approached us in 2015, and to Executive Editor Haze Humbert and Project Editor Janani Govindankutty and her team, who have seen the idea through to completion.

How to Use This Book

The book is divided into three Parts, each tackling a separate piece of the puzzle. The first section, "Understanding the Basics of Digital Entrepreneurship," authored by Penelope Muse Abernathy, consists of four chapters, and explores how the Internet has changed the business models for media enterprises. It is both a financial and strategic primer. It traces more than 550 years of innovation, identifies the prevailing business models of the past and present, and introduces the idea that successful entrepreneurs (as opposed to innovators and inventors) focus on getting the business model right. It has lessons on how to understand the difference between net income and cash flow, as well as examples of how to place a dollar value and rate of return on a media enterprise. It concludes by analyzing the various ways the Internet has attacked the traditional business models of media companies, and by identifying the strategic challenges and opportunities confronting all media entrepreneurs today.

Part II, "Creating Sustainable Strategies and Business Models," co-authored by JoAnn Sciarrino and Abernathy, develops a new customer-focused strategy roadmap for creating profitable and sustainable digital media business models. In the pre-digital age, successful media enterprises tended to control each of the processes involved in creating, packaging, producing, distributing, and selling their content to consumers. This led to inward-looking business strategies that focused on operational excellence and efficiency. The interconnectivity and immediacy of the Internet not only disrupted the economics of media enterprises, but also relationships with their customers—both their audiences and their advertisers. Strategies for companies in the digital space place the customer as the ultimate driver of profitability. Therefore, this section begins by posing five customer-focused strategic questions, and then establishing a step-by-step process for answering each question. This process provides the tools to define a company's unique value proposition, reach current and potential customers and strengthen relationships with them, utilize partnerships, and prioritize investments in key assets.

The concluding Part, "Leadership in a Time of Change," authored by Abernathy, focuses on the leadership challenges and opportunities facing media entrepreneurs today and in the near future. It concludes by asking readers to consider the possibilities that are yet to be realized around artificial intelligence, augmented reality, and blockchain, to name but a few. Each chapter has timely case studies focusing on media enterprises that are attempting to transform their digital media business models.

Our complementary website for this book, www.cislm.org/digitalentrepreneurs, has an extensive amount of supplemental material, such as instructional videos, essays by media leaders about significant issues they are confronting, and updates on topics covered in the book. In addition, at www.cislm.org/digitalstrategy, we have provided materials

(PowerPoints, study guides) for instructors using this book in either the academy or the profession.

As you may have concluded by now, this is not a classic economics textbook. Nor does it cover the sociological or policy implications of the disruption occurring in the media space. Those subjects require separate texts, and there are several excellent ones already. Rather, this book is about the business of media, so it relies on the language of business, often referring to readers and viewers as "customers," or "consumers of products and services." With apologies to journalists everywhere, we do not intend to diminish in any way the value of your vitally important work, communicating the news and information that feeds democracy at all levels of society. We are simply using business shorthand when we describe your journalism as "content" (undifferentiated from other types of content), or as a "product or service." However, since one of us is a journalist, we would also make the point that if you care about the future of journalism, you should learn everything you can about the business of media.

We hope that the book will be used in its entirety in both the academy and the profession, since we believe, for example, marketing students and journalism practitioners benefit from learning about the finances of media enterprises, just as those specializing in accounting and finance need to understand how putting the customer first contributes to bottom line performance. However, given the scope of this book, we also realize that there may not be enough time in a semester to cover all of the material we included. Therefore, we have envisioned each section as potentially a stand-alone entity that can be incorporated into the curriculum of existing marketing, strategy or journalism courses, as well as entrepreneurial centers.

This book reflects the insights gained from our strategy work with numerous media organizations, as well as what we have learned from our own professional experiences, research and teaching. We hope that what we offer in the following pages will be relevant for both the classroom and the profession, for college professors, as well as for those in the industry hoping to get funding for a new venture or transform their current media operations. We hope it both informs and inspires current and aspiring media entrepreneurs.

About the Companion Websites

This book is accompanied by two companion websites.

www.wiley.com/go/abernathy/StrategicDigitalMediaEntrepreneur

www.cislm.org/digitalstrategy

The Instructor Website (at www.wiley.com) contains:

- PowerPoints
- Lesson Plans
- Study Questions
- Syllabi

The Student and Professional Website (at www.cislm.org) contains:

- Videos and podcasts
- Essay and blogs by digital entrepreneurs
- Updates to the case studies and other relevant material

Part I

Understanding the Basics of Digital Entrepreneurship

In fact, no one can tell whether a given innovation will end up a big business or a modest achievement. But even if the results are modest, the successful innovation aims from the beginning to become the standard setter, to determine the direction of a new technology or new industry, to create the business that is—and remains— ahead of the pack. If an innovation does not aim at leadership from the beginning, it is unlikely to be innovative enough.

(Peter Drucker, "The Discipline of Innovation," *Harvard Business Review*, August 2002)

The Strategic Digital Media Entrepreneur, First Edition. Penelope Muse Abernathy and JoAnn Sciarrino.
© 2019 John Wiley & Sons, Inc. Published 2019 by John Wiley & Sons, Inc.
Companion website: www.wiley.com/go/abernathy/StrategicDigitalMediaEntrepreneur

Part I

Understanding the Concept of Entrepreneurship

1

Gutenberg to Zuckerberg: Innovation and Entrepreneurship

It is 1450 in the medieval town of Mainz in Central Europe. A former blacksmith and engraver is seeking investors for a secret project he refers to simply as "the work of books." Until now, Johannes Gutenberg, the youngest son of aristocrats, has led a rather peripatetic life shuttling among cities along the Rhine River as he seeks to make his own fortune. With money he inherited from his mother's estate, he's invested in a number of commercial ventures, including a plan to manufacture and sell handheld mirrors that are supposed to reflect a "holy light" on pilgrims visiting a 1439 exhibition of Emperor Charlemagne's relics in Aachen. Unfortunately, floods delay the pilgrimage for more than a year. As with many of his ventures, the profit he envisioned never materializes. With his inheritance gone, he has returned to the city where he was born and sets up a workshop in a building owned by a distant cousin.

Far from being discouraged, Gutenberg, who is now in his early fifties, is once again dreaming of striking it rich. Over the past decade, he has acquired a grab bag of skills, including metallurgy, and has invented several new manufacturing processes that he hopes to use in this new venture of printing and selling Bibles. But first, he needs an investor to advance him the funds. A local banker by the name of Johann Fust steps forward, lending Gutenberg 1,600 guilders (which is several hundred thousand euros in today's currency). Fust also introduces him to Peter Schoeffer, who signs on as an apprentice. Using the calligraphy skills he has developed working as a scribe in Paris, Schoeffer begins designing the typeface for the Bible while Gutenberg, the alchemist, attempts to bring all of his inventions together in a sequential printing process.

History recognizes Gutenberg as the inventor of the printing press. In fact, in his workshop, he invents, not one, but four separate products and processes. First, he develops a hand mold that he uses to cast individual letters of the alphabet. Once his moveable letters are cast in metal, they are fitted into a frame, and used to make multiple impressions of the same word onto a page. He then turns his attention to ink and paper, experimenting with formulas, adjusting the viscosity of the ink so that it bonds firmly with the paper, which also must be just the right thickness so it will not be shredded by the metal type. As a final step, he invents a new type of press—one with a screw that can be manually tightened using a wooden handle that compresses the type onto a flatbed surface onto which the image will be imprinted.

It takes several years of experimentation and adjustment to get the printing process just right. All the while, Gutenberg employs more than 20 people in his workshop because producing a quality reproduction of the Bible is a huge undertaking. Setting the 42 lines of type on each of the 1,282 pages requires at least a half day. Gutenberg attempts to cover his day-to-day payroll and operating expenses by printing a variety of other less

The Strategic Digital Media Entrepreneur, First Edition. Penelope Muse Abernathy and JoAnn Sciarrino.
© 2019 John Wiley & Sons, Inc. Published 2019 by John Wiley & Sons, Inc.
Companion website: www.wiley.com/go/abernathy/StrategicDigitalMediaEntrepreneur

prestigious materials, including indulgences, pamphlets, poems, and a Latin grammar book. By 1455, Gutenberg is finally ready to go to market, having produced almost 180 copies of his masterpiece. He tentatively decides to charge the princely sum of 40 guilders for each Bible.

Unfortunately, his investor has grown impatient. Fust sues Gutenberg for 2,000 guilders, claiming that over the past three years he has made no interest payments on the original loan of 1,600.

Gutenberg's apprentice, Schoeffer, testifies for Fust, who prevails in court. In addition to receiving a financial settlement from Gutenberg, Fust is awarded possession of almost all of the Bibles that have been printed, as well as the equipment in the workshop. With proceeds from the sale of the Bibles and using the tools and processes that Gutenberg had invented, Fust and Schoeffer set up their own workshop. In 1457, they become the first printers in Europe to publish a book stamped with their own branded imprint. On his own after Fust's death a decade later, Schoeffer becomes one of Europe's most successful and famous early printers, publishing his own version of the Bible, as well as catalogues and dictionaries that are sold through a far-flung network that stretches across the western half of the continent.

In contrast, Gutenberg's finances are apparently in tatters. In the years after the lawsuit, Gutenberg continues doing some minor print work, maybe even furnishing type for another Bible produced in 1459. He dies around the age of 70 in 1468, unknown outside his small circle of friends and former associates, the significance of his innovations largely unrecognized. He is buried in a churchyard cemetery near Mainz that has since been destroyed, his gravesite lost to posterity.

Gutenberg was the original "disruptive innovator." His inventions and improvements wrenched civilization from the age of the scribe whose works were available only to an elite few into a secular age of mass-produced, widely circulated texts that spawned social, political, and economic revolutions. Today, there are statues of Gutenberg throughout Europe, a university named after him, and a museum dedicated to him and his inventions in his hometown, right across from the imposing, 1,000-year-old Mainz Cathedral, under the spires where he set up his now famous workshop. In 2000, at the dawn of the third millennium, both scholars and journalists for the popular press that his inventions fostered proclaimed Gutenberg as one of the most important figures in the history of mankind.

Yet it was not until 50 years after his death that Gutenberg was finally acknowledged in historical texts as the inventor of typography and modern printing processes. From the vantage point of the twenty-first century, it is instructive to contemplate the supreme ironies of Gutenberg's life and the lessons it holds for today's digital innovators and entrepreneurs. Why were his innovations in printing processes and products—which revolutionized communication—unrecognized during his lifetime? Why did the world's first media innovator fail to capitalize financially on his own transformative inventions and become a successful media entrepreneur?

In this chapter, we will explore the difference between successful innovators and successful entrepreneurs. Among the questions we'll consider are:

- What is a media enterprise and what are the core competencies of economically successful media companies?
- What are the key transformative media innovations? How have business models for media enterprises changed over time in response to those innovations?
- What is the difference between a disruptive innovation and a sustaining innovation?
- What are the key mistakes that Gutenberg made? What are the lessons for today's media entrepreneurs?

Defining a Media Enterprise

Prior to Gutenberg, publishing was a solitary artistic endeavor. A wealthy benefactor would commission a scribe, skilled in the art of calligraphy, to hand-copy a text onto either parchment or paper. Most of the transcription occurred in the monasteries and most of the texts were of an exclusively religious nature. Transcribing a single book typically took at least a year, sometimes as much as two years, depending on the length of the text. Because the scribes were creating a new text by copying from an existing one (which most likely was itself a copy of the original document), they often codified errors that had been made by previous scribes in the new version, or they unintentionally edited in their own errors. Additionally, the quality of the actual reproduction depended on the calligraphy skills of the craftsman doing the transcription. Therefore, most accomplished scribes were considered "artists," and they tended to have only a handful of very wealthy clients who paid for their services.

After Gutenberg, publishing was a commercial endeavor. In contrast to the artist-scribe, a successful publisher needed to understand not only the economics underpinning every phase of producing a book, but also those involved in selling and distributing his products to many customers. Successful publishers began mastering the art and science of marketing, as well as manufacturing. They quickly developed a rudimentary understanding of such modern-day terms as "target market," "pricing sensitivity," and "competitive threat," while simultaneously moving toward a more efficient division of labor on the manufacturing side.

Economics is the study of how individuals and firms make choices, given that we have limited resources, such as time and money, available to us. Economists define a firm, or company, as an enterprise that converts raw materials into products or services, which are then distributed to consumers. Media firms straddle the line between traditional manufacturers of physical products, such as autos, and service providers, such as banks and financial institutions, since they create and distribute *both* products and services. An idea might well remain ephemeral—a momentary thought passing through in our own minds or a joke shared between two people and then forgotten—unless it is transformed (packaged) into a product that is distributed to others.

Media companies provide a service by creating or acquiring content that serves the needs and wants of society—such as information or entertainment. That content may then be packaged with other content to form a product, such as a newspaper, television show, or website. *Therefore, we can define a media enterprise—distinct from other firms—as one that is involved in acquiring or creating content, which is then packaged and distributed to various individuals and groups in society that will consume that content.* In business lingo, we can say that the creation, packaging, and distribution of content are the "*core competencies*" of a media firm.

The type of content produced by media enterprises determines the potential audience, and that, in turn, determines the business model of a specific media industry. Today's media companies produce a wide variety of content that has traditionally been grouped into four broad categories:

- *News,* such as the content in the *New York Times* and on the *NBC Nightly News* broadcast.
- *Information,* including business-to-business providers of proprietary research and analytics, such as Reed Elsevier's Lexis-Nexus for lawyers and Bloomberg's Business Wire for Wall Street traders.
- *Persuasion,* such as Ogilvy and Mather and other advertising and marketing agencies, or the commentary news shows on cable networks such as Fox.
- *Entertainment,* such as Viacom, with its cable channels and Paramount film studios.

Some media companies, such as the New York Times Company, specialize, providing primarily general interest news and information. Others, such as the Walt Disney Company, produce a variety of content that spans the spectrum from news to entertainment to retail. Therefore, Disney has a different business model than the New York Times Company. It also has a distinct model for each of its business divisions, which range from theme parks to movies. More and more, in the digital environment there has been a blurring of the lines between the four distinct categories, as media companies seek to engage audiences who want to interact with the content, both online and in-person, and in a variety of forms, including quizzes and video games as well as theme park rides. In the process, consumers have also become creators of content.

However, many of the underlying economics of today's media enterprises were established during the Gutenberg era when he began to separate the processes involved in publishing a book. Let's briefly consider the economics of each of the three processes—creating, packaging, and distributing content—for two types of publishers, a newspaper and a book publisher. First, a media enterprise needs to either create content or acquire it. A newspaper will hire a journalist to do original research and reporting that are then transformed into an article. Once the article is written, an editor will then package that content together with other articles written by other reporters. The package becomes an "edition" that is distributed to consumers—either physically (by carriers) or via the Internet. Book publishers, on the other hand, tend to acquire content, contracting with a specific author to produce a manuscript, or paying someone for the right to reproduce material that already exists. Once a manuscript is submitted, an editor packages the content into a finished book, which is then distributed through retail outlets—either book stores or online.

Both newspapers and book publishers incur significant costs as they create, package, and distribute content. Historically, consumers have been more willing to pay for certain types of information and entertainment than for general interest news. Book publishers cover their costs of producing content by selling directly to consumers. In contrast, newspapers, which traffic in general interest news, typically sell access to the audience the content attracts. They charge readers only a fraction of the costs associated with producing and distributing the content, and instead rely on revenue from their advertisers to cover the majority of the expenses and also provide them with a profit.

Even though they have two revenue models, both types of publishers need to have a thorough understanding of their audience: How large is the target audience? What is the best method for distributing content to that audience? How much are the consumers of the content willing to pay in order to receive it? Or, conversely, how much will someone else pay to have access to that audience?

This means that successful managers of today's media enterprises—whether commercial ventures or non-profit entities, such as the Public Broadcasting Corporation—must develop an economic mastery of the processes and procedures necessary to produce and distribute a firm's unique content. They must also possess a strategic understanding of how the various processes can be enhanced or disrupted by innovation.

How Innovation Drives the Business Models of Media Companies

Disruptive technological innovation has given rise to three distinct eras in communication: print, electronic, and digital. Over the past 550 years, each technological breakthrough has built on previous innovations and expanded the influence of the media industry and its reach. Each met an existing market demand or created a new one. Each technological breakthrough spawned new business models.

The Print Era (1450–1900)

This era is divided into two periods: pre- and post-1800. Figure 1.1 summarizes some of the main innovations in the print era. The early years of the print era coincided with the Renaissance movement of the fifteenth century, which had started in the city of Florence and created an interest among the educated classes in reading Greek and Roman classics. By 1450, there were a number of innovators across Europe attempting to solve the riddle of printing books on a press in order to meet a new market demand for secular texts that could be produced much more quickly and inexpensively than the manuscripts produced by scribes.

   We don't even know how the first printing press looked since all we have as guides are artists' renderings of wooden presses built in the late 1400s. By 1600, hand-operated wooden presses, very similar to the one we suppose Gutenberg had built 150 years earlier, were ubiquitous throughout the towns in Europe. An estimated 200 million books of varying quality were in circulation. The most expensive included engraved illustrations and maps, using a technique perfected and introduced around 1550. Simultaneously, pamphlets were evolving into newspapers. The first printed newspaper was published in 1605 in Strasbourg and the first English language newspaper in 1622 in London, followed by the first daily in 1702. However, despite incremental refinements in the printing process, books and newspapers published prior to 1800 looked very similar to those published in 1700. Publishing was not a mass medium and was often a side business.

   Innovations of the early nineteenth century—starting with the introduction of the steam-powered rotary press—vastly improved the quality and speed of producing printed material and heralded the arrival of the era of mass communication, as well as the establishment of modern-day media business models.

The Steam-Powered Rotary Press

After the introduction and swift adoption of the steam-powered press with rotary cylinders in the early 1800s, the business models of book publishers and newspaper publishers diverged, and a new media industry—advertising—was born. Prior to the early 1800s, newspaper publishers were limited in the number of copies they could sell by the capacity

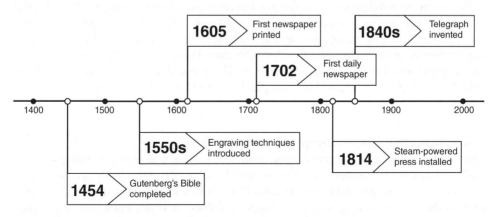

Figure 1.1 Timeline of some major innovations in the print era (1450–1900).

of hand-operated presses, which could only print about 3,600 page impressions a day. Circulation of a typical paper ranged from a few hundred copies to a couple of thousand and was confined to a small geographic area near the printer's shop.

The invention of the steam-powered press, which could print several thousand copies an hour, coincided with the Industrial Revolution and the mass migration of people throughout Europe and North America to cities. Businesses wanted to entice new urban residents to their establishments, and daily newspapers suddenly had the ability to distribute thousands of copies. The Penny Press era was born. Newspapers dropped the price they charged readers from 6 cents to 1 cent and made up the difference by charging businesses to advertise their goods and services. The lower price attracted more readers, which allowed newspapers to increase the price they charged advertisers. This established a new business model for both newspapers and the mass-circulation magazines that came on the scene shortly afterwards. In contrast to the book publishing industry, mass circulation newspapers and magazines increasingly relied on advertisers—not readers—to provide the majority of their revenue. Previously, newspaper publishing was a marginally profitable business, if that. After the introduction of paid advertising, it became a much more profitable enterprise, leading to the rise of the first media barons.

The Division of Labor and Economies of Scale

As publishing evolved into a modern-day business enterprise, a division of labor began to emerge. The steam-operated printing presses required skills very different from those in the past and led to a *division of labor*. Previously, one or two people—perhaps the printer and his apprentice—could write, compose, and then print a four-page weekly paper. The publisher of a multi-page daily paper, printed and distributed daily to thousands of people, could no longer be a master of all trades. He needed more people with specialized skills. He needed people to write and edit stories, set type (perhaps on the linotype machines that were invented in the 1850s), operate the expensive press, and then deliver and sell thousands of printed copies. By 1845, the *New York Herald* had a staff of 12 in the news room and 20 in the composing and press room. Large US and European daily newspapers in the 1850s and 1860s employed as many as one hundred people, and by the end of the century, famous writers and journalists, such as Horace Greeley and Nellie Bly, had become household names. The process of creating and packaging content had evolved into a profession—that of the writer and editor—while that of printing and distributing had become a craft.

The steam-powered presses were much more efficient than the hand-operated type, but they were also much more expensive. However, the more copies that were printed and circulated, the more advertising a newspaper could attract. Therefore, there was a tremendous incentive to grow circulation, and this, in turn, brought down the *marginal cost* of each paper that was produced on the new press. This is called *economies of scale* since fixed costs (the cost of purchasing and operating the press) are spread over more and more copies that are printed and distributed.

New Products (Telegraph, Photography, and the Typewriter)

Three other innovations improved the quality of the content that was being created, packaged, and sold to readers. The invention of the telegraph in the 1840s gave writers an ability to relay news and other information in a timely fashion, and led to the establishment of the first news co-operative, the Associated Press, in which a group of newspapers shared stories and information among themselves, defraying the costs for an individual enterprise. This is also an example of the *network effect*: the more papers that joined the Associated Press, the more stories that were shared, which benefited all the member newspapers in the cooperative.

Beginning in the 1870s, the adoption of the typewriter as the preferred method of writing stories greatly speeded up the process of both creating written prose and transcribing dictated content. The QWERTY typewriter keyboard, named for the first six letters on the top row, was invented and patented by a newspaper publisher, and was designed to prevent the keys on typewriters from jamming. This keyboard is an example of how a standard once accepted endures, even though more efficient alternatives are invented. Economists call this *path dependence*. Once enough industries have adopted a standard, and enough consumers are proficient with a certain way of doing things, we stay the course unless an alternative of vastly superior quality induces us to switch. So, the hundred-year-old QWERTY keyboard was incorporated into the first personal computers and remains a standard in the digital age.

The use of photography in publications began the transition from the print era of unbroken columns of type to the electronic era of images and moving pictures. It also created yet another journalism profession, that of the photojournalist. Engraved illustrations were the only artwork printed in books, newspapers and magazines prior to the 1850s. By the 1860s, rudimentary hand-engraving processes—some involving wood, others involving copper—allowed for the reproductions of art prints and the Civil War photos Matthew Brady in fine books and magazines (such as *Harper's Weekly*). The first halftone image (in which a photo is converted into dots of varying size) was published in a newspaper in 1873, and by the 1880s, photography was in widespread use in papers and magazines, bringing a you-are-there realism that was previously missing.

You did not have to be literate to appreciate a photograph. But perhaps more importantly, refinement and improvements in both cameras and film throughout the nineteenth century led directly to the introduction of moving pictures, which are really a series of still photos that appear to be moving when shown in rapid sequence on a screen. While reading was oftentimes a solitary endeavor, the consumption of motion pictures—and later radio and television shows—could be a communal one, enjoyed by many people simultaneously.

By the end of the nineteenth century, there were two established and distinct business models for media enterprises. Book publishers, and later motion picture producers, sold their content directly to consumers, while newspapers and magazines relied on advertisers to provide the majority of their revenue. A number of economic concepts that underpin today's digital enterprises had also begun to emerge, including economies of scale, the network effect, and path dependence.

The Electronic Era (1900–1990)

The technological innovations of the print era—especially the telegraph, telephone, and photography—laid the groundwork for the electronic era, which is divided into two periods, marked by the rise of radio and then television. Figure 1.2 summarizes the major innovations of the electronic era. The first AM radio stations of the early twentieth century ushered in a new era in mass communication, as they transmitted audio signals through the air as radio waves, which were received by thousands of antennas and then routed to thousands of individual radio sets. This new era coincided with a number of technological breakthroughs, such as the installation of electricity in most homes in the United States and Europe, leading to a quick adoption of this new medium. This

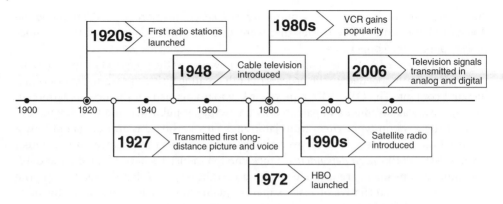

Figure 1.2 Timeline of some major innovations in the electronic era (1920–2006).

expansion of media enterprises into the broadcasting arena also led to the creation of totally new media enterprises which were regulated by the government and the creation of a variety of new business models.

The Broadcast Model

First with radio, and then with television, which was developed in the 1930s and 1940s, a networked system evolved. This system tied together multiple stations, which were required to have a government license to broadcast their signal across a region. In the UK. the British Broadcasting Company (BBC), founded in the 1920s and funded primarily by a fee charged to all households in the country, became the first non-profit, government-supported broadcasting organization. This model was adopted and is still prevalent in many countries today. In the United States, where a listener or viewer of a broadcast program could receive the over-the-air signal of a broadcasting network without paying any fee for the privilege, a for-profit model prevails. Even from its earliest day, the potential audience for radio and television shows was many times larger than that of the largest newspapers of the day. Therefore, early for-profit radio networks in the United States (such as CBS and NBC), and the for-profit television networks that succeeded them, relied solely on the revenue they received from advertisers who wanted to reach a large audience in a certain region.

The Cable Model

The wired cable companies that arose in the United States in the 1950s and the 1960s developed yet a different business model, charging a monthly fee to customers who signed up for their services. They justified this charge because their large antennas could receive broadcast signals from multiple stations across a wide geographic area—signals that were often too weak to be received by the smaller rooftop antennas perched on houses. Initially, most households that subscribed to a cable service could only receive two or three network channels. That began to change in the 1970s, when Time-Life launched Home Box Office (HBO), the first subscription-based television channel. The HBO signal was delivered via satellite transmission to cable operators throughout the country, who then retransmitted the programming to customers who paid an additional monthly surcharge. Simultaneously, Ted Turner, the owner of an outdoor advertising company in Atlanta, purchased a small, struggling, local ultra-high frequency (UHF) station, and also began delivering that station's signal to remote cable operators via satellite.

Other Business Models

Primetime television viewing peaked in the 1980s, a decade that witnessed the introduction of video cassette recorders (VCRs), video games (Pong), and the first cellular telephones, as well as the rollout of several new cable-only channels, including CNN, the first all-news station. These new channels, which were aimed at smaller, niche audiences, established another business model, relying on revenue from both advertisers, as well as from the cable operators, which paid a fee to the station owners to carry their programming. VCRs and video gaming introduced yet another business model, in which consumers paid twice—for the machine and then for the individual games or tapes.

The 1990s saw a continued ramping up of ancillary products and services, including the introduction of satellite radio (SiriusXM) and television (DISH and DIRECTV) providers, the swift adoption of the DVD player (and demise of the VCR) and the launch of TiVo (interactive TV services).

By the end of the century, two dominant economic models had emerged around the two largest electronic media segments—the networks and the cable providers. The original broadcast networks continued to rely overwhelmingly on revenue from advertisers who wanted to reach a mass audience. This made their business model vulnerable as new cable channels, and later the Internet, siphoned off customers. In contrast, the cable operators relied on revenue from consumers, and this put them on a collision course in the twenty-first century with digital services, such as Netflix and Amazon that also charge consumers a monthly fee for the privilege of streaming or downloading content. The number of cable subscribers in the United States peaked in 2012, while the number of consumers streaming content continues to grow.

The Digital Era (1990 to present)

The adoption and rapid spread of digital technology are often referred to as the Third Industrial Revolution—the first occurring in the early 1800s with the invention of steam-powered engines, and the second occurring at the turn of the twentieth century as mechanized manufacturing took hold. Like the electronic and print eras, the digital revolution in media occurred in stages, only this time it occurred over a much shorter timeframe. There are three main inflexion points that greatly influenced the speed with which this new technology was adopted. Figure 1.3 summarizes the major innovations in the digital era.

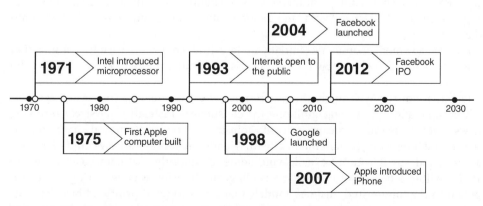

Figure 1.3 Timeline of some major innovations in the digital era (1970–2012).

The Chip

The first point occurred in the mid-1970s with the development of the microprocessor—or rather the chip that sits in our personal computers, smartphones and tablets, and serves as the brains of these mini-computers. The microprocessor was born out of an idea articulated by Gordon Moore in the mid-1960s. Moore observed that historically, the number of transistors on a circuit board had doubled every two years or so, due to advances in computer technology. He hypothesized that this growth could continue exponentially for some time into the future. Known as Moore's Law, this insight led him to found a company called Intel shortly afterwards. At the time, all computers at individual workstations were "dumb" terminals tethered to a large mainframe.

In 1971, Intel introduced its first microprocessor designed for use in a calculator the size of an index card. Throughout the 1970s, more and more applications were added. By the 1980s, the majority of computers being manufactured had the Intel chip. Even as the cost of manufacturing computing chips dropped dramatically, the capacity of the chips continued to increase exponentially. This led to rapid adoption of personal computers in the workplace throughout the 1980s. During the 1990s, the PC took up residence in our homes. By 2000, half of households in the United States had a PC; by 2010, 70 percent of homes had a personal computer.

Web 1.0

A second inflexion point occurred in the 1990s when the Internet was opened to commercial use, and communication suddenly became interactive, real-time, and global, at least for those who had access to a computer at either work or home. In only 20 years, the World Wide Web evolved from a network of computers called ARPANET (Advanced Research Projects Agency Network) set up in 1969 so mainframes at several West Coast universities could "talk" to one another, into a system of protocols and linkages to hypertext documents that could be accessed through client servers from anywhere around the world.

In 1993, it became official, with an announcement from CERN, the Swiss institute where computer scientist Tim Berners-Lee worked while implementing his design for the World Wide Web: the Internet could now be used by developers, as well as the public, for free. This effectively meant the Internet was open for business, as easy-to-use browsers and commercial Internet service providers rapidly became available. Suddenly personal computers could be used for a lot more than office tasks. You could email friends and family, purchase items online and search for documents and information stored in remote sites. Portals (such as AOL), commerce sites (including eBay and Amazon), and search engines (such as Magellan, Lycos, and Yahoo!) enticed more and more consumers onto the Web.

Most legacy media companies initially underestimated what a disruptive innovation this was. They tended to view the Internet as yet another system for distributing the content that they were already producing to consumers. They failed to realize that the interactivity of the Web made it a much more effective medium for certain types of advertising, and a more engaging one for consumers. Instead of passively receiving news and information, consumers could join in the conversation and share content they found interesting instantaneously with friends and family, or they could search for an item and buy it without ever leaving home. Despite the dot-com bust of the late 1990s, within a decade of its public unveiling, the Internet was delivering a one-two punch to the time-tested business models that had sustained print and broadcast, as well as news and entertainment enterprises. The newspaper industry watched helplessly as its most profitable business segment—help-wanted and real estate classified advertising—moved quickly to online sites, such as Monster and Zillow. As sales of books migrated online, Amazon became the thousand-pound e-commerce "gorilla" that could affect the profitability of book publishers and retailers. The piracy and sharing of copyrighted content online eroded sales of CDs and DVDs throughout the first decade of the twenty-first century.

Web 2.0

The third inflexion point is occurring now, with the rapid adoption of the smartphone and the dawn of the age of mobility. In 2016, more than two-thirds of the population in the United States owned smartphones, compared with less than a third five years before. The percentage was even higher among younger age groups, with more than 85 percent of those under age 30 owning one. The world's two largest markets are quickly catching up. By 2020, more than two-thirds of the residents in China and almost 60 percent of the population of India are forecast to have mobile phones.

With a smartphone in the back pocket or purse, a consumer today is always on and always texting, emailing, searching, shopping, or connecting with friends. Even though legacy media enterprises can distribute their content via the Web to more people today than ever before, their audience pales in comparison to the digital giants that have emerged in recent years. Google processes more than three billion searches a day, more than a trillion each year, with more than half coming from mobile devices. Facebook has more than two billion users, most logging on through their phones. Alibaba, the large Chinese e-commerce site, already accounts for more than 10 percent of all retail sales in that country, most being done by phone.

Not only do these digital giants reach more people than legacy media, they do it more effectively since their digital platforms allow for direct interaction with consumers and targeted messaging aimed at specific segments of a mass audience. Therefore, advertising revenue has followed consumers, moving rapidly away from traditional media. Newspaper advertising revenue in the United States has fallen below 1950 levels, and continues to decline. Television revenue is projected to decline from 40 percent of total ad spending in 2014 to less than a third by 2020. Digital advertising will rise from 28–45 percent during the same period. In 2016, mobile advertising worldwide topped one hundred billion dollars and accounted for 50 percent of all digital advertising spending. Three-fourths of the eight billion dollars in revenue that Facebook made in 2016 came from mobile advertising.

Increasingly, it is becoming a war on two fronts for legacy media companies, as the digital behemoths evolve and become even larger. In the late 1990s, the leaders of the large media conglomerates—Disney, News Corp, Time Warner, and Viacom—assured themselves that "content (not distribution) is still king," and that the digital start-ups, which excelled at aggregation or distribution of someone else's content, would need *their* content. But digital aggregators, such as Google, and distributors, such as Netflix and Amazon, are increasingly evolving into media enterprises that not only package and distribute the content of others, but also *create* their own unique content.

In 2013, for example, Netflix debuted *House of Cards*, a thirteen-episode drama available only to its 62 million global subscribers that cost $100 million to film and produce. Within three years, Netflix had created another 15 multi-episode dramas, 9 comedies and 13 animated series, plus it had picked up and then produced extra seasons of 7 popular series that had been canceled by cable networks. During the same period, Amazon produced more than 15 series and had more than three dozen in production. Netflix and Amazon are not only competing with one another for viewers, but also with other cable and broadcast networks, and with the legacy cable providers, such as Comcast and Time Warner.

Each of the three eras—print, electronic, and digital—has been more compressed than the previous one, as the time between the first stage (the breakthrough innovation) and the third (commercialization) shrinks. Only a quarter of a century has passed since the Internet was opened for business. But we are witnessing a proliferation of new business models and competitors that far exceeds the previous eras. The line has blurred between legacy media companies that have historically created, packaged, and distributed their own unique content, and the tech giants, such as Google and Amazon, who are now creating their own content, as well as aggregating and distributing the content of others.

What Is the Difference between Disruptive versus Sustaining Innovation?

Our digital era is replete with folkloric tales of innovators who made it big, seemingly overnight. Facebook started in a Harvard dorm room. Google was a Stanford research project begun by two PhD candidates. Apple was born in a garage. We often confuse creativity and inspiration with innovative breakthroughs, and assume that someone wakes up one morning with a brilliant idea and gets to work building the next invention. In reality, however, "most innovation—disruptive or not—begins life as a small-scale experiment," according to Harvard Business School professor Clay Christensen.

There are typically three stages in the lifecycle of a major innovation. First comes a long period of experimentation and research into new ways of doing things. In this stage, many people may be working on solving the same problem, each from a slightly different angle. Gutenberg may have actually developed a rudimentary printing process and press as early as 1440 in Strasbourg, but he needed another decade of experimentation and adjustment before he could bring all the elements precisely into alignment. Once the breakthrough has occurred, it is followed by an intense, fast-paced period when a number of new products are introduced that build on the breakthrough idea.

The final stage is commercialization. During this period, new entrants fight for market share, often displacing existing businesses and each other. Consider, for example, color television sets. Black and white television sets were invented in the 1930s, followed by color sets a decade later. The first broadcast of a television show in color occurred in the early 1950s. As the quality of color sets improved, more and more people opted to buy them. By 1972, sales of color televisions surpassed those of black-and-white models.

Christensen popularized the term "disruptive innovation" in his book, *The Innovator's Dilemma*, which was published in the mid-1990s, just as the Internet was taking off. We use that term frequently these days, using it to apply to any type of technological breakthrough that changes an industry's business models and competitiveness. The mantra for most companies in the digital age has become, "Disrupt or be disrupted." Not so fast, says Christensen, who has spent the last two decades refining his own research. He now differentiates between two types of technological breakthroughs: disruptive innovations versus sustaining innovations. Both types of innovation have the ability to significantly alter the customer experience and the business model of an industry, but in very different ways. Leaders of media companies need to understand the difference, so they can respond accordingly.

In this book, we will define a *disruptive innovation* as a breakthrough technological invention that creates new products, new industries, new business models, and new markets (i.e. new customers). For example, the invention of the printing press and related processes meant that books and pamphlets now could be quickly reproduced and circulated to thousands of people who had never owned a book before. This, in turn, created a publishing business with a very different organizational and financial model from that of the cottage-industry scribe era.

In contrast, a *sustaining innovation* makes products better. In the process, these sustaining breakthroughs may also create new business models and new markets. For example, the steam-powered presses developed at the beginning of the nineteenth century were a vast improvement over the hand-operated presses used for the previous three centuries. Books and newspapers could now be produced in greater volume and more efficiently, which brought down the price a customer had to pay. This, in turn, created new markets and new business models for both industries. The Google algorithm is another example of a sustaining innovation that was a major improvement over the labor-intensive search functions initially employed by Altavista, Yahoo!, and Lycos.

It's important to remember that not all innovations—whether disruptive or sustaining—succeed. In fact, most do not. Less than a third of all new businesses are still in existence five years after they are founded. Successful disrupters, according to Christensen, focus on getting the business model right, rather than the quality of the product. As we will discuss in later chapters, disrupters attack existing businesses first on the cost side, producing a new product in a much more efficient way. As they develop distribution channels and gain traction in the market, disrupters siphon off the customers and revenue of the existing business. Only when revenue begins to decline do most existing businesses realize the peril they are facing from the disruptive competitor that has flown under the radar, often for several years.

Existing businesses typically react much faster to the competitive threat posed by a sustaining innovation. Either they will attempt to improve the quality of the product they are offering, or they will acquire or adopt the new entrant and incorporate it into their product mix. Newspaper publishers, for example, grasped immediately the implications of the steam-powered rotary press and began adopting this vastly improved product. An early adoption rate by customers is really critical for a sustaining innovation. Therefore, instead of focusing on undercutting the costs of existing products, successful sustainers quickly develop distribution systems and sales processes that will allow them to amass an early market share. The faster the adoption rate, the more likely the sustainer will develop a successful business model, based on the revenue coming in from new customers.

There is an added advantage. With a quick adoption rate, the improved product may well become the new industry standard, effectively eliminating other competitors. For example, Lycos and Yahoo! very quickly ceded the search market to Google, which became the go-to source for consumers because its algorithm offered substantial improvements over the others' labor-intensive and often inconsistent methods. All this raises a question we will return to in future chapters: Is there a first-mover advantage for disruptive innovators? If so, under what circumstances? Most often, it pays to be the second or third entry into the market that provides the sustaining innovation.

Innovators and Entrepreneurs: A Comparison

Why did the world's first disruptive media innovator fail to capitalize on his own inventions? From a distance of more than 550 years, we can raise a number of questions about business decisions Gutenberg made. All of these are instructive for modern-day entrepreneurs.

In the popular press, the words "innovator" and "entrepreneur" are often used interchangeably. However, dictionaries offer very different definitions. An innovator, according to the Cambridge English Dictionary, is someone "who develops a new product, design, etc. or who has new ideas about how to do something." An entrepreneur, according to the Merriam-Webster Dictionary, is a person "who organizes, manages and assumes the risks of a business or enterprise." In other words, an innovator is an inventor while an entrepreneur is a business person.

Nevertheless, in today's digital era, it is possible to be both a successful innovator and entrepreneur since they share many of the same traits. Steve Jobs and Jeff Bezos immediately come to mind. A six-year study, conducted by professors at three of the country's leading business schools, sought to identify the "secret sauce" shared by successful "innovative entrepreneurs." After studying the habits of 25 well-known innovators and interviewing more than 3,500 executives and individuals who had started or worked for innovative companies, the professors identified five skills that make up the "DNA" of successful innovative entrepreneurs: associating, questioning, observing, experimenting, and networking. They concluded that the first two—associating and questioning—were the most critical skills.

- *Associating*: The ability to connect problems or ideas from different areas. For example, Gutenberg was able to connect what he learned from metallurgy to the production of moveable type.
- *Questioning*: The ability to ask provocative questions that challenge the status quo. The study noted successful innovators begin by asking "Why?" and then proceed to asking "Why not?" and "What if?" Gutenberg questioned why a printing press couldn't produce a book of the same quality as that of a scribe.
- *Observing*: The ability to gain insights by observing how others use an existing product and the frustrations they encounter. Gutenberg observed the inconsistencies in quality and the length of time it took to produce a Bible produced by a scribe, as well as the subsequent frustrations such lapses elicited from customers.
- *Experimenting*: The ability to engage in active learning in multiple environments. Gutenberg experimented with multiple products—ink and paper, moveable type, printing presses—and then connected the dots to bring all the processes together.
- *Networking*: The passion for meeting diverse people in diverse settings, with the goal of incorporating diverse perspectives and ideas into your experimentation and innovation. Gutenberg traveled up and down the Rhine, engaging in numerous ventures—from reflective mirrors to coinage. He incorporated many of these diverse perspectives into his experimentation with the printing press.

If Gutenberg possessed all of these traits, why then did he fail as an entrepreneur or business executive? Management shortcomings are the most commonly-cited reasons for entrepreneurial failure. As Peter Drucker observed in his 1985 book, *Innovation and Entrepreneurship*:

> Unless a new venture develops into a new business and makes sure of being "managed," it will not survive, no matter how brilliant the entrepreneurial idea, how much money it attracts, how good its products, nor even how great the demand for them.

In a 2017 study, Joseph Picken identified the "eight hurdles of transition" (Table 1.1) and prescribed the essential actions to be taken by entrepreneurs as they transition their companies from a nascent start-up to a business capable of sustained and profitable growth.

Table 1.1 Laying the foundation for a sustainable and profitable business.

Set a direction and maintain focus	Clearly define goals and objectives, but fine-tune the details of implementation as required
Position products/services for an expanded market	Refine your offering and fine-tune customer relationships as you expand your market
Maintain customer/market responsiveness	Develop processes to ensure that the organization remains flexible and responsive to customers
Build an organization and management team	Hire key skills and develop organizational capabilities to address the challenges of growth
Develop effective processes and infrastructures	Establish and adapt customer-facing, production and management infrastructures consistent with growth
Build financial capability	Beyond raising initial capital – demonstrate the ability to prudently manage financial resources
Develop an appropriate culture	Shape and reinforce a culture that supports the business purpose and strategy of the firm
Manage risks and vulnerabilities	Understand and proactively manage risks and vulnerabilities

Source: Picken (2017).

Using this template, we can ask the following questions:

- *Did Gutenberg understand the finances of his own operation and develop efficient processes?* Gutenberg does not seem to have thought ahead and managed either the revenues or costs of his operation. From 1450 to 1455, the only source of income for Gutenberg's enterprise came from the printing of indulgences, textbooks, and pamphlets. Most of Gutenberg's 20 employees appear to have been working on the Bible, not on the tasks that brought in revenue. If Gutenberg had employed a salesman to drum up more of this sort of hum-drum printing business, he might not have had to ask Fust for a second round of financing, which came with much more stringent terms than the initial cash outlay. On the cost side, he doesn't seem to have maximized his use of capital and his labor force. It's unclear how Gutenberg divided the work, or how many employees had specialized skills—such as type casting or ink formulation—that would have made the Bible-printing operation more efficient.

Lesson for today's entrepreneurs: Successful media entrepreneurs are focused on both the efficiency of their operation as well as cash flow (the money they have on hand to pay the bills). Book publishers, for example, balance the risk of publishing a book by an unknown author, which may yield little or no money, by simultaneously releasing titles by best-selling authors with a proven track record for sales. Printing firms today operate around the clock, efficiently utilizing all equipment. Employees have specialized skills and clear accountability for certain tasks. They understand how their work fits into the overall process. Everyone has responsibility for making sure there is a smooth transition between each stage from creation to packaging to distribution. In Chapter 2 ("The Story behind the Numbers"), we'll discuss what sort of information can be gleaned from financial statements, and in Chapter 3 ("What Is a Company Worth?"), we'll discuss how to calculate the financial value of an enterprise.

- *Did Gutenberg appropriately manage the risks and vulnerabilities inherent in a startup?* Gutenberg was intent on reproducing a Bible of the highest quality, equal to or surpassing texts produced by the best scribes in Europe. Critics today herald his two-volume Bible as an artistic masterpiece, using words like "beautiful" to describe both the type and design. But while Gutenberg was constantly adjusting the formulas and experimenting in his quest for artistic perfection, he blew through deadlines that he and Fust had agreed on. Artists strive for perfection without a clear notion of return on investment. In contrast, successful entrepreneurs understand there is a trade-off between quality and return on investment. They are constantly assessing whether something is "good enough" to go to market.

Lesson for today's entrepreneurs: Studies have shown that founders of start-up enterprises tend to significantly underestimate the time it will take them to get their product to consumers. As the adage goes, if something can go wrong, it will. This is especially true when designing and manufacturing a new product. That is why successful entrepreneurs engage in contingency planning, constructing various scenarios to understand the impact delay will ultimately have on the bottom line. They also hold themselves and their employees accountable to meeting deadlines and expectations. In Chapter 5, we'll lay out "A Strategy for Dealing with the New Business Imperatives," and in Chapter 10, we'll discuss "Investing in Key Assets and Capabilities" that drive profitability.

- *Did Gutenberg devote sufficient attention to positioning his product in the market and establishing sales and distribution channels that would allow him to respond to customer demand?* Based on accounts in the few court documents that survive, Gutenberg apparently devoted very little time to establishing an efficient system for pricing, selling, and fulfilling orders. Even before he had acquired Gutenberg's workshop and his Bibles, Fust was apparently lining up customers throughout Europe and establishing a reliable distribution system. A mere 20 years after taking over operation of the print shop where he had apprenticed under Gutenberg, Schoeffer had developed a sales and distribution network that stretched across Western Europe. Through this network, he pushed sales of books he both produced and authored—including a Bible and a guide to herbs—as well as those he printed for other writers and organizations. All carried his branded imprint, which was stamped on the cover and differentiated his publications from his competitors.

Lesson for today's entrepreneurs: This may have been Gutenberg's most fatal business error. Successful media entrepreneurs maximize sales and profits by focusing not only on the quality of the content that is produced, but also on the quality of their marketing, sales, and distribution systems. They estimate the size of the target market and optimal pricing, then use the most efficient channels to get their content to their customers and build loyalty. In Chapters 6, 7, 8, and 9, we'll discuss: "Defining a Unique Value Proposition," "Understanding Customer Relationships in a Digital World," "Reaching Current and New Customers," and "Competing in a Networked World."

- *How well did Gutenberg set a direction for his venture, maintain focus and choose the right partners and employees?* Some biographers have speculated that his apprentice Schoeffer was one of the world's first industrial spies, placed in Gutenberg's workshop by his angel investor, Fust, to learn the secret formula. They point out that Fust foreclosed on the loan just as the first Bibles were coming off the press, and that testimony in court from Schoeffer tipped the verdict in Fust's favor. The retail value of the Bibles, alone, was more than three times as much as the original loan of 1,600 guilders. With the proceeds from the sale of the Bibles, Fust and Schoeffer set up their own successful print operation, using the equipment they confiscated from Gutenberg's shop. Today we have copyright and patent laws that protect inventors from the theft of intellectual property by a competitor, and confidentially agreements that are binding on employees and potential investors. While Gutenberg lacked such legal protections, he doesn't seem to have taken adequate precautions to safeguard his "secret project," nor does he seem to have articulated a strategy with clear goals and objectives and devised a sustainable economic model for his enterprise.

Lesson for today's entrepreneurs: Things might have turned out differently if Gutenberg had chosen better business partners and had a focused vision for his enterprise, beyond that of simply producing a "beautiful" Bible. That is why founders of media start-ups today should proceed deliberately when seeking initial investors and choosing an initial management team. Reputable investors exhaustively cull through the entrepreneur's financial statement, before working with founders to establish agreed-upon targets on everything from launch date to audience metrics and projected operating expenses. Members of the management team need to understand their individual and interrelated roles and responsibilities, and work with the founder to define and refine a clear strategic direction for the company. In Chapter 4 we'll discuss "The Transformed Competitive Landscape," and in Chapter 11 we'll discuss "Entrepreneurial Leadership and Culture."

By the end of the fifteenth century, there were as many as eight million books printed by machine circulating in Western Europe. Early publishing entrepreneurs, such as Schoeffer, succeeded by building an integrated business model that we still employ today.

- They focused on producing, marketing, and distributing unique content that differentiated their shops from the other 200 or so competing publishers in Europe, and began pushing for rules, regulations, and industry guidelines that would protect their intellectual property from theft.
- They worked out a division of labor in the production process that kept their enterprise operating at maximum capacity, even as they looked outward and began developing marketing and sales expertise.
- They understood the underlying economics of each phase in the production and distribution cycle and began to calculate a rudimentary return on investment for each product they produced.

Gutenberg was a transitional figure—more innovative artist than entrepreneur. As such, he failed to grasp the underlying economics of the new processes and procedures he was inventing. Managers of today's media enterprise have to balance the costs involved in creating, packaging, and distributing content against the revenue expected from either selling content directly to consumers, or selling an audience to advertisers. This means that a successful media entrepreneur must develop an economic mastery of the processes and procedures necessary to produce and distribute a firm's unique content, and a strategic understanding of how the processes come together to create a book, television show, or online site that attracts paying customers.

Mark Zuckerberg: Innovator and Entrepreneur?

In February 2014, as Facebook celebrated its tenth anniversary, CEO Mark Zuckerberg declared that he was "even more excited about the next ten years than the last. The first ten years were about bootstrapping this network. Now we have the resources to help people across the world solve even bigger and more important problems."

Borrowing designs and programs from existing sites such as Friendster, Zuckerberg had famously launched Facebook on February 4, 2004 from his dorm room at Harvard during his sophomore year. Word spread rapidly around the campus about the new social networking site, which Zuckerberg described as a service that would help students at the large university "connect" with their friends and keep abreast of what they were doing. Within 24 hours, more than 1,200 Harvard students had registered; within one month, more than half of all students. Zuckerberg and a handful of his college dorm mates and friends began offering the service to other Ivy League schools and Boston-area universities.

Excited over the business prospects of this new social network he had created, Zuckerberg decided that summer to leave school and set up headquarters in a ranch house in Palo Alto. Peter Thiel, co-founder of PayPal, joined the board of advisers and became an initial investor, contributing $500,000 for a 10 percent ownership in the young company. He was joined a year later by Accel Partners, which made a $12.7 million investment. By fall 2005, Facebook had more than five million users, with more than 85 percent of college students connected to the network. Next Facebook targeted high school students. By the end of 2005, Facebook was active in more than 2,000 colleges and 25,000 high schools. In September 2006, it was opened to everyone over 13 years old with a valid e-mail address.

By then, Facebook had already received another round of money ($27.5 million) from venture capitalists. It was also beginning to receive unsolicited offers from other companies, including Yahoo!, which offered to pay one billion dollars to purchase the company, and Microsoft, which in 2007 bought a 1.6 percent stake in Facebook that implied a $15 billion value for the three-year-old social networking site. On the advice of his investors and board, Zuckerberg began looking for a seasoned executive who could help him develop a sustainable business model. (Unlike some of his contemporaries, such as the Google founders, Zuckerberg did not want to give up the CEO title, so he sought COO candidates.) In 2008, he hired Sheryl Sandberg, a Google advertising executive, for the position. After holding a number of brainstorming sessions with Facebook employees, she concluded that advertising should be the main source of revenue for Facebook and began working on building a sales structure.

As he had from the beginning, Zuckerberg continued to focus primarily on improving the utility of the site and the quality of the user experience. Noticing the rapid adoption of smartphones, the company moved swiftly to adapt its platform for mobile usage. Facebook also began to add capabilities by acquiring other companies, including WhatsApp (encrypted mobile messaging), Instagram (mobile photo-sharing), and Oculus (virtual reality).

In 2012, Facebook filed for an initial public offering (IPO) of its stock. Demand for the stock was high, and underwriters priced shares at 38 dollars each, giving the company a valuation of $104 billion, the largest of any newly public company yet. However, in what was perhaps an omen of the year to come, a computer glitch on the NASDAQ on the day of the IPO, May 18, delayed trading. Facebook stock struggled all day to stay above the opening price. Over the coming months, the stock fell as low as 18 dollars a share before beginning to rebound.

By 2014, two years after its debut, with the stock trading around 62 dollars a share, both its founder and investors were once again optimistic. Three years later, by February 2017, Facebook's stock price had doubled to $137 a share. By October 2017, Facebook had a stock market valuation of $497 billion, making it the fourth largest public company in the world, exceeded only by Apple, Alphabet (the parent company of Google) and Microsoft.

During the first ten years of its existence, there were several inflexion points when Zuckerberg and Sandberg made critical decisions that influenced the long-term viability of Facebook as an enterprise. This included Zuckerberg's choice of investors and COO, his focus on the quality of the user experience, Sandberg's decision to aggressively seek advertising revenue to support Facebook's business model, and the company's agile response to changes in the marketplace, such as the adoption of the smartphone by its customers.

We conclude this first chapter by comparing and contrasting the different fates of two media pioneers, Zuckerberg and Gutenberg.

- Is Facebook a disruptive innovation—like the printing press—or a sustaining one?
- Given the fast pace of innovation and technological change, what immediate and long-term challenges and opportunities will Facebook confront?
- How will its business model evolve?
- Finally, why did Zuckerberg succeed as an entrepreneur, in contrast to Gutenberg?

Summary

Gutenberg's invention propelled civilization and communication into a new era. Over the past 550 years, technological progress has occurred at an increasing pace. The print era lasted from 1450 to 1900, followed by the electronic era, which lasted for a century. We are still in the early years of the digital era, which began at the end of the twentieth century.

In each era, there are disruptive innovations—such as the invention of the Gutenberg press—and sustaining innovations—such as the steam-powered rotary press. Both types of innovation have the ability to alter the economics of a media enterprise.

Nevertheless, all media enterprises share common characteristics, processes and procedures. A media company is an organization that creates content, packages that content into a product or service (such as a book or television show), and then distributes it to consumers. Over the past two centuries, two types of media business models have emerged. Book publishers, motion picture studios, and video games sell their content directly to consumers. In contrast, newspapers, magazines, television stations, and digital giants such as Google and Facebook sell their audiences to advertisers.

Innovators and entrepreneurs share many of the same traits—including an ability to question the status quo. But, not all innovators are successful entrepreneurs. In this book, we will be exploring how founders of start-ups, as well as executives in legacy media companies, become successful entrepreneurs, as well as innovative leaders.

2

The Story Behind the Numbers

Imagine you are the editor of one of the largest book publishers in the world. You learn that an unpublished, 70-year-old manuscript by one of your best-selling authors has just been "discovered" by her lawyer. What sort of business and financial decisions will you have to make as you decide when, how, or whether to publish? If you decide to publish, how will you judge the financial success of this venture?

To Kill a Mockingbird, Harper Lee's first novel, burst onto the scene in 1960 and quickly became a best seller and a critical success. The book received the Pulitzer Prize in 1961 and actor Gregory Peck picked up an Oscar in 1962 for his portrayal of the lawyer Atticus Finch in the movie. Over the next five decades, the coming-of-age novel about social and racial justice in the South during the 1930s became a staple in classrooms around the country, winning over several generations of fans and selling more than 40 million copies. However, in 1964, dismissing the entreaties of fans who hoped she would write another book, Lee retreated to her hometown of Monroeville, Alabama, and "retired" as an author.

Therefore, an announcement by HarperCollins in February 2015 caught the literary world by surprise and immediately provoked controversy: a new novel by Lee had been discovered, and HarperCollins planned to publish it in July. The press quickly learned that *Go Set a Watchman,* described by HarperCollins as a long-lost "sequel" to *Mockingbird,* was actually the original, unedited draft manuscript of her Pulitzer Prize-winning novel.

Longtime friends questioned whether Lee, who was now 90 and living in a nursing facility, fully understood that her lawyer was negotiating the sale of the first draft of *Mockingbird.* Critics accused HarperCollins of placing profit over integrity, by releasing on July 14, 2015 "a not-very-good first draft … hoping to sell millions of books and boost the bottom line."

Why did HarperCollins decide to publish *Go Set a Watchman*? What drove the business decision about when to publish *Watchman*? How would executives at HarperCollins determine if the decision to publish was a successful financial venture?

Book publishing is the oldest of mass mediums, and it was one of the first to experience the disruptive effects of digital technology. Much about the industry has changed in recent years. However, the business imperative has not. Publishers who are not profitable do not survive. That is why successful publishing entrepreneurs have a deep and nuanced understanding of how each of the processes and procedures involved in producing and selling a book affect the bottom line and the long-term sustainability of their company.

The Strategic Digital Media Entrepreneur, First Edition. Penelope Muse Abernathy and JoAnn Sciarrino.
© 2019 John Wiley & Sons, Inc. Published 2019 by John Wiley & Sons, Inc.
Companion website: www.wiley.com/go/abernathy/StrategicDigitalMediaEntrepreneur

This is true whether they are managing a start-up enterprise or a legacy media company, such as HarperCollins.

In this chapter, we will explore how the economics of a media enterprise are reflected in a company's financial statements, identify some of the key information contained in each of these statements, and discuss what can be surmised about the financial challenges and opportunities media executives face. Among the questions we'll consider are:

- How do the underlying economics of a media enterprise flow through a company's financial statements?
- What does the income statement tell us about past and current profitability?
- What are a company's most valuable assets and most onerous liabilities?
- How does a company make and spend money?

The Basic Economics of Book Publishing

Over the past two decades, book publishers have confronted, and attempted to adjust to a new economic reality, driven by technological innovation. First, in the 1990s, they had to contend with the rise of e-commerce and online retailing giant Amazon, which disrupted their distribution and sales processes. Next, came the advent of e-books and the development of easy-to-use software that allows practically anyone with minimal training to publish his or her masterpiece. Taken together, these developments affected all the processes involved in producing books and had a significant impact on both expenses and revenue.

Roughly 2.7 billion books are sold annually in the United States, generating approximately $27 billion in revenue. According to industry estimates, the five largest English-language publishers, known as the "Big Five," account for between 50% and 80% of all sales and a similar amount of revenue (see Figure 2.1). Penguin Random House, the

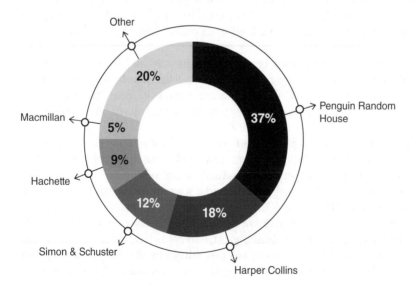

Source: Publishers Lunch Trade Magazine, 2015

Figure 2.1 Percentage of market share for the Big Five publishers, 2015.

largest publisher, employs more than 12,000 people and releases 16,000 new titles annually under 250 imprints. It has an estimated 35–40% market share. HarperCollins is the world's second largest consumer book publisher with operations in 18 countries and roughly a 20% share. It oversees the production and distribution of 10,000 titles under more than 120 imprints including Avon, William Morrow, and Harlequin. Over its 200-year history, this venerable media franchise has published works by talented authors such as Mark Twain, Maurice Sendak, H.G. Wells, and Agatha Christie, and popular titles such as *The Hobbit*, *Goodnight Moon*, and the *Divergent* series.

HarperCollins is one of five divisions in the News Corporation, a multimedia global conglomerate, headquartered in New York. In 2013, the parent corporation separated into two separate companies, each listed separately on the New York Stock Exchange. Twenty-First Century Fox includes the film and television assets and has annual revenues of $25–30 billion. The other company, which assumed the News Corp name, houses the various publishing enterprises and generates annual revenues of $8–8.5 billion (Table 2.1). Almost half of 2015 revenue in News Corp came from the United States and Canada, with the other half from Europe and Australia. The largest division in the recently reconstituted News Corp is the News and Information Services, with annual revenues of $5–6 billion. It includes newspapers in the United States, Great Britain, and Australia, as well as digital financial services. HarperCollins is the second largest division in News Corp with annual revenues of approximately $1.7 billion. In 2015, News Corp had three other smaller divisions with revenues ranging from $109 million (Digital Education) to $625 million (Digital Real Estate Services).

Every year, an estimated 700,000 titles are published in the United States. This includes 400,000 titles that are self-published. Since most books published ultimately sell only a few hundred or a few thousand copies, HarperCollins and its "Big Five" brethren, depend on a small number of blockbusters each year to cover all their expenses, including overhead. Book publishing is an industry with significant fixed marketing and distribution costs that do not vary, regardless of whether a book sells 1,000 copies or one million. Therefore, economies of scale are important so that these costs can be spread across thousands of titles.

This means each editor at HarperCollins is making a quick economic calculation, estimating the size and type of audience for a particular book compared with the upfront costs of producing and distributing the book. It may be up to two years between the time a book proposal is first approved by the editor and the bound copy is available and sold through online and brick-and-mortar retail outlets. Until a book is printed and released for sale to the public, HarperCollins has no revenue to offset against its expenses.

Table 2.1 News Corp divisions and revenue, 2015 (in million $).

Division	Revenue
News and Information Services	5,731
Book Publishing	1,667
Digital Real Estate Services	625
Cable Network Programming	500
Digital Education	109

Source: News Corp Annual Report, 2015.

Among the significant costs for publishers are:

- Marketing costs, including paying the retail chains for upfront display space for books.
- Advance royalty payments to the author. Not all books sell enough copies to cover the amount of a cash advance on projected royalties that a publisher gives to the author. When a book fails to "earn out" its advance, the publisher must absorb the costs.
- Unsold copies of hardcover and paperbacks that are returned by retailers to the publisher where they are remaindered (sold at very steep discount clearing out space in the warehouse for new releases) or destroyed. Roughly a third of books printed are returned to the publisher by the retail outlets.

Approximately 70% of all books sold today are print copies. But only a very small number of books—less than 1% of those printed—will actually be stocked on the shelves of most bookstores since even the largest brick-and-mortar chains have space for only 175,000 volumes compared to the three million stocked by Amazon. Depending on the genre, publishers will distribute their books through a variety of channels—including book clubs, large discount retail chains (Walmart, Costco), and specialty retailers (such as pet stores for books about dogs and dog owners). But the vast majority of books, especially best sellers, are sold at discounted prices through large bookstore chains (such as Barnes and Noble) or the online retail giant, Amazon.

Publishers have the potential to make more profit on e-books than print copies since there are fewer costs associated with the production and distribution of the content, and they do not have to account for returns on unsold books. To illustrate this point, *The New Republic* in 2014 published a graphic showing the discrepancies between the retail price, publisher profit, and profit margin of hardcover and e-books (Table 2.2). However, despite initial projections that e-books would rapidly replace print copies, e-book sales have plateaued around 30% industry-wide. Sales of digital books at HarperCollins have trended lower, around 20% of total sales.

Hardcover titles, which carry a list price of $26–30, tend to sell best around the holidays, such as Christmas and Father's Day, while fictional paperbacks, with a list price of $6–15, are popular beach reading. Authors typically receive royalties of 6–15% of the list price of hardcover or paperback books and up to 25% on electronic books. Only authors with proven track records, or well-known "celebrities" with large followings, will get a large advance payment against the royalties. Typically, sales of general interest books are highest in the first six months of a release. So, HarperCollins writes off advances that have not "earned out" in six months to a year. While the royalties for *Go Set a Watchman* were not disclosed, industry experts estimate that it was most likely in the 15% range, which means that for every million copies sold, the estate of Harper Lee received $3–4 million in royalties. (Lee died in February 2016, seven months after HarperCollins published *Watchman*.)

Table 2.2 Price of hardcover versus e-book, 2014.

	Hardcover	e-book
Retail price ($)	27.99	14.99
Publisher's profit ($)	5.67	7.87
Profit margin (%)	41	75

Source: *New Republic*, 2014.

General interest fiction and nonfiction titles tend to dominate all of the top dozen or so yearly best-seller lists, while children's and religious literature (both of which HarperCollins publishes under its 120 imprints) tend to sell consistently across many seasons. *The Girl on the Train* and a sequel to *Fifty Shades of Grey* topped Amazon's best-seller list for 2015, for example. That list of the top 20 best sellers included half a dozen mysteries, a couple of romances and history books, and an adult coloring book. The "Big Five" book publishers try to publish a wide variety of genres, hoping to have several dozen best sellers in any year. In the 12 months preceding the publication of *Go Set a Watchman*, HarperCollins had 214 titles on *The New York Times* print and digital best-seller lists, with 15 reaching the number one position.

Predicting which book will become a best seller is a big gamble. Any profit on a newly released title often disappears when unsold print copies of the book are returned by retailers. Publishers often refer to their "front list"—consisting of books that have been recently released—as a breakeven proposition (meaning the costs equal revenue) and their "backlist" as a profit center. The backlist consists of books released in prior years that continue to sell thousands of copies annually. The only costs are the royalties paid to the author and the printing and distribution expenses. By some estimates, the "backlist" accounts for a quarter of sales at large publishing houses. HarperCollins has more than 200,000 titles on its backlist, including *To Kill a Mockingbird*, which sells tens of thousands of copies each year because it is assigned reading in many junior and senior high school classes.

As a result, on both the cost and revenue sides of the equation, economies of scale determine the financial success of the "Big Five" publishers. On the revenue side, a Big Five publisher needs a couple of hundred best sellers each year, plus a backlist of several hundred books that sell consistently year-over-year, long after publication. This allows the publishing house to cover the costs of all the potential literary masterpieces that receive critical acclaim but sell so few copies that they are unprofitable. Specific genres—such as romance and mystery—are more likely to become best sellers and backlist profit centers. The more genres a publisher offers, the better the chances of having dozens of best sellers and a profitable backlist. Therefore, the "Big Five" are continually purchasing other publishers, and contemplating merging their operations. In 2012, HarperCollins considered merging with Simon & Schuster, the third largest English-language publisher. It also contemplated purchasing Penguin in 2013. Instead, in August 2014, it purchased Harlequin, which publishes more than one hundred romance titles a month, with strong readership in both Europe and Asia.

When Harper Lee's lawyer arrived at HarperCollins headquarters in New York in fall 2014 with the manuscript for *Go Set a Watchman*, the various executives at the company were still focused on integrating Harlequin into the book publishing division. They knew that this newly "discovered" manuscript was an unedited first draft that had been returned in 1957 to the author by an editor at one of their imprints, with suggestions for rewriting and reframing the plot from the 1950s to the 1930s. Still, they undoubtedly recognized immediately the potential economic impact that publishing the manuscript could have on both revenue and profits. Given the popularity of *Mockingbird*, this "newly discovered" manuscript would most certainly be a best seller. *Watchman* could also boost backlist sales of *Mockingbird*. Like *Mockingbird*, it might even become a staple in the classroom and become a perennial backlist star.

Therefore, they pushed ahead with the decision to publish. How would the publication of *Watchman* ultimately affect the bottom line of both the book publishing division and its parent, News Corp? The answer to that question can be found by analyzing the data found in the company's annual financial statements.

Digging into the Numbers: Understanding the Story behind Financial Statements

Numbers tell a story. The 2015 News Corp annual report states, "Historical results may not be indicative of future results [since] operating performance is highly contingent on many factors, including customer tastes and preferences." However, by understanding the factors, or key financial drivers, that influenced current and past performance, you can identify strengths and weaknesses, project future trends in revenue, costs and profits, and adjust strategy accordingly. In short, you can determine how well a business is actually doing by understanding how the economics of an enterprise flow through the financial statements.

In this section we'll closely examine News Corp's financial performance in the months leading up to the publication of *Go Set a Watchman*. This will help us understand why HarperCollins made the decision to publish and how that decision might affect the financial results of both News Corp and HarperCollins in the following year.

There are three main financial documents that companies produce: (1) the income (or earnings) statement; (2) the balance sheet; (3) and the cash flow record. Each of these documents tells a slightly different story:

The *income statement* will give you valuable information about how a company's revenues, costs, and profits are trending. You can use that information to compare its performance to its competitors and to its financial outcomes in prior years. But an income statement will not show you what liabilities might be looming in the immediate future—such as loans that are coming due or pension obligations that are suddenly ballooning. You need to consult the *balance sheet* to learn about that. Similarly, profits can fluctuate year-to-year, depending on when and how expenses that do not require an outlay of cash, such as depreciation, are recognized. To learn how much cash a company has on hand and how it earned that cash, you need to study the *cash flow statement*.

The size of annual reports can be intimidating. The annual financial report for News Corp typically exceeds 180 pages, the size of a small novel published by HarperCollins. The three financial documents account for less than ten of those pages. The remaining pages are devoted to the overview and summary of operations (80 pages) and the footnotes that follow. This verbiage often contains valuable insights into how executives made certain business decisions. For those who know what to look for, reading financial statements is like reading a good detective story.

A company's fiscal (or financial) year may or may not correspond with a calendar year. For example, the fiscal year for Apple begins in October and ends the following September while the fiscal year for the *New York Times* begins in January and ends in December. News Corp's fiscal year runs from July through June. Therefore, the 2015 annual report for News Corp covers the financial results for the *12 months prior* to the publication of *Go Set a Watchman*, which was released in July 2015.

In the next three sections of this chapter, we'll be examining News Corp's 2015 annual report which can be accessed at: https://newscorpcom.files.wordpress.com/2015/09/newscorp-fy2015-10k.pdf to gain key insights into what business challenges News Corp and HarperCollins were confronting prior to publishing *Watchman*. Finally, we will compare and contrast the results of News Corp's fiscal year 2015 (July 2014–June 2015) with fiscal year 2016 (July 2015–June 2016) to determine exactly what impact *Go Set a Watchman* had on the bottom line of both HarperCollins and its parent corporation.

We will be seeking insight into these questions:

- How have revenue and profitability been trending at HarperCollins and News Corp in recent years?
- How efficiently does HarperCollins operate?
- How does News Corp finance acquisitions?
- What are the biggest challenges confronting HarperCollins and News Corp?
- How important is financial success in the book publishing division to the financial success of News Corp?

What Does the Income Statement Reveal about Profitability?

The income statement is one of the most quoted in news stories. It is also known as the "Profit and Loss Statement," the "Statement of Revenue and Expense," or the "Consolidated Statement of Earnings/Operations." It shows the financial results for a certain period of time, either quarterly or annually, and gives a summary of a company's revenue, expenses, and profit. It is predicated on the matching principle, in which revenues are paired with related expenses during a specific period. It shows both an operating profit (which is the income generated before taxes and interest) and a net profit (which reflects what the company made after paying interest and taxes). We'll examine five key indicators—revenues, expenses, operating income, EBITDA, and net income, in Box 2.1.

Revenues

This is the first line on any income statement and is sometimes referred to as a company's "top line." It is the amount of money that a company received during a certain period (monthly, quarterly, or yearly) from selling its products or services. Revenue is the price of the goods sold times the number of units sold. Fluctuations are due to either the price of the product increasing or decreasing, or the volume (or number of units) sold moving in either direction. If volume is increasing and the price holds steady, that is usually a sign of increased consumer demand. However, if either volume or price is declining, that is usually a sign that a company is facing increasing competitive pressure.

Media companies often receive revenue from three or four different sources: from advertising (newspapers, magazines, television, and cable networks), from subscriptions (newspapers, cable providers, streaming services), from sales to consumers (books, movies, music), and from licensing, syndication, and other income (television and cable networks).

Box 2.1   Income Statement
Revenues – Operating Costs – Sales and General Administration (SG&A) – Depreciation = Operating Income (or EBIT, Earnings Before Interest and Taxes) + Other Revenues or Expenses (Impairments, etc.) –/+ Interest – Taxes = Net Income

You should always ascertain if a company has acquired another enterprise during the period covered by the income statement. Typically, in the comparison to the previous reporting period, revenues of the acquiring company will increase significantly because it has sold more units, thanks to the inclusion of the revenue of the acquired company.

What We Learn about Revenue at Harper Collins and News Corp

In Table 2.3, we see that the 2015 revenue from News Corp's five divisions (News and Information Services, Book Publishing, Digital Real Estate Services, Cable Network Programming, and Digital Education) totaled $8.6 billion, an increase of $59 million, or 1% growth, over the previous year. Both of the largest categories—advertising ($3.8 million) and circulation ($2.7 million)—were down a total of $218 million. However, the third largest source of revenue, sales to consumers or sales of books ($1.6 million) increased significantly by $220 million. According to the book publishing segment data provided in the News Corp annual report, the book division was up a total of $233 million (Table 2.4).

Even from this high-level analysis of News Corp's income statement, we can begin to understand how much HarperCollins contributed to the company's overall revenue increase in 2015. Even though sales from the book division accounted for only about 20% of total revenue for News Corp, the increase of $233 million year-over-year counteracted the decline in advertising and circulation revenue in the News division.

What drove the increase at HarperCollins? There are two ways for book publishers to dramatically increase year-over-year revenue: by publishing several runaway best sellers or by purchasing another company. By studying the management comments that come before the financial results, we learn that sales of HarperCollins's wildly successful *Divergent* series by Veronica Roth had declined dramatically, from 19.2 million units sold in 2014 to only 8.2 million in 2015. So, "the increase [in revenue]," according to the management overview, "was primarily the result of the acquisition of

Table 2.3 News Corp revenues, 2014 and 2015 (in $ millions).

Revenues	2015	2014	Change
Advertising	3,835	4,019	(184)
Circulation	2,654	2,688	(34)
Consumer	1,594	1,374	220
Other	550	493	57
Total	8,633	8,574	59

Table 2.4 HarperCollins revenues, 2014 and 2015 (in million $).

Revenues	2015	2014	Change
Consumer	1,594	1,374	220
Other	73	60	13
Total	1,667	1,434	233

Source: News Corp Annual Report, 2015.

Harlequin [in August 2014], which contributed $281 million ... [while] consumer revenues associated with print and digital book sales at HarperCollins's other divisions decreased $44 million." Without Harlequin's revenue contribution, the top line of both HarperCollins and News Corp would have been less than 2014. HarperCollins's revenue for 2015 would have been $1.3 million, and News Corp's total revenue for 2015 would have been $8.3 billion.

Expenses

Revenues should be matched against expenses in the same reporting period. There are three types of expenses that are typically recognized: (1) operating costs (sometimes referred to as cost of goods sold, or cost of production); (2) sales, general, and administrative costs (often referred to as SG&A); and (3) depreciation and amortization.

Operating cost is essentially the cost of using resources to actually produce the products or services that were sold. It includes raw materials, advances paid to authors, design and research on the product, and the salaries of those involved in the production (creation, packaging, and manufacturing) process. *SG&A* can include administrative salaries, selling expenses (such as advertising), and rent, for example. *Depreciation and amortization* form a "noncash" expense, in contrast to the other two expenses. It is an accounting method of spreading the cost of acquiring an expensive asset over the expected usefulness of the asset. Depreciation is used on tangible assets, a piece of equipment, such as a printing press, which will be operated for many years to produce many editions of a newspaper, while amortization prorates the cost of creating or purchasing intangible assets. For example, the cost of designing a new product is often amortized over the lifetime of a patent or copyright. There are a number of "generally accepted" accounting methods for recording depreciation and amortization, which can have a huge impact on both operating and net income. (The footnotes in an annual report explain which method or methods a company is using for depreciation and amortization.)

What We Learn about Expenses at HarperCollins and News Corp

In addition to increasing revenue, acquisitions often increase expenses significantly. Such was the case with Harlequin (Table 2.5). For News Corp in 2015, total expenses for the five divisions (including operating expenses, SG&A, and depreciation) decreased by $71 million. Based on information provided in the management summary, the News and Information division posted the most significant cash savings of $360 million, but that was offset by an additional $249 million in expenses, "as a result of the Harlequin purchase."

Table 2.5 News Corp expenses, 2014 and 2015 (in million $).

Expenses	2015	2014	Change
Operating	(5,025)	(5,139)	$114
SG&A	(2,756)	(2,665)	($91)
Depreciation	(530)	(578)	$48
Total	(8,311)	(8,382)	$71

Source: News Corp Annual Report, 2015.

Table 2.6 HarperCollins expenses, 2014 and 2015 (in million $).

Expenses	2015	2014	Change
Operating	(1,106)	(1,029)	(77)
SG&A	(340)	(208)	(132)
Depreciation	(52)	(36)	(16)
Total	(1,498)	(1,273)	(225)

Source: News Corp Annual Report 2015.

In addition to acquiring Harlequin's revenue, HarperCollins also acquired its expenses (Table 2.6). As News Corp acknowledges in its annual statement, it takes time to efficiently integrate a newly acquired company and realize projected cost savings. Including depreciation expenses, the book publishing division expenses increased $225 million in 2015 versus the previous year: $77 million in operating expenses, $132 million in SG&A, and $16 million in depreciation.

Operating Income (EBIT) and Margin

This is also referred to as operating profit or loss or EBIT (Earnings Before Interest and Taxes). This is a measure of how efficiently a company has been managed during the reporting period. Managers of businesses aim to increase operating profit year-over-year. If it is decreasing, investors will often look to see whether this is driven by decreases in revenue (which can signal lack of consumer demand for the products the company produces) or increases in expenses, which cannot be covered by price increases in the product. Industry analysts and investors like to compare the operating efficiency of a company within industries (book publishing, for example) and across industries (book versus newspaper publishing). To do this, they calculate an operating or EBIT margin by dividing the operating income by the total revenue generated during that period.

What We Learn about the Operating Income of Harper Collins and News Corp

While News Corp does not provide an "operating income" line for either the company or its divisions, this can easily be calculated by subtracting total expenses (operating, SG&A, and depreciation) from total revenue (Table 2.7). Due to costs savings of $360 million in the News and Information Services division and revenue increases of $220 million from HarperCollins, operating income for News Corp for 2015 was up $130 million to $322 million. The operating margin increased from 2.2% to 3.2%. However, many of News Corp's competitors—such as the *New York Times* or the Walt Disney Company—posted operating margins of 10% or more in 2015.

In Table 2.8, we see that expenses of more than $200 million associated with the Harlequin acquisition offset revenue increases of $223 million. Therefore, operating profit at HarperCollins increased only $8 million to $169 million, and its operating margin dropped from 11.2% to 10.1%.

EBITDA (Earnings Before Interest, Taxes, Depreciation, and Amortization)

Many media companies have significant noncash expenses (depreciation and amortization) that can depress *operating income*, as well as *net income*. Therefore, industry

Table 2.7 News Corp EBIT, 2014 and 2015 (in million $).

	2015	2014	Change
Revenues	8,633	8,574	59
Expenses	(8,311)	(8,382)	71
Operating profit	322	192	130
Operating margin (%)	3.7	2.2	

Source: News Corp Annual Report 2015.

Table 2.8 HarperCollins EBIT, 2014 and 2015 (in million $).

	2015	2014	Change
Revenues	1,667	1,434	233
Expenses	(1,498)	(1,273)	(225)
Operating profit	169	161	8
Operating margin (%)	10.1	2.2	

Source: News Corp Annual Report 2015.

analysts and investors use EBITDA calculations to estimate the amount of actual cash the company is generating from its operations and gain additional insight into the operating efficiency of a company or division. An EBITDA calculation adjusts operating profit by adding back depreciation and amortization. (EBITDA is not listed on the income statement.) An EBITDA margin is calculated by dividing EBITDA by total revenues. With an EBITDA margin, investors can compare the operating efficiency of a company to its competitors.

What We Learn about EBITDA at HarperCollins and News Corp

The annual statement from News Corp notes management's preference for using this measure instead of operating profit or margin: "Segment EBITDA provides management, investors and equity analysts with a measure to analyze operating performance of each of the Company's business segments and its enterprise value against historical data and competitor's data."

From Table 2.9, page 34, we see that excluding depreciation expenses of $530 million (a noncash expense mostly incurred by the News and Information Division), News Corp had EBITDA income of $852 million in 2015. This compares to an operating profit of only $322 million. Therefore, its EBITDA margin rose to almost 10% compared to an operating or EBIT margin of only 3.7%. This brings News Corp's efficiency more in line with its competitors, such as Bertelsmann (which owns Penguin Random House) or the New York Times Company. These two competitors posted EBITDA margins of between 13% and 15% in 2015.

In 2015, HarperCollins accounted for 17% of revenue for News Corp, but almost 25% of EBITDA (Table 2.10). As the largest division, News and Information Services, struggles to gain an economic footing in the digital era, News Corp relies on its second largest

Table 2.9 EBITDA for News Corp, 2014 and 2015 (in million $).

	2015	2014	Change
Revenues	8,633	8,574	59
Operating expenses	(5,025)	(5,139)	114
SG&A	(2,756)	(2,665)	(91)
Total News Corp EBITDA	852	770	82
EBITDA margin (%)	9.8	8.9	

Source: News Corp Annual Report 2015.

Table 2.10 EBITDA for HarperCollins, 2014 and 2015 (in million $).

	2015	2014	Change
Revenues	1,667	1,434	233
Operating expenses	(1,106)	(1,029)	(77)
SG&A	(340)	(208)	(132)
Book Publishing EBITDA	221	197	24
EBITDA margin (%)	13.3	13.7	

Source: News Corp Annual Report 2015.

division, HarperCollins to provide consistent year-over-year financial performance and overall stability to the corporation's bottom line.

Even though EBITDA increased $24 million at HarperCollins, its EBITDA margin is down slightly from 13.7% in 2014 due to the increased expenses that came with the Harlequin purchase. A 2015 EBITDA margin of 13.3% is slightly less than that of its direct competitor, Penguin Random House, the largest of the "Big Five" publishers. Penguin, which released 16,000 titles in 2015, had a 13.6% EBITDA margin on $452 million in operating income in 2015. Since sales of "major titles" drive most of the revenue of a book publisher in any fiscal year, this would suggest that HarperCollins editors would be seeking to publish as many best sellers as possible in Fiscal Year 2016 to offset the increased expenses that came with the Harlequin acquisition.

Net Income

This is often referred to as "net profit or loss," "net earnings," or, more colloquially, "the bottom line." Net income is usually mentioned in the first or second paragraph of any news story about the financial results reported by a company. However, the third and fourth paragraphs often list a number of adjustments to the net income for "one-time expenses" unrelated to the continuing operation of the business. For example, a company might recognize an income tax credit in one year and incur a significant income tax expense in the next year. Similarly, management often has discretion about when it recognizes noncash expenses (such as depreciation or impairment of assets) or when to set aside money for buyouts or impairment charges. That is why industry analysts, investors, and many companies, such as News Corp, prefer to use EBITDA calculations when comparing the annual financial performance of a company with that of its competitors.

Table 2.11 News Corp net income, 2014 and 2015 (in million $).

Net income	2015	2014
Operating income	322	192
Impairment charges	(455)	(94)
Equity and interest earnings	114	158
Other	75	653
Income tax	(134)	691
Net income	(78)	294

Source: News Corp Annual Report 2015.

Net income is calculated by adding to operating profit, or EBIT, any income that did not come directly from day-to-day operations (e.g., equity earnings in enterprises that are partially owned) and then subtracting a range of expenses, including interest payments, any one-time restructuring costs (such as money set aside to buy out personnel or shut down operations) and any taxes owed.

What We Learn about Net Income at News Corp

News Corp posted a net "loss" in 2015 of $78 million, despite having an operating income of $322 million and an EBITDA of $822 million (Table 2.11). Two corporate expenses caused this wild swing from a $294 million net profit the previous year. In contrast to 2014 when it had an income tax credit of $691 million, in 2015, News Corp owed $134 million in income taxes. (Taxes for large corporations—especially global ones like News Corp—can fluctuate a good deal, depending on a number of factors.)

But even with the tax expense, News Corp would still have posted a net income of $377 million, if not for $455 million in impairment charges. News Corp recorded a $75 million restructuring charge related to buyouts in its News and Information Services division and a noncash impairment charge of $370 million related to its Digital Education division. When companies realize that the value of an asset is less than the amount listed on the balance sheet, they must "write down" the value of the enterprise by taking a charge against earnings. News Corp had purchased Amplify, the digital education company, in 2011 for $390 million. By taking an impairment charge of $370 million, News Corp was now estimating that this division was only worth $20 million in 2015. In October (in fiscal year 2016), News Corp sold its education division for an undisclosed sum to a group of investors that included Laurene Powell Jobs, Steve Jobs's widow.

The Balance Sheet: What Are the Most Valuable Assets and Most Onerous Liabilities?

The *balance sheet* is separate from the income statement and provides insights into the value and type of a company's assets, as well as the liabilities looming on the horizon. Think of the balance sheet as a sort of inventory. The assets are the resources the company has at its disposal to use in creating its products and services. The liabilities section lists the obligations a company has to its creditors (debt), employees (pension), and

---

Box 2.2 The Balance Sheet

Current Assets (Cash, Accounts Receivable, Prepaid Expenses)
+ Long-term Assets (Property, Plant, Equipment, Book Value, Intangible Assets)
= Total Assets
Current Liabilities (Accounts and Notes Payable, Long-Term Debt Due)
+ Long-term Liabilities (Debt, Pension, Retirement Obligations)
+ Shareholder Equity
= Total Liabilities

---

shareholders. The assets and liabilities balance one another; that's why it is called a balance sheet (Box 2.2). There is typically no balance sheet for divisions within a company. Therefore, in this section, we'll be looking at the balance sheet for News Corp.

Assets

There are two types of assets listed on a company's balance sheet. *Current assets* can be used by the company during the coming year to produce additional income. It includes cash, income from stocks and bonds the company may have purchased, accounts receivable (revenue from sales that have not been collected), inventory, and pre-paid expenses. *Long-term assets* are often called fixed or capital assets since they are the source of the company's continuing cash flows and income. Unlike current assets, they are not expected to be "used up" within a year and expensed. These assets are either depreciated if they are *tangible assets* (plant, equipment, real estate) or amortized, if they are *intangible* (copyright, patents, brand reputation, or customer and employee relations).

Goodwill is a long-term asset and arises when one company purchases another enterprise and pays a premium price (based on either its stock price or its earnings or some other financial measure). If it turns out that the acquiring company overpaid for the asset—and the company can no longer be sold to another business for the original price— then the acquiring company will need to "write-down" the value of the asset, as News Corp did by taking *an impairment charge* of $370 million against the Digital Education division. (See the Net Income section above.) Many media enterprises carry a significant amount of intangible assets and goodwill on their balance sheet.

What We Can Learn about News Corp from its Assets

From Table 2.12, we learn that roughly a quarter (26%) of News Corp's assets are current. Its tangible long-term assets total $5 billion, including investments in financial securities ($2.3 billion), property, plant, and equipment ($2.7 billion), and $333 million in advances paid to authors for future books. It lists $5.3 billion in long-term intangible and goodwill assets, of which $896 million is attributed to the book division. HarperCollins paid $455 million for Harlequin. On its balance sheet, News Corp recorded $115 million in tangible Harlequin assets (including accounts receivable and author advances), $165 million in intangible assets (including imprints with an indefinite life), and $185 million in goodwill (the excess over the fair value of the tangible and intangible assets). As management points out in the annual report, it has in the past paid a premium when acquiring properties, including the Dow Jones Company in 2007. As a result, every year it calculates the fair market value of its various assets compared to the value listed on the balance sheet and adjusts both the intangible and goodwill amounts accordingly.

Table 2.12 News Corp balance sheet, 2015 (in million $).

Assets	Million $
Current assets	3,975
Long-term assets	11,118
• Investments	2,379
• Property/Plant	2,746
• Intangibles	2,242
• Goodwill	3,063
• Other	688
Total assets	15,093

Source: News Corp Annual Report 2015.

Liabilities

There are two types of liabilities on the balance sheet. *Current liabilities* are expenses that are due within the year. It includes accounts payable (bills owed to suppliers and vendors), accrued expenses (such as tax payments that are due but not yet paid) and any debt (such as notes payable to banks and finance companies or monthly payments due on long-term debt). *Long-term liabilities* include debt that is due a year or more out, as well as obligations to current and past employees, such as pension and benefits charges. Recent academic studies have shown that most companies finance at least 30% of their investments with debt. Interest expense (on the income and cash flow statements) increases as debt increases. In addition, creditors are often unwilling to lend more to a company that is heavily indebted, or, alternatively, they will charge a much higher rate of interest on subsequent loans.

In the liabilities section, the balance sheet will also provide some insight into the ownership of the company, and its *shareholder commitments.* There are typically two types of stock: preferred and common. Preferred shareholders have a priority over common stock holders in terms of claims on the company's assets (if it were to go bankrupt, for example), but often do not have voting rights. Those who own common stock do have voting rights, including the ability to select members of the board of directors. However, many companies have two or more classes of common stock (often referred to as Class A and Class B), in which the founders of the company are assigned more voting rights than others who purchase the shares on the open market. Examples of companies that have two classes of stock include the New York Times and Facebook.

What We Can Learn about News Corp from its Liabilities

From Table 2.13, we learn that News Corp has no debt on its balance sheet in 2015, in contrast to most of its competitors. Bertelsmann, which owns a controlling interest in Penguin Random House, carries $3.1 billion in long-term debt, and the New York Times Company lists $691 million. Even before News Corp was spun off as a separate company in 2013, the parent company with the same name (which included such diverse properties as MySpace, 20th Century Fox studios, and the Fox television network) carried only a small amount of debt and preferred to pay cash for its purchases whenever possible. Historically, this has had both competitive advantages and disadvantages. Without debt, News Corp does not pay interest expense, and this frees up

Table 2.13 News Corp liabilities, 2015 (in million $).

Liabilities	Million $
Current liabilities	2,155
Long-term liabilities	802
Retirement obligations	305
Deferred income taxes	166
Other	331

Source: News Corp Annual Report 2015.

more cash that can be used for more acquisitions. It also imposes a rigorous management discipline on assessing the price tag of potential acquisition targets since there is a financial limit—the cash on hand—as to what News Corp can afford to pay. On the downside, News Corp can be outbid by a company that is willing to pay more. Prior to its purchase of Harlequin, News Corp had attempted to purchase Penguin but was outbid by Bertelsmann.

Because of this preference for funding acquisitions with cash, the founder of the original News Corporation, Rupert Murdoch, has always insisted that he and other executives in the company need the latitude to move quickly when they spot a potential investment opportunity. This is why News Corporation has two classes of stock—Class A, which can be purchased by anyone, and Class B, which is owned and controlled by the Murdoch family trust. These Class B shares control almost 40% of voting rights. This means Murdoch and his sons James and Lachlan (who also work in the company) have much more latitude in choosing members of the board of directors or withstanding takeover attempts by corporate raiders than CEOs at a media enterprise, such the Walt Disney Company, which does not have a dual class of stock.

The Cash Flow Statement: How Does a Company Make and Spend Money?

Think of the statement of cash flow as a sort of bank statement that records all the cash flowing into and out of a company. It is divided into three parts: Cash from operating activities, investments, and financing (Box 2.3). Investors pay close attention to how much cash is being generated from operating activities since this is an important barometer of the sustainability of a company's business model. They also look to see how the company is spending its money by investing in new equipment or acquiring other enterprises, and whether it is using debt to finance its investments. Companies that are struggling will often raise "cash from investing" by selling properties they own. This temporarily solves the cash flow problem, but is not sustainable. Similarly, the dot-com start-up companies of the late 1990s relied primarily on "cash from financing" (IPOs and debt) to fuel their earnings growth. This is also not sustainable.

As is the case with the balance sheet, most corporations do not provide a cash flow record for their various divisions. Therefore, in this section, we'll be looking only at News Corp's cash flow record for fiscal year 2015.

Box 2.3   Cash Flow

Cash from Continuing Operations
(Net Income + Noncash Expenses + Changes in Working Capital)
= Net Cash from Operations
Cash from Investing
(Minus Capital Expenditures + Proceeds from Sale-Acquisitions)
= Net Cash from Investing
(+ Debt Issues - Debt Retired + Stock Issued - Dividends)
= Net Cash from Financing
= Change in Cash
Beginning Cash
Ending Cash

Cash from Continuing Operations

This is calculated in two steps. First, all noncash items (such as depreciation, amortization, and impairment of assets) are added back and earnings from equity holdings in other companies are subtracted. Then increases or decreases in current assets and liabilities (such as accounts receivable and payable, inventory and benefit obligations) are calculated and either added or subtracted. The resulting number is the cash from continuing operations.

What We Can Learn about News Corp's Cash from Continuing Operations

When all the noncash charges (such as depreciation and impairment of assets) are added back to the net loss ($78 million) recorded on the income statement, News Corp actually generated about $831 million in cash from its five divisions (Table 2.14). This number correlates closely with the 2015 EBITDA figure of $852 million for the company (Table 2.10). Therefore, EBITDA is usually a good approximation of the cash a company will generate from continuing operations, which is why News Corp places a strong emphasis on EBITDA in managing its various divisions and compensating executives based on their segment's EBITDA performance. Additionally, when making acquisitions and/or deciding to sell a division or property, News Corp says in its annual report that it evaluates and estimates the future cash flows and EBITDA of the company it is acquiring or divesting.

Table 2.14 News Corp net cash from continuing operations, 2015 (in million $).

Net (loss)	(78)
Adjustments	
Depreciation	530
Impairment	371
Other	8
Net cash from operations	831

Source: News Corp Annual Report 2015.

Cash from Investing Activities

This captures the amount of cash a company either earned or spent on investments. This includes cash spent to purchase equipment or other businesses (which is subtracted) and proceeds from selling properties or investing in long-term securities (which are added) to yield a net amount of cash from investing activities. This figure can fluctuate dramatically from year-to-year, depending on whether a company has spent a lot on purchases, or conversely, disposed of property and assets.

What We Can Learn about News Corp's Cash from Investments

News Corp is an actively managed company. It is continually disposing of underperforming companies or divisions and seeking acquisitions. Fiscal Year 2013, for example, was a big year for both acquiring and disposing of companies. In 2013, News Corp spent $2.1 billion on acquisitions—including a media investment company in Australia and Storyful, a social media news agency. At the same time, it received $865 million in cash by selling a group of community newspapers in the United States, the DJ Indexes, and SKY Network Television in Asia.

In Table 2.15, we see that Fiscal Year 2015 was a year for major acquisitions, with only minor dispositions. In addition to purchasing Harlequin for $455 million from Torstar Enterprises, News Corp paid $864 million for Move, Inc., which, through its website www.realtor.com and mobile applications, displays 98% of all properties for sale in the United States. Move was folded into the Digital Real Estate division. News Corp also spent $378 million in 2015 on major capital expenditures for its various divisions. Of this amount, $238 million was invested in software and equipment for the News and Information Services division, and only $12 million went to HarperCollins. (Unlike the News and Information division, HarperCollins has outsourced its printing and distribution functions. This decreases the need for substantial outlays of cash for capital assets, such as equipment, in the book division.)

Cash from Financing Activities

Net cash from financing activities is calculated by subtracting cash spent retiring debt, repurchasing shares of stock, and paying dividends to shareholders, and then adding cash raised from issuing debt. Investors and analysts keep a keen eye on the amount paid in dividends. How does the outflow of cash to pay dividends compare with the money produced from operations? Companies that are struggling financially often do not generate enough cash from continuing operations to pay dividends and instead will use cash

Table 2.15 News Corp cash from investing activities, 2015 (in million $).

Investing activity	Million $
Capital expenditures	(378)
Acquisitions	(1,190)
Other	(173)
Net cash investments	(1,741)

Source: News Corp Annual Report 2015.

from financing (borrowing money) or from investing (one-time cash payments from the sale of property).

What We Can Learn about News Corp's Use of Cash from Financing

In Table 2.16, we see News Corp spent only a small fraction of its cash on financing ($190 million) compared with the cash it spent on investments ($1.7 billion). Most large media companies pay a dividend on their common stock, either quarterly, twice yearly or annually. (Companies that do not pay dividends, such as Google and Facebook, reinvest all their earnings into company growth.) Like most other traditional media companies, News Corp pays out a portion of its earnings in dividends (10 cents per share, paid twice a year), which amounted to $30 million in 2015, or less than 1% of the cash it generated from operations. It also spent $129 million paying back its only loan.

Changes in Cash Flow

Cash from all three activities (continuing operations, investments, and finances) are added and subtracted together to calculate the net increase or decrease in cash. This is followed by two more lines on the cash flow statement which record the beginning cash balance and the ending cash balance. This is the amount of money the company has available to spend in the following year.

What We Learn about the Cash Flow at News Corp

From Table 2.17, we see that News Corp began 2015 with $3.1 billion in cash carried over from the previous year. It generated another $831 million from operations and then spent $1.7 billion on investments, including $1.2 billion on acquisitions. At year's end, it had almost $2 billion in cash that it could use in 2016 to acquire new properties or invest in current enterprises. According to the footnotes in the 2015 financial report, it also has the ability to tap into an additional $900 million in revolving credit, bringing the total amount of money that management can easily access to almost $3 billion.

Table 2.16 News Corp net cash from financing activities, 2015 (in million $).

Financing activity	Million $
Repayment loan	(129)
Dividends paid	(30)
Other	(31)
Net cash from financing	(190)

Source: News Corp Annual Report 2015.

Table 2.17 News Corp changes in cash flow, 2015 (in million $).

Net decrease	(1,100)
Cash at beginning	3,145
Cash at end	1,951

Source: News Corp Annual Report 2015.

By comparison, at the end of 2015, Bertelsmann, which had twice the revenue and EBITDA of News Corp, had only $1.3 billion in cash, and the New York Times Company had only $29 million. In short, News Corp, compared to its competitors, is cash-rich, has no debt and is able to move quickly to acquire other publishing properties. As the annual report states, "The company has evaluated, and expects to continue to evaluate, possible acquisitions and dispositions of certain companies."

Summary of Financial Results: 2015

News Corp's 2015 financial statements reveal much about the economics of book publishing and the challenges confronting both HarperCollins and News Corp as management considered whether to publish *Go Set a Watchman*. Among the insights:

- HarperCollins accounted for only a fifth of total revenues for News Corp in 2015, but the increase of $233 million from the book division compensated for the loss of a similar amount of revenue in the largest division, News and Information Services.
- The News and Information Services division, which houses the company's newspapers, is struggling to adapt to the digital era, with print advertising and circulation revenues declining much faster than increases from digital sources. This means that, in the short term, HarperCollins's consistent, year-over-year performance has a significant impact on both News Corp's top and bottom lines (its revenue and profitability).
- In evaluating the financial performance of its divisions, News Corp management relies heavily on the unit's current and projected annual EBITDA or cash flow.
- In order to consistently meet profit and EBITDA targets set by News Corp management, HarperCollins needs to publish a number of best sellers each year (which sell a million or more copies) and it needs to offer several genres of literature (so that it appeals to the widest possible audience).
- Economies of scale are important for the Big Five book publishers, which carry high fixed marketing, production, and distribution costs. Although it is number two in the market, HarperCollins is about half the size of Penguin Random House (in terms of revenue and EBITDA), and therefore has less room for error—when choosing best sellers or acquiring other companies.
- Unfortunately for HarperCollins, by 2015, the popularity of its *Divergent* series (which sold 19 million copies in 2014) was waning rapidly. By acquiring Harlequin, News Corp quickly added $281 million to the top line. Without the revenue from Harlequin, HarperCollins's revenue for 2015 would have dropped back to 2013 levels.
- However, HarperCollins also acquired Harlequin's expenses, which pulled down the division's operating profit and margins in 2015, compared to Penguin Random House.
- The best way for HarperCollins to offset the increased costs associated with the acquisition was to aggressively seek out and publish best sellers in 2016, such as *Go Set a Watchman*.

According to management statements in the 2015 annual report, "Major new title releases represent a significant portion of the Book Publishing segment's sales throughout the fiscal year." In other words, best sellers have an outsized impact on both revenues and profits. Therefore, we can surmise that *Watchman* was released in July (the first month of News Corp's 2016 fiscal year) so that HarperCollins and News Corp could recognize a full year of revenue and profit from what management anticipated would be a huge best seller.

Go Set a Watchman and HarperCollins: An Update

From the moment HarperCollins announced in February 2015 that it would publish *Watchman*, it appeared that the book would be a best seller. In the five months prior to publication, the book posted the largest number of preorders in HarperCollins's history, with the online retailing giant Amazon reporting the strongest demand for a yet-unpublished title since the release of *Harry Potter and the Deathly Hallows* in 2007. Advance orders for *Watchman* were so strong through all retail outlets that HarperCollins ordered the advance printing of 2 million hardcover copies. On July 14, 2015, at one minute past midnight, more than 90 bookstores and Amazon started selling the new novel.

Despite reviews that were "charitable at best, scathing at worst," the sale of 1.1 million copies in the first week after the release of *Watchman* set yet another post-publication sales record for HarperCollins. By Christmas, it had sold 1.6 million copies, roughly two-thirds of which were hardcover books. *Watchman* was a bestseller, but it had not attained the level of Scholastic Publishing's Harry Potter series, which sold 8.3 million copies of *Deathly Hallows* in the first day after its release. Even HarperCollins had produced bigger best sellers in recent years, including the *Divergent* trilogy, which sold more than 32 million copies and the Chris Kyle memoir, *American Sniper*, which sold 5.6 million copies.

Still, as the *Wall Street Journal* noted about its sibling division in News Corp, it was "a big haul in today's book world." Depending on the discount offered by sellers, the 1.1 million hardcover copies sold by the end of 2015 had already generated estimated revenue of $20–25 million, with the e-book copies generating an additional $5–7 million. In addition, there were other supplemental materials that were released and offered for sale, including a teacher's note and instructional manual for *Watchman*. Not only that, sales of *To Kill a Mockingbird*, HarperCollins's perennial best seller on its backlist, increased as much as 200 times in the weeks just before and after the release of *Watchman* as readers reconnected with a book they hadn't opened since high school.

Judging by these sales figures, publishing *Go Set a Watchman* was a successful business venture for HarperCollins and News Corp, despite the literary controversy it caused. Although sales of *Watchman* had already begun to slow by Christmas, News Corp reported in its 2016 financial statement that for the fiscal year (July 2015 to June 2016), *Go Set a Watchman* actually generated $42 million in revenue. (News Corp did not report the actual number of copies sold of *Watchman*. Industry analysts estimated 1.5 million hardback copies and an additional half a million e-books.) Several Harlequin best sellers contributed an additional $23 million to HarperCollins's revenue. But this was not enough to offset significant declines in other areas. The *Divergent* series sold only 2 million copies in 2016 compared with 8.3 million in 2015. Sales of the more profitable e-books also dropped at HarperCollins from 22% to 19%, and foreign currency fluctuations negatively impacted the bottom line by $39 million.

As a result, despite the strong performance of *Go Set a Watchman*, both revenue and EBITDA declined at HarperCollins in 2016. Revenue dropped $21 million from $1.667 billion, while EBITDA declined to $185 from $221 million. This brought the EBITDA margin for HarperCollins in 2016 down from 13.3% in 2015 to 11.2%.

Adding to the woes at News Corp, performance at the News and Information Services division continued to deteriorate and drag down both the top and bottom lines of News Corp. Advertising and circulation revenue in the News and Information Services group declined by $400 million. Revenues at News Corp sagged by a similar amount to $8.2 billion. Even though expenses decreased by $200 million, the EBITDA margin at the News and Information Services Group dropped to 4% from 10% in 2015. As a result, the EBITDA of News Corp dropped to 8.2% from approximately 10% in 2015.

Even allowing for the vagaries of the book publishing industry, HarperCollins's revenues and EBITDA were more consistent and predictable, year-on-year, than that of the News and Information Services Division. While literary critics may have scoffed, *Watchman* had been a significant contributor to both the top and bottom lines at HarperCollins, as well as News Corp.

Exercise: What's the Future of News Corp?

In June 2013, News Corp was spun off from its parent company with a promise from Chief Operating Officer Robert Thomson, that it would "cultivate a start-up sensibility even though we already work for the world's most established and prestigious diversified media and information company."

The establishment of News Corp as a publishing entity was, in many ways, an example of a business coming full circle and returning to its origins. Since the 1950s, the company, under the leadership of the ambitious Australian media mogul Rupert Murdoch, had grown from a couple of family-owned newspapers "Down Under" to a global enterprise that consisted of a variety of well-known media brands, including movie studios, television networks, and digital enterprises. Even though he considered himself a "newspaper man," Murdoch was intrigued by the international business potential unleashed by the digital age and understood that in order to succeed in the twenty-first century, a media conglomerate needed to pursue economies of scale and scope. So for three decades he had aggressively acquired media outlets around the world, and in 2005 shocked many in the industry when he purchased MySpace, which at the time was the largest social media site in the world, surpassing even Google in terms of visitors.

By 2010, however, Wall Street analysts and investors were beginning to voice concern that the woes of the newspaper industry in particular were dragging down the price of News Corp's stock. So, News Corp split into two entities, with 21st Century Fox housing the television, film, and supporting digital enterprises. This separation, Murdoch predicted, would "unlock the true value" of both companies and allow investors "to benefit from the strategic opportunities" of each company. The stock of the "new" News Corp debuted at around $15 a share, rose as high as $18 before settling in around the $12–14 range. By 2015, the two-year-old "publishing company" was composed of five divisions:

1) News and Information Services, with newspapers in the USA, Europe, and Asia—including such prestigious brands as the *Wall Street Journal* and *The Times* of London, popular tabloids such as the *New York Post* and the *Sun*, and 120 newspapers in Australia—as well as a North American direct mail and coupon marketing service.
2) Book Publishing, which included the venerable New York publishers Harper & Row, purchased by News Corp in 1987 and merged with British publisher William Collins & Son in 1990—hence HarperCollins.
3) Digital Real Estate Services, which consisted of a partial interest in REA—which operates websites in Australia, China, and Europe advertising commercial and residential listings—and Move, which operates similar websites in the United States.
4) Cable Network Programming, which consisted of Fox Sports, the leading sports programming producer in Australia.
5) Digital Education, which consisted of Amplify, a tablet-based instructional program for K-12 that incorporated the Common Core Standards into a multi-media presentation.

More than half of the company's total revenues ($4.6 billion) came from outside the United States, $1.9 billion from Europe and $2.7 from the Australian and Asian properties. But the biggest market was the United States with almost $4 billion in revenues. Consider the following questions:

- What is the contribution of each of the divisions to News Corp's overall revenue and EBITDA?
- What are the financial trends for each of the divisions?

In October 2015, after taking an impairment charge of $370 million against its digital education division, News Corp sold Amplify, which it had purchased for $390 million in 2011, for an undisclosed sum. Amplify, a tablet-based instructional program, had been conceived by a former superintendent of New York public schools as a digital alternative to traditional textbooks published by such major competitors as Pearson, Macmillan, and Houghton Mifflin. But Amplify struggled to ever gain a toehold in the educational market. Compare the business and digital challenges facing educational publishers to general interest consumer publishers, such as HarperCollins.

Summary

Every strategic decision is a gamble that carries with it risks and opportunities. Sometimes managers and executives of media enterprises make short-term decisions that boost revenue and profits for a year, for example, publishing *Watchman.* Other times, they make long-term decisions, such as purchasing Harlequin, betting that these acquisitions will boost both top and bottom line in the years ahead.

Each of the three financial summaries provides insight into the health and long-term sustainability of an enterprise. While past performance of a company is not necessarily indicative of future performance, recent trends in revenue, expenses and profitability, obtained from the *income statement,* provide clues about future performance of a company. The *balance statement* provides insights into a company's assets and liabilities, including debt and pensions. The *cash flow* record shows how much money companies make from continuing operations and how they have used their cash to invest in new ventures.

The publishing industry is in the throes of what the economist Joseph Schumpeter called "creative destruction." As this analysis of News Corp's annual financial statement shows, technological innovation has changed the economics of the publishing industry, affecting both the revenue and profits of divisions within companies and their parent corporations. There are no guarantees that the media giants of the twentieth century, such as HarperCollins and News Corp, will survive in their current form. Successful media entrepreneurs, buffeted by what Schumpeter called "the gales of destruction," understand how every strategic and tactical decision they make flows through the annual income statement, balance sheet and cash flow record. As we will see in Chapter 3, industry analysts and investors use the information in these financial records to decide how much a company is worth.

3

What Is a Company Worth?

Shares of Snap Inc. surged immediately upward on March 2, 2017, its first day of trading on the New York Stock Exchange. When the bell rang in the afternoon, signaling the end of trading, the parent company of the vanishing messaging app, Snapchat, had a market value of $34 billion. The 26-year-old founder and CEO of the company, Evan Spiegel, was suddenly a paper billionaire, and early investors in the social media company had reaped a tidy return. But questions hung in the air about the future financial performance of Snap and what that would mean for its market value down the road.

Would it be like Facebook, which had a market value of $390 billion on the day that Snap began trading, or more like Twitter, worth only $11 billion? Facebook and Twitter had followed very different paths over the past several years. When Facebook's stock debuted on the NASDAQ in 2012, shares initially soared from $38 to $45 a share, but then dropped back down to $38 at the close of trading. Over the next year, the price of Facebook stock dropped as low as $18 a share, before beginning a steady climb in late 2013. On the week that Snap went public, Facebook traded at $137 a share. The price of shares in Twitter, on the other hand, had more than doubled on its first day of trading in November 2013 to $45, giving the company a market value of $25 billion. But its price per share peaked at $69 in early 2014, and had fallen steadily since to approximately $16 a share in early 2017.

What determines the price of a share of stock, and ultimately, the market value of a publicly traded company? What is a fair price to pay for a company that is for sale? How do investors and industry analysts place a value on a company that is unprofitable? In this chapter, we'll explore the following questions:

- What are the factors that affect the value of a company?
- How do investors determine a media company's valuation?
- Who are today's media investors and what sort of return on investment are they seeking?
- How do you measure return on investment (ROI)?

What Affects the Value of a Media Company?

All companies, whether publicly traded or privately held, have a financial value. The worth, or market valuation, of a media company is based on its past performance and the credibility investors and shareholders place in the current management to deliver future earnings. If projections of future earnings decline, then the valuation

The Strategic Digital Media Entrepreneur, First Edition. Penelope Muse Abernathy and JoAnn Sciarrino.
© 2019 John Wiley & Sons, Inc. Published 2019 by John Wiley & Sons, Inc.
Companion website: www.wiley.com/go/abernathy/StrategicDigitalMediaEntrepreneur

placed on a media company also declines. For example, in the 1990s, before the widespread adoption of mobile devices, newspapers in small and mid-sized markets in the United States typically sold for 13–15 times earnings because they were considered de facto local monopolies with little competition for either readers or advertisers. Today they sell for 3–5 times earnings. This drop in value reflects the sharp decline in both advertising revenue and readership that newspapers have experienced in recent years. Newspapers are no longer de facto local monopolies since they now compete with digital giants, such as Facebook and Google, for both readers and local advertisers.

When referring to publicly traded companies, such as Snap or Facebook, the terms *market value* and *market capitalization* are often used interchangeably. Market capitalization, or market cap, is calculated by multiplying the price of a share of stock times the number of outstanding shares (i.e., the number of all the shares that have been issued, including those that are restricted or held by the company's owners or officers). Some companies issue many shares of stock, while others don't. In March 2017, when Snap went public, the Walt Disney Co. had almost 1.6 billion shares in circulation while Twitter had approximately 730 million. The price of the stock in a company depends on demand for the shares that are available to trade on a public exchange. The world's largest is the New York Stock Exchange, where Alibaba chose to list its shares in 2014. The second largest, the NASDAQ, founded in 1971, is where many technology companies, including Facebook, Apple, and Google, are listed.

Market capitalization takes into account both demand for shares and the number of shares available. It, therefore, becomes a proxy on investor sentiment in a company at a given point in time. If market capitalization is rising, investors are optimistic about earnings growth. In early 2017, as Snap prepared to go public, the three largest companies, measured by their market capitalization, were Apple, valued at $733 billion, Google at $587 billion, and Microsoft at $496 billion. Amazon at $405 billion was fifth largest, and Facebook at $396 billion was sixth. In other words, investors were bullish on technology stocks.

Market value or market capitalization is determined by both external and internal factors. As much as 90% of a company's valuation can be accounted for by external factors—such as the growth prospects for the industry segment in which a company operates. Therefore, legacy media companies, such as CBS Corporation, tend to have a lower market valuation than digital enterprises that are perceived as having better prospects for earnings growth. At the close of the first day that Snap began trading, CBS had a market valuation of $31 billon, less than half the market cap of Netflix, even though CBS's net income of $1.3 billion in 2016 was nearly ten times as much as Netflix's. In the eyes of investors, Netflix had greater potential to grow its customer base—and its future earnings—than CBS.

Nevertheless, how the management of a company capitalizes on opportunities or responds to competitive threats can significantly alter the valuation of both start-ups and legacy companies. When it became apparent in late 2013 that Facebook had successfully adapted its platform for ease of use on mobile phones, which were rapidly replacing desktop computers as the primary way to access the Internet, the price of the stock began climbing. Between July of 2013 and 2014, the price of Facebook stock almost tripled, from $26 to $70. Investors reasoned that the company was positioned for significant growth of both advertisers and users in the years ahead.

Here is how external and internal factors affect the value of a media company.

The Current and Projected Macroeconomic Environment

All media companies—and many technology companies—are cyclical, meaning that revenues from advertisers and consumers (and ultimately profits) tend to move in sequence with economic cycles, trending down during recessions and upward during recoveries. During the 2008 recession, the stock price of all media companies fell. CBS stock, which traded for $23 a share at the beginning of the year, traded for $8 in December. Its share price did not rise to $23 again until late 2011. Even Google stock, which had risen steadily since it began trading at $50 a share in 2004, fell from a high of $357 in December 2007 to $165 in November 2008.

The Industry Segment in Which a Company Operates

As a successful company moves from start-up to maturity, growth rates decline from high double-digits to single ones. In time, growth may actually begin to decline, as customers adopt new technologies. Industry segments follow a similar pattern of growth and eventual contraction. Therefore, companies in mature industry segments with steady but slowing growth rates—such as cable or broadcasting companies like CBS—tend to carry lower valuations than those in high-growth areas, such as streaming enterprises, like Netflix. Industry segments that have declining growth rates and are very competitive have even lower valuations. For example, Gannett Company, one of the largest US newspaper companies in terms of both circulation and number of papers owned, had a market valuation of only $1 billion in early 2017.

The Management and Strategy of a Company

Even in the best of times and in high-growth industry segments, many companies fail to meet investor expectations about growth in earnings and users. While Facebook's stock soared from 2013 onward, Twitter struggled. Twitter stock peaked at $69 a share in 2014 and then seesawed back and forth between $30 a share and $50 over the next year and a half. After a series of management stumbles and shake-ups at Twitter in 2015 and 2016, its stock began steadily declining and was trading at $16 a share in early 2017. When Snap went public, Facebook's valuation of $396 billion was 36 times that of Twitter.

Similarly, the strategy that an established company pursues can set it apart from its competitors in the same segment. In 2006, Disney stock was roughly comparable in price to that of CBS. Both traded for around $25 a share. In early 2017, Disney stock sold for $110 a share, and CBS for $69. With many more shares outstanding, Disney had a market cap of $177 billion, almost six times that of CBS's market valuation of $31 billion. The difference in market cap also reflected the difference in earnings between the two companies and the diversity of its assets. Disney's operating income of $14.2 billion in 2016 was almost six times that of CBS, which primarily relies on revenue and profit from its television-related properties—broadcast and cable networks, locally owned stations, and studios that produce shows for other networks. Disney operates in four different industry segments—film studios, theme parks, consumer products, and television networks. Each of the four segments can operate independently of one another, so that a strong performance in one segment can compensate for weak growth in another. However, each of the segments can also contribute to growth in another division. A blockbuster film—such as *Pirates of the Caribbean*—can lead to many profitable box-office sequels, new rides in its theme parks, and increased sales of movie-related merchandise in retail stores. Large diversified market-cap companies, such as Disney, with multiple streams of revenue and sizeable profits in each division, can absorb a flop or bad bet more easily than a smaller, less diversified company can.

How Investors Place a Price Tag on a Company

Most companies—other than those run as hobbies by their founders, such as blogs—have assets with some value to other people:

- to another company that wishes to acquire it;
- to major investors and lenders who hope to get a profitable return on funds they advance a company;
- to shareholders who have purchased stock;
- to underwriters setting the price of a share of stock in an initial public offering (IPO).

Therefore, establishing a credible valuation is important. The value placed on a company is a best guess about future earnings potential, based on available information, much of it found in a firm's financial statements. A valuation is a *forward-looking* assessment. Financial statements are *backward-looking* and quantify a company's performance over the past several years. Nevertheless, analysts, investors, underwriters, and lenders pore over several important line items on a financial statement: (1) looking for clues as to how a company will perform in the future; and (2) placing a value on the tangible assets (such as real estate and equipment) and intangible ones (i.e., copyrights and customer relationships). This process is called due diligence.

Media companies compete for share of wallet—the amount of money a customer spends on a product or service—as well as share of mind—the amount of time customers spend on a product or service. Especially for companies that depend on advertising revenue—including technology giants such as Google or Facebook—the size of the audience and its demographics ultimately drive revenues and earnings. Those with the largest audiences (i.e., scale) and those that can also target specific customer segments (i.e., depth) are most likely to attract advertising dollars in the digital space. Therefore, investors track both the number and type of users, as well usage—engagement with the site or application—since this will drive revenue and profits in both the short and long term.

Here are some of the financial trends investors focus on when trying to assess a company's current management and strategy and the impact these will have on future earnings:

- *Revenues from sales of products and services*: What is driving sales—new or improved products, geographic expansion into new territories, new customers, or recent acquisitions of other companies? Is the current market almost tapped out or is there the potential to continue growing, and at what rate? How much of the revenue is derived from one customer segment? How much revenue per employee does the company generate? How much competition does the company face for its customers? Is there downward pressure on pricing?
- *Costs incurred from creating, packaging and distributing content*: How high are the company's fixed costs? How judicious has the company been in managing costs—especially with its hiring practices? Is the company facing major capital expenditures? How reliant is it on one or two suppliers?

- *Debt and any other outstanding obligations*: Is the company carrying significant liabilities on its balance sheet—including looming pension obligations for an aging workforce, long-term real estate leases, or major loans that are coming due? Is it currently generating enough cash from continuing operations to cover these obligations?
- *Investments and acquisitions*: Is the company actively involved in research and development of new products and services? Will these new products attract more users or increase customer engagement? How are investments of any type financed? What is the rate of return on the various investments? Has the company acquired other companies? What was the strategy behind these acquisitions? How does it pay for the acquisitions? Were the acquired companies successfully integrated into day-to-day operations? Did the company sell divisions or parts of the company at a loss or a profit?
- *Earnings and cash flow*: How fast have earnings grown in recent years? Does the company have consistent earnings and predictable margins? How much of current or projected earnings is being generated by continuing operations? Do current investments in research and development of new products or services have the potential to significantly impact earnings and cash flow in the near future? Have recent acquisitions contributed to the company's earnings and cash flow? How has the company used the cash it has generated?

After analyzing a company's financial statements to answer these questions, investors, lenders, and underwriters then use one of several methods to establish the market value of both private and publicly traded companies.

- If it is an *established company* with a track record of consistent earnings, then the valuation is based on either a multiple of EBITDA (Earnings Before Interest, Taxation, Depreciation and Amortization) or its discretionary cash flow (i.e., the cash from continuing operations minus capital expenditures).
- If it is a *new company* with no earnings, then the valuation is based on a multiple of revenue or estimated future earnings.
- In some cases, with a *mature company* that has posted wildly fluctuating earnings or negative profit in recent years, valuation is calculated by using a multiple of book value (i.e., assets minus liabilities).

Here are the pros and cons of each method (Box 3.1).

EBITDA and revenue are the two most frequently used methods for evaluating media and technology companies. Large, established media enterprises are valued on average at 11.2 times EBITDA and at 2.4 times revenue. Technology companies, such as Google or Facebook, carry much higher EBITDA and revenue multiples.

Both EBITDA and revenue are calculated on a weighted, trailing average. Earnings and revenue for the last three to five years are often used, with the most recent earnings given a higher value (or weight) than earnings in the more distant past. For example, if you are calculating a weighted average based on the past three years of earnings, the most recent earnings would be multiplied by a factor of three, the next by a factor of two and the farthest by a factor of one.

As you will recall from Chapter 2, News Corp provides EBITDA calculations for all its divisions—newspapers, book publishing, digital real estate services, and cable network programming—as well as for the corporation. In its annual report, the company says that it uses EBITDA when assessing the performance of each division within the company. It also uses EBITDA when deciding whether to buy or sell a property. Let's look at how News Corp would be valued based on an EBITDA Multiple (Table 3.1, page 53).

Box 3.1 Pros and Cons of Each Method

EBITDA Multiple: Pros

- Easy to calculate by using the Income Statement (i.e., add back Depreciation and Amortization to Operating Income). Many companies actually list EBITDA in their annual financial statements.
- EBITDA is commonly used by investors and analysts to compare companies within the same industry segment.

EBITDA Multiple: Cons

- Past earnings are not always indicative of future earnings. The business environment can change.
- EBITDA is not equivalent to discretionary cash flow (cash from continuing operations minus projected capital expenditures). Therefore, EBITDA is not necessarily a good measure of actual cash being generated that can be used to grow future earnings.

Revenue Multiple: Pros

- Simple to calculate and, like EBITDA, is commonly used to compare companies within the same industry.
- It can be used to evaluate start-ups that are not yet profitable.

Revenue Multiple: Cons

- It does not consider profitability or cash flow.
- It is based on historical performance.

Cash Flow Multiple: Pros

- It projects future earnings, while discounting them, based on the time value of money.
- By examining all projections—costs, capital expenditures, etc.—an investor or acquirer can gain more insight into future risks.

Cash Flow Multiple: Cons

- The value can vary based on the projections since they are subjective.
- It can be difficult to use in negotiations with different groups due to varying projections.

Book Value Method: Pros

- Most useful for businesses that are capital-intensive. Also used with financial services businesses, such as investment banking firms.
- Can be compared to the stock price to determine if company is undervalued.

Book Value Method: Cons

- Most businesses are worth more than book value. Assets are recorded on a balance sheet at cost, not current value.
- It does not take into account profitability, cash flow, and future earnings potential.

Table 3.1 Placing a value on News Corp based on EBITDA multiple, March 2017 (in million $).

	2016	2015	2014	
EBITDA multiple (in $ millions)	684	945	963	
Weighted multiplier	×3	×2	×1	
Sum of weighted EBITDA	2,052	1,890	963	4,905
EBITDA weighted average (divide $4,905 by sum of multipliers: $3 + 2 + 1 = 6$)				817.5
Market cap of News Corp, March 2017				7,690

Source: News Corp Annual Report 2014/2015/2016.

The market capitalization of News Corp—$7.69 billion—is 9.4 times the EBITDA average of $817.5 million. Therefore, in March 2017, News Corp was being valued by its shareholders at a multiple of 9.4 times EBITDA. This is slightly below the industry average of 11.4, and it suggests that one or more divisions within News Corp may be pulling down the average. Most likely, it is the newspaper division, which has recorded declining revenue and earnings in recent years. As newspaper companies have struggled to transition from print to digital, their earnings multiples have dropped significantly. However, book publishers have fared much better. As we discussed in Chapter 2, the EBITDA for HarperCollins is comparable to that of its competitors. In its 2015 annual financial statements, News Corp indicated that it paid between 11 and 12 times EBITDA for Harlequin Books, which it purchased in 2014. Therefore, if you were to put a market valuation on HarperCollins, you would use an EBITDA multiple of 11 to 12. The average weighted EBITDA for HarperCollins from 2014 to 2016 was $165.6 million. This would place the market value of HarperCollins in March 2017 at an estimated $2 billion. Therefore, if News Corp decided to sell HarperCollins, it could expect to receive at least $2 billion.

The process for valuing a company, based on revenue, is very similar to that of the EBITDA exercise above. However, a much lower multiple is employed in the calculation. Revenue growth—along with costs—are projected forward and used as a proxy to estimate future EBITDA potential. This method is most often used to value a new company that has not yet turned a profit. Therefore, assumptions about both user growth and the revenue associated with users are critical to establishing a fair market value for a company that is about to go public, like Snap, or about to be acquired by another company. Both Google and Facebook, which have been very active in purchasing other smaller private tech companies, often use the revenue multiple method to establish a price for those enterprises.

Let's do another valuation of News Corp, based on its revenue over the past three years (Table 3.2). In contrast to early-stage companies, such as Snap, which have high-growth rates, revenue for News Corp has been relatively stable, and actually declined in 2016. Therefore, you would expect the revenue valuation for News Corp to be lower than its EBITDA valuation.

If you divide the weighted average revenue of $8.4 billion by the market cap of $7.69 billion, you determine News Corp is trading at 1.1 times revenue. This is half of the industry average of 2.4 times. The newspaper division accounted for two-thirds of the company's revenue in 2016, and has declined significantly over the past three years. To offset the decline in revenue in this division, News Corp has made significant cost

Table 3.2 Placing a value on News Corp based on revenue multiple, March 2017 (in million $).

Revenue multiple (in million $)	2016	2015	2014	
Revenue	8,292	8,524	8,486	
Weighted multiplier	×3	×2	×1	
Sum of weighted revenue	24,876	17,048	8,486	50,410
Revenue weighted average (divided by 6)				8,401

Source: News Corp Annual Report 2014/2015/2016.

reductions, which is why its EBITDA margins have not decreased by a similar amount. However, a revenue valuation does not take into account those cost reductions. As a result, with the revenue method, News Corp has a much lower valuation than with the EBITDA method.

As these two valuation exercises on News Corp illustrate, putting a price tag on a company involves both quantitative analysis, as well as qualitative judgment. All methods for evaluating a company rely on the numbers that are in a company's annual statements. But, in the end, assumptions about growth in revenue, costs, and liabilities determine projected earnings and cash flow. Past performance is not necessarily indicative of future performance. The strategy that management pursues can make a substantial difference in the long-term viability of a company—whether it is a start-up, such as Snap, or a legacy company, such as News Corp. That's why placing a value on a company is about predicting the range of possibilities that could impact a company, both positively and negatively.

Who Are Today's Media Investors?

Anyone can purchase a share of stock in a media company that is traded on an exchange, such as the New York Stock Exchange or the London Stock Exchange. Increasingly, however, the shares of most companies are owned not by individuals, who buy shares through a broker, but by *institutional investors*, who invest money for other people. Institutional investors include banks, pension funds, endowments, mutual funds, and, in recent years, hedge funds and private equity funds. They basically pool money from many investors and then funnel this money into purchasing shares of specific companies. On a typical day, institutional investors account for more than half of the volume of shares traded. As a result, they can exert significant influence on both the overall movement of the stock market, as well as the price of shares and the market valuation of companies. One study found that, by 2007, institutional investors held almost 60% of the stock in publicly traded media companies. Table 3.3 provides a sampling of media and technology companies and the percentage of shares owned by institutional investors in March 2017.

Over the past two decades, three types of investors have played a very important role in shaping the market value of media companies: venture capitalists, hedge-fund operators, and private equity fund managers. In general parlance, these investors are referred to as "the smart money" since it is assumed they are better informed about the risks than individual investors, and also better able to spot deals. However, there is little empirical evidence that, over the long haul, their investment portfolio performs better than the stock market average.

Table 3.3 Today's media investors: percentage of shares owned by institutional investors.

Company	Percentage of shares owned by institutional investors
CBS	79
Comcast	85
Disney	62
Facebook	72
Google/Alphabet	70
News Corp	96
New York Times	66
Twitter	45

Source: Information on historical stock prices and investor information can be accessed for each company at https://www. google.com/finance?q=NYSE%3ASNAP&ei=JsGMWfmZFJO1m AGy_Z7QCw and http://www.marketwatch.com/investing/stock/.

What exactly do each of these three different investors do and how does their presence shape the economics and finances of today's media enterprises? What sort of return on investment (ROI) are they seeking? And what is the time frame for achieving that return?

Venture Capitalists

These investors provide seed money to fund early-stage companies in exchange for partial ownership in the company. Founders of start-up media enterprises typically seek initial financial support first from a group known as "angel investors." These are typically individuals—friends or family members, as well as wealthy individuals, who supply money to support salaries for a small management team, proof of concept and prototype development and testing. Valuations of the company during the angel round are usually driven by subjective appraisals of the management team, the value proposition, estimates of the time-to-market, path to profitability, and estimated capital expenditures. The primary goal in this stage is to hire a talented initial team and develop a proof of concept that will attract investors for the next, more formal round of investment.

Venture capitalists typically enter in the next round of funding, often called the mezzanine level or Series A. In return for as much as a 50% ownership in the firm, a venture capital firm will expect the management team to continue developing and testing the product, hire additional talent needed to bring the product to market, and begin business development efforts. Recent research by Harvard University professor Ramana Nanda found that more start-ups are getting a first round of financing, however, fewer are getting funding for next round. As a result, more than one in five start-ups fail before receiving a second cash infusion. By the Series B—or the balcony level—the goal is building scale and revenue traction. In this stage, typically one or more firms will furnish financing, which will be larger than in the previous round. There may also be a Series C round, with another cash infusion in return for ownership. This round is focused on strengthening the balance sheet, including operating capital to achieve profitability, acquire another company, or develop new products. The last round signifies the start of an exit strategy for most venture capitalist investors.

More than half of all start-ups never make it to the five-year mark, and only a third make it to the ten-year mark. In general, value capitalists tend to invest with an expectation of selling their shares in a start-up within three to five years. At that point, venture capitalists typically place a valuation on the surviving start-ups, based on revenue and projected EBITDA. Additional funding may be sought to shore up the balance sheet and profitability as the venture fund determines the best exit strategy: Should the company issue an IPO or be purchased by another, larger company? As we discussed in Chapter 1, Facebook received three different major rounds of funding—including an initial $500,000 from the founder of PayPal, $12.7 million from the venture capital firm Accel Partners, and an additional $16 million from Microsoft that valued the firm at $15 billion. Because the valuation of a company at this final stage of funding is based on sales and a best guess on future EBITDA, it may or may not relate to the actual IPO price of the shares or to the eventual selling price. For example, at the close of the first day of trading in 2012, Facebook had a market valuation of $100 billion.

Like Microsoft, many media companies have their own venture capital fund. This includes Comcast, Verizon, Reed Elsevier, Time Warner, and Hearst. Corporate venture funds participated in almost one-fifth of the more than 3,600 venture capital deals in 2014. In some cases, these corporate venture funds will continue to "hold" instead of "exiting." In 2005, Jerry Yang, the founder of Yahoo!, invested $1 billion for 40% ownership of a start-up e-commerce site in China that was "killing" Yahoo's own site in China. The start-up was headed by Jack Ma, a former government translator who had been assigned to give Yang a tour of the Great Wall in 1997. Both parties benefitted, according to Ma and Yang, who were on stage together at Stanford in 2015, reminiscing about the deal. Ma says he received management and strategy advice from Yahoo that he would not have received from a "non-corporate" venture capital fund. As for Yahoo, that initial $1 billion investment was worth $20 billion when Alibaba listed its shares in an IPO offering in 2014.

Hedge Fund Operators

Once a company has done an IPO and is publicly traded, it will likely attract a second type of investor, the hedge fund operator. By 2015, three years after the IPO, more than 133 hedge funds had purchased sizeable stakes (of 1% or more) of Facebook stock. Hedge funds proliferated in the 1990s and first decade of 2000 as an investment alternative to mutual funds. Like mutual funds, hedge funds are classified as "institutional investors" since they pool money from other individuals and institutions (such as universities or pension funds) and invest in stocks, bonds, and other types of equity. However, they typically invest in a broader range of instruments (including derivatives or shorting stock), seeking a higher rate of return, regardless of whether the market rises or falls. Since risk is correlated with return, they are often restricted to high net worth individuals and institutions, with at least $1 million net worth. A hedge fund is a limited partnership with a fund manager, who, unlike a mutual fund manager, receives a percentage of the investment returns. One of the criticisms of the hedge funds is that this system of compensation can encourage the fund manager to seek out riskier investments and employ leverage (i.e., use debt) in order to get a higher return on investment.

Hedge fund operators often employ a dual strategy of "buy and hold" and "buy and sell." The long-term strategy (called "going long") usually involves buying stock in companies judged to have the potential for a higher than average ROI when compared to the stock market or their industry peers. The short-term strategy involves purchasing stock with leverage, selling it, and then buying it back when the price falls. (This is called "shorting" the stock.) Hedge fund manager John Paulson, for example, became famous for correctly betting against the mortgage industry in 2008.

Because of this dual "long-short" strategy employed by hedge funds, the fund managers tend to be "activist" shareholders of stock that they hold—especially if they calculate it is falling short of projected returns. They acquire a sizeable percentage of the shares and then use their financial stake to seek seats on the board of directors, and then lobby for appointment of a new management team and/or a strategy to "unlock the value" of an underperforming company. Often that strategy involves selling the company or parts of the company. In 2005, the manager of a Legg Mason hedge fund, Private Capital Management, acquired 19% of the outstanding shares in Knight Ridder, the second largest newspaper company in the United States in terms of circulation. He then joined with two other hedge firms that together held an additional 20% stake and "put the company in play," forcing it to sell off its assets. In 2006, McClatchy Newspapers, a much smaller company with only one-third as many newspapers as Knight Ridder, bought the company, paying $67 a share—considerably less than the hedge funds had calculated. Still, it represented a 26% premium over the $53 price a year before. The hedge funds "exited" the market and Knight Ridder ceased to exist.

In 2008, Legg Mason's Capital Management, which had acquired a 4.4% stake in Yahoo, took the opposite stance, opposing the sale of the company and the ousting of CEO Jerry Yang, which was advocated by another hedge fund manager, Carl Icahn, who had a 5% stake. Yang resigned later that year, and Icahn quietly left the board the following year when the new CEO failed to take his advice. In recent years, Icahn has acquired significant stakes in a number of media and technology companies—including Time Warner, eBay, Apple, and Netflix—and has a mixed track record of success. In 2006, for example, he unsuccessfully pushed to break up the AOL Time Warner conglomerate into four separate companies—publishing, cable services, Internet, and film/television. Two years later, after Icahn had sold his stake in the company, a new CEO began implementing the break-up strategy advocated by Icahn, spinning off AOL, Time Warner Cable, and Time Inc. as separate companies.

Most CEOs and CFOs spend a considerable amount of time managing the expectations of institutional investors—especially activist hedge fund managers who buy up significant shares of a particular company. Often, as was the case at Yahoo, they take diametrically opposing views. Other times, as was the case with Knight Ridder, they band together to force change. Critics say that these activist hedge funds force managers of media companies to make decisions that may boost short-term gains for their own funds, but hamper long-term sustainability of the company. Regardless, since they now own a significant portion of stock in media companies, managers of publicly traded companies have to reckon with them and try to chart a financial course that delivers an acceptable ROI and a strategic course that allows the company to grow in the years ahead.

Private Equity Fund Managers

Once a company is "put into play," as Knight Ridder was in 2006, private equity funds will most likely take a look at the company's prospectus and decide whether to make a bid on the company. In contrast to venture capitalists, which invest in start-ups, private equity firms tend to buy existing companies. These can be private companies, as well as publicly traded ones, such as Knight Ridder. As with hedge funds, private equity managers pool the funds from other high net worth individuals and institutions, to make large investments in private companies or to "buy out" all the stock in publicly held companies and make them private. Private equity is exactly as it sounds: equity (part ownership) of an investment fund that cannot be purchased or traded on an exchange.

Private equity funds often focus on buying distressed properties and reviving them through a combination of cost-cutting and "better management" before selling them either to another firm—or taking them public again, issuing another IPO. These funds typically require their investors to commit to a long holding period (of five to seven years) before they can withdraw their money. However, private equity companies are often criticized for both their use of leverage and a short-term focus on ROI. Many of the companies acquired by private equity firms are saddled with a significant amount of debt, with the assets of the company used as collateral. This is called a leveraged buyout. As a result, private equity funds can make a large number of acquisitions without having to commit a lot of money to any individual company they purchase. Without significant funds invested, private equity managers can simply shed underperforming properties in their portfolio and move on to the next acquisition. This strategy is summarized as a "buy 'em, hold 'em and flip 'em" strategy. After the sale of Knight Ridder in 2006 and the subsequent recession in 2008, private equity companies have aggressively purchased newspapers in small and mid-sized markets across the United States, and implemented significant cost reductions. Newsroom employment, for example, had declined by more than one-third by 2015, lower than at any time since the numbers were first tracked in 1970. Investment entities—most of which are private equity companies—now own all or portions of 2,000 of the nation's 7,500 papers. Many papers have been sold two or more times since.

Regardless of the pros and cons, these three types of investors are a fact of life, with a significant stake in media companies. The average share of stock is held for only nine months today, compared with nine years in the 1970s. The unrelenting focus by institutional investors on ROI means that managers and owners of both public and private companies have a new imperative to grow and grow quickly—revenue, profit, and cash flow—all of which is assumed to ultimately drive shareholder return of both public and private companies.

How Do You Calculate a Return on Your Investment?

How much would you pay to own a company founded in 2011 by Stanford classmates who designed a disappearing photo app as a class design project? One of the earliest and largest investors in Snap was the venture capital firm, Benchmark, which, beginning in 2013, invested a total of $24 million in return for a 12% stake. Later investors paid more and received less of a stake, but were still eager to get on board. In 2016, in its last round of financing before it went public, Snap raised $1.8 billion, including $169 million from four mutual funds run by Fidelity Investments. Shut out of the last round, NBC Universal, instead, made a deal to buy $500 million of stock in Snap in the March 2017 IPO.

At the close of the opening day of trading, early stage and late stage funders appeared to have made very profitable decisions. Benchmark's profit alone was estimated to be $3–4 billion. But, how about the individual investors, who scrambled to own a piece of Snap at $24 a share on opening day? Would this prove to be a wise investment or had they entered the game too late? Over time, how would both the big and small shareholders in Snap calculate a return on their investment?

The large brokerage and securities firms employ research analysts to develop earnings estimates for publicly traded corporations and make recommendations on whether to buy stock in a specific company. Typically, analysts specialize in covering an industry sector, so the same analysts that cover CBS will likely cover Disney. Likewise, the same who cover Facebook will also cover other social media companies, such as Twitter. This allows them to compare the financial performance of peers and competitors quarter to quarter, year to year. These analysts develop their earnings estimate with quantitative models that take into account a company's past financial performance, trends within the industry sector (i.e., is demand for a product or service increasing?) and the macro-economic environment.

Once they have worked through several scenarios, they then set a target price for the stock, based on whether they conclude earnings will rise or fall. They make one of five recommendations:

- Buy: This stock is expected to outpace others in its industry sector. Also known as a "strong buy."
- Overweight or outperform: This indicates a particular stock is expected to post above average returns in its industry sector. Also known as a "moderate buy."
- Hold: The stock in this company is expected to perform at the same level as other stocks in its sector, or as the market as a whole.
- Underweight or underperform: The expected return on this stock is below the industry sector average.
- Sell: The stock is not expected to rise in price and may continue to fall in value. Implicit in this recommendation: even if you paid more for the stock than it is now worth, you should consider selling and salvaging whatever you can.

Table 3.4 shows how analysts assessed four stocks in March 2017, as Snap issued its IPO.

In reality, the majority of stocks in established companies, even those that are underperforming compared to their industry competitors, have a recommendation of "hold" or higher. Note the recommendation on Twitter in Table 3.4. Even though Twitter had an average target price lower than its current price of $15.56—indicating that most analysts felt the stock was overvalued—22 out of 39 research analysts still had a "hold" recommendation on the stock. Only 13 analysts had issued an "underweight" or "sell" recommendation.

Since grade inflation affects stock ratings, investors often employ other metrics to determine whether to buy or sell stock. Two of the most commonly used calculations are *earnings per share* (EPS) and the *price/earnings* (P/E) ratio. Both give some insight into a firm's current profitability.

Table 3.4 Four stock analyses as Snap issued its IPO, March 2017.

Company	# of analysts	Average rating	Current price ($)	Average target price ($)
Facebook	46	Buy	137.00	158.00
Google	34	Buy	827.00	986.00
News Corp	12	Overweight	12.95	14.87
Twitter	39	Hold	15.56	14.64

Source: http://www.marketwatch.com, accessed March 6, 2017

- *Earnings per share* (EPS) represents the amount of profit for each share of common stock held by shareholders. Many investors consider this the most important variable that determines the share price. It is calculated by dividing a company's net income by the number of outstanding common shares (net income/number of shares). In general, the higher the EPS, the higher the price of a share of stock. In March 2017, Google's EPS was $28.26 and each share was worth $835. Disney had an EPS of $5.54 and a share price of $111.
- *The P/E ratio* can be calculated by dividing the price of a share of stock by the earnings per share (price/EPS). Most stocks on the US exchanges have a P/E ratio of approximately 20, which, in theory, means an investor should be willing to pay $20 for every $1 in future earnings. If companies have a high P/E ratio, it typically indicates that investors expect it to produce higher future earnings growth than another company with a lower P/E ratio. After Facebook reported higher than expected mobile revenue in 2016, its stock increased in price and as a result its P/E ratio climbed to 72 times current earnings. During the same period of time, Google's P/E ratio was approximately 30 times and CBS had a P/E ratio of 19 times current earnings. This difference in P/E ratio among the three companies suggests that investors anticipated that Facebook earnings would grow at a rate significantly faster than CBS and Google.

Both metrics are simple to calculate and allow investors to compare the performance of companies across industries, regardless of size. But they have their significant drawbacks. First, the earnings figure used to calculate both EPS and P/E is net income, which includes taxes, interest, and noncash items such as depreciation, which can vary widely from year to year. Second, both EPS and P/E can vary depending on the number of shares a company has issued. (Management can increase earnings per share by buying back shares.) Finally, both are snapshots of current profitability and may not represent future prospects.

This is why most investors use a combination of metrics to evaluate established businesses that also includes trailing, weighted EBITDA, as well as revenue growth over time, and projections of trends in the industry. Additionally, managers of a portfolio of stocks may also take into account the "beta" of a security. Beta measures the tendency of a stock to respond to swings in the market as a whole. A beta of "1" means the stock tends to move in tandem with the market. Facebook had a beta of .67 in March 2017, indicating its stock price had not reacted to recent dips or peaks in the market. Disney had a beta of 1.20, which, theoretically, indicated that its stock had been 20% more volatile than the market.

Established companies, as well as start-ups, issue stock because they want to raise money to invest in new products and services, and grow revenue and profitability over time. Shareholders buy stock in a company because they hope to share in the company's profitability. Underwriters handling the IPO for a new company that is unprofitable, such as Snap, set the target price for a share of stock by using the revenue multiple method discussed previously, along with complex modeling formulas that project user growth and potential earnings. The trick is to price the shares so there is sustainable demand for the stock on opening day, but not so much investor enthusiasm that the price rises to unrealistic multiples of revenue growth in the days after the IPO, as Twitter's stock did.

The lead underwriters of the Snap IPO—Morgan Stanley and Goldman Sachs—initially indicated that, based on investor demand, the shares for the IPO would be priced between $14 and $16. On the day of the IPO, March 1, 2017, the target price was raised to $17 a share, which gave the company a market value of $24 billion. On March 2, the first day of trading on the NYSE, the stock opened at $24 a share, and rose to $29 a share the next day before falling back down to just under $24 a week later.

Early investors in the firm, venture capitalists like Benchmark, were clear winners in the early days of trading. Benchmark's investment of $24 million in Snap was worth $3.2 billion at the close of trading on the first day. Later investors, like Fidelity and NBCU, had also reaped significant gains on their shares, acquired for $17 or less. But what about the investors who bought at $24 dollars or higher? Would this be a profitable investment for the small investor?

Let's consider the trajectory of two other stocks: Facebook and Twitter. Suppose you had purchased one share of stock each in Facebook and Twitter on their first day of trading and sold the two shares on March 2, 2017, the day that Snap went public. How would you calculate a return on your investment in these two start-ups?

In the weeks leading up to Facebook's IPO in 2012, several analysts argued that a $38-per-share price was too high, given the company's recent metrics (including revenue and user growth rates). On the first day of trading, Facebook stock closed just barely above its opening price, and it fell as low as $18 a share over the next year before beginning to rebound. However, if you had purchased a share of Facebook stock for $38 and held onto it until Snap went public in 2017, a share purchased for $38 on opening day was worth $137. You had a gain of $99.

Hoping to avoid a repeat of Facebook's first weeks, underwriters priced Twitter's IPO shares at $26. As soon as Twitter began trading on the New York Stock Exchange on 2013, the share price shot up to $45, before closing at $40. Six weeks later the price had climbed to $69 a share. It then began a relentless downward tumble in early 2014. A share of Twitter stock purchased at $40 a share on opening day in 2013 would have been worth $16 in 2017. You had a loss of $24.

You calculate a return on your investment (ROI) on the two stocks by subtracting the cost of the shares of stock from the proceeds on the investment, and then dividing that answer by the cost of the investment (Box 3.2). Because the answer is expressed as a percentage, you can easily compare a return on various investments.

On the surface, return on investment (ROI) is a fairly simple calculation. However, the above ROI calculations do not take into account two important economic and financial variables: *opportunity costs* and the *time value of money*.

Let's consider the *opportunity costs* of buying Twitter stock, instead of investing the money in another stock. What if, instead of purchasing one share of Twitter stock at $40 a share on Nov. 8, 2013 (the day that company went public), you purchased another share of Facebook stock, which was then trading at $48. In that case, you would have a very positive ROI on your purchase of two shares of Facebook stock compared to the negative ROI when you bought both Facebook and Twitter (Box 3.3, page 62).

Box 3.2 ROI = Profit Divided by Cost

- ROI on the Facebook investment: $99 (the gain on the stock)/$38 (the cost of the investment) = 260% ROI.
- ROI on the Twitter investment: You have a loss of $24 (you bought the stock at $40 and it was only worth $16). This is a negative ROI.
- ROI on the combined Facebook and Twitter investments: You have a net gain of $75 on the two stocks ($99 gain on Facebook minus $24 loss on Twitter)/$78 (the cost of the two stocks, $38 for Facebook and $40 for Twitter) = You have a gain of $75 and a ROI of 96%.

Box 3.3 ROI on Facebook Investments in 2012 and 2013

- You had a gain of $188 of both stocks ($99 on the stock purchased in 2012 and $89 on the stock purchased in 2013).
- You paid $86 for both shares ($38 in 2012 and $48 in 2013).
- $188 gain/$86 cost of stock = 219% ROI.

In this case, you not only lost $24 on the Twitter stock, but also missed out on a gain of $89 on a Facebook share purchased for slightly more ($48) at the same time. So, the opportunity costs of choosing to invest in Twitter stock are even greater than the accounting loss ($24).

Calculating *the time value of money* diminishes your ROI even further. Simply stated, given inflation and other risks, the value of a dollar today is greater than a dollar four or five years hence. Inflation from 2012 to 2017 was low compared to rates in the previous two decades. Nevertheless, the annual average rate for those five years was between 1 and 2%. So, even if you had chosen to invest in Facebook, instead of Twitter in 2013, dollars you received in 2017 would have been worth less than the dollars you invested in Facebook stock in 2013, as well as the dollars you invested in 2012. You still have a positive ROI, but it is discounted for the time value of money (Box 3.4).

Box 3.4 ROI Calculation on Facebook Investments, Discounting for 2% Inflation

- If an investor paid $38 for one Facebook share in 2012, he/she is paying $41.96 in 2017 terms (assuming 2% annual inflation). $38 x (1.02) ^ 5 = $41.96.
- If an investor paid $48 for one Facebook share in 2013, he/she is paying $51.96 in 2017 terms (assuming 2% annual inflation). $48 x (1.02) ^ 4 = $51.96.
- Adjusting for the time value of money, the ROI is 200%. $188 / ($41.96 + $51.96)

In a similar fashion, a manager of any firm is constantly evaluating and analyzing options for using the earnings at his or her disposal, and then choosing which option is more likely to yield a better profit over the next several years.

In calculating an ROI on major investments—such as taking a major stake in Snap—all of the following three methods are used since they take into account both opportunity costs and the time value of money: net present value, internal rate of return, and profitability index.

Net Present Value

Suppose you invested $1 million in a start-up company and received a 50% share of ownership. This enterprise is sold five years later for $2.5 million, yielding a profit of $250,000 (or a 25% gain).Let's consider how to calculate ROI on this investment using net present value (NPV) (Box 3.5). This method takes into account the time value of money by

---

Box 3.5 NPV Calculation of $1 Million Investment, Assuming 2% Inflation

$NPV = C_1 / (1 + r)^t$
Cash gained (C_1) = $250,000
Discount rate (r) = 2%
Time periods (t) = 5
Present value of cash gained = $226,432.70

---

discounting future cash flows to what they are worth in today's dollars. Five years have elapsed since your investment in the start-up. The ROI has to be adjusted for an average inflation of 2% in the intervening years, which brings down the $250,000 gain to $226,432.70.

Internal Rate of Return

This method builds on the net present value (NPV) calculation. It not only takes into account the time value of money, but also establishes a targeted rate of return, also called a hurdle rate. Let's assume your company is evaluating a five-year project that requires a one million dollar investment. It has the following expected cash flows: Negative cash flows of $30,000 in year one and $30,900 in year two, followed by positive cash flows of $31,827 in year three, $32,782 in year four, and $1,250,000 in year five. Let's also assume the hurdle rate in this case is 5%. We can calculate the *internal rate of return* (IRR) by finding the rate at which the NPV of the project is equal to zero (Box 3.6). The IRR must be equal to or greater than the hurdle rate of 5% in order for a project to get the go-ahead. The IRR is 4.5%, which is lower than the hurdle rate. Therefore, you should not proceed with the project.

Profitability Index

This method builds on the IRR method and allows an investor to compare many different projects, projecting an IRR for each one and then choosing whichever has the highest rate of return. Let's suppose you want to compare the ROI of two projects, assuming an inflation rate of 2% (Box 3.7, page 64). You can buy a 50% stake in a start-up that you anticipate will be sold in five years for $2.5 million. Or, you can invest $1 million in the development of a new product with projected cash flows of $25,000, $400,000 and $600,000 in years three through five. Which is the better option?

As these examples illustrate, every decision that a manager—or an individual shareholder—makes has an associated opportunity cost, which is the profit or value of the option that was given up in order to invest in the other one. Opportunity cost and the time value of money are economic concepts that are not recognized in a company's financial statements. However, it is front of mind for analysts and investors who pore over a company's annual statements, evaluating not just the recent performance of an enterprise, but also the decision-making acumen of the managers.

Those who bought Facebook stock on opening day and held onto their stock for at least two years had a nice return on their investment. But, it took almost a year a half for the Facebook stock to rebound to its opening price. The rise in share price was ultimately

---

Box 3.6 IRR Calculation with Hurdle Rate of 5%

Cash flow in year 0: -$1,000,000 / (1 + 2%) ^0 = -$1,000,000
Cash flow in year 1: -$30,000 / (1 + 2%) ^1 = -$28,700
Cash flow in year 2: -$30,900 / (1 + 2%) ^2 = -$28,280
Cash flow in year 3: $31,827 / (1 + 2%) ^3 = $27,866
Cash flow in year 4: $32,782 / (1 + 2%) ^4 = -$27,459
Cash flow in year 5: $1,250,000 / (1 + 2%) ^5 = $1,001,655
IRR = 4.5%. You should not proceed with the project.

Box 3.7 Profitability Index

Profitability Index for Project #1

Cash flow in year 0: -$1,000,000 / (1 + 2%) ^0 = -$1,000,000
Cash flow in year 1: $0 / (1 + 2%) ^1 = $0
Cash flow in year 2: $0 / (1 + 2%) ^2 = $0
Cash flow in year 3: $0 / (1 + 2%) ^3 = $0
Cash flow in year 4: $0 / (1 + 2%) ^4 = $0
Cash flow in year 5: $1,250,000 / (1 + 2%) ^5 = $1,132,164
Profitability index: $1,132,164 / $1,000,000 = 1.13

Profitability Index for Project #2

Cash flow in year 0: -$1,000,000 / (1 + 2%) ^0 = -$1,000,000
Cash flow in year 1: $0 / (1 + 2%) ^1 = $0
Cash flow in year 2: $0 / (1 + 2%) ^2 = $0
Cash flow in year 3: $250,000 / (1 + 2%) ^3 = $235,581
Cash flow in year 4: $400,000 / (1 + 2%) ^4 = $369,538
Cash flow in year 5: $600,000 / (1 + 2%) ^5 = $543,438
Profitability index: ($235,580 + $369,538 + $543,438 = $1,148,556) / $1,000,000 = 1.15
Based on these projections, project 2 has a higher profitability index. Therefore, select project 2.

---

propelled by the company's shift in strategy, away from desktop to mobile platforms, which placed Facebook on a new growth trajectory of both revenues and profits. In 2016, four years after its IPO, Facebook had revenues of $26.6 billion and net income of $10.2 billion. Those who bought Twitter were not as lucky. As user and revenue growth slowed and then plateaued, Twitter's management seemed to flounder. In 2016, three years after its IPO, Twitter posted revenues of $2.5 billion and a net loss of $456 million.

How long should Snap investors hold on to their shares before selling? Metrics such as EPS and P/E ratios, as well as recommendations from Wall Street analysts, offer some guidance about the direction of the company and its prospects for future growth. Ultimately, the ROI for any investor—whether venture capitalist or individual stockholder—will depend on a variety of factors. When did they invest? How much did they invest? How long did they leave their money in this investment? Were there other options that might have yielded greater returns?

Exercise: Divining the Future Value of Snap's Stock

In early 2017, there were more than 150 start-up companies valued by venture capital firms such as Benchmark, a major investor in Snap, at more than $1 billion. In the business world, such companies—with high valuations based not on their current financials, but on their future prospects—are called *unicorns*. They are so-called because they were considered a rarity until recently. However, by 2015, unicorns were becoming so plentiful that a partner in Benchmark worried that a "bubble" was developing. When it burst, he predicted there would be a lot of "dead unicorns"—along with some very disappointed late-stage investors.

Snap's March 2017 IPO was the biggest in the United States since Alibaba's in 2014. There was much pent-up demand for both the IPO shares and the publicly traded ones. With IPO shares priced at $17 a share, Snap's valuation was $24 billion. When shares closed at $24 on the first day of trading, its valuation had climbed to $34 billion.

Despite the demand for the stock, a number of analysts questioned whether Snap was overvalued right out of the gate. They pointed to a number of cautionary signs:

- User growth was slowing. Although Snapchat had 158 million daily users, its year-over-year growth rate had slowed from 7% in the second quarter to 3% in the third quarter. Growth seemed to have slowed at the very point that Facebook's Instagram released a new app very similar to the Stories feature on Snapchat, which allowed users to post disappearing videos or paste heart-shaped icons over their eyes. Instagram had 150 million daily users of its app, almost as many as the entire user base of Snapchat.
- Its price-to-sales ratio far exceeded such high-growth stocks as Facebook and Google. Snap had generated $404 million in revenue in 2016. A $34 billion valuation at the close of the first day of trading was 84 times revenue the previous year. By comparison, Facebook's valuation was 14 times revenue, and Google's was 6 times. As one analyst pointed out, even assuming that Snap's revenue grew at 50% over the next four years, it would still be trading at a higher price-to-sales ratio than either of those tech giants.
- Snap was bleeding money. The company had not turned a profit since its establishment as a commercial enterprise in 2011, and the losses were growing. It had lost $515 million in 2016 compared to $379 million in 2015. Adding to the confusion about the long-term strategy of the company, the founders had indicated in the prospectus circulated before the IPO that Snap might never turn a profit.
- Snap was facing fierce competition for both advertisers and millennials, the heaviest users of Snapchat. Instagram, which Facebook had purchased in 2014 for $3 billion, had 300 million daily users in 2017, twice as many as Snap. Potential advertisers could get much greater reach and narrower targeting of customers through Facebook and Google.

Adding to the concerns, those who bought shares of the company on the New York Stock Exchange had no voting rights on major business decisions made by the company, including sale of assets, mergers, and acquisitions, and the make-up of the board of directors. In an highly unusual move, the two founders of the company—26-year-old CEO Evan Spiegel, and 28-year-old CTO Bobby Murphy—retained 90% of the voting rights, with the other 10% going to early investors, such as Benchmark. (In comparison, Zuckerberg and the founders of Google had retained only slightly more than 50% of the voting rights in their company.) Investors were placing almost complete confidence in the business acumen of the young founders, who were described by the press and Wall Street analysts as "secretive" about their long-range strategy for Snap. This led to speculation that early investors would quickly sell their IPO shares, driving down the price for nonvoting investors.

In its first quarterly earnings report in May 2017, Snap posted a $2.1 billion loss, and shares tumbled 20% to $18 a share. The loss was driven in part by a whopping $2 billion payout, related to IPO stock compensation. But, even adjusting for this one-time hit—which significantly exceeded on a percentage basis the amount both Facebook and Twitter paid out on their IPOs—there were signs that Snap was struggling. It added only 8 million daily users in its first quarter, and only 44 million over the previous year. It was the slowest year-over-year growth for the ad-supported site since its inception. Its 166 million users tended to be engaged, staying on the site an average of 30 minutes, using its augmented reality features. However, analysts pointed out that Snap was making only 90 cents per user. Facebook, which reported 200 million daily users for Instagram, had made $4.23 per user. CEO Spiegel resisted suggestions that Snap should more aggressively grow its user base through push notifications and similar methods, saying it wasn't "sustainable over the long term." Several analysts, who had projected higher user growth rates for Snap, openly questioned whether Snap could "elbow its way into a crowded social media market" and began to wonder if Snap was following the path of Twitter.

Snap shares continued to decline over the summer months. In August, the lockdown period expired—investors and employees were able to sell their shares—and Snap reported disappointing second-quarter earnings, as user growth continued to slow. Shares fell below $12 a share before climbing to $14 a share, giving it a market cap of $17 billion (or half of its opening day valuation). Even worse, some analysts were predicting shares might fall below $10 a share before Snap bottomed out. As one analyst described it, "2017's hottest IPO has quickly become its worst."

- If you had been a venture capitalist, would you have invested in Snap prior to its IPO? Why or why not?
- The founders of Facebook, Google and Snap retain more than 50% of the stock's voting rights. Consider the pros and cons of this sort of arrangement.
- Compare the trajectory of the stock price of Twitter and Facebook to Snap during the first six months of trading. What caused the price of all three stocks to fall below their IPO target?
- Under what scenario would Snap be worth $34 billion, its market cap at the close of the first day of trading?

Summary

The market valuation of any media company is determined by both external and internal factors. External factors—such as the economic environment and industry sector in which a company operates—have historically exerted an outsized impact, determining as much as 90% of a company's market valuation. That is because most media companies are cyclical, with revenues and profits mirroring the ups and downs of the economy. Also, companies in rapidly expanding and innovative industry sectors tend to grow more rapidly than those in mature and stable industries. However, decisions made by managers of a firm can make a big difference in the financial performance and valuation of both a start-up or legacy company, such as a book publisher.

The fate of media companies lies increasingly in the hands of institutional investors. This includes venture capitalists, hedge fund operators, and private equity fund managers. Venture capitalists typically fund start-ups, while hedge fund and private equity fund managers tend to focus on established companies. These three types of investors typically have an expectation for a quick return on their investments. This often prompts media companies to focus on near-term growth.

There are a number of financial tools used to place a valuation on both private and publicly traded companies. Analysts, investors, and lenders pore over the annual financial statements looking for trends in revenue, costs, profits, and cash flow. They determine the value of a company, using one or more of these methods: EBITDA multiple, revenue multiple, discretionary cash flow, or book value. Established media companies are typically valued based on the EBITDA method. Most start-up valuations are based on some combination of a revenue multiple and projected EBITDA.

Whether you are a shareholder in a publicly traded company or an investor in an early-stage company, you will calculate return on investment (ROI) using the same financial tools. ROI is a very simple calculation but it must be adjusted and discounted to account for opportunity costs and the time value of money. More complicated tools—such as net present value, internal rate of return, and the profitability index—allow investors to discount future cash flows because of inflation, and to consider what other options might have yielded a better return.

Most start-ups and "unicorns" fail to pass the test of time, despite the phenomenal success of Facebook and Google in recent years. What made them different? Why were they able to reach scale and profitability when others weren't? Will their sky-high market valuations continue? What are the lessons for other start-up and legacy media enterprises? These are all questions we will consider in Chapter 4.

4

The Transformed Competitive Landscape

Tom Freston seemed to work magic with the MTV brand. Beginning in 1987 when he was appointed CEO, he oversaw the rapid expansion of the then six-year-old cable music video channel. By 2006, MTV Networks had grown into a global conglomerate of channels and networks that were popular with teens and young adults, including Comedy Central, Nickelodeon, BET, CMT and VH1. It distributed such in-demand cable shows as *South Park*, *The Daily Show with Jon Stewart*, *SpongeBob SquarePants*, *Rugrats*, and *Beavis and Butt-head*.

So, in January 2006, when Freston became CEO of Viacom, expectations were high that the stock of this newly formed company, which included Paramount Pictures as well as MTV Networks, would soar under his deft guidance. Viacom (short for Video and Audio Communications) had been spun off from its sibling, CBS Corporation, which included the CBS broadcast network, some television and radio stations, and the subscription channel Showtime, as well as an outdoor advertising division and the Simon & Schuster book publishing company. Industry analysts predicted that splitting the corporation into two separate publicly traded companies would "unlock the value" of the stock price of the two entities, allowing them to rise and fall independently of one other. Viacom was seen as the hip youngster, most likely to thrive in the digital age, while CBS was viewed as a collection of mature legacy companies. The CBS network, once known as the "Tiffany network," had recently finished last in primetime ratings.

Viacom's stock debuted at $43 a share, CBS at $25. But confounding the expectations of Wall Street, the price of Viacom stock began falling. By September, Viacom's stock was down almost 15% while that of CBS had risen more than 10%. Only nine months after naming him CEO—and only one month after expressing strong support for him in a meeting with Wall Street analysts—Chairman Sumner Redstone ousted Freston. Pressed to explain his reasons, Redstone faulted Freston's lack of a "growth strategy" and the failure of Viacom to acquire the social media network MySpace, which had been purchased by News Corp in July 2005 for $580 million. Redstone promised that the new CEO Philippe Dauman, a Viacom board member and head of a private equity firm, would be "more aggressive and entrepreneurial," especially in seeking out Internet investments that would bolster the price of Viacom's stock.

A decade after the spin-off of Viacom, the stock price of CBS had risen from $25 a share to roughly $60. However, Viacom stock was trading at the same price in 2016 as it had in 2006, hovering around $40. Why did the stock price of the aging sibling outperform the hip youngster?

In this chapter, we'll discuss the imperative that all companies face to grow or be left by the wayside in a rapidly changing media landscape. We'll explore the challenges and

The Strategic Digital Media Entrepreneur, First Edition. Penelope Muse Abernathy and JoAnn Sciarrino.
© 2019 John Wiley & Sons, Inc. Published 2019 by John Wiley & Sons, Inc.
Companion website: www.wiley.com/go/abernathy/StrategicDigitalMediaEntrepreneur

opportunities confronting management at each stage of a company's development, and how that affects the types of growth strategies that managers can profitably pursue.

Among the questions we'll consider are:

- What are the various stages in the typical life of a company? How does this affect a company's ability to grow customers, revenues and profits, and the strategies that it pursues?
- How can companies grow revenues and profits?
- How fast must companies change their business model in order to survive?
- How did the Internet challenge the economics of existing media companies?
- What will be the business models going forward?

What Are the Various Stages in the Life of a Company?

When Tom Freston was ousted as CEO from Viacom after only nine months, at least one Wall Street analyst questioned if it was "unfair" to make him the "scapegoat" for Viacom's woes, as well as the malaise affecting cable networks in general. "Viacom's networks are already number one with kids and music. Where do you go from there?" he asked. However, other analysts questioned whether Viacom could continue to attract a young audience to television when many were already turning to the Internet for their music and entertainment.

The rise and fall of MTV and Viacom as the go-to destination for young viewers parallel that of the cable industry. In the late 1940s and early 1950s, communities around the United States began installing tall antennas on mountaintops and other towering structures to enhance over-the-air reception of newly licensed regional television stations. Residents in those communities were connected, via cable, to the towers and paid a fee to watch the handful of network-affiliated channels that were available. Growth in the early years was slow. By 1962, there were 800 cable companies in the country, but only 850,000 customers. Satellite transmission in the early 1970s changed the trajectory for the industry by allowing cable operators to distribute signals from distant stations as well. In 1976, entrepreneur Ted Turner began beaming, via satellite, the signal of his small independent station in Atlanta—which carried a steady diet of movies, reruns of old television shows, and live feeds of the Atlanta Braves games—to cable subscribers in Nebraska, Virginia, and Kansas. Following in Turner's footsteps, dozens of cable channels that accepted commercials were established in the late 1970s and early 1980s, including ESPN in 1978, CNN (Cable News Network) and USA Network in 1980, and MTV (Music TV) in 1981.

In the 1980s, the industry spent billions on the wiring of the country and creating new programming for cable subscribers. For several years, revenues and profits doubled annually for both cable networks and cable operators, according to the Museum of Broadcast Communications. By the end of the 1980s, over 53 million households in the United States subscribed to cable and the number of "cable stations," offered exclusively to subscribers, had increased from 28 in 1980 to 79. Regulation in the 1990s, which required cable operators to begin selling their programming to wireless and satellite broadcasting companies, slowed the actual growth of subscribers, but not the growth of satellite channels. By the end of the 1990s, there were 68.5 million cable subscribers, and 170 cable channels, most of them, like MTV, targeting a niche market.

MTV initially carried music videos 24/7, with VJs, or video jockeys, introducing the music segments, interviewing musicians, and announcing upcoming concert dates.

Programming for the channel evolved in the 1980s to include live broadcasts of music awards programs and major concerts, as well as news and game shows. Under Freston's stewardship in the 1990s and early 2000s, MTV added reality shows—such as *The Osbournes*, which followed the day-to-day life of Black Sabbath musician Ozzy Osbourne and his family—and comedy shows, such as *Punk'd*, with actor Ashton Kutcher playing pranks on other celebrities. By 2006, the MTV/Viacom television brand included a host of other networks—featuring comedy, cartoon, and retro television shows—popular with young adults and teens.

As the number of cable household subscribers exploded in the 1980s and 1990s, viewership of MTV and its sister cable channels grew in tandem. But as cable growth slowed in the early 2000s, and adoption of the Internet skyrocketed, viewership plateaued. The 2006 upfront market—when television networks pitch their shows and sign advance contracts with advertisers—had been weak for all cable networks, and especially for Viacom's younger audience, which was migrating online to watch videos and download music on their iPods and MP3 players.

The issue of growth confronting Viacom in 2006 had been faced previously by other industries, most recently by broadcast television. Viewership of primetime shows carried by the major broadcast networks—CBS, NBC, and ABC—had peaked in the early 1980s, as the number of cable networks and channels proliferated. As a company, such as Viacom, becomes bigger and more mature—and as the market becomes more and more saturated with competitors—growth is harder to sustain. There are several stages in the life of a company or industry. In this section, we'll consider them:

The Foundation or Pioneering Stage

Both the company and the industry are in its infancy, much as the cable industry was in the 1950s and 1960s. The market is small. The majority of potential customers do not yet realize they need or want the product. The focus of management is on getting early adopters to use the product. Development and build-out costs associated with a new technology can be very high. Because of this, there is often a high failure rate of companies that enter the market at this early stage.

Rapid, Accelerated Growth

There are often "bugs" and defects in newly developed technologies. So, first-movers often don't succeed in gaining a significant toehold. Instead, the next generation of companies, with enhancements to their products, ushers in a stage of accelerated growth. Neither Google nor Facebook were first-movers, but significant improvements in their products led to widespread consumer adoption and phenomenal growth of their nascent industries. Similarly, satellite transmission changed the game for cable operators in the 1970s and 1980s. Cable subscribers not only got better reception than homes with rooftop antennas, but also had access to a growing number of "exclusive" channels. Both year-over-year revenue and audience growth in this stage are often in the high double digits, even triple digits. Those who are first to gain a toehold with a breakthrough product, such as Google or Facebook, can achieve a significant share of market and begin to establish barriers to entry. As development costs come down, existing firms in the industry begin to move toward sustainable profitability. According to industry estimates, annual operating margins of cable operators during the 1970s exceeded 40%. Encouraged by the new economics, new companies enter the market, leading to further growth of the industry and the development of customer segmentation. Companies that enter the market during this phase often begin by targeting a specific niche. MTV and a handful of other cable networks that debuted around 1980—CNN, ESPN, CBN (Christian Broadcasting Network), and USA (featuring talk shows and children's programs)—each served a different niche audience.

Mature Growth

Demand continues to grow, although revenue and audience increases are in the low double or high single digits. Earnings growth still exceeds the market average, but becomes more predictable. The market leaders continue to solidify their position and increase audience share, focusing on creating product extensions that attract new customers, and deepening the engagement and loyalty of current ones. For example, during his tenure, Freston oversaw the creation and/or reformatting of a number of cable channels, including Comedy Central, MTV2, and VH1. He also expanded the Viacom brand into international markets, with Nickelodeon, MTV, and VH1 becoming household names around the world. During this mature growth phase, new firms still enter. Also, some small firms begin to piggyback on the success of the market leaders, for example, building games or applications off existing online platforms. Zynga, founded in 2007, launched its most successful game, Farmville, in 2009 on the Facebook platform. Others, such as LinkedIn, focus their growth efforts on providing specialized products for niche audiences.

Maturity

During this phase, the growth rate for the industry segment is typically in sync with overall macroeconomic trends. Revenue growth for the industry slows to the rate of GDP. Of all the stages, this one is usually the longest for market leaders. During this stage, market leaders typically pursue two different strategies simultaneously. They attempt to create barriers to entry that discourage new competitors; often this is done by acquiring competitors and building market share. Additionally, they attempt to construct barriers to exit for their customers, making it prohibitively expensive (either in dollars or time spent relearning a new system) to switch to an alternative. Since revenue growth is now in single digits, profits mostly depend on a company's ability to control costs with its various products. Smaller firms may begin to exit the market, or be acquired by larger companies. Consolidation leads to steady earnings for the big players. That also leads to a blind spot in that executives in mature profitable companies may not recognize future competitors.

Decline

As demand for a mature product or content lessens, revenue and margins decrease, often slowly at first, and then accelerating dramatically. When this occurs, most often customers have moved on and adopted a new product, which has, in turn, created a new industry and new nimble competitors for the mature company. If companies do not have a strategy for following their customers, they will not be able to follow the money. By 2006, some industry analysts had begun to question whether Viacom could continue to attract a young audience to television when many preferred to listen to their music on MP3 players and iPods.

According to news accounts, Freston was dismissed as CEO of Viacom, at least in part, because he did not move fast enough to purchase MySpace, which was the largest social networking site in the world by the summer of 2006. Instead, News Corp acquired it for $580 million, in a move widely envied by other media executives. Viacom Chairman Redstone told an interviewer that losing MySpace was "humiliating." At the time, News Corp CEO Rupert Murdoch remarked that in the years ahead his acquisition would either be a "$500 million mistake or…look very smart." News Corp more than covered the cost of the acquisition by signing a $900 million contract with Google in 2006 to place advertising on MySpace. In retrospect, however, the dynamics of the social media landscape were already beginning to shift, as Facebook opened its user-friendly site to more and more people, including anyone 13 years old with an email account. By 2009, Facebook had eclipsed MySpace as the most popular social network. In 2011, Murdoch pronounced the acquisition a "huge mistake" when he placed the company on the market, asking $100–200 million. It sold for $35 million to an advertising company.

Would the fate of Viacom have been any different if it had purchased MySpace in 2006? Could Viacom have used MySpace to reposition its cable networks for growth in the digital age? In the next section, we'll consider the ways that companies grow revenues and profits.

How the Imperative to Grow Affects Strategies

A study of 1,870 companies done in the late 1990s found that over a ten-year period—during the longest period of macroeconomic expansion that the United States had experienced since World War II—only 13% of companies had grown at an average yearly rate of more than 5.5%, the average growth rate of the country's Gross Domestic Product (GDP). During the same period, industry analysts had predicted that companies would grow at an average of 12% a year, based on forward-looking guidance from CEOs.

The focus on short-term shareholder return on investment by institutional investors brings a laser-like focus on decisions that executives make about how they will grow the company. Given the outsized expectations of investors about earnings growth, CEOs of media companies know that failing to deliver can lead to dismissal. As a company matures, it becomes very hard to achieve earnings that exceed the rate of growth in GDP. The pressure to match the double-digit growth of their youth can prompt executives at mature companies to make bad decisions about how to grow. Therefore, this imperative for companies to grow and grow quickly has led to increasing turnover in the executive suite. Since 2000, the average CEO tenure in the United States and Europe has declined to less than five years. Between 2007 and 2012, Yahoo, for example, had six different CEOs, as the mature company struggled to regain the mojo it had in the early years, after its IPO in 1996.

Companies can grow revenues, and potentially profits, by adding:

- New products or services, either by acquiring them or developing through internal research and development. Apple, for example, built on the success of the iPod with the iPhone and iPad.
- New geographic markets. In the 1990s, the *New York Times* rejuvenated its earnings by expanding beyond its home market and repositioning itself as a national newspaper. Similarly, the large media conglomerates, as well as the new tech giants, have attempted to expand into high-growth global markets, such as China and India.

- New customer segments. When the financial publishing company Dow Jones—which owned the *Wall Street Journal*, Barron's and the Dow Jones News Wires—purchased CBS MarketWatch in 2004, it added a new group of customers—day traders—to its mix of executives and professional Wall Street traders who subscribed to their other publications and products.
- New technologies, skills, or businesses. These are then integrated into the core business. Facebook's acquisition of the photo-sharing app, Instagram, allowed it to leapfrog other competitors vying for supremacy in mobile delivery of content, which, in turn, led to higher earnings from mobile advertising.
- New channels that either boost sales or better integrate the product mix. Disney's template expands across many platforms. A popular movie results in the licensing of toys and other items sold through retail channels, as well as, potentially, a new ride in one of its theme parks.

There are three growth strategies available to companies. They can focus on organic growth, relying on internal research and development efforts. They can seek out partnerships. Or, they can acquire other companies. Each has advantages and disadvantages.

Organic Growth

Organic growth, especially involving new products or product extensions, provides the greatest and most consistent return to shareholders over the long term. Apple is the classic example of a company that has relied almost exclusively on organic growth. But organic growth requires an upfront investment in research and development without a guaranteed financial return. Many products never make it out of the lab; others fail to gain traction. Even when products do make it into the marketplace, the time from conception to first sale can extend for long periods of time, with no revenue to offset the development costs. Organic growth (through innovation of product and service design) is especially difficult for mature companies, which are typically in defensive mode, building barriers to entry that will ward off competitors and help them consolidate market share of the current product.

Partnerships

Partnerships, in which two or more companies form another corporation, allow mature companies to test and jumpstart an innovative product or service. But partnerships usually dissolve or evolve fairly quickly, with one partner taking the dominant role. Hulu, the advertising-supported streaming service, launched in 2008 as a joint partnership between ABC, Fox, and NBC, all with roughly a third ownership. In its earliest years, it allowed the three networks to gain a toehold in the streaming market and to test various strategies—including advertising and subscription-based models. But tension among the partners about what content should be available, and when, quickly arose. As a condition of government approval of its purchase of NBC in 2011, Comcast agreed to become a silent partner, and delegated decision-making to the other two partners. By 2013, Hulu was struggling financially, as it had been surpassed by the streaming services of Amazon and Netflix. Five years after the launch, the three partners put Hulu up for sale in 2013, but reversed course when they did not get what they perceived to be a fully valued offer. With Hulu off the market, the partners agreed to invest an additional $750 million in content creation and acquisition, in the hopes of seeking additional partners or making Hulu a more attractive acquisition for another media company.

Acquisitions

Acquisitions are the quickest way to boost year-over-year growth of revenue from new customers and new markets. However, numerous studies have shown that most acquisitions fail to increase the earnings of the acquiring firm over the long term. As a result, there is a loss of shareholder value. There are a number of reasons why acquisitions have such a low success rate. Often the acquiring company makes poor assumptions about cost savings or revenue growth that will result from the combination, and overpays. As a result, the acquiring company then does not invest in the company it has just purchased. Failure to integrate the cultures and operations of the two companies also dooms acquisitions, as well as poor management. Finally, a lack of discipline in either selecting potential acquisitions or setting target acquisition prices leads to disappointing results.

In *The Curse of the Mogul*, the authors found that over the period from 1993 to 2006—a time when large media companies were growing primarily through acquisition—shareholder return for the media conglomerates lagged behind the market average. They questioned the logic of many of the acquisitions, saying they were driven by "sham" sources of competitive advantage, including the "value of the brand name" or the "talent" in the acquired company. True sources of competitive advantage, they concluded, came from economies of scale, customer captivity (including habit and switching costs), cost differentials (from proprietary technology), and government protection. But even these had "an Achilles' heel," they concluded. Therefore, media companies needed to be focused on constantly reevaluating and updating their assumptions about how best to grow when pursuing even those acquisitions that delivered one of these competitive advantages.

According to studies done by the consulting firm Bain & Company, companies are most likely to achieve above-average growth rates from organic efforts or through partnerships and acquisitions when they focus on "adjacency expansion." In other words, they look for new products, geographic markets, customers, businesses, and channels that build on the core competencies they already possess.

The computer networking tech giant, Cisco, which has successfully integrated many acquisitions into the larger corporation, lists a multi-step process for deciding whether to acquire or partner with another company:

1) There needs to be a common vision between the two companies.
2) You must produce short-term wins immediately, or people at both companies will lose interest.
3) There must be long-term strategic potential; this means the company must be purchased at "just the right time" and must fulfill a long-term need.
4) There needs to be good chemistry between the people at the top of both companies.
5) Geographic proximity helps a lot since it gives people at all levels of both companies the opportunity to interact frequently.

Studies show that organic growth (developing new products and services internally) is more likely to result in long-term earnings growth. But organic growth is hit-and-miss. Partnerships usually dissolve and rarely lift earnings significantly. So executives of mature companies, as well as "young" companies, increasingly look to acquisitions. Google is known for being especially acquisitive, buying eight companies in December 2013 alone, and often averaging a purchase a week during a typical month. With earnings still growing, Google can afford to make mistakes and still recover. But for mature companies, it is much harder to recover from such mistakes.

How the Pace of Change Affects Strategies in the Digital Age

Consider the swift growth and decline of Yahoo. With its IPO in 1996, which occurred only a year and a half after the company was founded and incorporated by two Stanford graduate students, Yahoo had a market valuation of $848 million. At the time, it was one of the largest ever for a newly-formed tech company. Eight years later, in 2008, when it rejected a buyout offer of $44 billion from Microsoft, it had already reached maturity and its earnings were stagnating as Google and others eclipsed it. In 2017—only 22 years after it was founded—Yahoo was purchased by Verizon for $4.5 billion.

Standard & Poor's 500 is a list of the companies with the largest market valuation (or market cap) traded on either the NASDAQ or New York Stock Exchange. In the 1970s, a company on the S&P 500 had an average lifespan of 50 years. This means that it took roughly 50 years for a company to move through the five developmental stages mentioned in a previous section. Today the average lifespan of a company on the S&P 500 has declined to 16 years.

The S&P 500 is often used as a benchmark by economists to calculate the rate at which a company must change its business model if it is to survive and thrive in the twenty-first century. Such a calculation suggests that if a company is to keep pace with change in the S&P 500, then it must average an annual rate of 6% (100% divided by 16 years, the average lifespan of a company on the list). This increasing pace of change in the marketplace means that companies must be constantly reevaluating their strategies and business models.

In the book, *Creative Destruction: Why Companies that Are Built to Last Underperform the Market*, published in 2001, authors Richard Foster and Sarah Kaplan identify four stages in the evolution of a company's thinking and culture. In the first two stages—foundation and growth—the organization is outwardly focused and on the offensive. Executives and employees are intent on serving new and potential customers. They redesign the product or service based on customer feedback, continually test marketing techniques, and recruit a "team" of experts to manage and coordinate all aspects of the business—including sales, finances, production, and distribution.

Once the company reaches the third stage—dominance—employees begin to change the way they view the world. Organizations with a dominant market share start making defensive—instead of offensive—moves. As growth slows, executives and employees in successful companies become intent on protecting their position in the market by fending off competitive threats that might siphon off their customers. They make incremental improvements to their products and services, seek economies of scale by acquiring competitors and start-up enterprises, and, in general, become increasingly risk-averse. Senior management no longer functions as a "team," but as a group of individuals responsible for separate divisions in the company, each with separate goals. Unless the senior executives make a concerted effort to reignite an outward focus on the marketplace, the organization turns inward.

By the final stage—cultural lock-in—leadership in the organization has typically been handed over to the next generation. Organizations in this stage are focused on their existing business and assume dynamics in the marketplace are relatively stable. As a result, organizations in cultural lock-in fail to see the emergence of potential competitors that "can eat their lunch," according to Foster.

This is especially true when organizations face a disruptive innovation—such as the Internet. As we discussed in Chapter 1, a disruptive innovation in the media space is a breakthrough technological permutation that encourages the creation of new products

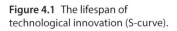

Figure 4.1 The lifespan of technological innovation (S-curve).

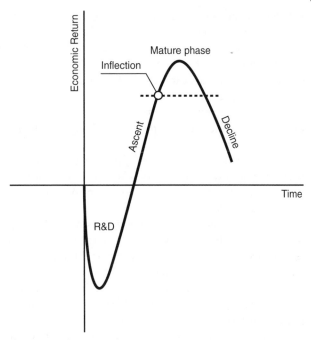

Illustration adapted from: Foster, 1986

and services and the development of new business models. In contrast, a sustaining innovation simply makes products better, and in the process, allows existing organizations to improve their profitability. Existing organizations typically react quickly to the competitive threat posed by a sustaining innovation. Either they acquire the other company or adopt the new technique. On the other hand, disrupters often fly under the radar for some time, ignored by existing companies.

The lifespan of a technological innovation is often referred to as an S-curve, with four phases. The *research and development* phase requires a significant cash outlay and investment in talent, with uncertain return since prospects for failure are high. In the *ascent* stage, expenses are recouped, as the commercialization of the technology begins. In the *mature* phase, profits are high and relatively stable. The emergence of a new technology usually brings about the final stage, *decline*, as both the usefulness of the technology and profits decrease (Figure 4.1).

In his book, *Innovation: The Attacker's Advantage*, Richard Foster noted, "Rarely does a single technology meet all customers' needs. There are almost always competing technologies, each with its own S-curve...Often several new technologies vie with each other to replace an old technology." Companies that manage to survive a disruptive technology, he concluded, "invest in research in order to know where they are on relevant S-curves and know what to expect from the beginning, the middle and the end of these curves."

Foster is often credited with applying the "creative destruction" theories of economist Joseph Schumpeter, articulated in the mid-twentieth century, to the computer/technology revolution that was in its infancy when *Innovation* was published in 1986. Schumpeter saw creative destruction as capitalism's way of reshuffling the deck and renewing itself. He argued that innovation drove economic growth, even though, as a by-product, it destroyed the business models of incumbent companies and industries. Foster contended that legacy businesses and industries could survive if they reimagined and reinvented their business models.

In his second book, *Creative Destruction*, Foster identified three types of responses by legacy companies when confronted with a disruptive innovation. In the beginning, most organizations underestimated the long-term impact of the technological innovation and made *incremental changes*, modifying existing products and services. As profits in the incumbent enterprise began to decline and customers gravitated to the new technology, organizations often made *substantial changes* to their cost structure, reducing expenses by 10% or more. Companies that survived a major disruption committed to what Foster termed "*transformative change*." Speed was of the essence. They sought to "keep pace with the market," using the S&P 500 as a proxy for how fast they needed to change. This meant they put in place a business plan to aggressively restructure their revenues and costs at an annual average 6% rate.

For existing organizations, the focus is on managing the transition from one technology to another. In order to compete on the cost side with start-ups, they need to shed the legacy costs associated with the old technology as aggressively as possible. However, many of their existing customers are also in transition. So existing companies have to maintain the old technology and costs in order to maintain the loyalty of existing customers, even as they are attempting to build new capabilities and new business models for producing and distributing content.

Foster notes two tipping points that determine whether an existing company will survive a disruptive innovation. The first comes when customer behavior begins to change and accommodate the new technology. Typically, early adopters of a new technology tend to be younger. For example, gen Xers and millennials, the primary target audience for MTV Networks in 2006, were the early adopters of MP3 players and iPods, and they flocked to the user-generated videos on YouTube, when it was established in 2005.

The second tipping point comes when economics start to work in favor of the disrupter. Once the new organization is profitable on a marginal basis, it can cut prices to such an extent that it drives the incumbent business toward bankruptcy or irrelevance. Because of its massive scale (reach) and its considerable digital capabilities (targeting), Google, for example, has decimated both advertising and circulation pricing in newspapers. It has undermined paid subscriptions by allowing its many users to link to interesting articles in hundreds of newspapers absolutely free. Even worse, it established a low ceiling on digital advertising rates, which leaves newspapers with the option of replacing profitable print advertising with unprofitable digital advertising. Similarly, streaming services undercut the pricing ability of cable providers who rely on the fees paid by consumers to then pay cable networks for the right to carry their channels.

This means that existing media enterprises need to have a three-pronged strategy to respond to a disruptive innovation. They need a strategy to shed costs (associated with the old technology), acquire new customers, and build new sources of revenue. Stated another way, they need to follow the technology, follow their customers, and follow the money. Figure 4.2 shows traditional attacks and how media enterprises can respond to them.

The hurdles to achieving sustainability in the new world order differ for start-up media enterprises. The Internet changed the cost side of the equation overnight for media organizations. Existing companies—the market leaders in news, information, and entertainment—had made huge capital investments in equipment and infrastructure to support production and distribution of their content. Previously, this served as a barrier to entry.

Figure 4.2 Media response to disruptive attacks.

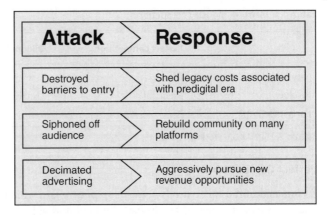

But aspiring media entrepreneurs no longer need to raise the funds necessary to purchase a printing press or build a video production studio. Instead, their priority is on building scale quickly, acquiring customers so they can then begin to acquire revenue. Disruptive innovations are typically adopted first by tech-savvy enthusiasts and visionaries. However, these early users and adopters typically comprise less than a fifth of the market potential for a new product. In order to reach sustainability and viability, innovators need to attract a mainstream audience, which values ease of use and functionality, according to Geoffrey Moore, author of *Crossing the Chasm: Marketing and Selling High-Tech Products to Mainstream Customers*. So, for new entrants, the primary costs are for development, sales, and marketing.

Clay Christensen noted in *The Innovator's Dilemma* that successful disruptive innovators focus on getting the business model right first, rather than on the quality of the product. So early iterations are often of inferior quality compared to products produced by existing businesses. However, because the Internet is a "hot" medium instead of a "cool" one—interactive, instead of passive—feedback from customers is almost instantaneous, which allows for quick adjustments in the product. It also means that those who enter the market behind the initial innovator can learn from the mistakes of the first-mover and build a product that is much easier to use, and therefore more likely to attract a larger audience. The first iteration of MySpace in 2003, for example, mimicked the most popular features of Friendster, founded in 2002. However, the developers of MySpace used rapid application software tools to both develop and build out their site. So within the span of a few months, the features and functionality of MySpace surpassed that of Friendster. As a result, MySpace had supplanted Friendster as the go-to site for young adults and teens by 2005 when it was purchased by News Corp.

How the Internet Challenged Existing Market Structures

Why do existing media companies have difficulty identifying and responding to a competitive threat? In part, it has to do with the market and economic structures that evolved for media companies in the twentieth century.

Economists sort industry segments by the amount of competition they face. It ranges from industries that are deemed to be "monopolies" to those who are considered to face "perfect competition" (Table 4.1). At the dawn of the digital age in the 1990s, legacy media companies tended to be grouped on either end of the spectrum.

Table 4.1 Matrix of industry competition.

	Perfect competition	Oligopoly	Monopoly
Number of firms	Many	Few	One
Product	Identical	Usually differentiated	N/A
Barriers to entry	No	Yes	Yes

Source: Adapted from Hoskins, 2004.

Perfect Competition

At one end of the spectrum is *perfect competition*, in which there are no barriers to entry, and products are viewed as almost identical and substitutable. In perfect competition, there are many buyers and sellers, supply and demand are in equilibrium so firms cannot control the market price of their products, purchasers have complete information about the products and pricing, and firms earn just enough profit to stay in business. Perfect competition is most often considered a "theoretical" state since businesses continually try to differentiate themselves from their competitors through the content they produce and the marketing tactics they pursue.

The magazine industry served as an example of *almost* perfect competition in the pre-digital world. The most successful magazines occupied niches—business, lifestyle, and celebrity news, for example. However, if a niche appeared to be profitable, competitors often rushed to introduce products into those niches, dragging down the overall profitability of all companies as the market share became smaller. For example, with business news, three general-interest business magazines—*Fortune, Forbes,* and *Bloomberg Businessweek*—competed against one another and other niche publications ranging from the *Economist* to *Fast Company.* In perfect competition, the loyalty of customers serves as the *only* bulwark against competitive thrusts.

Monopoly or Oligopoly

At the other end of the spectrum are *monopolies,* where one firm has almost exclusive control over a market, or *oligopolies,* in which a handful of firms dominate. Both monopolistic and oligopolistic enterprises can regulate the supply and pricing of a product or service, and keep competitors out of the market by erecting barriers to entry. Such firms can reap significant profits, while consumers have little or no control over the supply of the product and service or the prices they pay.

Some media monopolies and oligopolies are government-sanctioned and regulated. Because of the upfront capital expense involved in laying cable to thousands of households, many municipalities gave the early cable operators the right to be the exclusive provider of those services in their communities. Similarly, the Federal Communications Commission was set up in the 1930s to regulate the licensing of frequencies and spectrum. The three main television broadcasting networks—ABC, NBC, and CBS—were oligopolies from the 1950s to 1980s. In the United States, the FCC—which regulates interstate communication of radio, television, wire, satellite, and cable—and the Department of Justice—which passes on mergers and acquisitions, making certain they don't violate anti-trust provisions—have the most direct impact on media enterprises.

For the most part, government regulations aim to encourage competition for audience and advertisers, and to prevent one media company from exercising too much control over any aspect of the production or distribution of content, thereby erecting a barrier to entry for other firms. In 2015, Comcast, the largest cable/broadband provider in the country, was forced to call off its merger with Time Warner Cable, the third largest, when government regulators raised concerns that almost two-thirds of all US households would be served by the combined company. Similarly, owners of broadcast stations have been prevented from buying newspapers in the same market.

Despite government attempts to thwart or regulate monopolies, in certain markets one media company can dominate. These are called *de facto monopolies*. This type of structure often occurs in shrinking, isolated markets, with high barriers to entry. Such is the case with newspapers in the latter part of the twentieth century. When competing afternoon papers folded, the surviving morning newspapers in small and mid-sized markets in the United States often became de facto monopolies. The cost of acquiring a press—which ran into millions—prevented new competitors from entering the market. As a result, the surviving paper became the main provider of news for residents in the community, as well as advertising for local businesses. This meant local newspapers could set the price it charged both advertisers and readers.

Regardless of where they fell on the spectrum—competitive, like magazines, or monopolistic, like community newspapers—media enterprises in the twentieth century increasingly relied on three economic strategies to hold down costs and boost revenue: *vertical integration*, *economies of scale*, and *economies of scope*.

Vertical Integration

From the earliest days of Gutenberg, media enterprises were vertically integrated. In other words, they controlled and managed all the processes involved in producing and distributing their content. Newspapers hired reporters to create the news stories, editors and designers to package the material, and then used presses to print copies and trucks to distribute them. Media conglomerates formed in the 1980s and 1990s, such as CBS or Viacom, sought to produce their own television shows and then distribute the programs through their various broadcast and cable networks. Original programs for HBO might be created by Warner Brothers Studio and distributed through Time Warner Cable.

Economies of Scale

In its original form, *economies of scale* was a manufacturing term that referred to the marginal cost of producing an additional unit. The fixed cost of creating and packaging content for a book, for example, was the same—regardless of whether it was consumed by a few people or many. Therefore, the more people who bought a book, the more the average cost per unit of producing and distributing the content decreased. As costs went down, profit increased. As growth began to slow in the latter half of the twentieth century, consolidation in the media industry increased, and economies of scale took on a new meaning. Book and magazine publishers, for example, began buying one another and gaining cost efficiencies by combining production and editing operations, as well as back office and administrative tasks. Larger corporations had more control on the price they paid suppliers, as well as the price they charged consumers. They were also able to reach and target many more consumers with their content. At its peak in the 1990s, Time Inc., for example, published more than 200 magazine titles, ranging from mass circulation titles like *Time* and *People* to niche products like *Horse and Hound* and *Practical Boat Owner*.

Economies of Scope

Media conglomerates also pursued *economies of scope*, producing multiple products aimed at capturing a wider audience and more revenue. News Corporation and CBS, for example, produced television shows and movies, as well as books and newspapers. As with economies of scale, firms with diverse products could realize a number of efficiencies, including shared overhead and joint sales and distribution of related products. In addition, they could reformat material in one product (a book) for use in another (movies or television shows).

In the 1980s, just as the first large media conglomerates were being formed, Harvard professor Michael Porter's book, *Competitive Advantage: Creating and Sustaining Superior Performance*, became a business bible. Porter identified five competitive factors that could have a significant impact on a company's profitability:

1) Customers: How much were they willing to buy and pay?
2) Suppliers: How much were they able to charge?
3) Existing firms competing for the same customers: How much market power did these have?
4) New entrants: Could firms that had recently entered the market siphon off your customers?
5) Substitute products: Could firms that weren't even in the same sector create a product good enough to meet your customers' need?

By pursuing economies of scale and scope, as well as vertical integration, media enterprises could devise strategies to deal with the first three factors—customers, suppliers, and existing firms. But these economic strategies did not allow them to deal with new entrants or substitute products, especially one as intrusive and disruptive as the Internet. Additionally, as Richard Foster points out, it is very difficult for firms that have monopolistic or oligopolistic structures to maintain their competitive instincts. Their markets have been relatively stable. Disruptive innovations most often occur on what Foster calls "the periphery," and fly under the radar for some time. By the time an incumbent firm recognizes the threat posed by this new entrant, the market may have already reached a tipping point. Such was the case for the newspaper industry. The price of publicly traded newspaper stocks suddenly fell off the cliff in 2006, as investors and analysts realized the business models were broken.

Historian Donald Shaw notes that whenever an existing mass medium is displaced by a new one, the once-dominant market leaders initially and wrongly "assume that only an 'adjustment' in strategy is needed." What they fail to realize is that the business environment has irrevocably changed.

Has the Internet Changed Everything? What Is the Business Model Going Forward?

What is the future for books, newspapers, movies, and television shows in an always-on interactive age? Can their business models evolve to meet the demands of a digitally savvy generation? Or will they be supplanted by such tech giants as Google, Facebook, and their yet unknown successors?

Traditionally, media enterprises were defined either by the products they produced, such as books or television shows, or by the method in which they were delivered. However, the Internet has blurred the line between products, with video games evolving into movies, and vice versa, or newspapers producing videos and documentaries for their websites. All of these—video games, movies, television shows, and newspapers—can now be delivered to a single device of your choosing, whether a wide-screen television, a laptop, or a mobile phone.

In 2009, the economist Eli Noam surveyed the media landscape and concluded that the economics of media enterprises was shifting. In Noam's view, in the digital age, the premium is on attracting, retaining, and growing an audience, getting the right content to the right audience efficiently and continuously. As a result, he believes successful media firms in the twenty-first century will be either specialists or integrators:

- *Specialists* will develop a core competence around one of the processes involved in creating, packaging, selling, or distributing content. In the digital era, each successful specialist firm understands what unique value it adds to the process of producing, distributing, or marketing content and then develops a business model that maximizes profit through focusing on its core competency.
- *Integrators*, on the other hand, will oversee and organize all the processes, ensuring that the content that has been created and packaged is also distributed to either the widest possible audience, or a targeted one, in the most cost-efficient way possible. In addition, integrators will understand the variety of revenue possibilities in this interactive, always-on age, maximizing profit for both themselves and the specialists.

Such a media ecosystem, with specialists and integrators, places a premium on horizontal—not vertical—integration of the processes. Even before the digital era, some media enterprises—such as movie studios and book publishers—were already moving toward such a horizontal model, contracting with other firms to write scripts and market films, or to print and distribute their books. This means firms, such as newspapers, that are currently vertically integrated are disadvantaged and need to move quickly to shed or outsource a process that no longer pays for itself.

Also, large media conglomerates, such as CBS, which rely on economies of scope (with multiple divisions, such as book publishing, television networks, and film studios) could also be disadvantaged if there is not a clear rationale for each division. McKinsey consultant Angus Dawson has identified five questions that "incumbent" companies need to "step back" and ask:

1) Do the businesses we own make sense in the way in which the world is unfolding, and are they going to create value?
2) Are we the best owners of those businesses?
3) Where do we need to think about investing?
4) What's the bar on the capabilities that we have, and how much has it gone up?
5) Are we going to end up being out-competed by somebody else who just reconceives what's possible?

But if there are fewer financial benefits to vertical integration and economies of scale in Noam's horizontally-integrated media ecosystem, economies of scale still count. Specialists can be large enterprises, he concedes, especially those that produce content distributed and sold to several large integrators or multiple customer and industry segments. However, the largest firms are "mainly coordinators, integrators of the specialist firms, the branders of the final product, and often the marketers."

All this sets up a very different competitive environment for media companies. Using Porter's competitive framework, the large integrators—such as Google—can place pressure on the profits of specialists, just as buyers and suppliers did in the pre-digital era. Are they friends or enemies, partners or competitors? Day-to-day, month-to-month, specialists must keep a watchful eye on the periphery for new entrants and substitute products emerging in the integrator space as well as in their own area. In other words, the successful media firm is both innovative—constantly reimaging and reinventing itself to meet the changing needs and wants of its customers—and entrepreneurial—understanding the interconnected economics of the digital media ecosystem.

In a 2002 article published in the *Harvard Business Review*, management consultant and author Peter Drucker wrote, "Most innovations…especially the successful ones, result from a conscious, purposeful search for innovation opportunities, which are found only in a few situations." He advised entrepreneurs to look for opportunities within their own company or industry, as well as among their customers and the outside world because "the potential for innovation may well lie in more than one area at a time."

In the following chapters, we will be exploring how a media enterprise—whether specialist or integrator, start-up or legacy—can create a sustainable business model that is both innovative and entrepreneurial. Drucker concluded, "No one can tell whether a given innovation will end up a big business or a modest achievement…[But] if an innovation does not aim at leadership from the beginning, it is unlikely to be innovative enough."

MTV, *Vice*, and the Future of Viacom

Would the fates of both Viacom and MySpace have been different if Viacom had purchased it? Former CEO Tom Freston says "No." In many ways, he and Philippe Dauman, his successor, are a study in contrasts, a first-generation founder and builder versus the second-generation defender of the legacy.

Freston joined the company in 1981, shortly after it was founded, and as CEO from 1986 onward led it through its years of rapid growth. He describes himself as a risk-taker, who gave a national platform to musicians, such as Michael Jackson and Madonna, and comedians and actors, such as Jon Stewart and Judd Apatow. "I encouraged the interns and executives to think of themselves as a motorcycle gang who was reinventing television for young people," he told CNBC in 2016. Through 2004, Viacom enjoyed quarter-to-quarter earnings growth.

As Viacom matured and growth slowed, Freston began looking to acquire a social media company. By owning a social media company, he reasoned, Viacom could interact directly with millennials, and strengthen Viacom's bond with its existing customers, the gen Xers. Before making a losing $500 million offer for MySpace, Freston says he offered Mark Zuckerberg $750 million for Facebook and was turned down. Facebook, not MySpace, was the "crown jewel" that got away, he contends, and history proved him right.

When he succeeded Freston as CEO in 2006, Dauman vowed he would "never" miss another "trophy" acquisition. However, from 2006 to 2016, Dauman pursued a classic defensive strategy designed to protect Viacom's existing content, instead of expanding it to other platforms. In January 2016, SpringOwl Asset Management, which owned an undisclosed stake in Viacom, presented a 99-page slide show to the board of directors detailing why the company's performance lagged behind all its industry peers. Viacom, under Dauman, had "made virtually no digital investments or acquisitions," and it significantly lagged behind its peers in OTT (over the top) offerings, the investment group pointed out. Viacom had missed the media industry's shift to digital, the report concluded.

With Dauman's tenure as CEO hanging in the balance, Freston weighed in on his successor's mistakes and missed opportunities in an interview with CNBC. He cited Dauman's unsuccessful lawsuit against the Google-owned YouTube for copyright infringement, which indicated that Viacom was "not ready for the future of digital." But, perhaps the biggest mistake, Freston said, was Dauman's decision in 2006 to sell Viacom's half stake in Vice Media for $3 million.

Vice magazine had been established in Canada in 1996 and covered music, drugs, and trends in the youth culture. By 2006, the print magazine circulated on five continents. At the urging of the filmmaker Spike Jonze, Vice executives approached Freston for advice about establishing a strong digital video presence—and asked for some initial funding. By 2016, the digital and broadcasting media enterprise was worth $4.5 billion, based on investments by other large media conglomerates, including News Corp and Disney, which owned almost 25%. Its brand extensions included Vice News, Vice Sports, Fightland, Garage and Viceland (the first cable network launch by a digital video operation).

It was not the money Viacom left on the table by selling Vice in 2006 that concerned Freston. Rather, it was the sense that Viacom had missed out on the opportunity to learn how to transition its youthful brand into digital spaces. Citing the suite of channels that Vice had developed, Freston said, "Vice has taken the old Viacom playbook and built a great youth media business for today's world." If Dauman had kept Vice, instead of selling it, Freston said, Viacom "would have a much-needed platform in the digital world. They'd have a home for the Nickelodeon graduates."

In late 2016, Viacom named Bob Bakish, former head of its international division, as the new CEO. Two months later, he announced his turn-around strategy, which involved shifting resources to six "flagship" networks with global reach. These were MTV, Comedy Central, Nickelodeon, Nick Jr., BET, and Spike (rebranded as Paramount). Other networks without global potential—including VH1 and TV Land—would lose resources. He also said he was considering, once again, buying a stake in Vice. Bakish promised "big moves in the digital world." The question that hung in the air: Would it be enough to make up for a lost decade?

Exercise: Was Yahoo's Short Life Pre-Ordained?

In the 1990s, before the birth of Google and Facebook, Yahoo ruled Silicon Valley. Like other start-ups in the area, the idea for the company had been conceived in 1994 as a class project by two Stanford University classmates—Jerry Yang and David Filo. It was a portal, like AOL, the dominant player at the time. One sign-on brought you to "the web." But it was more than that. It was an attempt to bring order to the many websites on the web. Yahoo stood for "yet another hierarchically organized oracle." Yahoo was a sort of digital Dewey-Decimal type listing of pages by subcategories (business and art, for example). The Yahoo hierarchy was put together by a diverse group of young, tech-savvy "surfers"—so named because they surfed the web for the most credible listings.

In the go-go era of the dot-com boom, Yahoo received its first round of financing in 1995 and went public the following year, with one of the largest market valuations for any start-up tech company to date. With money from its IPO, Yahoo began acquiring other tech start-ups and building out the infrastructure. In 1997, it launched free webmail and within a short period of time, it had 25 million email users compared with only five million for AOL, which charged for its services.

Its highest market valuation came just before the dot-com bust—$125 million—comparable to AOL, which merged with Time Warner in 2000. Like AOL, Yahoo's revenue and income came from banner ads. But a new competitor was already emerging from the periphery—one that derived its revenue not from banner ads, but from search ads. By 2001, the new Yahoo CEO, Terry Semel, a former News Corp executive, realized the future was increasingly moving away from human-driven search toward an algorithmic function, such as the one employed by Google, which had been incorporated in 1998. After being rebuffed in his attempt to buy Google for $3 billion in 2002, he acquired two other search firms, Inktomi and Overture. However, the predominant share of Yahoo's revenue continued to come from banner ads.

After Google went public in 2004, it quickly became the dominant search firm—pushing Yahoo and Microsoft into second and third place. By 2008, when Microsoft's $44.6 billion offer to purchase Yahoo was rejected, Google had more than a 50% share of the US market and was rapidly gaining dominant market share across the globe. Meanwhile, Yahoo had pursued a succession of investments and acquisitions across a variety of industries, including photo sharing, e-commerce, and music sites. The one that proved most prescient occurred by happenstance in 1997 when Yahoo founder Jerry Yang visited China and his guide was the English-speaking entrepreneur, Jack Ma. In 2005, Yahoo invested in Ma's start-up Chinese site, Alibaba.

The inability of Yahoo's management to craft a strategy that responded to the Google threat, and the rejection of Microsoft's offer to buy Yahoo, ignited a shareholder revolt. Between 2007 and 2012, Yahoo had six CEOs, with each successive executive (some of whom were in the job for only a few months) trying to right the ship. Marissa Mayer, one of the first employees at Google, was recruited in 2012 to great fanfare. Her first acquisition was the blogging-social networking site Tumblr. But, despite numerous acquisitions, she also failed to right the ship.

In 2016, the board announced it was "exploring all strategic options," which was coded wording that invited other companies to make bids on acquiring the company. By then, 89% of Internet users resorted to Google for their searches; only 3% used Yahoo. Verizon submitted the winning bid of $4.5 billion. This bid was for the Yahoo properties only. Yahoo's stake in Alibaba was now worth more than $40 billion.

Yahoo was first listed on the S&P 500 in 1999. Only 17 years later, it ceased to exist as a stand-alone company. As we conclude this chapter, it is worth considering these questions:

- What were the inflexion points? Hindsight is twenty-twenty. How did Yahoo respond? How should it have responded?
- Terry Semel saw the threat that Google posed and tried to buy the company. Did Yahoo make the right decisions immediately after the offer to buy Google in 2002 was rejected?
- Would Yahoo's fate have been different if it had been purchased by Microsoft?
- Change happens quickly in the digital age. Did Yahoo's executives correctly identify competitors "on the periphery"? Did the firm respond in the appropriate fashion?

Summary

All companies face the imperative to grow and change with their customers, or be left behind. There are three ways to grow—through research and development of new products, through partnerships, and through acquisitions. In the early years of a firm's life, revenues are often double or triple the previous year. But as a firm matures, growth in revenue and profits becomes harder to maintain. Therefore, in the latter part of the twentieth century, mature media companies increasingly relied on acquisitions as the primary means of growth, with mixed results.

Disruptive innovations, such as the Internet, typically attack cost structure first, and then begin siphoning off customers and revenue. Therefore, incumbent media companies need a three-pronged strategy for shedding their legacy costs, attracting new customers, and building new sources of revenue. They need to follow the technology, follow their customers, and follow the money. Start-ups, on the other hand, must first focus on attracting loyal customers in order to attract revenues and achieve long-term viability.

The culture in an organization often changes in tandem with the life stage of a firm. Successful start-ups create products and services that meet unfulfilled market needs or wants. In the early years, they employ offensive strategies, seeking to build market share. Mature firms, with a dominant position in a market, however, are defensive. They are constantly trying to fend off attackers and preserve their market share. As a result they often fail to see and respond to competitive threats emerging "on the periphery" until it is too late.

In the twentieth century, media companies typically achieved dominance by pursuing vertical integration, economies of scale, and economies of scope. The emergence of large aggregators and integrators—such as Google and Facebook—has significantly changed the economics of media companies in the twenty-first century. Economies of scale still matter, but the competition is more intense.

The pace of change has picked up considerably in recent years. The S&P 500 is often used as a proxy for change in the marketplace as a whole. The average lifespan of a company on the S&P 500 has fallen to 16 years, which suggests that, in order to keep pace with change in the marketplace, firms need to reinvent themselves and their business model every 16 years. In the new world, the emphasis for media companies is on attracting, retaining, and growing audience. Therefore, successful media entrepreneurs must also be innovative leaders, constantly scanning the horizon for opportunity.

Part II

Creating Sustainable Strategies and Business Models

Customers rightfully expect the undivided attention and resources of businesses that compete to serve their needs. So it is vitally important to be clear about who is—and who is not—a customer...Choosing a primary customer is a make-or-break decision. Why? Because it should determine how you allocate resources. The idea is simple: Allocate all possible resources to meet and exceed your primary customer's needs.
(Robert Simons, *Seven Strategy Questions, Harvard Business School Press, 2010*)

The Strategic Digital Media Entrepreneur, First Edition. Penelope Muse Abernathy and JoAnn Sciarrino.
© 2019 John Wiley & Sons, Inc. Published 2019 by John Wiley & Sons, Inc.
Companion website: www.wiley.com/go/abernathy/StrategicDigitalMediaEntrepreneur

Sustainable Strategies and Business Models

5

A Strategy for Dealing with the New Business Imperatives

This is a tale of two media companies, both with iconic names that are recognized around the world. One was founded in 1856 and has been largely owned and operated for the past 125 years by members of the same family, with the sixth generation now at the helm. The other company was founded in 1982 by a Wall Street bond trader, who became mayor of New York City in 2002, and then returned to the firm in 2013 in his former role as CEO. Leaders of both the New York Times Company and Bloomberg, LLC, crafted strategies in the latter years of the twentieth century that distinguished them from their competitors and propelled their companies to record revenues and profits.

In the 1980s, Bloomberg unveiled a new computerized system that allowed Wall Street traders and analysts to access current market data and news, while simultaneously performing complicated calculations and financial analysis of various investment options. The Bloomberg terminal was a disruptive technology that dislodged longtime market leaders from their dominant positions. By the end of the 1990s, the Bloomberg terminal was ubiquitous in the big Wall Street investment houses, as well as many of the boutique firms, and founder Michael Bloomberg routinely made the list of the wealthiest people in the world.

In the 1990s, the *New York Times* simultaneously developed and launched an online edition, nytimes.com, while redesigning its print editions, using color for the first time, and vastly expanding the footprint of the national edition, which became widely available from coast to coast. The success of both print and digital ventures propelled the stock of the New York Times Company to a peak of $52 a share in 2002, and gave the firm a market valuation of $5 billion.

But "past performance is no guarantee of future results," to quote the warning included in the prospectus for most investments traded on public exchanges. Disrupters such as Bloomberg can be disrupted. Established and prestigious print journalistic enterprises such as the *New York Times* can fail to develop a sustainable digital business model. Today, both companies confront significant challenges as they attempt to craft business strategies that identify and take advantage of opportunities available in a dramatically changed—and continuously changing—media environment. Since the average life expectancy of companies has declined dramatically in recent years, neither start-ups nor established companies have room for error.

Media enterprises need to respond to the challenges posed by the rapidly evolving digital landscape by developing new strategies, new competencies, and new business models. In this chapter, we develop a strategic framework that can be used by both start-up and existing companies seeking to create a profitable and sustainable digital business model.

The Strategic Digital Media Entrepreneur, First Edition. Penelope Muse Abernathy and JoAnn Sciarrino.
© 2019 John Wiley & Sons, Inc. Published 2019 by John Wiley & Sons, Inc.
Companion website: www.wiley.com/go/abernathy/StrategicDigitalMediaEntrepreneur

Among the questions, we'll consider in this chapter are:

- What are the emerging business models for media companies?
- How do you create a business plan for start-up media enterprises?
- What are the strengths and weaknesses, as well as opportunities and threats, that confront existing media companies?
- What are the components of a sustainable digital business model for both start-ups and legacy enterprises?

What Are the Emerging Business Models?

In the latter part of the twentieth century, there were four types of media enterprises: (1) news organizations; (2) information providers; (3) persuasion and commentary suppliers; and (4) entertainment outlets. The type of content produced determined the audience. Each type relied on a different business model to achieve long-term profitability. Most, however, were vertically integrated. In other words, the enterprises controlled every step of the process from content creation to content distribution. Therefore, the most efficient enterprises tended to be the most profitable.

News Organizations

News organizations such as the *New York Times* and other news publications distributed content to a mass audience, often in geographic proximity to the media enterprise. The aim was to attract as large an audience as possible, without regard to demographic targeting. News publications were veritable "supermarkets," according to Tom Rosenstiel of the American Press Institute. The editorial focus was on producing "general interest" content that would appeal to the majority of the audience and cover a range of topics from breaking news to lifestyle and sports. Publishers kept the price to the consumer low, relying instead on selling their audience to advertisers who wanted to reach a mass audience with their message. As a result, advertising provided the predominant share of revenue for news organizations—as much as 85%. This was and remains primarily a B2C (business-to-consumer) model, which means that consumers are the end-users of the products (newspapers and news magazines) produced by the media companies. However, because of the low price point set for consumers, news organizations have had very little flexibility in raising the cover price of their products and services, even as print advertising declined dramatically.

Information Providers

Information providers such as Bloomberg created and delivered a variety of information—including proprietary research, data, and analysis—often to a specific audience with specialized needs and interests. This included professionals, such as those in law, medicine, and business, as well as academics. Most of these organizations operated on a B2B (business-to-business) model, which meant the purchasers of the content were other commercial enterprises. The revenue came not from advertisers, but from the end-users themselves. Because many businesses were early adopters of digital technology, most of these B2B information providers transitioned away from print to online delivery of their content in the 1980s and 1990s. Therefore, unlike many B2C news organizations, they have not been saddled with significant print legacy costs. Their main competitive challenge in the digital era is remaining an indispensable source of information for the businesses they serve. If they do, they have significant pricing leverage.

Persuasion and Commentary Suppliers

Persuasion and commentary suppliers included advertising agencies, such as Ogilvy and BBDO, as well as cable news channels, such as Fox and MSNBC. The ad agencies operated on a B2B model, charging clients a fee for the content they produced and distributed (i.e., placed in other media outlets). They were often a one-stop shopping center for their clients, providing all the services necessary to implement a marketing program. Cable channels operated on a combination B2B and B2C business model. They received a fee from cable operators who paid to carry them on their systems, and they received revenue from advertisers who wanted to reach the audiences they delivered. In contrast to general news organizations, they tended to attract a niche audience, instead of a mass one. The niche audience was often much more engaged than the mass audience attracted to network news shows. However, the size of their audience tends to fluctuate, depending on the interest in breaking news and politics.

Entertainment Outlets

Entertainment outlets such as Disney and NBC Universal created a variety of mass media products and services, including general release movies, broadcast network television shows, and theme parks. They also produced products aimed at a niche market, including indie movies, video games, and programming for their cable networks. Some products, including movies and video games, were sold directly to the consumer. Other products, including the network television shows, relied primarily on the revenue received from advertisers who wanted to reach a mass audience, supplemented by licensing and other types of fees received from media enterprises who wanted their content (e.g., reruns of old television shows). Whether selling directly to consumers (like the movie studios and book publishers) or selling their audience to advertisers, the economics of the entertainment industry primarily relied on blockbuster hits.

Creative Destruction

Creative destruction in an industry typically occurs in successive waves. Both the B2C and B2B business models had vulnerabilities that have become immediately obvious in the Media 2.0 era. As discussed in Chapter 4, a disrupting innovation often attacks the cost structure of an established industry first. The technology of the Internet destroyed traditional barriers to entry—such as the need to spend millions of dollars purchasing a printing press or investing in a movie studio. This meant consumers could become creators, and small B2B or B2C media enterprises could flourish *if* they offered the right product to either consumers or other businesses. The interactivity and instant connectivity of the new medium also raised customer expectations about what sort of content media companies should provide, while simultaneously lowering expectations about what customers should pay for that content. It has siphoned off the audience for most B2C media enterprises, which has affected the revenue they can get from advertisers who want to reach a mass audience. In other words, the digital revolution has threatened both the customer and revenue base of most media companies.

In order to survive and thrive in the new environment, both traditional media companies and start-ups must develop new core competencies around attracting and retaining audiences, and align their costs with their value drivers. Although vertical integration drove the profitability of media organizations in the past, economist Eli Noam, author of *Media Ownership and Concentration in America*, argues that horizontal integration is most important in the Media 2.0 environment. Successful media companies will focus on what they do best, and will outsource the rest. Book publishers were early adopters of horizontal integration, contracting with various authors to create the content, and with large printing companies to produce and distribute their books.

Instead of four or more business models determined by the type of content that a media enterprise is producing, Noam hypothesizes that there will be two types. Successful media enterprises will be *integrators*, such as Google and Facebook, aggregating and collecting content from multiple sources onto their platforms and then distributing it to a vast audience. Or, they will be *specialists*, creating content for a smaller niche audience and/or providing a specialized service—such as aggregation of content on a specific topic. In Noam's scenario, the largest B2C firms will be integrators, who will have the capability to target specific segments within their mass audience. The size of their audience and the scale of their operations will dwarf those of the specialists, which are focused on creating, packaging, and distributing news and information to much smaller, but engaged audiences. In the Media 2.0 world, both Bloomberg and the *New York Times* would be specialists, according to Noam.

Marketing and technology consultant Shelly Palmer offered a similar prediction about digital business models when interviewed by *strategy + business* magazine. He believes that successful media companies will be either really large, platform-based, with immense scale and capabilities to reach vast audiences, or tiny, flexible, and independent. Mid-sized companies will be squeezed since they will not have the ability to reach a mass audience like the large enterprises, or the unique targeting capabilities of the small ones.

In the past, media enterprises received revenue from one to three types of sources: (1) consumers who paid to receive the content (subscriptions); (2) other outlets and companies who wanted the content produced by the media company (licensing, syndication and fees); and (3) advertisers who wanted to reach a certain audience. Palmer predicts that in the digital space, successful B2C media enterprises will figure out a way to make money from *all three sources*. As a result, news organizations, for example, may well employ some of the techniques utilized by entertainment companies to engage and connect with the consumers of their content so they can charge their subscribers more, and not remain primarily reliant on advertising.

Regardless of which scenario prevails—Noam's or Palmer's—both point to the need for a different way of thinking about and constructing business models that will lead to success. Both point to the need to connect with customers. As Noam says, the premium for media companies in the digital space is on attracting, retaining, and growing an audience, getting the right content to the right audience at the right time. Media companies will be data-driven, collecting and analyzing data on their customers in order to understand them and their preferences better. "Data will be cash, and it should be treated like cash," Palmer says. "You need a data P&L," and everyone in the company needs to know how to use the insights it provides. Therefore, successful media companies will need to develop core competencies in three different areas: (1) the creation of content that engages audiences; (2) the cultivation of new and diverse revenue sources; and (3) the savvy use of technology to connect with customers, regardless of where they are.

Creating a Business Plan from Scratch

The strategic and financial challenges confronting mature companies trying to transition to new business models, such as the *New York Times* and Bloomberg, are different from those of start-ups. So let's first consider how the founder of a newly-formed digital media enterprise would put together a business plan. The first order of business is getting funding for the venture.

Until recently, many of the business plans for the digital start-ups relied heavily on financial models that pushed a company to reach scale quickly, regardless of profitability. Now, however, many venture capitalists are asking for a strategy behind the numbers that will ensure profitability and sustainability. Therefore, a business plan for a start-up should address this strategic question: What are your potential customer's critical needs and expectations, and how will your firm meet those needs in a way that distinguishes you from your competitors?

The adoption rate of an innovation affects the long-term economics of start-up enterprises. Maloney's Rule posits that a new technology must attract more than 16% of potential customers in order to become profitable. The earliest customers of a new product are called *innovators* and *early adopters*—and together they comprise only 16% of a potential customer base. Start-ups must also attract mainstream users—often called the *early majority*—in order to become profitable. (On the flip side, for legacy enterprises, the first tipping point in their own business models occurs when their current customers begin switching to the new technology. They represent a mainstream (majority) acceptance of the new technology.)

Harvard Business School professor William Sahlman recommends in *Creating Business Plans* that companies seeking investment funds organize their business plans into four parts: (1) information on the macro-environment; (2) information on the opportunity you're proposing; (3) the potential risks and rewards of this venture; and (4) the people who will be bringing the idea to fruition.

- *Context*: What are factors that you cannot control? This is the environment in which your business will operate. It should take into account demographic trends, macro-economic shifts (such as interest rates, projected inflation), the regulatory environment, and the industry outlook (projected growth rates, competitors, barriers to entry, overall profitability, and special challenges).
- *Opportunity*: What are the factors you can control? This includes your target customer, the size of the market, and your potential market share. What are the innovative ways in which you are responding to customer needs and wants (i.e., your unique value proposition)? How does your product or service differentiate you from your competitors?
- *Risks and rewards*: This involves cataloging everything that can go right, and perhaps more importantly, everything that can go wrong. This is often called scenario planning, in which you calculate a breakeven financial point on high growth, low growth, and no-growth opportunities. In each scenario, you anticipate how your firm will respond to the opportunity or challenge, and, just as importantly, how your current and potential competitors respond. Will they copy your idea and underprice you? How can they move to limit your upside opportunity? What is the window of opportunity? How will you measure success in three years or five? What is the delta (difference) in ROI (return on investment) between the most realistically optimistic scenario and the most realistically pessimistic one? (See Chapter 3 on how to calculate ROI.)

- *People*: What are the key capabilities that you need in place to ensure success? This is really a review of the three Ps: people, processes, and procedures. Do you have the right people in leadership roles? Do you have the ability to hire the right people as your company grows? Do they have the knowledge, skills, and resources to succeed? If not, can you provide the training needed? Is your firm organized in such a way as to capitalize on opportunity and quickly recover from setbacks?

Thanks to cloud computing, it is easier and less expensive than ever to come up with a business plan and start a company, since server space and development tools can be rented, instead of purchased. As a result, Harvard Business School professor Ramana Nanda found that the number of media outlets that received funding from venture capitalists doubled from 2006, when Amazon introduced its web-based services, to 2010. However, many fewer companies were likely to receive the second round of funding. As a result, in the period from 2002 to 2010, 43% of companies failed before receiving the second round of funding, with the failure rate increasing significantly after 2006. Additionally, firms with first-round funding received less strategic guidance from venture capitalists, who were inclined to hold off on placing someone on the board of directors until after the second round of funding. On the positive side, the valuation of firms that made it to the second round of funding increased substantially.

All this places an increased premium on start-ups gaining traction fast. This also suggests that successful founders will take a long-term, strategic view of the entire industry segment—and consider the context in which they will be operating three to five years from initial funding. This is exactly the sort of forward-looking strategic view that the consulting firm PwC advises leaders of existing firms, such as the *New York Times* or Bloomberg, to do. This viewpoint anticipates that the tremendous pace of change and disruption will continue, and perhaps even accelerate in the media industry. Therefore, leaders of start-ups, as well as leading legacy companies, should ask: What are the big trends sweeping across the industry? What are the most disruptive outcomes of these trends? How can my company anticipate and react to the highest risks?

What Are the Strengths and Weaknesses of the Current Business Model?

While start-ups create their business plans on blank canvases, existing media companies, like the *New York Times* and Bloomberg must be mindful of the current legacy business, which pays the bills. So, before crafting a new strategy, existing businesses typically make

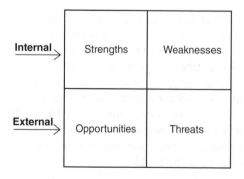

Figure 5.1 SWOT matrix.

Box 5.1 SWOT Analysis

- *Strengths* are capabilities and resources at a company's disposal that allow it to succeed. It is important to identify not only what a company does well, but why it succeeds. If a company has high profit margins, is that due to the popularity of its products or an efficient cost structure? Examples of strengths include strong brand recognition and customer loyalty, talented employees, patents, popularity of the product or service, efficient cost structure and supply chain, diverse income streams, well-established partnerships, a history of innovation, and entrepreneurial success.

- *Weaknesses* are the areas where a business needs to improve to be more competitive. It is important to acknowledge all vulnerabilities that could affect bottom line performance or a return on future investments. Examples include a diminishing market share, high cost structure, high levels of debt, lack of capital or cash for investment, weak brand recognition, a reputation for poor customer service, high turnover of employees, a lack of up-to-date technology capabilities, and an aging product line.

- *Opportunities* are the market and macro trends that a firm can capitalize on. These are options or scenarios that allow a company to significantly improve its performance. Examples include demographic shifts, new regulations or deregulation, identification of an unmet customer need, changes in a competitor's strategy, acquisitions or new partnership possibilities, restructuring, the opening of new markets, and expansion of existing product lines.

- *Threats* are the forces outside a company's control that can negatively impact a firm's performance. Perhaps the best way to identify threats is to pose this question: What could realistically change for the worse? Examples include entrance of a new competitor, increased competition from lower-priced products, shifts in consumer tastes, rising costs and no pricing flexibility, and legislation or regulation that threatens the lifespan of an existing product or service.

---

an inventory of both the positive and negative attributes of their current business models. A so-called time-honored *SWOT analysis* utilizes a matrix approach to identify two internal factors and two external ones that can significantly influence profitability and future growth trajectory (Figure 5.1). The internal factors are classified as strengths and weaknesses, and the external ones as opportunities and risks (Box 5.1).

There are limitations to using a SWOT analysis since it is a subjective exercise, dependent on the biases and perspectives of those involved in the process. A SWOT analysis also does not compare and quantify upside or downside potential for the various opportunities or the impact of doing nothing. More sophisticated financial analysis is always needed to determine an ROI. However, it is a valuable starting point in assessing the long-term viability of a current business model and some opportunities available for growth. Let's use a SWOT analysis to consider the current business models of both Bloomberg and the *New York Times*.

Current Bloomberg Business Model

Bloomberg is a B2B (business-to-business) firm, selling directly to customers in the financial services industry. Its founder, Michael Bloomberg owns almost 90% of the privately held company. In 2016, it had estimated annual revenues of $8–9 billion, and profits of more than $3.5 billion. (This suggests an profit margin of roughly 40%.)

The driver of 85% of the revenues for the company is the Bloomberg terminal, which has unique analytical abilities valued by its customers, especially Wall Street traders and analysts. Bloomberg does not discount the price of its terminals ($2,000 a month per terminal), regardless of the number a company purchases. By using the terminal, customers in the financial services industry can get instantaneous updates on news that might affect the market, while simultaneously using Bloomberg's extensive data to analyze the performance of various financial instruments. At the beginning of 2017, there were more than 320,000 terminals in financial offices around the world.

Bloomberg is a classic *closed network*. A customer needs to pay for the terminal in order to get access to the company's unique services and products. According to a *Fortune* article written in 2006, Bloomberg tends to retain its customers—not necessarily out of *affection and good will* for the terminal, which can be cumbersome to use. Instead, they *fear* losing a competitive trading advantage if they do not have access to Bloomberg's data and analytics. Bloomberg, which received a $10 million buyout when the investment house Salomon Brothers was purchased in 1981, teamed up with three other investors to develop a terminal that could be used to track market information *and* calculate the price of financial instruments.

The Bloomberg terminal was a very disruptive innovation when it arrived on the scene in the 1980s. In short order, it displaced the market leaders—Dow Jones News Services and Reuters. Bloomberg holds a dominant market position—more than a third of the market—with Thomson Reuters, a publicly traded company with $12 billion in annual revenues, lagging significantly behind. Despite numerous efforts in recent years to catch up, the Thomson Reuters Eikon is considered inferior to Bloomberg's in terms of its analytical and trading functions. Over the past three decades, Bloomberg has added numerous services and features—aimed at enhancing the reliance of its customers on the terminal and other sources of Bloomberg-produced news and information. This includes the establishment of a robust news service that includes online, television, radio, and print (*Bloomberg BusinessWeek*).

In addition, Bloomberg has established other data management and subscription services, including Bloomberg Law, which serves lawyers and competes with LexisNexis, and Bloomberg Government, which serves lobbyists and tracks congressional and regulatory changes in Washington. Despite some recent efforts to diversify and seek new customers for its products, Bloomberg's profitability still depends on the health of the financial services industry. Growth in subscriptions to its financial terminals slowed in 2009—in the wake of the 2008 Great Recession—and again in 2012. As the dominant market leader in the financial industry, Bloomberg must continually focus outward, trying to stay innovative and prevent the emergence of a competitor that builds a better mousetrap. If that happens, then the disrupter can be disrupted.

Let's do a SWOT analysis on Bloomberg.

Strengths

- Established market position with dominance in the financial information systems. In early 2017, Bloomberg provided real-time financial information to more than 327,000 subscribers worldwide.
- Extensive data layer makes the company the strongest player in the industry. A market share of 33.3% in 2015 (vs. Thomson Reuters at 24.3%).
- Diverse products and services offerings, including financial products, enterprise products, and media products.

- Brand considered "reliable" by Wall Street customers, giving Bloomberg pricing leverage with its terminals.
- Strong presence across digital platforms. In early 2016, Bloomberg.com recorded digital traffic of 27 million unique visitors.

Weaknesses

- Bloomberg's fortunes tied to strength of Wall Street.
- Profits tied primarily to the terminal.
- May be reaching market saturation with terminals, resulting in slowing growth.
- High cost of terminal may limit growth outside financial services.
- Privacy scandal in 2013 at Bloomberg (reporters at Bloomberg News were using company's terminals to monitor subscriber activities).

Opportunities

- Projected strong growth opportunity in US capital markets—US debt market reached $1.6 trillion in high-yield and investment-grade insurances in 2017, from $1.5 trillion in 2014.
- Rising consumption of online content—Bloomberg delivers premium content across numerous digital platforms. *Bloomberg News* publishes more than 5,000 original stories on an average day.
- Significant partnerships, e.g., Twitter offers 24/7 streaming video and news in partnership with Bloomberg.

Threats

- Emerging alternatives, including Markit's federated messaging platforms and Symphony, an instant messaging platform. Thomson Reuters and many banks, including Goldman Sachs and Bank of America, are supporting the new platforms.
- Alternatives are expected to put pressure on Bloomberg to lower the price of the terminal.
- Negative trends in magazine publishing industry—global print consumer magazine subscriptions are expected to decline at a compound annual rate of 2% through 2020, putting pressure on print products, such as *Bloomberg Businessweek*.

Current *New York Times* Business Model

In contrast to Bloomberg, the *New York Times* is a B2C (business-to-consumer) media enterprise. It is one of three national print newspapers, circulated throughout the United States—along with the *Wall Street Journal* and *USA Today*. It carries a range of general interest information, including politics, culture, and sports, as well as business news. The readers of its print edition tend to be affluent, well-educated, and influential decision-makers in both the business and political world. However, the news industry is in flux. As a result, the *New York Times* faces strong competition for both audience and advertising from a range of media outlets, including online ventures (such as Vice and Buzzfeed), as well as more traditional broadcast outlets.

Over the past three decades, the *New York Times* made several major acquisitions that had a negative ROI (including the *Boston Globe* and About.com). Simultaneously, the company sold most of its non-newspaper properties, including its magazines and television stations, as well as its smaller, regional newspapers. So, in contrast to other B2C media companies—such as News Corp (which owns the *Wall Street Journal*)—it is almost exclusively reliant on income from the *New York Times*. In 2016, the New York Times, a publicly traded company, had $1.5 billion in revenue and $102 million of operating income—an operating margin of 7%.

Even though it has made substantial progress in transitioning to digital delivery of its newspapers, the primary driver of profitability remains the print edition. Because it enjoys strong customer loyalty, the *New York Times* is able to charge more for a subscription to either its print or digital edition than any other general interest circulation newspaper in the United States—as much as $800 for a print subscription and more than $300 for a digital edition. As a result, more than half of its revenues come from circulation, an anomaly in the newspaper business. However, despite its strong brand appeal, the *New York Times* has not been able to replace rapidly declining print advertising revenue with increases in digital advertising revenue. In the first quarter of 2017, for example, print advertising fell 18% compared to the previous year. Although digital advertising was up 19%, overall ad revenue was down 7%. Analysts estimate that more than 60% of 2016 revenues came from the print edition. Additionally, the *New York Times* continues to carry significant fixed production and distribution costs tied to the print product.

Let's do a SWOT analysis on the New York Times company.

Strengths

- Multiplatform presence has driven digital growth, which has provided meaningful diversification of revenue. Circulation revenue accounts for more than 60% of total revenue.
- Digitally savvy audience, among the most affluent and engaged of any publishing company.
- Strong growth of paid digital subscribers, willing to pay a premium price—$250–325 yearly.
- Number of digital subscribers to various products (including crossword)—2.2 million in early 2017.

Weaknesses

- Lack of scale as compared to peers (NYT with $1.5 billion in 2016 vs. News Corp with revenues of $8 billion in 2017). Lack of scale limits ability to compete effectively and might impact investor confidence.
- Concentrated geographic presence—highly dependent on US domestic market. News Corp generated 54% of revenues from outside the United States in FY15.
- Pressures on both print and digital advertising revenue. Advertising revenue accounts for only a third of total. Print advertising continues to decline.
- Market for digital display advertising continues to experience challenges due to abundance of available advertising inventory and a shift toward automated, real-time bidding.
- Continued reliance on print paper for the majority of its revenue. High costs, tied to union contracts and related to printing and distribution of print edition.

Opportunities

- Growth in smartphone market. NYT has been building on its mobile initiatives.
- Growth in online advertising. US digital advertising is expected to hit $113.2 billion by 2020. NYT has a strong portfolio of digital assets.

- Global expansion. Rebranded *International Herald Tribune* as *International New York Times*. Publishing alliances include *Chinese Monthly*.

Threats

- Very competitive market. Competing for audience in both national and international markets and with digital alternatives, such as Google News and huffingtonpost.com.
- Competing for digital advertising revenues with other ad-supported websites.
- Declining print circulation—expected to decline at least 1% annually, 2015 to 2020. Print subscription is double that of digital-only subscription.
- Increasing paper prices. Rising wood pulp prices—expected to increase at annualized 5% through 2020.

As these two SWOT analyses show, both Bloomberg and the *New York Times* face significant potential threats in the near future. Bloomberg is operating in a relatively stable market with a dominant share, but slowing growth prospects. Its fortunes are tied to Wall Street and its profits can turn significantly due to macroeconomic shocks, such as the 2008 recession. Additionally, there is always the possibility that a new competitor will emerge that dislodges Bloomberg from its market-leading position.

The *New York Times* confronts an even more uncertain future. The consumer publishing industry is in a dynamic transition from print to digital. There are few barriers to entry, so there are numerous new entrants on a yearly basis. Legacy companies such as the *New York Times* must also attempt to shed legacy costs tied to the print world, in an attempt to free up the money to invest in digital initiatives. To make matters worse, it is not at all clear which of several digital scenarios will ultimately yield the greatest ROI.

Given the fast pace of change in the media industry, both the *New York Times* and Bloomberg are continually reevaluating their strategies and modifying their business plans. In 2014, the *New York Times* published an Innovation report, co-authored by Arthur Gregg Sulzberger, a member of the sixth generation of the family that purchased the newspaper in 1896. The report stated emphatically that the *New York Times* was "winning at journalism," but needed "to become a more nimble, digitally focused newsroom that can thrive in a landscape of constant change." It mapped out strategic goals of significantly growing the *New York Times* audience, working with the business side to enhance the "reader experience," and reorienting the newsroom so that it was a "digital first" organization. The latter goal "means reassessing everything from our roster of talent to our organizational structure to what we do and how we do it." Although annual revenues for the company declined slightly from 2014 to 2016, in its letter to shareholders, executives pointed out the significant growth in digital subscriptions, giving the *New York Times* a combined three million print and digital subscribers—the most ever in its history. It noted a number of new journalistic platforms—including a virtual reality project and the launch or expansion of its podcasts and themed "sections"—and the purchase of two boutique digital marketing firms. In late 2017, the 37-year-old Sulzberger was named publisher of the newspaper, succeeding his father.

During the same time period—2014–2016—Michael Bloomberg was also attempting to reorient his company. Almost immediately upon his return to the company in 2014, he began a reorganization of the newsroom that led to the layoffs of 90 people in 2015. A memo. from the editor explained the shift. The company was returning to its roots—focusing on the financial professionals who provided 85% of total revenues. This meant that it would back off covering topics such as sports and education, and would instead focus on six main areas: business, finance, markets, economics, technology, and policy (government and politics). Bloomberg was for journalists with "a passion for business, finance and markets," the editor's memo said. "So if you are not intrigued by how people make money...or yearn to practice 'gotcha journalism' on investment bankers...then Bloomberg is probably the wrong place for you." Bloomberg would focus once again on providing data and shorter pieces since "people on a terminal are short on time." Given its global reach, there would be more emphasis on locally translated stories and the use of social media.

Existing media companies, like the *New York Times* and Bloomberg, must strike a delicate balance between preserving revenues and profits from the legacy business, which still pays the bills, while trying to transition to a new model. To get around this conundrum, strategy experts often recommend starting with "a blank sheet of paper" and asking this question: If we were building this company today, how would we build it? That's what we'll attempt to do in the next section.

What Are the Components of a Sustainable Digital Business Model?

> "Your strategy is your promise to deliver value: the things you do for customers, now and in the future, that no other company can do as well."

This definition of strategy from the consulting firm Strategy&, captures the essence of the shift in business models for media companies over the past two decades. Pre-digital strategies for media companies tended to focus on achieving operational excellence and efficiency. They were inwardly focused. Successful entrepreneurial media companies in the digital space—existing companies as well as start-ups—will be outwardly focused, prioritizing the end-user, the *customer*, instead.

In their book, *Business Model Generation: A Handbook for Visionaries, Game Changers and Challengers*, consultants Alexander Osterwalder and Yves Pigneur created a business model "canvas" that served as "a shared language for describing, visualizing, assessing and changing business models." This canvas—a simplified, one-page diagram with nine components—considered both internal and external factors (i.e., strengths and weaknesses, opportunities and threats) that could affect the success of a strategy. It prompted entrepreneurs to perform a SWOT analysis on: customer segments, value propositions, channels, customer relationships, revenue streams, key resources, key activities, key partnerships, and cost structure.

Given the customer-focused imperative that media enterprises confront in the digital era, we've adapted their model, and those of recent authors, including Robert Kaplan and David Norton (*The Strategy-Focused Organization*) and Robert Simons (*Seven Strategy Questions*) to develop a more outwardly-focused strategic framework. This can be used by leaders of start-ups crafting business plans from scratch, or legacy enterprises, attempting to rapidly transition to more of a digital business model. The strategy framework consists of five questions that correlate with the five primary components of a digital business model for both large and small B2B and B2C media enterprises.

1) What is the unique value proposition your enterprise offers current and potential customers?
2) What are your most promising (and profitable) current and potential customer segments?
3) What are the best channels for reaching current and potential customers and enhancing your relationship?

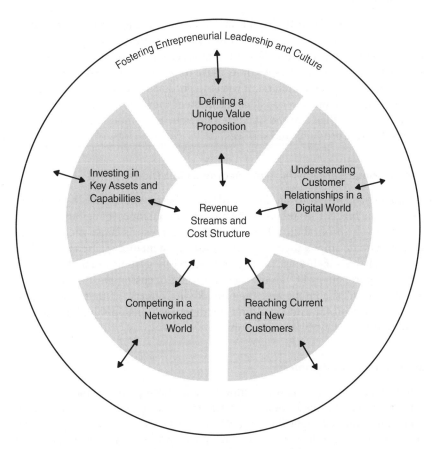

Figure 5.2 The components of a digital media business model.

4) When should you compete and when should you collaborate in a digitally networked world?

5) What are your key assets (including people and capabilities) that will deliver value for your customers and drive long-term profitability and sustainability?

The business model we are using in this book (Figure 5.2) is an integrated and iterative one in which the various components feed into and continuously shape both internal and external outcomes. Therefore, we've represented it as a circle in which the arrows extend in both directions, assuming continuous feedback and adjustment when necessary. The five components of the strategy influence costs and revenues, and vice versa. Similarly, all five components must be integrated into a coherent strategy. This in turn influences, and is influenced by, organizational structure, culture and leadership. In the chapters that follow, each of the five components in Figure 5.2 will be discussed in greater detail, as well as tools and processes for assessing your current position in the market and future prospects.

Defining a Unique Value Proposition

The creation of a new strategy and business model for any enterprise begins with the articulation of how a company's products and services create value for the customers who buy them and use them. A media enterprise must establish a unique value proposition in order to differentiate itself from the competition and establish a sustainable business model. The Internet has disrupted the traditional value proposition that media enterprises delivered to their consumers, putting downward pressure on pricing and also changing consumer expectations about how they interact with content. In Chapter 6, we'll explore strategic tools and processes you can use to profile your customers' wants, needs, and motivations, and then match them with the products and services you offer. It is important for media companies to consider the content they deliver as both a "product," as well as a "service." What are the benefits that your customers uniquely receive from interacting with your products and services?

Understanding Customer Relationships and Segments in a Digital World

The Media 1.0 era focused primarily on the size of the audience in determining financial winners and losers. The bigger the audience, the more potential for revenues and, if costs were managed effectively, profitability. The Media 2.0 era rewards those media enterprises that can differentiate among their customers, sorting them into segments based on a range of characteristics—including demographics, psychographics, and behaviors. Successful media entrepreneurs will "target" specific groups of customers, directing their creation and distribution of content and their marketing efforts, at these groups. In Chapter 7, we'll explore tools for understanding customer relationships and for calculating the strategic value of various types of customers.

Reaching Current and New Customers

Today, customers create, purchase, and consume content through many channels—traditional ones (such as purchasing a book at a brick-and-mortar retail outlet) or digital ones (by downloading a mobile application or accessing material through an aggregator). How do media companies use these numerous channels to attract new customers and enhance the relationship with existing ones? In Chapter 8, we'll explore tools for mapping the customer journey, designing and delivering content that engages, and evaluating the efficiency and effectiveness of the various channels.

Competing in a Networked World

We now live in a networked world. In order to survive in the digital era, media companies must learn how to take advantage of the new economics of networks and partnerships. The economist Noam envisioned two types of media organizations in the digital age: the large integrators that aggregate and distribute content (such as Google and Facebook) and the smaller specialists that create content (such as the New York Times). This dynamic can create a "contested space"—with both the integrators and the specialists competing for the same customers. In Chapter 9, we discuss how media enterprises can thrive in a networked world by understanding when to collaborate and when to compete.

Investing in Key Assets and Capabilities

Strategy is about marrying the key resources that a company possesses, such as its tangible assets and its assorted capabilities, with the expectations of its customers. How do the leaders of media enterprises use the limited resources and assets that they possess to best advantage so that they meet the expectations of their customers and maximize their return on investment? In Chapter 10, we develop a framework to help media entrepreneurs identify the key assets in their organization and then prioritize investments in capabilities that will ultimately drive profitability.

In the 1995 business classic, *Competing for the Future*, authors Gary Hamel and C.K. Prahalad encouraged leaders to "create and dominate emerging opportunities." Successful media enterprises will have an agile organizational structure, and a leadership attuned to moving quickly. The goal of any digital media strategy is to fully utilize the new capabilities unleashed by new technologies to attract new audiences and develop new sources of revenues, ultimately driving profitability and sustainability.

Exercise: How Arianna Huffington Thrives in the Digital World

It began with an interest in politics. In 1995, Arianna Huffington, then married and living in Washington, began writing a nationally syndicated political column for newspapers. Her divorce prompted a move to Los Angeles in 1998, a shift in her political allegiances (from conservative to progressive), and a newfound interest in the web. She began posting blogs on her website, a new phenomenon in the late 1990s. After losing a bid to become governor of California in 2003 and writing about the 2004 elections, she became convinced there was a need online for a progressive site similar to the conservative *Drudge Report*. With $2 million in funding, she and a former AOL executive, Ken Lerer, founded Huffington Post in 2005 as a platform for aggregating and featuring not only her blogs, but those of others as well. Almost immediately the blogging site proved "sticky"—in part because of Huffington's skill at soliciting blogs from well-known writers and celebrities. The bloggers offered opinions and often linked to stories produced by other mainstream news organizations. Also, in contrast to other sites, the editorial and technology staff sat side by side, learning from each other how to increase traffic to the site through search engine optimization (SEO).

By 2010, Huffington Post had a collection of more than 3,000 bloggers who wrote 300 posts a day, and between 12 million and 20 million unique monthly visitors. Yet profitability still eluded the company. In 2011, AOL purchased the Huffington Post for a reported $315 million, and Huffington stayed on as president and editor-in-chief until 2016, when she left to form a new online enterprise. By then, Huffington Post had more than 81 million monthly visitors, 13 editions around the globe, and more than 1,200 daily posts. The site had also finally turned profitable.

Huffington's new venture was called Thrive Global, described in venture funding material as "a consumer and corporate well-being productivity platform." Through her two books—*Thrive* and *The Sleep Revolution*—and extensive personal appearances, Huffington had already promoted a conversation around health and wellness topics. Now she hoped to turn the conversations into both a B2C and a B2B enterprise.

Her consumer business model relied on a hub approach, offering editorial content (accessed for free and with paid subscriptions), e-commerce (wellness pillows and candles), and live events featuring sports celebrities. While other consumer sites focused on just one topic, Huffington planned to cover the waterfront. On the corporate side, she planned to set up a consultancy that would send "trainers" into companies to hold workshops and retreats to address stress, depression, and burnout. Huffington launched her new business with $7 million in venture funding and a staff of seven, which was expected to expand to 50 within a year's time so the company could "have a global impact on millions of people."

Based on what we discussed in this chapter, consider these questions:

- How would you compare the business model of Huffington Post (before it was sold to AOL in 2011) to that of the *New York Times* prior to 2014?
- What are the strengths and weaknesses of Huffington Post today? Will it continue to survive and grow without the founder?
- Using the four-part framework for constructing a business plan for a start-up, evaluate Thrive Global's B2B and B2C model. What do you think of its chances for profitability and sustainability?

Summary

"Today is the slowest rate of technological change you'll ever experience in your lifetime," technology consultant Palmer advises his clients. The fast pace of change in the market, driven by both consumer expectations, as well as technological innovation, complicates matters for both start-ups who are trying to gain traction and profitability, and for traditional media companies attempting to move more aggressively into the digital space.

In the pre-digital era, media companies typically produced four different types of content—news, information, persuasion/commentary, and entertainment—and had a variety of business models. Prognosticators see two dominant types of media enterprises emerging in the digital space—large integrators, which aggregate content from many sources, and smaller specialists that create their own unique content that will be consumed by specific types of customers. Successful media enterprises—whether large or small—will have a diversified revenue stream.

Founders of start-ups should craft a business plan that takes into account factors you can control and those that you can't. This then allows you to consider the risk and reward of each potential investment, while also determining whether you have the right people and processes in place to succeed. Before crafting a new strategy, the leader of a legacy media enterprise needs to first identify the strengths and weaknesses of the current strategy and business model. The SWOT framework provides a snapshot of the positives and negatives, while also highlighting potential threats that may need to be addressed and opportunities for growth.

In the digital era, all successful media enterprises—start-up as well as legacy firms—will have a primary strategic focus on delivering unique value to their customers. In this chapter, we offered a customer-focused strategic framework that can be used by leaders of both new and established media enterprises to develop a sustainable and profitable digital business model with five key components.

6

Defining a Unique Value Proposition

Netflix was at a crossroads in 2011. Founder and CEO Reed Hastings was considering a strategic pivot away from the company's successful policy of providing DVD rentals to subscribers by using the US mail service. Over the previous decade, Netflix had disrupted the video rental industry with a cheaper, more convenient alternative to brick-and-mortar video stores. However, Hastings correctly recognized the future of video rentals was online streaming, and he was anxious to stay on top of the trend by phasing out mail delivery of DVD movies and investing in streaming capabilities. To facilitate the online strategic shift, Netflix publicly announced it was separating DVD rentals from its four-year-old streaming business and increasing monthly subscription fees for customers who wanted to continue to receive DVDs. Longtime Netflix subscribers revolted at the sudden change. Over the next few months, Netflix lost 805,000 of its 20 million subscribers and its stock plunged 77% to below $65 a share. In 2010, Hastings had graced the cover of *Fortune* magazine, having been named "Business Person of the Year." In 2011, he was parodied on *Saturday Night Live* as a clueless executive.

Fast-forward to December 2015: Netflix claimed more than one hundred million subscribers and had a market valuation of $60 billion, with its stock trading at $124 a share (the equivalent of more than $700 a share after a 7:1 stock split a few months earlier). In the interim, Netflix had pivoted toward yet another new business model, offering subscribers original streaming content that was receiving both critical and customer acclaim. Not only had Netflix become the first Internet content distributor to win a major TV award for its original series, *House of Cards*, but it was posting the highest revenue per employee among all of the mega cap technology companies, including Apple, Facebook, Google, and Amazon.

Why did these two strategies provoke markedly different responses? The answer lies in how Hastings evaluated his customers' needs and Netflix's ability to meet them. This process is called *defining a unique value proposition* and is critical for any media enterprise because it enables a company to craft strategies that give them long-term and sustainable competitive advantage. In this chapter, we consider the following questions:

- What is a value proposition?
- What research techniques and tools help you decide how to improve your product?
- How do you create value that matches your target customers' wants and needs?
- How do you set pricing and translate value into profit?

The Strategic Digital Media Entrepreneur, First Edition. Penelope Muse Abernathy and JoAnn Sciarrino.
© 2019 John Wiley & Sons, Inc. Published 2019 by John Wiley & Sons, Inc.
Companion website: www.wiley.com/go/abernathy/StrategicDigitalMediaEntrepreneur.

The Netflix Story: Three Value-based Strategies

Early one morning in 1997, Reed Hastings discovered a copy of the VHS tape *Apollo 13* in his bedroom closet. When he returned the VHS tape to a rental store, the software entrepreneur learned he owed a $40 late fee. As he pondered how to break the news to his wife, Hastings began imagining a better model for at-home entertainment—one without late fees that capitalized on newly-created DVDs. Hastings' insights led to the founding of the video-streaming company Netflix. During its short history, Netflix has adopted three different business models. At each turn, Hastings has attempted to follow the technology, follow his customers, and follow the money—the key components of any successful digital media strategy. Netflix began as a mail service, disrupting the market leader Blockbuster by focusing on providing timely delivery of DVDs through the US mail. Hastings next moved to phase out DVDs and deliver movies and television programs directly to a customer's TV or mobile device via streaming. Most recently, Netflix has become a creator of original television shows and movies. In formulating the company's strategies, and in recovering from potentially disastrous business missteps, Hastings has continually reconfigured the unique value proposition offered to customers, as he attempted to differentiate Netflix from its competitors.

Disruption One: Sidelining Blockbuster

In the late 1990s, most at-home movie watchers rented VHS cassettes from a local video rental store, such as those in the large Blockbuster franchise. Video stores lacked a wide selection of DVDs because people balked at the initial $600 price tag of a DVD player, introduced in the United States in March 1997. In setting up his company, Hastings hoped to appeal to this high-income customer base—the early adopters of this new, expensive technology. But he first had to crack how to deliver DVDs. Hastings explained to the *Financial Times*, "I went out, bought a whole bunch of CDs and mailed them to myself to see how quickly they would come back and what condition they would be in. I waited for two days— and they all arrived in perfect condition."

Armed with this solution, Hastings launched Netflix in August 1997. However, Netflix struggled to retain new customers. Movie-watchers grew frustrated they were spending in-store prices for a slower delivery time. So, Hastings rolled out a subscription-based service, allowing customers to rent an unlimited number of DVDs for a monthly fee of $18. This compared favorably with the price a consumer would pay for renting just four DVDs from Blockbuster during a one-month period. Netflix tapped into customers' desire to watch as much as they wanted for as long as they wanted, avoiding late fees associated with in-store entertainment. Netflix also introduced a proprietary recommendation system that suggested older in-stock movies that were often unavailable at local video stories.

By 2000, the price of DVD players had dropped below $100; by 2003, they sold for less than $50. As DVDs increasingly replaced VHS cassettes, Netflix achieved its first operating profit in 2003. The year before, Netflix went public, with its stock debuting at $15 a share. By 2010, Netflix had more than 20 million subscribers and a DVD library with 100,000 titles. By comparison, the typical video rental store had only 3,000 titles. So, while the price of Netflix stock climbed, shares of Blockbuster tumbled. In 2010, Blockbuster was delisted from the New York Stock Exchange when shares hit an all-time low, and shortly afterwards it filed for bankruptcy.

Disruption Two: Flubbing the Transition to Streaming

Even as Netflix massed an unparalleled DVD library, customer preference was shifting toward watching programs delivered over the Internet, instead of through the mail. In 2006, Amazon launched a streaming service, and in response Netflix began offering streaming in 2007. By 2011, two more services—Hulu and Vudu—had been founded. Hastings realized that the future was online and announced in a blog post that he was separating DVD rentals from the streaming service. But Netflix's streaming capabilities lagged behind that of its competitors. While Netflix had an extensive DVD library of more than 100,000 tiles, it had only 20,000 titles available for streaming, compared to more than the 110,000 streaming titles offered by Amazon. (Amazon Prime customers, who paid $75 a year in 2011, could view 10,000 of those titles for free, and they paid as little as $2 to view other streaming titles.) In order to continue to have access to Netflix's extensive DVD library, customers had to create two accounts with two different domain names, pay two credit card billings and navigate two sets of ratings and preferences. Further antagonizing longtime customers, Hastings effectively increased the price of a monthly subscription by 60%. Prior to the split, Netflix customers paid $10 a month ($120 a year) for unlimited access to both the DVD and streaming libraries which had a total of 120,000 titles. After the split, they had to pay $8 a month for each service, or $16 a month to receive both services. Netflix customers abandoned the service in droves, enticed by the lower subscription and rental prices on other streaming services, as well as the larger availability of their online libraries.

Disruption Three: Using Unique Content to Create Value

Scrambling after the public flop, Hastings considered a new way to promote the Netflix brand. He decided to create original content, much as a television or movie studio would. In a 2016 interview with *Business Insider*, he admitted, "It seemed crazy...At that point, we were still buying DVDs." But he hoped making and owning shows would give the company an advantage over other streaming competitors. In 2013, Netflix unveiled the critically acclaimed *House of Cards*, an American political drama that it produced for $100 million. A number of other shows quickly followed, included including *Orange is the New Black*, the most popular streaming series of 2016. The company also revised its pricing, offering three subscription options—ranging from $8 a month to $12—based on a customer's preference for the quality of the streaming video and the number of screens that could be watched simultaneously.

The company's annual revenue rose to $8.8 billion, as Netflix surpassed Time Warner's HBO as the biggest subscription-video service. Hastings told CNBC that the company would spend as much as $6 billion yearly on original content to counter the "awfully scary" Amazon, which had also begun to create original movies and television shows. In an attempt to strengthen its content, Netflix acquired the comic-book publisher Millarworld in August 2017, allowing it to capitalize on the popularity of characters such as "Kick Ass" and "Old Man Logan." As of 2017, Amazon Prime boasted more than 20,000 TV and movie titles that Prime subscribers, who now paid $99 a year, could view for free. While Netflix had only 7,000 titles, it offered more television shows than Amazon, and its programs earned more awards giving Netflix a unique value proposition that enabled growth in both international and domestic markets.

Why All Companies Need Unique Value Propositions

As the Netflix example illustrates, if you want to win customers for a product or service, you first need to understand their needs and wants. Only by deeply knowing customer needs and wants can you position yourself to offer unique value. Reed Hastings understood this when he created a DVD by-mail business, allowing customers to easily access movies not available at their video stores. In describing this process, Hastings said: "When there's an ache, you want to be like aspirin, not vitamins. Aspirin solves a particular problem someone has, whereas vitamins are a general 'nice to have' market. The Netflix idea was certainly aspirin."

Authors Robert Kaplan and David Norton underscore that a customer's perceived value in a product or service creates the "essence of strategy." Marketing professor Irvine Clarke calls unique value propositions the "fulfillment of customer needs." Similarly, business theorists Alexander Osterwalder and Yves Pigneur define value propositions as "creating products and services customers want."

All of these definitions speak to the importance of unique value propositions for both start-up and mature organizations. For start-up organizations, as Netflix was in 1997, the challenge is to invent new products or services for a particular customer segment. In contrast, existing organizations, as Netflix was in 2011, must develop ways to either improve their value proposition or invent a new product. Improving an existing bundle of products or services for a particular customer segment is the most common approach. This involves the same steps as creating a value proposition, but employees consider how they can leverage current resources and capabilities.

There are several frameworks for evaluating the potential value of a product or service, and how it compares to other products in your own portfolio or those of competitors. Some of the concepts—such as the BCG grid and the Product Life Cycle—are best applied to existing organizations. Others—the checklist of value components and value-proposition mad-lib—can be applied to all organizations.

Frameworks for Existing Organizations

In the 1970s, the Boston Consulting Group's (BCG) founder, Bruce Henderson, developed a two-by-two matrix that plots a product's market share against the industry's annual growth, called the BCG grid. Henderson originally created the BCG grid to analyze an entire business portfolio of a multi-product or multi-business corporation. The matrix enables business units, brands or products to be evaluated on the basis of market share and annual growth, to plot the relative positions. Those business units that enjoy high market share and high growth are identified as *stars*; those business units that have low market share and low growth are identified as *dogs*; those business units that have high market share and low growth are identified as *cash cows*; and finally, those business units that have low market share and high growth are identified as *problem children*. Henderson posited that a product was "high" growth when its cumulative annual growth rate was 10% or higher, and it had a "high" market share when it achieved 25% or higher.

BCG consultants used this framework to recommend investment strategies. Revenues generated by *cash cows* were used to fund *problem children* in the hopes they would become *stars*. *Dogs* would be divested and the money also would be reinvested into *problem children*. Using this framework, entrepreneurs in established companies can either attempt to turn a dog (a product or service with low profits) into a star (a product or service with high profits), or divest it entirely.

In addition to the BCG framework, Raymond Vernon's product life-cycle theory is a key concept for understanding revenue potential. The life-cycle (Figure 6.1) charts products

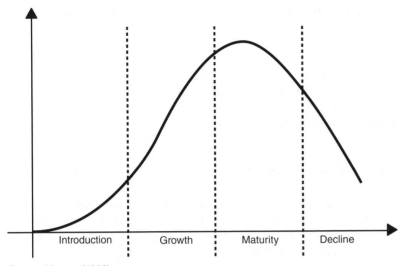

Figure 6.1 Product life-cycle.

from "birth" to "death," using the stages of "introduction, growth, maturity, and decline." The life-cycle stages are similar to the BCG grid in that products in their initial (introductory) stage are often "problem children" (as pertains to the BCG matrix) and require the highest resource commitment, if they are to survive. Using the product life-cycle to evaluate your portfolio of products provides the same guidance as the BCG framework: products in the mature stage fund products in the introduction stage and declining products are divested to invest in new products.

Frameworks for All Organizations

Whereas the BCG grid and product life-cycle are best applied to existing organizations, you can use the questions and frameworks below to more critically examine entrepreneurial ideas. Start-up organizations can draw on these tools to solidify their unique value propositions and mature organizations can also use them when considering how to launch a new product or reinvent an existing product's value proposition.

- Is your product or service newer than others on the market?
- Does your product or service perform better than others already?
- Is it better customized to a target audience than other products?
- Is your product or service less expensive? If not, what justifies the additional price?
- Is your brand stronger than your other competitors in the market?

You can also use the "mad-lib" approach to test your value proposition. Management consultant Geoffrey Moore introduced this approach in 1991 in his book *Crossing the Chasm: Marketing and Selling High-Tech Products to Mainstream Customers*. In this scenario, you fill in the blanks, completing two sentences:

> My product is <u>for</u> (short description of your target customer) <u>who</u> (short description of the problem vexing your customers). <u>Our</u> company (short description of the solution your product provides) <u>so that</u> (short description of the value created by the new product).

Here's how we could apply the "mad-lib" approach to Hastings's 1997 idea to launch Netflix:

> Netflix is:
> For high income customers
> Who recently bought a DVD player and cannot find DVDs in video stores.
> Our company will mail DVDs to your door
> So that you can enjoy a wide selection of rental DVDs.

Steps to Creating a Value Proposition

Using the above frameworks, you can begin to understand how your goods or services might appeal to customers. Now let's examine how to create a unique value proposition. First you identify your potential customers' wants and needs, and then you need to design products and services that create perceived value for your targeted customer.

What motivates your target customers? What frustrates them about current goods and services? Before launching a new business or line of services, you need to dive into your target customer's needs, wants, emotions, and motivations. This will give you a complete view of your customer and strengthen your value proposition.

But how do you dive into your customer's head? Table 6.1 is a brief overview of four research methods. With information gleaned from any of these research methods, you can use a series of tools to create a unique value proposition. In 2014, authors Alex Osterwalder and Yves Pigneur published a sequel to their book on *Business Model Generation* (discussed in the Chapter 5), called *Value Proposition Design: How to Create Products and Services Customers Want*, which featured a "value proposition canvas." The "canvas" was a two-part diagram that allowed entrepreneurs to visualize the process of creating value for customers, and then determine what features mattered most.

Table 6.1 Research methods to understand your consumer.

Type of research	What it is	Best when
Secondary and syndicated research	Analysis of previous research on a target customer and analysis of data performed by a firm. Syndicated research is often purchased by multiple clients who share costs and results.	Seeking contextual information, such as demographic, behavioral and attitudinal data. Looking to minimize and/or share costs with other companies.
Ethnographic research	Primary research observing customers in their own environments using products and services to do or complete certain jobs.	Have a long time horizon and need to understand how existing products and services are used. Helpful for spotting customer wants and needs.
In-depth interviews	Interviews between a respondent and an interviewer where interviewer asks probing questions to understand behaviors, attitudes, and motivations.	Hoping to produce an "empathy map" to immerse yourself in a user's environment.
Focus groups	Discussions led by a moderator of small group participants with common characteristics to understand behaviors and attitudes	Want to uncover participant needs, wants and emotions.

We've modified Osterwalder's and Pigneur's canvas by posing an additional question, "What is the purpose of your product or service?" This question acknowledges the key role in communication that media companies play in informing and entertaining society. In the exercises below, let's apply this model to the value proposition for Netflix in 2011, as Hastings weighed which type of streaming and DVD strategy to pursue. First, we will create a value creation customer profile for Netflix, then a value offering map and finally attempt to align the wants and needs of the customer with the value map of the products and services Netflix designed.

Step One: Creating a Value Creation Customer Profile

This exercise helps identify the target customer's wants and needs, emotions, and motivations by asking some questions:

- *What does the customer want and need to accomplish?* As you answer this question, keep in mind that economists define a *want* as a desire and a *need* as anything needed for survival.
- *How do your customers feel when they are trying to solve a problem? How do they want to feel?* Answering these questions highlights your customer's *emotions.* When considering emotions, you should think about both their "pains"—obstacles frustrating them—and their "gains"—what they are hoping to accomplish.
- *Why is the customer acting in a certain way?* This is the most difficult, but also the most crucial question to answer: What is your customer's *motivation?* Motivations can be emotional, social, and economic. Customers can have more than one motivation.

Putting all these factors together allows you to create a value creation customer profile, as in Figure 6.2. In his research on the value creation customer profile, Osterwalder instructs that after you have fully identified the three domains, you should prioritize them from strongest to weakest. He also recommends segmenting your target customers into various groups, and using complete descriptions for wants and needs until you have a robust narrative of each target customer segment. (We'll discuss customer segmentation in Chapter 7.)

Figure 6.2 Value creation customer profile for digital media companies.

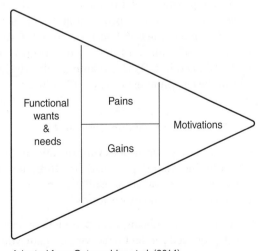

Adapted from Osterwalder et al. (2014).

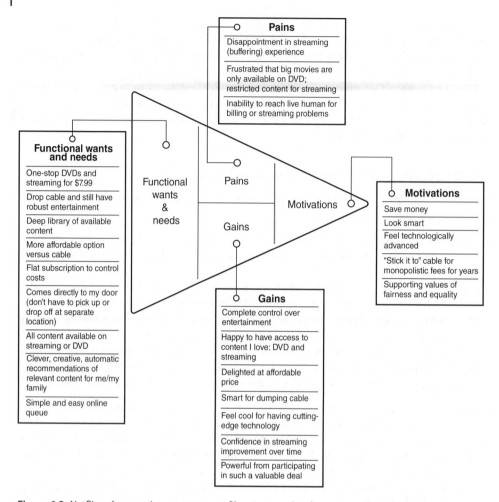

Figure 6.3 Netflix value creation customer profile prior to split of streaming and DVD business.

If you apply the model in Figure 6.2 to the Netflix example, you can imagine what a value creation customer profile might look like for a Netflix customer in 2011, prior to the separation of the DVD business from the streaming service. In Figure 6.3, notice how the value profile answers the key questions about Netflix customers: (1) What do they want and need in a DVD/streaming subscription? (2) What are the positives and negatives in the customer experience? (3) What are the factors motivating Netflix customers?

Step Two: Creating a Value Offering Map

A value offering map applies your product to the target customer's wants and needs. The value offering map (Figure 6.4) has three parts: products and services, emotions, and motivations. Successful value offering maps address the most important customer wants, needs, emotions, and motivations.

1) Why are you offering your products or services? *Motivation* provides grounding to the proposed product or services. Again, you should focus on the motivations that are essential to the product or service and omit those that are non-essential.

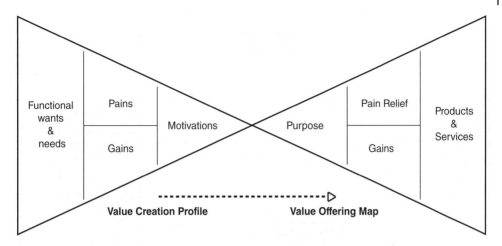

Adapted from Osterwalder et al. (2014).

Figure 6.4 Digital media value offering map.

2) How will you stoke the customer's positive emotions and quell negative ones? *Emotion solutions* describe how you will relieve the customer's pain and help them achieve their goal. When examining this aspect, it is important to focus on solutions only for emotions that are essential.
3) How will you address the customer's wants and needs? This is reflected in the *products and services*, which include tangible and intangible items. As you apply your product or service to the framework in Figure 6.4, you should ensure you are adding only the products and services that apply to the customer target and hone in on the most specific emotions and motivations. Successful value propositions are about making trade-offs, regarding which wants, needs, emotions, and motivations will be addressed and which should be omitted.

Let's apply this to the Netflix example in 2011 when Hastings wanted to transition customers to streaming. As you can see in Figure 6.5, Hastings miscalculated and did not offer any "pain relievers" for customers who wanted to order DVDs *and* have access to streaming through Netflix.

By mapping the Netflix value offering, you can identify: (1) the purpose of the offering; (2) how you might address customers' negative emotions; and (3) how you might address wants and needs with products and services.

Step Three: Aligning the Customer Profile and Offering Map

Once you've produced a value creation customer profile and value offering map, you are ready to determine how the two overlap. You should align or adjust the two until they work together. Alignment occurs when meaningful customer wants, needs, emotions and motivations are addressed by a solution customers care about. If alignment cannot be achieved, then you need to go back to the drawing board.

Compare the value creation customer profile in Figure 6.2 with the value offering map for Netflix in 2011 (Figure 6.3). In the Netflix customer profile (Figure 6.3), you can see that customers were previously happy with the combined streaming and DVD monthly subscription. They had relatively few points of "pain." However, Netflix's value offering of

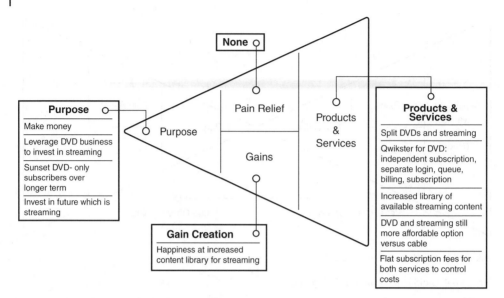

Figure 6.5 Netflix value offering map after the split of streaming and DVD business.

splitting DVDs and streaming services did not alleviate their pain. Instead, it created a new source of pain and frustration. Now customers who wanted access to the DVD library, as well as online streaming, had to create a separate account, login, queue, search, billing, and subscription for their DVD account while maintaining their old information for their streaming account. Moreover, Netflix increased its monthly subscription price for customers receiving both DVDs and streaming content by 60%, charging more for the increased hassle. While customers will generally resist any price increase, it is worth noting that increases accompanied by the removal of "pains" or the creation of meaningful gains will generally make it more palatable—which is not the value proposition Netflix created in 2011. After hundreds of thousands of people canceled their subscriptions and Wall Street responded by punishing the company's stock, Netflix CEO Reed Hastings formally apologized on September 19, 2011:

> I messed up…It is clear from the feedback over the past two months that many members felt we lacked respect and humility in the way we announced the separation of DVD and streaming, and the price changes. That was certainly not our intent, and I offer my sincere apology. I want to acknowledge and thank our many members that stuck with us, and to apologize again to those members, both current and former, who felt we treated them thoughtlessly.

On October 10, 2011, Netflix dropped Qwikster. "It is clear that for many of our members two websites would make things more difficult, so we are going to keep Netflix as one place to go for streaming and DVDs," CEO Reed Hastings wrote in his announcement. "This means no change: one website, one account, one password…in other words, no Qwikster."

Since the customers' needs and wants (the value creation customer profile) did not match the value Netflix was offering with the new streaming service (the value offering map), a new strategy was needed—both to entice current DVD customers to switch to streaming and to attract entirely new customers to sample and subscribe to its streaming operation, which in 2011 was much smaller than Amazon's. Hastings therefore needed to go back to the drawing board. He enhanced the value proposition by adjusting both the product and price. By offering original award-winning content—not found on any other service—he gave customers a reason to sign up or stay connected. Additionally, he revamped his pricing options, making them more comparable to competitors such as Amazon Prime and Hulu.

Translating Value into Profit

Let's now consider pricing, which is an integral part of the unique value proposition. Customers expect products with higher price tags to connote higher quality and deliver greater value. There are three primary pricing models: cost-based, demand-based, and value-based.

- *Cost-based pricing:* With this model, a product is priced to cover the cost of manufacturing it. Therefore, price is determined by calculating the cost of producing or providing it (including expenses related to raw materials, personnel, and delivery, for example). Obviously, a company cannot continually price below the "cost of goods sold" and make a profit. Therefore, all companies rely, in some form, on cost-based pricing, which serves as a "floor" when setting price. Companies that employ cost-based pricing as a strategy often have slim profit margins and depend on doing a large volume of business in order to drive both revenues and profitability. Examples of low-cost firms include Ryanair, the budget airline, or the discount retailer Walmart, which strive to be the lowest-cost producers in their industry segments.
- *Demand-based pricing:* This is based on the consumer's demand for a specific product or service, and the availability or supply in the market place. This is the classic supply-and-demand curve. Under this model, the customer's willingness to purchase the product at different prices is compared and then a price is set that matches supply with demand. For example, Disney recently unveiled a new demand-based pricing scheme for its amusement parks. Tickets to Walt Disney World cost up to 20% more during holidays than during slower periods of the year, when families with school-aged children are less likely to want to visit the park. Similarly, tickets on airlines typically cost less during off-peak times, such as the weekend.
- *Value-based pricing:* In contrast to cost-based or demand-based models, value-based pricing is a relatively new concept. It is based on the value that a customer perceives the product or service providing. Value-based pricing allows a company to maximize profits by offering different pricing schemes to specific consumer groups. Customers who receive less value, pay less. Those who receive more value, pay more. In order to implement a value-based pricing approach, a company must understand the value they are actually offering various customer segments versus the customer's perceived value of the product.

Thomas Nagle, founder of the Strategic Pricing Group, expands on the benefits of value-based pricing in his (2014) book, *The Strategy and Tactics of Pricing*. Nagle notes that the purpose of value-based pricing is "not simply to create a satisfied customer but to price more profitably by capturing more value." Nagle also clarifies the relationship between value propositions and an effective pricing strategy. He writes that by creating and establishing a clear value proposition, value-based marketing discourages customers from making easy comparisons between products based on price alone, and instead encourages them to consider the actual value of the product delivered.

There are several examples of value-based pricing in cases we have already studied. For example, Bloomberg is able to maintain a steep price for its terminals because it is perceived by financial traders as giving better insights (i.e., delivering better value) than its competitors. Similarly, the *New York Times* is able to charge much more for a subscription than a local newspaper because it is perceived to offer much richer content. However, the New York Times also tiers its pricing, offering lower-priced subscriptions to students—in the hopes of convincing them to pay more once they start earning a salary. Table 6.2 highlights four examples of value-based pricing.

In addition to these value-based examples, media companies have also used several other types of pricing models. Cable companies, for example, have employed bundled pricing quite effectively. The idea of bundling and unbundling services can be traced back to the 1960s, when Nobel Prize-winner George Stigler described how profits could be increased by combining the pricing of two goods. Pricing experts Yannis Bakos and Erik Brynjolfsson considered the bundling of information goods on the Internet in the late 1990s, and concluded that it can be highly profitable, particularly when customers are using a large number of goods and have a difficult time determining and comparing the pricing of individual goods.

It is important to note that when buying a product or service, the bundled price almost always benefits the seller, whereas the unbundled price benefits the buyer, primarily due to the transparency over the particular options. Beyond lack of transparency, bundling also benefits the seller as users are supporting the extensive catalog of other products or services. Cable companies sell bundled packages that include hundreds of channels, even though most households actually only watch an average of 17 channels per week. Having customers simply pick the channels that they would like to watch would make niche programming more expensive and unprofitable. Moreover, whereas a customer may be happy to pay the overall bundled price, once individual prices are provided, the customer may be displeased at the cost of each particular component.

Table 6.2 Examples of value-based pricing.

Pricing type	What it is	When it's used
Customized	Adjusting the price according to the value the product or service delivers to the customer	Customized pricing is very common in B2B sales of computer software, for example. Similarly, popular US television shows sell for more in one country than another.
Group rate	Dividing consumers into two or more groups or markets having different price elasticities	Newspapers such as the *New York Times* routinely offer a student rate substantially reduced from the regular rate
Tariff-plus	Charging the consumer a flat or lump-sum fee for the right to buy a product or service in addition to charging for in-demand features	Amazon Prime customers paying $99 a year have access to more than 18,000 streaming titles but pay extra for titles outside of the Prime library. Similarly, some amusement parks charge an entrance fee and a fee to ride popular rides.
Tiering	Selling goods or services together in a package	This is commonly practiced by cable television companies, which package channels together into cable tiers such as basic or premium

Similarly, media and technology companies have tended to employ one of two pricing strategies when introducing a new product. Apple has used a *skimming* strategy when introducing its new products and innovations. It charges the early adopters a premium price for the privilege of being one of the first to own the latest version of its iPhone, for example. In contrast, other software and hardware companies have employed a different strategy. They introduce the product at the lowest possible price (sometimes below the cost of producing it), in the hopes of gaining rapid market share and displacing existing competitors. The price of DVD players, for instance, declined dramatically over a period of five years, from $600 to less than $50, displacing videocassette players. Netflix was perfectly positioned to benefit from the penetration pricing strategy pursued by makers of the DVD player. By 2003, the year that Netflix turned profitable, half of all households in the United States had at least one DVD player. By 2004, two-thirds of all households had DVD players.

All customers have a notion of what they are willing to pay for a product or service. We call this a reference price. Using the research methods (depth interviews and focus groups) and the tools described previously—the *Value Creation Customer Profile for Media Companies* and the *Value Creation Map for Media Companies*—it is often possible to gain extensive insight into what sort of value customers place on a product or service. If there is a gap between the value that a certain product is delivering compared to the customer's perceived value or reference price, then a company has two options: it can attempt to educate the customer about the value a product provides or adjustments must be made to the product offering or the price to make it align with customer expectations.

Advertising and marketing efforts have historically played an important role in educating consumers about the value of a product or service. Skillful marketing can create an awareness for the need, desire, and demand for a new product, encourage purchase and re-purchase, and, perhaps, most importantly, it can differentiate a product from an existing one by attributing more value to it. For example, in the early 2000s, the *Harvard Business Review (HBR)* was able to substantially increase both newsstand sales of the monthly business periodical, as well as the price it charged, by changing the customer's perceived value of the magazine and the reference price. Previously, the *HBR* was displayed on racks at the airport newsstands next to other periodicals, such as *Vanity Fair* or *Fortune*, which sold for $4.99. By arranging to display the *HBR*, which was printed on high-quality paper with colorful graphics, closer to paperbacks, which sold for $13.99, the circulation marketing executive was able to increase the cover price for each issue to $14.99. Newsstand sales doubled as business travelers looking for reading material for the long flight ahead compared the value in a paperback mystery to the content in a monthly issue of *HBR*.

If the consumer cannot be convinced that the value offered by the product is worth the price tag, then adjustments need to be made to either the product offering or price to bring it into line with customer expectations. Hastings, in admitting his mistake, made just such adjustments. He understood that Netflix could not compete with Amazon in terms of the quantity of streaming titles. Therefore, he began focusing on quality to justify the subscription price. Although he initially hoped to maintain the monthly $16 subscription price (for access to both the DVD and online library), he realized that he also needed to adjust the price to meet perceived customer value. His solution was to tier the pricing, similar to the scheme used by cable companies, with a basic, intermediate, and premium service.

Disruptors of Media Value Propositions

Netflix disrupted the value proposition of physical video stores in the early 2000s. But by 2011, the Netflix DVD business model was itself in danger of being disrupted by streaming. Let's conclude by examining how the Internet works to continually alter and, in many instances, undermine the value proposition of existing media enterprises such as Netflix or the *New York Times.*

For nearly one hundred years, the unique value propositions of traditional media enterprises focused on achieving excellence and competitive advantage in three broad domains:

- *Distribution*: Traditional media companies such as newspapers and television networks invested in superior delivery platforms to meet reader or viewer wants and needs. Such platforms also allowed them to reach the largest audience possible.
- *Performance*: They also attempted to differentiate themselves from competitors by creating unique content that the consumer could not find anywhere else.
- *Price*: Because the actual cost of producing and distributing the content was subsidized by advertising sales, audiences for newspaper, magazine, and television paid an artificially low price for the value they received.

The Internet began to erode these value propositions on a myriad of fronts. It offered even more convenient distribution at the lowest price of all–free. A 2011 Federal Communications Report, *The Information Needs of Communities*, points to three examples of innovative online products and services that led to the erosion of the financial performance of newspapers: Craigslist and eBay in 1995, followed by AutoTrader in 1997. These three start-up organizations initially attracted only a niche segment of customers. However, over a decade, the value propositions of all three improved along performance and distribution dimensions such that consumers begin to embrace the new services. Classified advertisers took notice and shifted their advertising online, undermining the profitability of newspapers. Innovative entrants that challenged broadcast media followed a similar pattern, beginning with YouTube and Reddit in 2005.

Harvard Business School professor Clay Christensen called value proposition disruptions the "Innovator's Dilemma." Scholars and practitioners have, for the most part, been focused on innovations that disrupt demand patterns by offering customer-based solutions. This is exactly what such digital entrants as Craigslist and YouTube did. Here are some examples of demand-side disruptors of existing media companies.

- *Platform competition*: Today's media consumers have easy access to the web (at work and at home), mobile devices, free newspapers and on-board TV, and other alternative media channels. While the Internet enables local newspapers, radio, and television stations to reach long-distance users from outside the market, national and pure digital media companies, along with other regional start-up websites, can penetrate into the local market and compete with traditional media for customers and advertising. Additionally, because consumers can easily access content on the web, traditional media outlets can end up competing with their own websites.
- *Changes in consumer behavior*: The Internet has enabled a seismic shift in the relationships between consumers, retailers, distributors, manufacturers, and service providers. It presents many companies with the option of eliminating the role of intermediaries

(newspapers or television shows that rely on revenue from advertisers to cover the cost of the content they produce) and communicate directly with their customers.

- *Customers' willingness to pay for digital content*: The Internet has fostered a dramatic increase in consumer-generated media, desktop publishing, and branded content, for example. As a result, supply has outstripped demand, and consumers become less willing to pay for basic content they can get elsewhere.

Traditional media companies have experienced not only these demand side disrupters of distribution, performance, and price, but also "supply side" disruptors. A supply side disruptor occurs because the response by the organization is only partially pre-ordained by external conditions. The choices that top managers make are the critical determinants of whether the organization recovers and addresses the demand side disruptors with their own customer-based innovation. Executives often hesitate to respond aggressively to the demand side disruptions, fearing that they will prematurely undermine their current business (the cash cow in the BCG matrix). Additionally, they are saddled with legacy costs associated with the pre-digital era—such as capital-intensive equipment, organizational structures and divisions, and personnel who do not have the skills to make the transition.

Traditional media organizations have evolved to have operationally excellent processes and structure, which breed cultures of administration and analysis, not prospecting. In other words, they are internally focused and defensive of their position, instead of externally oriented and offensive. This internal, defensive focus impedes innovation and often prevents traditional media enterprises from pivoting with agility. The key to recovering from any disruption or misstep is returning to a customer focus and recreating a unique value proposition.

Reed Hastings recovered from a serious business miscalculation in 2011 that could have destroyed his company by understanding that the product and service he was offering did not meet his customers' expectations. He apologized, then quickly regrouped and created a new unique value proposition for Netflix.

Exercise: Assess Netflix's Value Position in 2017

Is Netflix poised to displace traditional Hollywood movies, as some business analysts predict? Or are competitors such as Amazon and HBO an increasing threat to the 20-year-old company?

Assume you are Reed Hastings' chief marketing officer and you have been asked to review the company's unique value proposition. Prepare a presentation using tools such as the BCG grid, the value proposition mad-lib, and the value creation customer profile to give an assessment of whether Netflix needs to update its unique value proposition to maintain customers. Consider the questions:

- What type of research might be best to understand your target customer?
- How would you assess your target customers' behaviors, attitudes, and motivations?
- After establishing whether Netflix needs to update its value proposition, what is your take on whether Netflix should modify its pricing scheme?
- What are the hypothetical future disrupters that would harm Netflix's unique value proposition?

Summary

Successful media entrepreneurs identify and continually reassess their unique value proposition, which can be defined as "the fulfillment of your (current and potential) customer's needs and wants." They use tools such as the BCG growth share matrix to decide whether a product is a star and has a promising future, or a dog and should be improved or divested. They thoroughly research the customer target, taking into account their emotions and motivation for choosing a particular product or service.

The key to crafting a unique value proposition is to first identify a customer's most meaningful wants, needs, emotions, and motivations. This can be done by using a value creation customer profile. After understanding a customer's set of wants, needs, emotions, and motivations, you should next create a value offering map, focusing on the "pains" or "gains" that the customer will experience by purchasing your product or service. Do the wants and needs of the customer identified through the value creation customer profile align with the value offering map? Are there product or service solutions that can address customer wants, needs, emotions, and motivations? If not, then you need to go back to square one.

Pricing is an important component of value equation. We discussed three types of pricing: cost-based, demand-based, and value-based. Of the three, value-based pricing (which is based on the value that a customer perceives a product or service provides) has the most potential to increase profitability.

Demand disruptors—such as changes in consumer behavior and the proliferation of delivery platforms—can destroy the business model of both traditional and start-up media enterprises, and dramatically alter a product's value proposition. This why it is essential for media companies to constantly update their value creation customer profiles and value offering map, ensuring they are providing a unique value proposition that will enable them to make a profit.

7

Understanding Customer Relationships in a Digital World

Like Reed Hastings at Netflix, Charlie Ergen, CEO of Dish Network, staked his career on disrupting the media industry. Ergen began by hawking satellite dishes out of his truck in Colorado, appealing to rural residents who weren't able to access cable. In 1980, he founded EchoStar, which sold satellite television systems and dabbled in space exploration. After the company launched a satellite in 1995, he debuted Dish Network, offering subscription television services to frustrated cable customers and those in rural areas without access to cable. By 2015, Dish Network had become a Fortune 250 company, with more than $15 billion in annual revenues.

Despite such success, Ergen and his team, including Roger Lynch, who was then the executive in charge of advanced technologies, worried about how Dish could attract and retain "cord-cutter" and "cord-never" customers abandoning traditional television for over-the-top (OTT) content accessed via the Internet. In 2013, one in ten households had cut the cord and transitioned to streaming TV. By 2016, that number had jumped to one in five, and analysts predicted it would reach one in two by 2025. These cord-cutters skew younger and represent a growing trend. In 2017, MediaShift reported that nearly one-third of millennials had cut the cable cord entirely and more than half of them used streaming more than traditional TV.

Dish hoped it had found an alternative when it launched Sling TV, an Internet TV service aimed primarily at 18-to-35-year-olds. When it debuted with Lynch as CEO, Sling offered a skinny bundle of 30 streaming channels for $20 per month, allowing customers to personalize their experience through packages such as "Kids Extra" or "Lifestyle Extra" for an additional $5 per month. Sling became the first service to live stream major sports, news, and other paid programs through an internet platform. The *Wall Street Journal* commented that Sling was "the most hopeful sign yet that cable providers are losing their chokehold on home entertainment." On a subscription basis, Sling TV boasted cheaper rates than traditional cable television operators, as well as satellite providers such as Dish, although the total cost could vary due to Internet costs.

Why would Dish offer a cheaper subscription service that could cannibalize its core business? The answer lies in understanding segmentation and targeting. In this chapter, we will explore these concepts, which are key to strengthening your relationship with your audience. Successful media entrepreneurs understand the importance of "segmenting" customers into distinct groups, and then directing their marketing efforts, services, and products at these targeted segments. Finally, they position their products to ensure an advantage over their competitors. In this chapter, we will build on the concepts of how

The Strategic Digital Media Entrepreneur, First Edition. Penelope Muse Abernathy and JoAnn Sciarrino.
© 2019 John Wiley & Sons, Inc. Published 2019 by John Wiley & Sons, Inc.
Companion website: www.wiley.com/go/abernathy/StrategicDigitalMediaEntrepreneur

to define a unique value proposition and learn how media companies can more effectively reach current and new customers. We will discuss the following topics:

- How to approach customer segmentation.
- How to define a target market.
- How to use the adoption curve for targeting and positioning.
- The different types of customer relationships in the media industry.
- How to evaluate the profitability of each customer segment.
- How to measure and build loyalty and engagement.

Segmenting Customers

When marketing experts refer to "segmenting," they mean dividing your customer base into distinct groups with specific needs, attitudes, and behaviors. The subgroups should all share a common set of characteristics. There are five common ways to segment a market or audience: geographic, demographic, attitudinal, behavioral, and psychographic. Segmenting an available market into subgroups typically involves a combination of these five variables.

- Geographic: County of origin, city, state, neighborhood, climate.
- Demographic: Age, gender, family size, family life-cycle, income, education, religion, and race.
- Attitudinal: Perceptions toward a product or service, willingness to recommend, purchase intention.
- Behavioral: Usage, benefits, user status, user rates, comments, revenue or purchase levels.
- Psychographic: Lifestyle, social class, personality and motivations.

Let's apply these theories to Sling TV. When Sling launched in 2015, its CEO Roger Lynch highlighted the importance of segmenting. Lynch forecast Sling would avoid being dragged into the traditional TV package because it was aimed at specific customer segments. Using the variables above, Sling's marketing team divided its customers along two variables—their *attitude* toward paid television and their *demographics* such as age, income, and education. With these two variables, Sling identified three customer targets:

- *Cord-nevers:* These were people who had never bought paid television (cable or satellite). They were younger, better educated, more affluent, and more likely to be males living in an urban area.
- *Cord-cutters:* These were people of any age who had given up on traditional television but still wanted to have the channels they loved. Like the cord-nevers, they tended to be younger than the typical Dish customer. They were more likely to have a family.
- *Supplementers:* These were people who had paid television, but wanted more access to more content. They could be of any location, age, or family status.

Some may be tempted to "over-segment," which is counterproductive because it is usually not profitable to discretely target and position products and services for all segments. There are four tenets of effective segmentation.

The first rule is to ensure the customer segment is *accessible* to the firm or organization. This means the segments can be easily reached and served, based on what this segment wants to achieve. For example, let's say you are starting an e-newsletter about healthy cooking. There may very well be a segment of extroverted, empty-nest, urban-dwelling, male vegans who would subscribe to such a newsletter, but this segment would be difficult to reach and target.

The second rule is that the segments must be *responsive*. This means that each segment will respond differently to products, services, and communications. Each segment must be independently differentiable. Cord-nevers, cord-cutters, and supplementers all have different attitudes toward pay TV, ensuring they are true customer segments.

The third rule is that this segment must have *tactical reach*. Marketers must be able to design marketing tactics and plans to reach segments. A 2016 ad illustrates how Sling used messaging to appeal to the cord-cutter segment, trying to lure them away from pay TV. Actor Danny Trejo, a perpetual villain in films and television shows, opened with, "People say I'm scary," and then followed with "I'm not nearly as scary as pay TV."

The final guideline of effective segmenting is that the segments must have *purchasing power*. Marketers should be able to use predictive forecasting to determine if there is enough purchasing power in the segment to profitably sell the product. In the case of Sling, market research from Nielsen shows that in just one year (2015–2016) over-the-top/broadband only households increased by an additional 2.5 million while cable households sank by 1.8 million.

Targeting Customers

After segmenting your customer base, you then need to decide which segment you want to target and serve. You need to be confident about your target market because it underpins your strategy, which will decide your business's success or failure. Your company can target only one segment, or several, but most marketers choose both primary and secondary targets. For example, Sling chose cord-nevers as its primary target, and cord-cutters and supplementers as its secondary targets.

The most common way to evaluate a segment is to measure its size and its growth potential. A segment that has a slightly smaller size, but a very strong growth rate may be more attractive than a larger segment with a flat or negative growth rate. For example, when Hastings founded Netflix as a DVD-by-mail service, he was targeting a segment—DVD owners—that was small in 1997, but had strong growth potential.

Next, you should consider each segment's structural attractiveness. Weigh the level of competition, substitute products, power of buyers, and power of suppliers. This is especially important in the media industry where a number of disruptors have created products that overlap with other players, creating "contested boundaries." Sling's cord-cutting segment, for example, was already being served by Netflix, Hulu, Vudu, and Amazon. However, while Sling shared overlapping, contested boundaries with these large and formidable competitors, it offered ESPN programming, not offered by competitors and highly coveted by male millennials.

Finally, you should combine qualitative and quantitative analyses to determine whether targeting the segment will help your company achieve its objectives. In the case of Sling, targeting cord-nevers and cord-cutters helped supplement the list of subscribers to Dish, which was dwindling.

You might consider factors such as the audience's viewing and digital behavior. Are they distracted? Do they prioritize viewing on demand? Considering the audience's behavior can help you segment based on attitudes and digital personalities. Figure 7.1 segments customers based on how they prioritize their access to the content and their emotional attachment to the platform. This example, which comes from marketing experts, Saul Berman and Lynn Kesterson-Townes, illustrates how a media and entertainment company could segment and target by attitude and digital personas. Looking at this matrix you see that the two largest segments are the extremes: those with low access to content and low

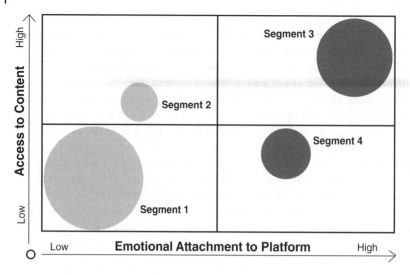

Adapted from Berman and Kesterson-Townes (2012).

Figure 7.1 Media and entertainment sample segmentation.

emotional attachment to the platform compared with the segment that has high access to content and strong emotional attachment.

The final step is to consider how you will position your product to your targeted customer segments. Simply put, positioning should be based on the target audience's needs and wants. Positioning is the place a product occupies in a consumer's mind relative to similar products. This is embodied in the positioning statement, which helps define the product in a simple declarative sentence. When crafting your positioning statement, you should consider sources of differentiation from competitors. You can differentiate your product along any of these dimensions: content, distribution, service, image, personality, and price. For example, Sling positions itself as "the only live TV service that gives you choice, customization, and control you deserve."

Your product should also have at least four, but ideally all of these characteristics: it must be important to the target market, distinctive, superior, communicable, preemptive, affordable, and profitable. Consider how Sling TV stacks up against these seven characteristics. It offers ESPN streaming, which is *important* to its target market of millennial male cord-nevers and cord-cutters. It is also *distinctive*, because it was the first OTT service marketing "a la carte TV" where you could pick your own channel line-up. Sling claims to be *superior* because customers can watch it anytime, anywhere, just by downloading the app. Finally, Sling appeals to customers based on its *affordability*, claiming to have a "price you can't beat."

Applying Targeting and Positioning: Types of Purchasers in the Life-Cycle of a Product

Let's now consider how to apply these targeting and positioning concepts to marketing. One of the most common approaches is to use the Diffusion of Innovation curve. Communication specialist Everett Rogers introduced this theory in the 1960s to explain who adopts technology and how they use it. According to Rogers's theory, a product will encounter five types of *purchasers* as it moves through its adoption life cycle: *innovators*, *early adopters*, *early majority*, *late majority*, and *laggards*.

By using the Diffusion Curve (see Figure 7.2), you can estimate the size, growth potential, and structural attractiveness of your target customer segments. Each consumer's willingness and ability to adopt an innovation or new technology depend on their awareness, interest, evaluation, trial, and adoption. People can fall into different categories for different innovations: a millennial might be an early adopter of WhatsApp, but a baby boomer may be an early adopter of the iPad.

Once a product has attracted *innovators* and *early adopters* and effectively reached 16% of its target market, Australian marketer Chris Maloney recommends changing the message from one based on scarcity to one based on social proof. This, he says, will accelerate purchase by the early majority segment and create a viable *tipping point*—the critical mass of purchasers necessary to achieve profitability and sustainability for your product.

Here's how Rogers assesses how people respond and adapt to new technologies:

- *Innovators* are social creators and the first to purchase a product or service. Rogers argues they represent only 2.5% of all purchases of the product or service. They don't shy away from trying completely new products or technology and will pay a premium for this benefit. Surprisingly, innovators are unlikely to thoroughly research and consider new purchases. Sales to innovators are not usually an indication of future sales

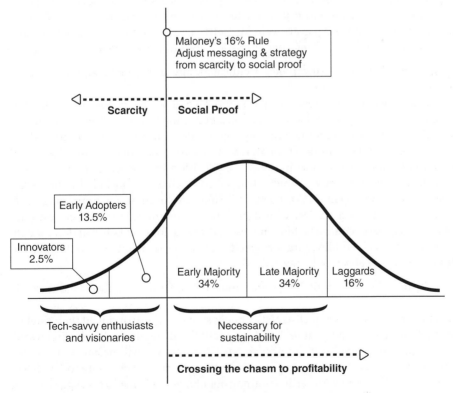

Source: Adapted from Maloney (2010) and Rogers (1962).

Figure 7.2 Maloney's 16% rule and the diffusion of innovation.

because innovators tend to purchase simply because a product or service is new. If innovators dislike the product, they can torpedo it on social media and through word of mouth.

- *Early adopters* are visionaries, social creators, and more integrated into the social system than innovators. They make up 13.5% of purchases. This target, more than any other, has the greatest influence and social capital in media. Early adopters know they must make grounded decisions if they want to safeguard their social status.

- *Early majority* consumers are pragmatists, social critics, and collectors. Representing 34% of purchasers, they wait for a product to become mainstream. These consumers are cautious, and likely to respond best to marketing strategies based on customer testimonials. In order for a product to achieve scale and sustainability, it must attract early majority purchasers.

- *Late majority* purchasers are conservatives, social joiners, and spectators. They comprise another 34% of sales. They tend to purchase when a product has become widely adopted, and is usually in its mature phase.

- *Laggards* are skeptics and socially inactive, according to Rogers. They represent 16% of total sales. Laggards purchase a product toward the end of its life cycle, waiting for the price to come down.

If you have a new product or service, such as Sling in 2015, you probably want to target innovators and early adopters with your messaging. These groups have the highest degree of opinion or thought leadership and can help persuade more customers to purchase, allowing your product to achieve critical mass support. Early adopters, especially, tend to be more social and more aspirational than later purchasers. Consider, for example, how crucial early adopters of DVD players were for Netflix's initial success in Chapter 6. Early adopters tend to have the following characteristics, according to Rogers:

- *Demographics*: They are younger, better educated, upwardly mobile and have higher social status than later adopters.

- *Personalities*: Early adopters tend to have a more favorable attitude toward change and can handle uncertainty, as well as abstractions, better than later adopters. Early adopters are likely to respond best to marketing communications based on scarcity and the promise of being trend-setters. Through research, Dish found that "cord-cutters" and "cord-nevers" were frustrated with traditional television service, which they perceived locked them into long-term contracts, had veiled pricing, and included unnecessary channels. Using the slogan, "Take Back TV," Sling produced an ad comparing cable companies to childhood bullies, with each bully representing a common customer complaint: long-term contracts, hidden fees, and paying for channels you don't watch. This positioning helped Sling target a specific customer segment: 18- to 35-year-old males who did not subscribe to pay TV.

The majority of early adopters of Sling were younger than Dish subscribers, and the early messaging spoke to their frustration with traditional television service. But Sling also appealed to a smaller segment of Dish Network consumers, who abandoned their satellite subscription for a cheaper alternative. Speaking about this dynamic, Dish CEO Ergen said: "There's no question [Sling] will cannibalize our [Dish's traditional] business." However, "We know that millions of people every year are cutting the cord. We're better off with half a loaf—$20 a month—than with getting nothing out of that customer." This suggests Sling TV will employ a different marketing message as it moves more mainstream, and attempts to attract older, more conservative purchasers—including more Dish subscribers.

Categories of Customer Relationships

Once you have selected the customer segment or segments that you will target for your products and services, you need to determine the type of relationship your organization will have with the customer. You should clearly delineate the type of relationship you want to establish with each customer segment so that your firm can provide appropriate support to nurture a relationship. There are three reasons for developing a relationship. You hope to acquire a new customer, retain an existing one, or upsell an existing customer (i.e., convince them to pay more for a premium product). The tactics you employ will vary, depending on your objective. For example, Sling used aggressive pricing and the promise of favorable distribution to attract early customers. On the other hand, cable providers are focused on customer retention and increasing the average revenue per user. Therefore, they offer attractive bundles, with the most appealing and expensive bundles priced to encourage upselling to faster Internet speeds with premium programming.

In their 2013 book, *Business Model Generation*, Alexander Osterwalder and Yves Pigneur identify six categories of customer relationships which may co-exist in a company's relationship with a particular customer segment. These are highlighted in Table 7.1 and range from self-service to dedicated personal assistance.

In the case of Sling, researchers found that the customer segments were most attracted to relationships based on personal assistance (for technical difficulties) and self-service (for streaming live television). They used these insights to tell consumers they could drive their own viewing experience but Sling would provide personal assistance whenever technical problems cropped up.

Table 7.1 Types of customer relationships.

Type of customer relationship	Characteristics
Personal assistance	The most traditional customer relationship; the customer can communicate easily with a customer service representative to get help during or after the sales process
Dedicated personal assistance	A more improved version of personal assistance; a representative is assigned to a particular customer or client. Organizations form this type of relationship when they want a deep and intimate connection with the customer over time.
Self-service	Customers are provided with the means to help themselves; the organization does not have direct contact with customers
Automated services	This relationship leverages data, gleaned through behavioral or personal online profiles, to give customers access to customized self-service. This data provides more customized opportunities for upselling and retention.
Communities	A relatively newer form of customer relationship, with organizations facilitating conversations among customers and prospects to exchange information and solve problems
Co-creation	This moves beyond the traditional customer-vendor relationship to jointly create value for the organization and customer, typically through a closed community of members

Source: Adapted from Osterwalder et al. (2013).

The customer relationships that will best fit your organization's value proposition have a direct influence on the customer experience. This is why it is crucial to outline and support the relationship each customer segment expects. Otherwise, customers will feel dissatisfied. For example, during the growth phase of the cable industry, cable operators gave away set-top boxes and routers. The customer relationship during this phase was mostly a self-service type of relationship, with occasional personal assistance for technical issues. This type of customer relationship worked for the growth phase because customers were so eager to obtain the new product. However, once the market became saturated, cable operators switched to a customer retention and upselling strategy, but did not offer a different customer relationship. This led to widespread dissatisfaction with cable operators, making the cable industry among the worst in customer satisfaction for nearly a decade. Only recently have cable operators shifted to the personal assistance-type of customer relationship, redesigning customer support functions and installation services.

Considerations in Designing Customer Relationships

When media companies describe and measure the "health" of the customer relationships they have created for their target segment(s), they may use one or several of the following common descriptors:

- *Customer satisfaction* is used to describe and measure how products or services supplied by an organization meet or surpass a customer's expectations. In its simplest form, planning or achieving excellence in customer satisfaction means that a media organization has exceeded the promised product/service value proposition that the customer expects. Customer satisfaction is typically measured in a survey completed by respondents from the targeted segments.
- *Customer loyalty* is used to describe and measure the degree to which a customer segment will repurchase an organization's product or service. More specifically, loyalty measures the overall consistently positive physical attribute-based satisfaction and perceived value of the entire experience, which includes the product or services. Customer loyalty is typically measured by a survey completed by respondents from the targeted segments.
- *Engagement* is used to determine the degree of attention, effort, or involvement between a brand (or media organization) and the target segments. As such, customer engagement is built and rebuilt (or destroyed) with every brand interaction, whether that's making a purchase, reading a tweet, joining a loyalty program, receiving an email, passing by a billboard, stumbling onto an online review, having a conversation with a friend, or any other exposure that generates involvement. Engagement is typically measured by mapping online interactions and other involvement by customers and prospects.
- *Emotional (brand) attachment* is used to determine the highest degree of emotional attachment between a brand (or media organization) and the target segment(s). Fast-moving target audiences operating in frenetic environments of multiple devices, channel blur, and collapsed transaction times have created unprecedented complexity for marketers, as well as media enterprises. One of the most rigorous measures of the "health" of a customer relationship is brand attachment. Brand attachment forms when the target audience believes that the brand is part of who they are, feels a personal

connection, and automatically and naturally has positive thoughts and feelings about the brand. Products or services with high brand attachment have five times the number of digital interactions and also have significantly higher customer loyalty than brands with lower brand attachment. Emotional attachment is typically measured by media organizations by either administering surveys to customers or by extracting raw conversations from social media and applying linguistic algorithms to evaluate them.

Evaluating Profitability

You need a system for evaluating the profitability of each customer segment. A key metric is the Customer Lifetime Value (CLTV) calculation, which measures the profitability of individual customers and customer segments over the entire period in which the customer deals with the firm, from acquisition to abandonment. Most service and retail marketers already recognize CLTV as one of the most important key performance indicators. However, it is not as widely used among media organizations because it is often difficult to collect accurate data.

In a digital world, CLTV can be calculated on a per-customer basis, but is more typically determined for an average customer in each of its target segments. CLTV helps organizations understand long-term value versus short-term gain, and can be more informative than average profit (ROI), especially related to acquisition or retention cost decisions. Figure 7.3 is a simple calculation of the ROI method for a large online entertainment rental (streaming) service.

Considering that the cumulative profit for an average customer of this online entertainment rental service shown in Figure 7.3 is $420, what would you spend to acquire a customer—$50, $150 or $300? If we follow the traditional transaction or ROI (Return on Investment) view, we could select any of the three acquisition costs (because they are all less than $420). But, if we are following the CLTV method (see Table 7.2), our answer would depend. The reason is that not all customers are alike! Our online entertainment rental service has three different segments of customers that have different consumption and usage patterns, and therefore different value to the media organization.

Clearly, we could spend much more to acquire the "Ms. Best" segment of customer than the "Ms. Average" customer, and we would not want to spend anything to acquire the "Ms. Negative" customer segment.

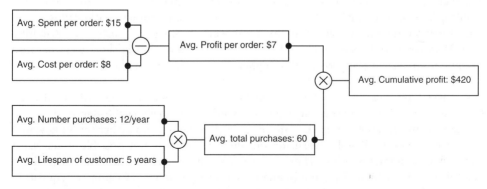

Figure 7.3 Simple Return on Investment (ROI) calculation for an average customer at an online streaming company.

Table 7.2 Customer Lifetime Value (CLTV) calculation for three customers of an online streaming company.

	Ms. Best	Ms. Average	Ms. Negative
Average order ($)	22.50	15	12
Cost/order ($)	12.50	8	7
Profit/order ($)	10	7	5
Purchases/year	26	12	3
Lifespan	10	5	1
Lifetime profit ($)	2,600	420	15
Acquisition costs ($)	300	150	50
Profit/customer ($)	2,300	270	(35)

The simplest formula for calculating CLTV is as follows:

Annual Profit Contribution per customer (for each year) times the *Customer Retention Rate* (for each year) minus the *Initial Cost of Customer Acquisition*

In order to use this formula to calculate CLTV for each segment, a media organization will need to know:

- the initial cost of customer acquisition;
- the annual revenue contribution per customer (including all sources including advertising that is attributed to the customer);
- the annual direct costs and fulfillment per customer: (including advertising costs);
- the annual customer retention rate.

As you can see, CLTV is a function of both the revenue generated by the segment through transaction frequency and amount, as well as the cost to acquire, serve, and retain customers. Therefore, the type of relationship that a media organization may establish by customer segment will have a direct impact on CLTV. For example, self-service and automated service types of customer relationships may require significantly more up-front costs in systems and labor, but the costs to maintain, serve, and retain beyond the initial investment are much lower. Conversely, dedicated personal assistance will likely require a smaller up-front cost, but the cost to maintain, serve, and retain on a monthly basis will be much higher than the other types of customer relationships.

Let's explore how we would apply this framework to Sling TV. Customers switching from Dish Network to Sling will spark a decline in revenue in the short term because revenue from Dish at $90 per-month is higher than revenue from Sling at $20. However, we need to use CLTV to measure the revenue and cost of Sling TV's customer value on Dish's overall business. According to Ergen, Sling's lower billing revenue will be offset by three factors: improved ad revenue, lower acquisition, and lower cost to serve.

Financial analysts noted that the improved ad revenue per subscriber for Sling would come from tailored digital advertising on Sling, which was not possible under Dish Network's traditional offering. They also assessed that the lower customer acquisition per subscriber for Sling TV would enhance company revenues. Customer acquisition costs are significantly lower because, unlike Dish, Sling doesn't need to schedule an appointment, do a credit check, send over a truck, and install a satellite dish.

Therefore, CLTV reveals that replacing a $90-per-month customer who has flat or declining ad revenue *and* is expensive to acquire and serve, with a $20-per-month customer who has increasing ad revenue, and costs less to acquire and serve, is not as terrible as it would appear. Sling TV cord-nevers and cord-cutters represent a large and growing segment that is structurally attractive and helps achieve company objectives. Moreover, cannibalizing Dish's own subscribers is better than losing subscribers to the competition, whether that is a traditional cable company or a newer technology streaming service.

The Importance of Customer Loyalty

As the CLTV calculation illustrates, longtime customers, who make many purchases during the time they are associated with a firm, ultimately drive overall profitability for a company. In his 1996 book, *The Loyalty Effect*, former Bain consultant Frederick Reichheld established that a 5% increase in customer retention could yield anywhere from a 25–95% improvement in a company's bottom line. In searching for the key to retention, Reichheld found that there was very little connection between customer satisfaction rates and retention, or between a company's growth in revenues and profits. Similarly, when companies used only financial metrics to assess success, they focused on growing the bottom line regardless of whether profits in a single year represented the rewards of building long-lasting relationships with customers, or the consequences of abusing them.

Therefore, he concluded, it was important for companies to both measure and track customer loyalty over time because loyal, longtime customers tend to buy more products and services, pay more for the value they perceive a product delivers, and they cost less since firms don't have to continually acquire new customers. Reichheld also hypothesized that loyal customers "sell more"—they recommend the product or service to others. "The tendency of loyal customers to bring in new customers is particularly beneficial as a company grows...," he said. "In fact, the only path to profitability may lie in a company's ability to get its loyal customers to become, in effect, its marketing department."

So how can companies track loyalty? Reichheld researched this question for more than a decade and ultimately concluded that most B2C (business-to-consumer) companies can effectively gauge and track the overall loyalty of current customers by asking one simple question: "On a scale of one to ten, with ten being highest, how likely are you to recommend [company X] to a friend or colleague?" Reichheld used a ten-point scale because it offered more nuance and gradations than a five-point scale, and less confusion for the respondent than a hundred-point scale. (Both five-point and hundred-point scales are often used when customer satisfaction surveys are conducted.)

Since people tend to be overly generous in assessing their experience with a company, he determined that only those people who rated their company experience at a 9 or a 10 were loyal customers. He called these people "promoters." They have a high level of engagement and emotional attachment to the product or service. Those who gave a rating of "7" or "8," he classified as "passives" or "fence-sitters," customers who were currently satisfied but not emotionally attached to a brand, and therefore, subject to being lured away by a competitor. Those who gave a rating of "6" or less, he classified as "detractors," unhappy campers who were very dissatisfied and probably dissing the product to anyone who would listen. Working with the software company, Satmetrix, Reichheld used this question to then produce a rating called the *Net Promoter Score* (NPS). To

Table 7.3 How to calculate a net promoter score (NPS) (%).

Calculation	Example (%)
% of promoters	68
% of detractors	41
Net promoter score	27

calculate a NPS, a company subtracts the percentage of promoters from the percentage of detractors (Table 7.3).

Reichheld's research suggests that an average business has an NPS of 27%, but that number fluctuates significantly depending on the industry segment (see Table 7.4). For example, as a group, specialty stores and online shopping sites have some of the highest NPS scores—an average of 60 and 56, respectively. Tablet computers and online entertainment sites also receive high scores from loyal customers. At the low end of the scale, however, are Internet service providers with a NPS of 2 and cable company providers, with a NPS of 3. Typically, media products—such as newspapers, magazines or films— range between a NPS of 19 to as high as 50.

Since its introduction, Reichheld's net promoter metric has been adopted by hundreds of companies. This includes fast food franchises, auto dealers, and rental car companies, as well as insurance companies, and brokerage houses. The NPS can be used to measure current loyalty and compare your company's performance to others in the same segment, as well as identify potentially attractive customer segments to target with new products, based on the demographics, media consumption patterns, and psychographics of loyal customers. This information can then be used to design products that attract new customers. Alternatively, the NPS can be used to diagnose problems in the current business model and come up with solutions.

Using the NPS framework, let's examine why Dish would cannibalize its own business. According to data compiled by Satmetrix, the average NPS for cable or satellite television companies is 3. This industry ranks at the very bottom of the NPS scale, only slightly above Internet service providers. Various industry analysts speculate that Dish Network's NPS is even lower than the industry average—perhaps as low as −3—based on Dish's quarterly reports. Since 2012, Dish has lost an average of 400,000 customers. In contrast, Sling subscribers increased from 169,000 in 2015 to two million in 2017. By tracking the loyalty of these new Sling customers, Dish may be able to make timely course adjustments in strategy and tactics that will engender loyalty and emotional attachment to this new product so that Sling customers will recommend it to their friends and colleagues.

Dish's pivot to Sling TV shows the value of using NPS metrics to track customers' habits, preferences, and loyalty. Keeping up with changes in customer media consumption and monitoring their loyalty and attachment to current technology are key to protecting your business model and maintaining a unique value proposition. Netflix recovered from a serious customer misstep and transformed its business model by producing original streaming content. As a result, in 2017, Netflix had a NPS of 62, considerably above the online entertainment industry's average score of 46.

In recent follow-up research, Reichheld has found that companies with the highest customer loyalty often grew revenues at more than twice the rate of their competitors. That is because loyal and engaged customers, who form emotional attachments to a brand will, over time, buy more, pay more, cost less, and, most importantly, sell more by recommending it to their friends and colleagues.

Table 7.4 Net Promoter Score Leaders by Sector and Average Sector NPS Scores.

Sector	Avg. NPS by Sector	NPS Leader by Sector	NPS Leader Score
Online Shopping	56	Amazon	73
Tablet Computers	53	Amazon	66
Online Entertainment	46	YouTube and Netflix	62
Laptop Computers	39	Apple	62
Smartphones	36	Apple	60
Cable/Satellite TV	3	Verizon Fios	27
Internet Service	2	Verizon Fios	21

Source: Adapted from Satmetrix, *US Consumer 2017: Net Promoter Benchmarks at a Glance.*

Exercise: Analyzing the Sling TV Strategy

Dish Network's segmenting of its customers by creating Sling TV's "skinny bundle" demonstrated that "cannibalizing" one's own business can be smarter than it looks. Even though Sling's billing revenues were equally "skinny" compared to Dish, CEO Charlie Ergen noted that this was offset by improved ad revenue for the company and lower costs—both to acquire and to serve Sling customers. In 2017, the *Wall Street Journal* reported that Sling TV propelled Dish Network to achieve its first positive period of net customer additions in several years.

Let's consider the following questions:

- Dish CEO Charlie Ergen said he would rather cannibalize his current customer base with a new product such as Sling than lose them to a competitor. Keeping in mind the lessons of Chapters 5 and 6, what, if any, options were there for Dish, other than cannibalizing its own customers with the Sling offering? Would these options have been as successful as Sling?
- How can you apply Rogers's Diffusion Theory to both Dish's and Sling's target customer segments? How does this influence your overall strategy for these two products over the next five years?
- Where would you place both of these products on the BCG matrix in Chapter 6 (problem child, star, cash cow, or dog)?
- If you were in charge of Sling TV's corporate strategy, how would you approach segmenting, targeting, and positioning the product in this next phase? How would you continue to differentiate between Sling and its competitors, and between Dish and its competitors?

Summary

Successful media entrepreneurs understand the process of dividing an available market or audience into distinct groups with specific needs, attitudes, and behaviors to create customer loyalty. The most common ways to segment the market are geographic, demographic, attitudinal, psychographic, and behavioral. Media entrepreneurs should use these factors to determine which segments they are best poised to serve.

After segmenting the market, media entrepreneurs should position their product or services for targeted customers. They should seek to answer these questions: How can we give the target audience what they need and want? How can we differentiate ourselves based on content, distribution, service, image, host, or price?

A key framework for understanding targeting and positioning in the media is the Diffusion of Innovation, which suggests adopters of any new innovation can be characterized as innovators, early adopters, early majority, late majority, and laggards. A media organization can use this framework to strategize their target customer segment and delineate the type of relationship it wants to establish. When establishing a customer relationship, the media company should consider the degree of functional versus emotional connection that the organization plans to achieve.

The final step to creating a strong customer relationship is to understand how to evaluate profitability. Media organizations should calculate a customer's lifetime value (CLTV), which is based on the initial cost of customer acquisition, and the annual revenue contribution per customer, direct costs, fulfillment per customer and retention rate. Loyal and engaged customers, who are emotionally attached to your brand or product, will buy more, pay more, sell more, and cost less, leading to increased growth in customers and profits.

8

Reaching Current and New Customers

Nobody has a bigger appetite for statistics and armchair quarterbacking than fans of American football's NFL, the burrito supreme of live sports audience reach. So, let's sit back, fasten our headsets, and crunch the yards, rushes, and passes. Which of the following was true about the 2016–2017 NFL season?

1) Nielsen ratings for NFL games hit a 30-year low, losing 8%, or more than one million viewers.
2) NFL TV advertising revenues hit a record high, and TV distribution rights will earn the league a guaranteed $50 billion through the time they expire in 2022.
3) Sling TV credited massive subscriber bulk-up to *NFL RedZone*, an ad-free channel offering "whip-around" coverage of simultaneous games, sometimes using a split screen.
4) *NFL RedZone*'s big season was linked to the 40 million Americans who played Fantasy Football, tuning in less to follow the fortunes of teams, and more to follow the stats of individual players.

If you answered that 1, 2, 3, and 4 were all true, you are beginning to understand the case for fragmentation, or what *Atlantic* magazine more aptly termed the "atomization" of entertainment media. The NFL, as the granddaddy of live sports broadcasting and defending champion of the most lucrative TV rights in the world, is Exhibit A. Year after year, it has been the superstar of audience draw. Upward of 90% of football fans have never attended a game, and so television rights sold to CBS, Fox, and ESPN, and by extension, ad revenues, have been the driver for the league. That makes the NFL more a media enterprise than a trade association, and until recently, the league remained one broadcast phenomenon too brawny, too unstoppable to fall victim to disruption.

With that winning streak now in jeopardy, the NFL illustrates how media interests must reconsider how they reach both new and existing audiences. In Chapter 7, we looked at segmenting customers. In this chapter, we will explore the following:

- What are the various channels for acquiring and retaining customers, and how can media entrepreneurs learn to evaluate channels?
- What is "human-centered" design and customer journey mapping, and how can they help brands pivot in creating, aggregating, and planning content distribution?
- How does channel mix change as media consumption shifts and brands outgrow their target audience and attempt to reach new audiences?
- How does customer experience affect loyalty and brand attachment?

The Strategic Digital Media Entrepreneur, First Edition. Penelope Muse Abernathy and JoAnn Sciarrino.
© 2019 John Wiley & Sons, Inc. Published 2019 by John Wiley & Sons, Inc.
Companion website: www.wiley.com/go/abernathy/StrategicDigitalMediaEntrepreneur

The Problem of Drift

In terms of segmenting, the NFL has maintained an enviable pass completion record to its intended receiver. We'll call that target customer "Bill." He's 48, makes more than $50,000 a year, and consumes football mostly through broadcast, the familiar three-and-half-hour Sunday afternoon ritual uniquely suited for advertising beer, pickup trucks, and pizza. The problem is, Bill is getting older. Distributing abundant content during the season, with multiple televised Sunday games, and the addition of Monday and Thursday nights, has only highlighted the NFL's trouble in holding fans' attention, reaching not just new viewers, but Bill as well.

American media companies love pro football nearly as much as they love profits, and analysts in the popular press were quick to dismiss the NFL's ratings fumble as an anomaly, a mere rounding error in the grand scheme of almost 60 years of NFL TV earnings. Among the reasons cited for the 2016 ratings plunge: football viewership was competing with a ratings-generating US presidential election, including two Sunday night debates. Viewers were frustrated with the NFL experience—the concussion controversy; player protests during the National Anthem; and a record number of interruptions of play for relatively minor penalties, including what umpires termed "excessive celebration" by players, antics that were essentially crowd-pleasing. At the same time, fans complained that there were too many commercials. In 2016, the number of ads per NFL game reached an all-time high of 70, according to Nielsen, up from 64 in 2008.

Still, if these were problems isolated to the NFL and to American audiences in the last quarter of 2016, why was TV viewership also falling off for the Olympics? And what about soccer, the "other" football? Premier League TV viewership fell 11% in 2016, according to Bloomberg, and this was despite fierce rivalries among the big six teams and two extra marquee games. Rather than a blip, this was the latest in a downward trend. Viewership had fallen by 22% since the 2010–2011 season, according to Bloomberg's reading of UK Broadcasters' Audience Research Board data. Asked Bloomberg's Gadfly: "When both 'footballs' are struggling for attention like this, you have to wonder whether the game is up." But is it the game itself, or the channels by which the game attempts to reach Bill, and his English cousin, Benny? The hard truth is that media consumption habits are changing for his younger friends and family—maybe for Bill himself. As NFL media executive Brian Rolapp observed, the act of watching has changed because of the ad-free experience of Netflix and its 15-second load time, rendering the pace of NFL games glacial in comparison. If the sea change is in fact reaching the pinnacle of live sports broadcasting, it's time to rethink the channels.

What Are the Channels in Marketing?

As the NFL example suggests, media entrepreneurs must first assess their channels to reach current and new customers. Experts define a marketing channel as the path or route that goods or services travel from initial creation to reach the end consumer. In media, marketing distribution channels are either direct or indirect. A direct distribution channel is one for which the sale of a product or service goes directly from the originator or producer to the final customer with no middle entity involved. An example of direct distribution might be when a Carolina Panthers fan plunks down $80 for a pair of home game tickets in the nosebleed section at Bank of America Stadium. An indirect distribution channel is one for which the sale of a product or service goes through an intermediary to reach the final consumer, for example, when the NFL sells TV rights to ESPN, which then resells its coverage to cable providers such as Comcast and DirecTV, who then distribute that content to subscribers. In media, distribution channels generally comprise the following (although not all channels for all media companies are featured):

- Direct distribution channels:
  - retail outlets owned by your company;
  - wholesale outlets of your own;
  - sales force compensated by salary, commission, or both;
  - website/web sales;
  - branded app (directly owned and operated by the company);
  - direct sales via your own catalog or flyers (e.g., "direct response").
- Indirect distribution channels:
  - retail outlets owned by an independent merchant or chain;
  - wholesale outlets of independent distributors or brokers;
  - online media aggregators/distributors/platforms.

Evaluating Customer Acquisition and Retention by Channel

Now that you understand what a channel is, it is time to start thinking about how media organizations can use them to shore up their customer base. In a 2007 article on customer relationships in *Review of Marketing Research*, Ruth Bolton and Crina Tarasi argue that a media organization should use an optimal mix of channels to acquire and retain customers, and should consider how to do so profitably. Most media organizations use the classical definitions of customer acquisition and retention, and report and track these as a percentage, over a time series as well as by channel. The *Harvard Business Review* defines a customer acquisition rate as the percentage of people targeted by a marketing effort who ultimately become customers. Customer retention rate is the duration of a customer's relationship with the media organization. These are simple metrics of marketing performance and are widely used in media, especially since the advent of digital. That's partly because these two metrics are easy for media organizations to understand and track and partly because they are accurate proxies of performance.

To apply this formula, let's say that Acme Media Co. was interested in evaluating acquisition and retention rates in the fourth quarter for two channels: direct response and website. Acme can easily compute the percentage of customers it acquired through these channels and the number retained through the following calculation:

1) Assume that the *total* (mixed channel) percentage of new customers acquired for the period was 7%, and the percentage retained was 88%.
2) Upon separating out the two channels, Acme learns that direct response yielded 13% acquisition, versus 1% from the website. Meanwhile retention from direct response was 95%, versus 78% from the website.
3) By one metric, Acme's direct response was more successful than its website, but what about cost effectiveness? For the full picture, Acme must also evaluate the cost of each channel in acquiring and retaining customers, to find the average short-term cost to acquire or retain.

As discussed in Chapter 7, it is also critical for media organizations to measure and track a customer's lifetime value (CLTV), especially when evaluating channels. While the cost of acquiring a new customer may be higher in the short term in a certain channel, that customer's long-term value may exceed other lower-cost channels. To help you think about how to evaluate the proper channel, consider that there are typically four outcomes of evaluating channel cost and CLTV retention, ranked by customer type:

1) easy to acquire and easy to retain (low costs, high CLTV);
2) difficult to acquire but easy to retain (high costs, high CLTV);
3) easy to acquire but hard to retain (low costs, low CLTV);
4) difficult to acquire and difficult to retain (high costs, low CLTV).

The consequences of measuring acquisition and retention performance, cost, and CLTV by channel for media organizations are clear. If a certain channel only targets customers who are very difficult to acquire, the company may end up with a small number of new customers who may also be difficult to retain, which may depress CLTV. Therefore, it's important not only to measure channels independently, but also to understand that with some channels, such as digital, it may be easier to acquire new customers but those customers offer lower overall CLTV. On the other hand, they may provide positive revenue growth due to the sheer number of potential customers that digital channels represent.

Changing Customer Behavior and Media Consumption

Next, let's consider how media organizations can leverage changing consumer behavior and media usage to attract and retain customers through appropriate channel mix. Powerful, irrevocable forces are shaping the modern digital consumer, and media organizations stand at the center of these tectonic shifts, even as they work to create, aggregate, and deliver content. Silicon Valley venture capitalist Mary Meeker, who tracks noteworthy Internet and tech developments, argues that four trends will shape media consumption through 2020:

- time spent with technology;
- user-generated content (UGC);
- digital innovation/disruption;
- mobile phone use.

Let's take a detailed look at each of these changing behaviors.

Time Spent with Technology

Despite forecasts in 2010 that consumers would spend *less* time with technology as Internet and mobile penetration increased and traditional media consumption decreased, the reverse occurred. Midway through this decade, consumers in fact were spending significantly more time with technology than they did five years earlier. Not surprisingly, the nearly one-hour increase in time spent with technology was from digital, with the mobile (non-voice) channel (37.2%) driving most of the increase, from 48 minutes per day in 2011 to *nearly three hours* by 2015. However, even this dramatic documented increase in time spent with technology does not represent all time spent with that medium, even without accounting for multiple-screen viewing (or multiplexing). E-readers, connected game consoles, smart TVs, and other connected devices also increased (7.8%) over the same five years, which demonstrates that consumers seek instant and constant access to digital media. As senior marketing analyst Paul Verna noted in an *eMarketer* report, "Without movies, TV shows, games, photos, books, magazines, newspapers, video clips and music, few would care to own a tablet, a connected console or an internet-enabled TV."

Additionally, while total time spent with technology is increasing, it should be noted that the fastest-growing segment was digital video viewership, regardless of where it is watched. While consumers may be spending less time with TV, that doesn't mean that they are watching less video. As time with TV decreases, time with online video goes up.

User-Generated Content (UGC)

User-generated content (UGC) is any variety of content, including discussion forums, blogs, wikis, posts, chats, tweets, podcasts, digital images, video, audio files, advertisements, and other forms of media created by users of an online system or service, frequently made available via social media websites. The growth of UGC is expected to continue to expand, fueled by the ubiquity of smartphones, Internet access, and social media. A recent article in the *Journal of Marketing Management* suggested that UGC is an emergent tool of engagement, influencing buying behavior. The scale is mind-numbing: each *minute*, over 347,000 Twitter tweets are sent, according to Ishbel Macleod at *The Drum*, and each *minute*, 2.7 million YouTube videos are viewed and 300 hours of video are uploaded.

Even though UGC has been around since 2005, there are several recent categories that have significant implications for media organizations: video, sound, and written stories.

- *Video*: The fastest growing area of UGC is the capture of consumer experiences at live events, such as Coachella (40 million views in three days) and the Olympics (30 million views in one day) through video storytelling. In 2014, the technology conglomerate Cisco forecast that video would account for 80% of all consumer web traffic over the next few years. The barriers to entry are extremely low and the tools needed to create and distribute the final video are easily accessible, turning amateurs into experienced videographers and YouTube into the largest video media company on earth.
- *Sound*: It's not just video that is attracting the talents of consumer creators. Bloomberg noted in 2015 that over 150 million consumer creators were registered on SoundCloud, with the majority of content coming from creators who do not have associations with professional rights holders. The number of SoundCloud creators increased 33% from the previous year and was expected to grow by double digits for the next five years.
- *Written stories*: With all the growth in video and sound UGC, it may seem surprising that ordinary text is also experiencing growth in UGC. WattPad, a writing social community, where users post articles, stories, fan fiction, and poems, has over 40 million active authors who have created nearly 130 million stories. WattPad has a highly engaged community, with users spending 13 billion minutes per month on the site and an average of more than 30 minutes per session, with 90% of the site traffic coming through mobile.

For media organizations, the surge in UGC, and especially the rise of video UGC, may increase the competition for an engaged audience. In 2016, media experts noted in the *Columbia Journalism Review* that even though many media organizations still consider UGC an unprofessional nuisance with questionable value that adds to media clutter, the last decade revealed that UGC can have an advantage over professional (media-produced) content when it comes to speed and accessibility. These two advantages have led the BBC and others to create formal internal programs to solicit, source, verify, and distribute UGC in their programming when appropriate.

Digital Innovation/Disruption

Digital innovation (or disruption) has been happening since the creation of the Internet. Early innovators, such as eBay, Amazon, and Alibaba improved the customer shopping experience through attractive graphical interface, long-tail product availability (usually not carried in inventory), excellent delivery systems, and value pricing—all conducted seamlessly from a consumer's desktop. Essentially, the rise of e-commerce, coupled with use of search engines, put competitive pressure on local retailers. The implication for media organizations was that a significant proportion of local and national retail advertisers began to cut traditional advertising budgets and consumers began to decrease spending in classified advertising in favor of Craigslist and other sites. While this "first-generation" digital disruption was relegated to products and traditional shipping delivery, we are now in the midst of the second-generation digital innovation disruption. This time, the revolution is in offering *services* such as Airbnb, Uber, and Thumbtack. Optimized for mobile and offering on-demand local delivery, this generation will create additional competitive pressure for media organizations by continuing to decrease traditional print advertising dollars, decrease consumer use of classifieds, and, in some cases, decrease the need for specialized content and digital marketing services. This brings us to perhaps the most significant change—the smartphone in your hand.

Mobile Phones

In 2016, YouTube's CEO trumpeted that the online platform reached more 18-to-49-year-olds than any other broadcast or cable TV network. And three guesses as to how they were watching: a 2015 Pew Research Center *State of the News* study reported that 39 of the top 50 digital news websites have received more web traffic from mobile devices than computers. For media organizations that generate revenues from a two-sided platform (i.e., subscriptions and advertising revenue), this is sobering news. The increase in consumer time spent with technology in digital—especially mobile—has contributed to the precipitous decline in total revenues. The reason? Digital media advertising revenue per thousand impressions (RPM) is much lower than traditional print advertising RPM.

The encouraging news, in spite of the daunting math? An estimated $25 billion opportunity exists in the gap between time spent with mobile technology and mobile advertising. Therefore, savvy media entrepreneurs and marketers who understand the shift in consumer behavior and media consumption are finding new ways to create sustainable media business models that are not dependent on twentieth-century economics. Many media and technology organizations are inventing new types of ad-supported formats optimized for mobile. Notable examples:

- Pinterest Cinematic Pin (the promoted video ad moves as the user scrolls);
- Facebook Carousel Ad (user scrolls right to view multiple promoted images/ads);
- Vessel 5-second ad (super-short form promoted video ads);
- Google local inventory ad (user presented with product searched as available in store nearby).

Another innovation in ad-supported formats optimized for mobile are the promoted ads with "Buy" buttons in social media. Twitter, Facebook, Google, and Pinterest all have integrated "Buy" buttons to minimize user friction to purchase. Finally, with designers recognizing that few users will rotate their phones to view an ad in horizontal "landscape" mode (and even fewer view video landscape ads to completion), Snapchat popularized full-screen vertical view ads in mobile, upping the view completion rate by a factor of nine, and both Instagram and Facebook followed suit.

Tools to Reach Your Customers

Now let's explore tools to help media enterprises reach current and new customers. Consider the example just cited above. Reorienting video to vertical was a radical aesthetic change, and not a change that content producers made on a whim. In fact, many professional photographers resisted the portrait format, initially seeing it as amateurish, anti-cinematic, and cumbersome to shoot. Why do it, then? Well, because users have migrated to mobile, smartphone screens are vertical, and switching to horizontal is hard to do with one hand. This is an example of putting the customer experience at the center, and two powerful tools help media entrepreneurs do just that: *human-centered design* and *customer journey mapping.*

Human-Centered Design (HCD)

Popularized by Stanford University, Human-Centered Design (HCD) is an innovative research and design methodology that develops solutions to problems by involving the human perspective to create new products or systems. Timothy Brown, CEO of the global design firm IDEO, which pioneered this problem-solving process, argued in 2008 that involving the human perspective means building a deep empathy with the target audience. Brown saw the process in three integrated phases:

- *Inspiration*: this phase uses immersive observation techniques such as ethnography to observe and understand the target audience.
- *Ideation*: learning from the inspiration phase informs brainstorm ideas and design concepts or prototypes.
- *Implementation*: this phase formulates and executes plans and tactics to bring the solution to market.

Think of products that disrupt conventions, large and small, and you see the fruits of human-centered design: Apple's first mouse. Toothpaste tubes that stand on end. The Swiffer. Fred Dust, a partner at IDEO, encourages the use of human-centered design to uncover insights that form the basis of innovation: "There's value to spending real time with the people you're designing for, in context. Don't let your judgement or preknowledge override the people you're designing for...empathy [maps] gets to better solutions."

Elements of human-centered design should be used regularly to design products and services that will attract new and retain current customers, as well as determine the best channels for reaching them. Many media organizations have successfully used human-centered design to help attract new and retain current customers through a new channel. Notable examples range from new concepts to solve old problems—for example, automatic cloud file syncing that allows users to access or update their documents anywhere—to new channels and platforms to solve new problems. For example, Kickstarter has become a powerful online fund-raising tool for nonprofits and entrepreneurs hoping to attract investors to their products or services. By using Kickstarter, they bypass traditional channels, such as venture capital funding or small business loans. HCD also helps in the redesign of existing products with the customer in mind. Take, for instance, the *Washington Post* mobile app for iOS and Android: the sleek format allows users to "swipe up" through stories like a stack of cards and feels virtually ad-free, apart from the subtle integration of sponsored content from the Post's BrandStudio.

Customer Journey Mapping in Media

Customer journey mapping is an immersive discovery technique that is typically part of the inspiration phase of the HCD process. Paul Boag, author of *The User Experience Revolution*, has explained that customer journey mapping visualizes and represents in detail target users before, during, and after as they attempt to use the new product or service for the problem it is intended to solve. This helps designers identify which channels to use during which phase (before, during, or after) to complete the activity.

One of the most useful frameworks for mapping this process is the McKinsey Customer Journey Model, published in 2009. The two concentric circles that make up the McKinsey model (Figure 8.1) provide the general framework of a target customer's journey from awareness through purchase and beyond. The channels illustrated on the outside of the McKinsey Customer Journey Model demonstrate that there are a myriad of channels that should be identified at each significant point in the target customer's journey. To gather detailed information from a target customer to create the map, experts recommend observational research techniques, such as ethnographies and immersive interviewing, or discovery techniques such as depth interviews (discussed in Chapter 6) and digital diaries.

In creating a detailed customer journey map, many researchers separate the McKinsey figure into four broad phases of inquiry. Parsing out the phases as follows gives the investigator added efficiency and accuracy:

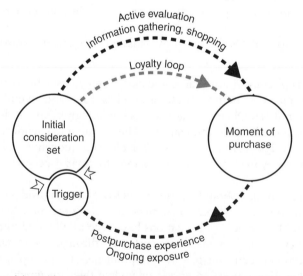

Source: Adapted from "The consumer decision journey," June 2009, *McKinsey Quarterly,* www.mckinsey.com. Copyright (c) 2009 McKinsey & Company. All rights reserved. Reprinted by permission.

Figure 8.1 McKinsey consumer journey map.

- *Formulation*: In the early phase of the customer journey, a target customer may have become aware of and may have formed an opinion about a brand, product, or service. This phase also includes the transition from awareness into the target customer's consideration set, which usually occurs after some trigger or event.
- *Pre-commerce*: This phase ensues once the target customer has a brand, product, or service in the consideration set. This is the phase where information gathering, active evaluation, interaction, and browsing/shopping, and in some cases, free trials occur.
- *Commerce*: The shortest phase begins at the moment the target customer makes a purchase and ends when the customer *perceives* the end of the purchase.
- *Post-commerce*: After the purchase, and there are two paths. (1) Buyers can become customers with ongoing exposure to the brand without action, until some future trigger pulls them back into the journey; or (2) they can become loyal customers of the brand and transition to the inner circle of the loyalty loop, where they influence others (through identified channels) and repeat purchase(s).

The McKinsey model takes into consideration the experiences the target customer has with the brand, experiences that may impact long-term loyalty after an initial purchase. Today, when nearly every media organization has many direct and indirect competitors, the loyalty loop is a more accurate picture of how the target audience may reevaluate the decision to purchase. In media, purchase can indicate either a hard purchase (such as a subscription or paywall transaction), or it can indicate a soft purchase (such as consuming content by reading an article or watching a video).

Many factors can affect the target audience's decision to purchase from a media organization for the second, tenth, or fiftieth time. A competitor might be offering shorter curated content through the target audience Twitter feed. The content might be offered in video. The quality may vary. Customers' experience with the media platform where the content resides might impress or frustrate them, and their continued exposure to your brand's ad messages versus your competitors' all factor into the decision whether or not to "purchase" media content. Customer journey mapping is used to uncover these reasons, and more.

To consider how customer journey mapping works, think back to the example of the NFL. The league has long focused on adding and retaining viewers through broadcast rights to intermediaries like CBS and ESPN. This distribution channel has been extremely successful for the NFL because it has been the most viable channel to reach the primary target audience as well as the most lucrative. Using customer journey mapping with the primary target audience, television broadcast is an excellent channel for retention of the target because the vast majority watches network television regularly and therefore most of the marketing to the target audience is concentrated on paid television media. Because the broadcast channel successfully reinforces existing target audience behavior, and the majority of the target audience repeats "purchasing" (i.e., viewing) behavior many times per season, the NFL's reliance on broadcast as a channel has served existing customers through the loyalty loop of the McKinsey model. The rub is that broadcast may not be a viable channel to attract new customers to the NFL, as we saw earlier in this chapter.

When a media company has outgrown or saturated a channel, it will often pivot either its entire value proposition or it will use its existing value proposition and seek a new customer segment and channel. The most common approach is to use the existing value proposition and seek a new customer segment and channel, which can be identified by using HCD. That includes completing a customer journey map for the new customer segment in order to identify the most appropriate new channel(s).

Evaluating Effectiveness and Efficiency of Channels to Reach New and Current Customers

The selection of the marketing channel for a brand, product, or service, including the discovery work of HCD and customer journey mapping, takes longer than any other decision related to the elements of the marketing mix. But the benefits make it worthwhile. Speed of delivery, guaranteed supply, frictionless convenience, accessibility, and other factors may improve the relationship between buyers and sellers and enhance customer loyalty. That is why media organizations are beginning to focus more on channel management in order to deliver their content, brands, products, and/or services to the right audience at the right time in an effective, efficient way. This is win-win. A successful channel strategy enables a media organization to create more perceived value to the target audience.

The challenge, of course, is dealing with the burgeoning number of channels media organizations face. The nearly constant barrage of requests to evaluate and consider incorporating more channels into the marketing mix can be overwhelming. That's why knowing how to evaluate the effectiveness and efficiency of a channel before including it in the marketing mix will reduce costly mistakes and increase the likelihood of selecting channels wisely. A tool we use in this selection process is a *channel brief* created for each channel and each target segment. Typically, this means fashioning multiple channel briefs, each of which can be referenced and updated over time, rather than starting from scratch with each change of the mix. A channel brief succinctly summarizes a channel within the context of a target audience, and analyzes the channel's potential to meet the media organization's goals. As the name "brief" implies, this is typically a one-page document, and it usually contains eight sections:

- *Buyer or target audience persona*: Different target audiences interact differently with specific channels, and so each one-page brief is built around one clear target audience. The persona should provide not only a functional and demographic description of the target audience, but also include and illustrate the audience's life stage, emotions, motivations, and aspirations.
- *Channel*: Indicate the specific channel the brief covers. (See the list of direct and indirect channels suggested at the beginning of this chapter.)
- *Channel frequency and customer journey map*: Summarize the frequency of contact with the channel for each of the customer journey phases. No need for the target to interact with the channel for all four of the customer journey phases, which each have a different purpose (e.g., awareness or education.) Commonly, different channels are prominent in different phases.
- *Channel goal*: Clearly define the channel's desired results for your content, brand, product, or service. If the channel is prominent in more than one phase of the map, there can be multiple goals. These can include lead generation, reach, brand awareness, click-throughs, unique visitors, downloads, etc. To help guide these expectations, syndicated data services sell licenses to media organizations. The licenses allow access to industry channel data, enabling media organizations to set competitive but realistic goals.
- *Channel performance*: Based on the goals being set, report the current channel performance. This should be reported and evaluated as a time series (current/versus

previous/versus trended) to identify issues of efficiency and effectiveness. A recommended practice, in addition, is to compare channel performance to industry and competitive benchmarks.

- *Value of channel to organization*: Indicate at least one tangible or intangible benefit the channel provides that the organization can't access otherwise.
- *Value of channel to target audience*: Identify the tangible/intangible benefit to the audience.
- *Budget*: Identify costs associated with the channel, including hard and soft costs.

How Customer Experience Affects Loyalty and Brand Attachment

In media, the trend has been to go beyond the basic functional elements of content or price to creating engaging, lasting customer experiences that set a product or service apart. This was not emphasized in the past, when marketers primarily focused on core product attributes. In the 1980s, the differentiator was quality; in the 1990s, it was brand; in the early 2000s, it was service. Currently, customer experience is at the forefront, and these emotional and value aspects are often embedded within the distribution channel, for example, with interactive participation platforms that extend the content experience digitally.

A good media brand experience provides engaging, memorable, "lived" moments, and these are highly personalized. The customer tends to cherish these experiences before, during, and long after engaging with the content. This creates what we call a "ladder of customer loyalty" from the lowest to the highest customer expectations being fulfilled. At the lowest rung of that "ladder," the customer is satisfied and predisposed to purchase (or consume) again. The ladder continues upward in a sequence of customer satisfaction until reaching the highest rung, which is the emotional connection between the customer and the brand, often called *brand attachment*. Customers at this level have a positive, emotionally bonded experience, consider the brand indispensable (also called *brand prominence*), and even consider the brand part of who they are (*brand-self connection*). They are often willing to pay a premium price. Hence, exceptional customer experiences that reach this top rung will have a sustainable competitive advantage over competing brands/products.

Media organizations that neglect the influence and impact of the customer experience do so at their own peril. They risk creating a transactional or quasi-loyal relationship that may be forgotten as quickly as a more compelling offer appears.

This is why the principles of *Total Customer Experience* (TCE) within the selected channels are so important. Brands able to transcend loyalty to build brand attachment and emotional connection have more digital interactions and higher purchase intention than loyalty alone. Put simply, TCE is the augmented experience that media organizations create to connect emotionally with target audiences. While content in one sense is a tangible and impersonal category of goods, media organizations understand that involvement and experiences are inherently intangible and personal to customers. This gives media organizations the ability to connect people emotionally with a media brand, product, or service.

Exercise: How Can the NFL Reach a New Audience?

Although the NFL is still king of live sports events, we've seen that the league recognizes it must accelerate growth and attract new customers. To do this, NFL marketers must turn to Human-Centered Design in luring an entirely new segment: millennials who get their sports and entertainment from Internet-connected devices, especially smartphones. With this in mind, the NFL in 2016 sold the rights to ten of their Thursday night games to Twitter for $10 million. In 2017, the league sold the same streaming package to Amazon for $50 million. Analysts see these moves as the beginning of a pivot, in advance of the TV broadcast contracts.

So now, it's your turn to be offensive team coordinator. Pull out the playbook, check the channel roster, and before calling the NFL's next play, consider these questions:

- How can the NFL research what channels to use to reach younger customers watching on smartphones?
- How can the NFL move customers up the "ladder of loyalty?" What is the role of user-generated content in attracting and retaining customers?
- What would a customer journey map look like for the NFL? How would you write a channel brief?

Summary

In short, media organizations must perpetually evaluate how to keep and reach new customers, and in this chapter, we've offered strategies and tools for doing so. We learned how to identify channels for acquiring and retaining customers, and how to use tools like human-centered design and customer journey mapping to think about effectiveness and efficiency in our content distribution. In seeking to engage customers, we've kept in mind the macro trends that are disrupting how people consume media: time spent with technology, user-generated content, digital innovation/disruption, and above all, mobile access.

To successfully navigate these shifting winds, media entrepreneurs must understand how these channels change over time as media consumption shifts. Adjusting to strike the right channel mix is especially important for organizations that generate revenues from a two-sided platform. This is the counterintuitive part. The increase in consumer time spent with technology has contributed to a decline in total revenues.

9

Competing in a Networked World

Approaching its fiftieth birthday party, *Sesame Street* is chugging along with as much steam as ever. PBS reported that an estimated five to six million preschool kids between ages 2 and 5 still tune in each week to devour the adventures of characters like Bert and Ernie, Cookie Monster, and Oscar the Grouch, with the requisite daily allowance of ABC's and 1-2-3's mixed in.

In many ways, the mission has remained the same since 1969 when Kermit the Frog emerged from the primordial soup of VHF antennas and "pay TV" to host the most successful educational children's program in history. But everything aside from the mission has changed. A half century in, the platforms by which *Sesame Street* reaches its audience have evolved and mutated, reshaping not just the distribution network, but the business model and the creative process itself. Where public broadcasting stations were once the main delivery system, *Sesame Street* now reaches many of its young viewers through HBO and video on demand, giving the premium channel first dibs on the latest programs—in exchange for the money that the Sesame Workshop, the nonprofit production organization, needed to produce them. Sesame meanwhile has launched a website and apps including STEM mobile games and a cloud-based, vocabulary builder powered by artificial intelligence (AI), in collaboration with IBM. All these efforts put Sesame in the learning technology business, not to mention the movie, toy, and merchandise licensing business. And in 2016, the production company unveiled a corporate underwriter-funded YouTube channel that is designed to drastically cut costs, boost innovation, and provide nimble audience analysis to inform creative decisions. The YouTube channel, executives believed, would be to the current generation what PBS was to children in the past.

In the evolving media landscape, survival of the fittest means survival of the most adaptable. And what could be a more adaptable, early-adopting audience than one made up of preschoolers? As YouTube's global head of family and learning, Malik Ducard, told NPR: "One thing 'Sesame' has consistently and effectively done from their beginning... was to really harness new media and technology and new formats in every generation." If the medium is the message, this was a teachable moment. As actress Christina Hendricks, known for her role in the AMC television series *Mad Men*, explained to Elmo on an episode of *Sesame Street*: "Technology is a tool that helps you do things."

That's a facile concept, but the implications for how media companies monetize these personalized, overlapping, always-on tools are complex and increasingly problematic, particularly for news companies. In the example of *Sesame Street*, we see that perpetual innovation creates networks of new relationships that seem contradictory: a public broadcaster partners with a premium subscription channel; copyrighted content bankrolled by old-line charitable foundations is shared on YouTube. In such a world—a "Me

The Strategic Digital Media Entrepreneur, First Edition. Penelope Muse Abernathy and JoAnn Sciarrino.
© 2019 John Wiley & Sons, Inc. Published 2019 by John Wiley & Sons, Inc.
Companion website: www.wiley.com/go/abernathy/StrategicDigitalMediaEntrepreneur

Media" or "Infinite Media" age—how would *Mad Men*'s Don Draper, creative director for the fictitious advertising agency Sterling Cooper, not just survive but thrive?

This chapter slices that question into three parts:

1) In a media environment that has shifted from finite content/infinite attention to the reverse—infinite content/finite attention—what are the economics for media organizations, particularly as tech behemoths such as Google, Amazon, and Facebook seize a disproportionate share of revenues?
2) How have traditional boundaries between media organizations competing for that attention become contested, or at least blurred?
3) Along those blurred lines of business relationships, how can media organizations use collaboration to protect themselves from the threats these changes pose?

In the age of *Mad Men*, the lines between content-producers, advertisers, and audiences were each as clear-cut and immutable as the part in Don Draper's hair. What scholars call the "mass media" era, stretching from the 1840s to 1990s, revolved around reaching people where they were, either in terms of geography or media channels. The model was operational excellence built around efficient infrastructures. The goal was to mass-produce content and distribute it to a large audience, typically through a single channel, and the financial formula was basic. Media companies held all the cards: content creation, production, sales, distribution, and most important, audience. Advertisers wanted to reach the audience. Therefore, advertisers paid media organizations a lot of money. The result was a jackpot for media companies. With profit margins this wide, why partner, let alone share?

The answer, as we saw in Chapter 1's whirlwind journey from Gutenberg to Zuckerberg, is that the world has changed. With the advent of the Internet, media companies no longer have the monopoly on production and distribution, supplying limited content to satisfy the attention of an unlimited audience (Figure 9.1). Now, in the age of infinite or

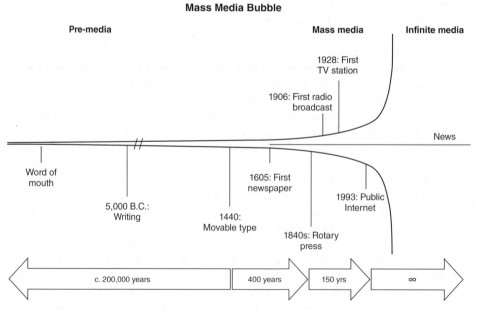

Mass Media Bubble

Pre-media   Mass media   Infinite media

1928: First TV station

1906: First radio broadcast

News

Word of mouth

1605: First newspaper

1993: Public Internet

5,000 B.C.: Writing

1440: Movable type

1840s: Rotary press

c. 200,000 years   400 years   150 yrs   ∞

Source: Adapted from Gray, S., www.mediareset.com.

Figure 9.1 The mass media bubble.

"Me Media," supply and demand have traded places: there is unlimited content competing for a scarce amount of attention. Now, as never before, audiences can access virtually any information, entertainment, or news they want, when they want, from a variety of sources, most of them free. Media companies are no longer the default solution to reach audiences. The result is that advertisers have options to reach audiences—online display ads, mobile advertising, targeted advertising, and sponsored content.

Why is this important? As we've seen, advertising revenues follow engaged audiences. When brands and consumers are publishers and anyone can get virtually any information, news, or entertainment they want at any time, savvy media organizations build for the "Me Media" era. They create premium content on multiple platforms, and do so cost effectively. The result is a business model shift from operational excellence to innovation, by delivering relevant, adaptive content to attract people, what we sometimes call the "few to few" approach. With apologies to Kermit the Frog, it's not easy being green. But as we'll see from the numbers, green is all there is to be.

Media Economics on Steroids: How to Measure Infinity?

While we have addressed the dramatic changes in consumer behavior in the "infinite media" era, we still need to consider how audiences have fragmented across a broad spectrum of digital news, information, and entertainment content. For example, in some local metropolitan markets, Google, the most popular website by visits, commanded 10–15% of average monthly website visits (from within designated market areas) in 2015, followed by Facebook with 7–12% of visits, according to research done by Morris Communications. It's not surprising that Google and Facebook lead in average monthly website visits. But more staggering is the number of websites users visit in many markets in an average month. There is a vast sea of outlets with ever-smaller audiences, most attracting less than 2% of visits. Where does all this leave local news sites, the former gatekeepers that came between advertisers and audiences? In the age of "Me Media," they garner on average *less than one-half of 1% of total visits.*

Pew's *State of the News Media 2015* found that the proliferation of platforms serving up articles and videos, news, entertainment, and sports, increased dramatically from 2011 to 2015. According to Pew, this, in turn, has made traditional publishers more dependent on Google and Facebook for driving attention and traffic. Outlets needed these platforms to stay afloat. And to understand the enormity of the sea change, take a look at the following measures, keeping in mind that in 2017, there are 7.2 billion people on the planet.

- *Reach*: Google's parent company, Alphabet, has seven products surpassing one billion users each, including Android (Google's mobile operating system), Gmail, YouTube, and Google Maps. Meanwhile, in 2017, Facebook was closing in on two billion users worldwide, according to the company's SEC filings and industry estimates. And one more headline: that number had *doubled* since 2015.
- *Engagement*: Google's number of daily users is estimated at 1.5 billion, Facebook's at 1.28 billion. At Facebook, year-to-year growth has been about 20%.
- *Dominance*: As of 2017, Google.com processed 3.5 billion searches daily (40,000 per second). At Facebook, Zuckerberg estimated that out of every minute spent on a smartphone, 20 seconds of that was spent on Facebook.

Clearly, that's a lot of "OK Google" requests, likes, shares, and cat videos, which all add up to audience engagement. And audience engagement means—you guessed it—advertising dollars. In 2017, *eMarketer* reported, the Silicon Valley "duopoly" of Google and Facebook was on its way to controlling 60% of online advertising. Importantly, that curve is growing steeper. In the third quarter of 2016, digital ad revenue grew by almost $3 billion over the third quarter of the year before. That was good news—except to smaller media companies. As reported by analyst Jason Kint and echoed by counterparts at the Interactive Advertising Bureau (IAB), 99% of that ad revenue growth went to Google and Facebook, and 1% went to what Kint called "Everybody Else." The writing is no longer on the wall for media organizations: it's on a sign with big red letters that spell "DANGER."

Clearly, the big three of tech companies—Google, Amazon, and Facebook—have siphoned off profits from content creators in music, books, news, TV, and movies. Now, they are poised to make inroads into other parts of the economy such as grocery stores (Amazon, with its purchase of Whole Foods) and transportation (Alphabet's Google, with the introduction of self-driving cars). The comparative strength of these AI forerunners in turn "begets strength," as venture capitalist Kai-Fu Lee predicted in the *New York Times*. "The more data you have," he wrote, "the better your product; the better your product, the more data you can collect; the more data you can collect, the more talent you can attract; the more talent you can attract, the better your product."

Apart from the job-killing aspect of artificial intelligence (think, self-driving Ubers) is the more immediate concern: the concentration of profits in the hands of a few companies, with neither recourse nor competition. Take, for instance, Facebook's and Google's advertising revenues. When TV and newspapers were still dominant advertising platforms, there were third-party monitors such as Nielsen or the Audit Bureau of Circulation to independently evaluate reach. Until recently, the dominant online platforms have avoided third-party auditing. However, in 2017, Procter & Gamble, the largest purchaser of advertising in the world, began demanding that the digital giants provide independently audited measurements of ad effectiveness.

There are a couple of important takeaways here for media organizations. From the consumer point of view, the 40-year-old theory of *Media System Dependency* (MSD) still applies. In a nutshell, the theory developed by Sandra Ball-Rokeach and Melvin DeFleur states that the more dependent people become on the media they consume to have their individual needs fulfilled, the more important the media will be to people. That sounds intuitive, but consider MSD through the added dimension of social media. Social media not only provided yet another channel for publishers to share content; it empowered users to create and share their own content, making them both consumers and producers. The more dependent individuals are on social media, the more often they talk with others offline about the topics to which they pay attention to on social networking sites. What is more, habitual and heavy social media use fosters dependency on online media to the detriment of non-online alternatives.

The second takeaway, then, is the new way media organizations, especially news organizations, think about their so-called "competition." Take Google, for example. Is it a media company's friend or enemy? In the early days after Google went public in 2004, the technology behemoth fit the definition of friend. It simply aimed to move users, as the *Wall Street Journal* put it, "out of Google and to the right place on the web as fast as possible." For media organizations building content for burgeoning digital audiences, Google helped build web traffic and get content in front of larger audiences than media companies could have dreamed of reaching on their own. For a time, this resulted in higher ad revenues, and the addition of AdSense allowed companies to place relevant ads on their websites.

It was a friendly collaboration so far. But it wasn't long before Google, recognizing a lucrative opportunity, added to its own advertising business. First, it purchased the start-up Where 2 Technologies based in Sydney, Australia, and renamed it Google Maps. As it was, the free GPS app was optimized for local advertising; add in mobility with the birth of the Apple iPhone, and Google Maps exploded. Two years later, in 2006, Google bought yet another platform to leverage for advertising, YouTube. Next, it bought DoubleClick, giving Google the software to optimize and track display ads, enabling advertisers to measure the effectiveness of their rich media, search, and online ads.

By now, you are doubtless detecting a pattern. Somewhere along the line, Google wasn't the media company's friend anymore, and began to look more like an enemy. In a potential preview of government intervention to come, EU regulators in 2017 fined Alphabet $2.74 billion after concluding that Google favored its own ads over those of competitors, a finding the company disputed and appealed. In many cases in our networked world, how thinly drawn is the line between friend and enemy? And for media organizations that must contend with today's technology giants—Google, Facebook, and Amazon—in order to survive, does the line become blurred? Let's take a look at a new kind of collaboration, that's neither friend nor enemy. In the snarky phrasing of Alexa Young's bestselling young adult heroines, they are "frenemies."

Contested Boundaries: Battle of the eBooks

It was a B-school textbook case of frenemies: Amazon and Apple's entry into the e-reader market. The competition came with the emergence of technology allowing users to download book titles ranging from the classic (e.g., *To Kill a Mockingbird*) all the way to the pulpy (e.g., *Faketastic*, from the Frenemies novels.) Both Amazon and Apple wanted in. The first question: Was the market big enough for the two of them? The second question: Could one survive without the cooperation of the other, or to put it in B-school-speak, without "key vertical input?"

In the beginning, Jeff Bezos launched the e-book customer's best friend, the Amazon Kindle, a monochromatic but highly functional gadget that debuted in 2007. All was well until 2010, when Steve Jobs introduced the popular, multi-talented new girl at school, Apple's first-generation iPad, which included the iBook interface with iTunes. The rivalry for readers' attention was on, but with a complicating factor: each rival had something the other wanted and needed. Amazon wanted access to the growing community of iPad users. iPad owners wanted to use their Apple-made tablets to read titles they bought from Amazon's well-stocked e-library.

The partial solution? In an almost-classic case of collaboration, Amazon created a Kindle app for the iPad and other Apple devices. Apple, in turn, allowed the app, despite its history of spurning third-party apps on its devices (think, Google Voice.) But we did say *almost* classic collaboration. Apple stopped short of making iBook accessible to Kindle users. In other words, the new girl had her limits, and that, in short, is the definition of frenemies. The two rival platforms sought a certain degree of compatibility to expand their individual resources and capabilities. Together, they gained more value than they could have apart, competing head-to-head. But that is not to say that they liked it.

It's that ambivalence—the blurring of conventional lines between competitors—that characterizes contested boundaries. As media companies navigate the complex, interconnected world, it is important to understand what makes a good media partnership, which we define as an alliance between two or more entities for a specific purpose. This alliance may be a contractual, exclusive relationship, or it can be merely a mutually beneficial relationship that expands the media company's resources and/or capabilities, in the manner of the e-book example. A few FAQs:

- *What kinds of media organizations can partner?* These can include advertisers, freelancers, distributors, contractors, and suppliers.
- *What is a competitor?* This is an entity that supplies a similar product or service, which offers either advertisers or audiences an alternative.
- *So, my competitor is my enemy?* This is where the media industry gets tricky. An enemy may be non-conventional and not a competitor, as such. A threat can emerge when a different industry—say, a technology company like Google—encroaches on the boundaries of media organizations through shared or similar activities. That's when things become contested. One-time friends become enemies. Former enemies join forces. Think of it as high school, but with a better lunch menu.
- *So how does this work out (or not work out) across the market?* From a media publisher's point of view, the interdependence with online platforms, as well as entertainment content creators has come with strategic, economic, and distribution challenges caused by contested boundaries. In business, a contested boundary occurs when two or more entities dispute, contend, or compete in a perceived or real market. For media organizations, the growing interdependence with online and content creation firms has created four primary contested boundaries. These give the leaders on each platform (and the leaders' challengers) the chance to become the platform that media organizations rely on to reach customers. But again, that reliance is problematic, hence the "contested" part.

Display Advertising

For a case in point, referring to Table 9.1, let's look at the first and probably most significant boundary that media companies contest with Google and Facebook: display advertising. Display advertising is a type of online advertising that comes in several forms, including banner ads, rich media (e.g., video, audio), and other interactive elements, positioned in a variety of locations on a website. In the United States, digital display ad spending eclipsed search ad spending for the first time in 2017. Digital made up 36.7% of total media ad spending in 2016 and will account for around half by 2021. Mobile is likely to be the main driver of this growth, commanding more than 70% of digital spending.

How has Facebook garnered such a large share of the display advertising market and how has this created media interdependence? Display advertising was not the reason

Table 9.1 Media revenue contested boundaries.

Media revenue contested boundaries	Leading platform	Challenger platform
Display advertising	Facebook	Google
Retail advertising	Amazon	Facebook
Mobile search & apps	Google	Apple
Entertainment	Netflix	Amazon

Mark Zuckerberg created Facebook, but as the largest news, entertainment, and information distribution platform in the world, it has a massive audience of users that advertisers are keen to target.

In what advertisers consider the demographic sweet spot of millennials, more than 60% get their news from social media, and Facebook provides a sizeable and growing share of Internet traffic, with 1.28 billion daily users, as of 2017. As we saw with Google, Facebook's growth has sprouted new revenue-producing tools for advertisers. For example, Facebook's ad network retargets based on user characteristics, attitudes, and behavior, seeking greater refinement to reach highly targeted audiences. For media organizations, this that advertisers that may have traditionally advertised through media now go directly to users through platforms. So, while Facebook may have started as a friend to media organizations, allowing them to distribute their content to targeted audiences through collaboration, media organizations increasingly view Facebook as the enemy, poaching display ad dollars that were once the lifeblood of media organizations.

As of 2017, this situation has reached critical mass, and this created new complications. As legacy news companies continued to bleed journalism jobs, just as Facebook and Google's parent company posted record profits, new threats emerged to the other parts of the picture: news consumers, and by extension, advertisers themselves. For consumers, the threat was both "fake news" propagated by political operatives or simple pranksters, neither of which a platform like Facebook was equipped to combat. And for advertisers? As *New York Times* CEO Mark Thompson told investors, the threat was that companies would find their display ads next to "dishonest or tawdry content." (This turned out to be a problem for Google's automated auction system for selling ads at the beginning of YouTube videos. Major advertisers pulled their spots after discovering that they ran at the beginning of videos that contained hate speech, racist, or otherwise disreputable content, a problem Google promised to fix with new screening technology.) The question still to be resolved was whether friends who had become enemies could become friends again. If a duopoly such as Facebook and Google relies on premium content it gets for free (such as quality journalism), what happens when the supply of that content dries up?

Retail Advertising and Cookies

The second contested boundary for media organizations is with Amazon and Facebook for online retail advertising. Online retail advertising, which seeks to sell small quantities of goods for personal use, is dominated by Amazon. What do we mean by "dominated?" As of 2017, Amazon has $80 billion in online sales; that's about six times the figure posted by the number two online retailer Walmart, with $13 billion.

A site like Amazon is a place where partner retailers can operate, subsuming traditional media inserts and other forms of media advertising. Today, online retail advertising is facilitated by retargeting from browser cookies, small traces of data a website sends to a user's computer to help the site remember the user's browsing activity and form fields such as names and credit card numbers. Miguel Helft and Tanzina Vega's 2010 article in the *New York Times* explained that *behavioral retargeting* (or simply *retargeting*) is a means for advertisers to appeal to consumers based on their previous actions. An online digital action is generally a browser page request that returns the page with a cookie sent from the server and stored in the user's web browser. The cookie is then used for future marketing purposes. For example, imagine that you searched for Nike sneakers on Amazon, closed the Amazon browser, then a few days later, visited the ESPN website. It's no coincidence that the ESPN page includes an Amazon ad featuring the precise Nike sneakers for which you shopped earlier. Through the magic of cookies, you've been retargeted.

Retargeting through cookies is not new, but worth noting is Amazon's continuing dominance of the domain, despite some forays by Facebook into the realm. With Amazon's extensive advertising network and retargeting technology, as well as delivery capabilities that can be used effectively by advertiser/retail partners, media organizations are competing even in local markets for these online retail display advertising dollars. That makes, Amazon (and to a lesser degree, Facebook) a "frenemy" of media organizations, because both compete for the same revenues.

The Mobile Market

The pitched battle for the mobile search market has multiple fronts, each hotly contested. A little background: ever since 2015, smartphones have outpaced all other searches, surpassing projected growth rates. As for retail, according to forecasts in the Forrester report, purchases made through consumers' smartphones were estimated at $60 billion in 2016, and by 2021 are projected to hit $152 billion in purchases, about a quarter of all online retail. Perhaps even more noteworthy is the estimated trillion-dollar role mobile searches already play in influencing *offline* purchases. That means comparing prices, reading product reviews, checking store hours, item availability, and coupons. This is a win for Google, right? Yes—and no.

Where the blurred lines exist are between browsers like Google, websites such as Amazon, and associated apps consumers can download like Amazon Shopping or Etsy. So, let's say you want to buy a fidget spinner through your phone. Sure, you can Google "fidget spinner," and, on any given day, the search engine will return 43.1 million results in .56 seconds, with the top results being a row of "Product Listing Ads" including seven nearby retailers (assuming your phone's location is turned on). But there are other options for the fidget-spinner shopper. You can bypass the Google browser and go straight to your Amazon Shopping app, complete a one-click purchase, and save 78% without going anywhere. Or maybe that's too much work. Why not just ask Siri?

So, quicker than we can say, "Hey, Siri, find me a fidget spinner"—or whatever the next Hula-Hoop fad might be—we see the increasingly contested (and sophisticated) overlap between browser, app, and retail advertiser. Because mobile search is often locally triggered, local businesses are investing more advertising dollars into mobile search and apps because users that are searching are more transaction-oriented; that is, they know what they want to buy, and a search provides the means to do so. And with mobile search becoming increasingly voice-activated, and more and more dominated by Siri through the Apple Ad Network, Google, Apple, Amazon, and others further become frenemies of media organizations. The platforms help engage audiences with relevant content, but compete for advertising dollars.

Video on Demand

Perhaps nowhere do these contested boundaries appear in more dramatic relief than in the entertainment sector. Whereas media organizations once had a friendly collaboration with streaming services like Netflix, Amazon Instant Video, and Hulu, now these services appear as threats. They have increasingly become producers of original content, with such commercial and critical hits as *House of Cards, Orange Is the New Black, Transparent,* and *The Handmaid's Tale*. So even as the Internet streaming services helped media companies such as CBS or AMC distribute to new audiences of cable "supplementers," "cord-cutters," and "cord-nevers," Netflix and its imitators have now encroached into production, technological innovation, marketing strategies, and partnerships that shrink media audiences and therefore negatively impact advertising revenues.

How does this occur? Netflix, for one, in 2017 planned to spend $6 billion on programming, second only to ESPN ($7 billion) but well ahead of NBC ($3.4 billion.) That spend builds for Netflix a competitive advantage that becomes self-fulfilling. Attracting more subscribers enables Netflix to afford more content. In a similar move, Amazon Studios released the Oscar-winning *Manchester by the Sea*, its first feature film in theaters (simultaneously streamed). The streaming services' moves into premium original content in turn attract even more subscribers, what *Business Insider* termed "a vicious cycle," the self-perpetuating pattern.

Netflix, moreover, is expanding beyond just movies and television series, and has committed to purchasing non-sports content that has high quality programming and good pricing. In a final turn of the screw, that includes journalism. For example, transformational original content included *Making a Murderer* and *The Keepers*, documentary series that, in a previous era, would have been the domain of news media organizations' investigative reporting. Or, consider other video content from independent filmmakers that distribute their work to a Netflix or an Amazon, competing with human interest stories featured by traditional news media outlets on their (owned) platforms. For these reasons, we can expect Netflix and Amazon to expand even beyond entertainment content, becoming frenemies of a host of media organizations by drawing audiences away with potentially more relevant and engaging video content.

The New Economics of Networks and Networking

The baffle of overlapping and competing interests, like the rat's nest of wires tangled up behind your entertainment center, can only lead us to one thing: *The 4-Hour Workweek*. Well, maybe not literally, but the case study of how first-time author and time-management guru Tim Ferriss landed his bold self-help guide on every bestseller list is a story of how to leverage what we call the "snowball" effect.

A little more than a decade ago, Ferriss was laboring in obscurity running a nutrition supplement company, with nothing to suggest that he was about to become an international author with a book translated into 35 languages. Without the benefit of offline advertising or public relations, Ferriss catapulted his book to success with some key strategies. First, he created a viral idea that appealed to a perceived problem in the lives of a specific demographic—tech-savvy young men on the East and West Coast—and gave the problem a name: "lifestyle design." Second, before launching *4HWW*, he elicited a strong emotional response (both for and against his ideas.) Third, he found out where his demographic went online, chose the least crowded channels, and made personal connections with the influencers in these channels. He spoke at SXSW. He fostered demographic communities around the book via forums, for example, "*4HWW* for Programmers" or "*4HWW* for Students." In fact, the book started as blog, then became a book that was heavily promoted by influential bloggers and YouTube celebrities. As these networks began to gain traction and momentum, *4HWW* was featured on *The Today Show* and Amazon. The 4HWW phenomenon, which led to a "4-Hour" empire of related rapid-learning titles (*The 4-Hour Body, The 4-Hour Chef, Tools of Titans*) is an example of snowball growth. In this model, media organizations build agile, organic networks to take advantage of relevant content that they may promote, aggregate, or reconstruct to engage audiences.

As we've discussed in previous chapters, the fundamental shift in media from scarcity to abundance in the twenty-first century has dramatically changed the economics of media. In short, the abundance (and consumption of) new micro-media are unbundled from the traditional media model of content aggregation. This inverted media economy, in which content is abundant and attention is scarce, has also driven advertising prices dramatically lower. The reason? We have a greater supply of content, coupled with people consuming more media, particularly online (see Chapter 8 Reaching Current and New Customers). This, in turn, has driven ad prices lower.

Micro-content has, in large part, driven the expansion of networks and networking by media organizations to work with online partners and entities that are creators, aggregators, micro-platforms, and re-constructors, to reach audiences. This differs dramatically from the era of content scarcity, when media organizations would create and promote their own content with a monopolistic "if we build it, they will come" mentality. This approach initially had very high value and low output, but output was expanded through exclusive line extensions (e.g., blockbuster growth).

An example of blockbuster growth is Bloomsbury's publication, promotion, and release of *Harry Potter and the Sorcerer's Stone*, first as a book, then as a movie, as a theme park, and as merchandise. Today, micro-media is introduced with low value and output, but then experiences what is known as "snowball" growth or "virality." This occurs when other content producers and aggregators share, repackage, or promote the content, eventually gaining enough popularity that a high-traffic aggregator or media organization will feature the content.

Interestingly, snowball growth of micro-content has slightly altered the Media 2.0 Supply and Demand economics in recent years, such that advertising prices are shifting upward (see Table 9.2). To illustrate, the cost per thousand (CPM) price of Google AdWords has supported the theory that as the demand for blockbusters drops, and a growing number of snowballs become viral and achieve scale, the demand curve becomes an "S" curve, pushing prices up, from approximately $4 CPM in 2011 to $12 CPM in 2015. The higher price available in a snowball economy is good news for media organizations, and a key reason that networking can enable more favorable economics.

Two leading networking strategies that can enable snowball growth for media organizations are *clustering* and *social exchanges*. These strategies provide stability and scale to media organizations' economies of production, distribution, and coordination without adding additional fixed and carrying costs of owned scale.

Table 9.2 Increase in cost of Google AdWords: 2013–2016.

Service	2013	2014	2015	2016
Cost per click (CPC) ($)	0.92	1.02	1.58	2.14
Click through rate (CTR) (%)	0.50	0.90	0.80	1.16
Cost per thousand impressions (CPM) ($)	4.70	8.81	12.07	24.74

Source: Hochman (2015).

Clustering

Clustering is a traditional networking strategy whereby firms, generally from the same industry, locate together in close physical proximity. For example, Silicon Valley, located at the southern part of the San Francisco Bay area in Northern California, is home to many of the world's largest high-tech corporations and thousands of start-up companies that have all "clustered" together as a means for small companies to enjoy some of the economies of scale usually reserved for larger firms. Even though clusters provide many benefits, the degree of interaction and subsequent advantages vary widely by the members of the clusters.

Media companies have a different definition of clustering from industrial or high-tech companies, because mediated content distribution is not rooted in a physical location. Robert Picard describes mediated content as "motion pictures, television programs/videos, broadcasts, audio recordings, books, newspapers, magazines, games, photography and designs, websites and mobile content." Picard finds that media clustering works well when contract labor and specialized services or skills are readily available when media organizations need to expand. For example, book publishers may rely on contract editors or writers when they have excessive book contracts to fulfill. Media organizations primarily cluster to gain ready access to labor (and to a lesser degree, specialized skills or techniques) so that when their business needs expand and contract, they can meet these needs on a contract or project basis. This enables media organizations to access talent and skills only when needed.

Similarly, advertising agencies may hire contract creatives, account managers, and researchers when they are pitching or have won new business. Because of the continual pattern of expansion and contraction, media service firms and individual contractors may locate near those media firms that may require their services, but because of the specialized production common in media industries, coupled with the development of digital and communication technologies, physical location is no longer a prerequisite for media clustering. *Virtual clusters* that depend more on social networks than location have emerged, enabling media organizations (mostly those associated with content production) to use clustering as an effective strategy to create interdependence in both local media and virtual clusters.

Social Exchanges

Social exchanges are based on Social Exchange Theory (SET), which sociologist George Homans developed in 1961. The purpose of a *social exchange* is to prompt and channel economic activity for members, and exchanges come in three forms: direct, generalized (indirect), or productive. A direct exchange occurs when each party's outcome depends directly on the other's behavior. These are the most commonly thought of exchanges, like trading favors. Conversely, the benefit of a generalized exchange is not reciprocal. The return on a generalized exchange is provided by someone else. Finally, a productive exchange relies on cooperation and participation made by both parties to achieve any benefit—like dancing or acting in a play. The social exchange theory suggests that parties create and preserve relationships for expected rewards and positive outcomes.

What, then, is the difference between a social exchange and clustering? Social exchanges are often formed on a relationship basis; clustering generally involves being part of a larger "many-to-many" network. Additionally, social exchanges often center on distribution and coordination, whereas clustering applies to production. For example, if a film script called for a particular prop, such as an automobile, the studio may call upon Ford for a product placement partnership in the film. As a member of the film studio's exchange network, Ford's relationship has created the opportunity for this product placement partnership exchange, which provides both economic as well as social outcomes.

The Art of Collaboration in a Competitive World

In a competitive world, media organizations need to identify and evaluate potential partnerships on the basis of value created or gained, while minimizing any negative impact from shared contested boundaries. For ad-supported media companies, this means, as the PwC 2015 *Media and Entertainment's Key Trends* puts it, the "development of a robust digital toolkit to build premium inventory whether in targeted and tagged site areas, interest-specific e-newsletters or registration-required applications…that give consumers control, community and interactivity." The process of identifying and evaluating potential partners is an art, rather than a science, and involves five integrated phases: (1) situation assessment; (2) target audience; (3) value creation; (4) economic evaluation; and (5) measurement.

- *Situation assessment*: In the first phase of network partnership identification and evaluation, the media organization creates a list of available firms that may be able to strategically complement the firm's current resources and capabilities to achieve a given strategic objective. For each of the potential available firms, the media organization then assesses each one to determine the degree to which they may be able to depend upon, trust, and share a common economic or social commitment with the firm.
- *Target audience*: In the second phase of network partnership identification and evaluation, the media organization does an analysis of each firm's target audience. This analysis can include both qualitative and quantitative research to fully understand the target audience perceptions, behaviors, and motivations. Collaboration is often more successful when the media organization and potential partner firm share a common target audience.
- *Value creation*: In the third phase, the media organization researches, conceptualizes, and evaluates the potential partner firms on the basis of value creation. That is, which resources and capabilities will the potential firm bring to the media organization and what will these capabilities create or add to the competitive position for the media organization? This portion of the value creation phase illustrates the rewards for both the potential firm and the media organization. The other important value to consider is the value to the target audience. The media organization must be able to identify how the target audience will be served by the proposed collaboration with the potential firm. This portion of the value creation phase is important because in today's highly networked world, media organizations must create win-win opportunities for both the firm and the target audience. Otherwise, the endeavor is unlikely to succeed.
- *Economic evaluation*: In the fourth phase, the media organization evaluates the economic benefit of the potential partner firm. This phase relies on the previous phases to ascertain approximate size, scope, and revenue generation, as well as estimating commensurate costs of the potential project to ascertain the net economic benefit to the media organization. It should be noted that not all partnerships in a networked world need to clear a standard profitability hurdle for the media organization. Some partnerships are created to initially build firm interdependence in nascent markets, with the goal of expanding the value creation in subsequent years when the market burgeons.

For example, several media organizations including Condé Nast and Vice Media have expanded into augmented and virtual reality both for storytelling and as a possible avenue for selling future advertising. While they have forged partnerships with companies that make virtual reality headsets and software, they have yet to turn a profit from these ventures. These types of partnerships are investments in future growth, and should be considered thoughtfully during this phase of partnership identification and evaluation.

- *Measurement*: If the media organization determines the potential partnership is viable to execute strategically, operationally, and profitably, it proceeds to the fifth and final phase of network partnership identification and evaluation: measurement. In this phase, the media organization determines the metrics it will use to evaluate the effectiveness of the partnership.

By practicing the art of collaboration in a competitive world, media companies may move from creating impressions to building one-to-one relationships in real time, either directly or on behalf of advertisers. In a networked world, media organizations do not have to exclusively build or provide all resources and capabilities within their own organization. Rather, through thoughtful and effective partnering, partnerships serve to expand digital toolkits and offer more value to consumers.

Exercise: Making "Frenemies"

In 2017, American legacy newspapers and their parent companies, faced with plummeting ad revenues and the existential problem of "fake news," renewed their appeal to the duopoly of Google and Facebook to save journalism by sharing the online platforms' profits. The newly-formed industry trade group News Media Alliance, consisting of small, medium, and large member news organizations in the United States and around the world, called on the public and the US Congress to act on what it called the "anticompetitive behavior of the digital duopoly." The alliance, while recognizing news organizations' dependence on Google and Facebook's ability to bring news content to a large audience, argued that the so-called duopoly in turn depends on news companies. These companies demanded something in return for providing this expensive-to-produce journalism: a fair share of Google and Facebook's ad revenues.

Try the following thought exercise:

1) Identify in this picture the friends, enemies, and potential "frenemies."
2) How you would you collaborate with the "frenemies" you identified? Frame your answer using the five collaborative tools listed previously.

Summary

In this chapter, we learned how best to partner with other media and technology companies. We detailed changes in the media landscape, explaining how it has shifted from "mass media" to "Me Media" and what this means for how media companies compete and collaborate with one another. Successful media entrepreneurs understand these dynamics and how theories such as Media System Dependency can drive their viability as a media organization. This theory takes on an additional layer of complexity in the Media 2.0 environment, where traditional publishers are even more dependent on platforms such as Google and Facebook, and the once-clear distinction between "friends" and "enemies" becomes blurred.

In this new environment, the economics are the inverse of the old media world: content is abundant and attention is scarce. Micro-content can balloon overnight, transitioning from a tweet to a blog to a podcast to a book. This dynamic—the snowball economy—can shift advertising prices upwards and has the potential to provide stability and scale to media organizations. In order to best compete in this competitive world, entrepreneurs must identify and evaluate potential partnerships, relying on five integrated phases where they consider *situation assessment, target audience, value creation, economic evaluation,* and *measurement.*

10

Investing in Key Assets and Capabilities

Some companies operate in rich media environments, with audiences composed of technologically savvy conversationalists and critics, who are active consumers, as well as creators, of content. Other media enterprises operate in an environment where their audiences are more oriented to passively consuming content on fewer platforms. Their customers tend to be media spectators, instead of creators.

Strategy is about marrying the key resources that a company possesses, such as its tangible assets and its assorted capabilities, with the expectations of its customers. Consider the strategic choices confronting leaders at these four small companies, two start-ups and two century-old community newspapers. All four have annual revenues in the millions or less, but they face the same issues as billion-dollar media enterprises.

theSkimm was founded in 2012 by two young producers at NBC, who had met in Rome while college students. With $60,000 in seed money, they launched a free daily email newsletter that targeted urban women, ages 22–34. The newsletter summarized the most important news and trends of the day in a conversational, casual tone. Its brand promise: we'll tell you what you need to know so you don't embarrass yourself when you are talking with friends. By 2017, the company had multiple online products (including Skimm Guides and Skimm the Vote), a staff of 45, and five million subscribers to its daily newsletter. Analysts estimated it had $4.4 million in annual revenue, much of it from advertising messages targeting subscribers. In early 2017, the founders received $8 million in venture capital from 21st Century Fox to invest in video. This infusion of cash values the company at $55 million. *TheSkimm's strategic priority*: deciding how best to invest the new round of capital for the greatest ROI.

Scalawag was founded as a nonprofit magazine in 2015 by three recent college graduates with a Kickstarter campaign that raised $31,500 and allowed them to publish their first issue. The magazine, which is printed four times a year, has more than 1,000 subscribers. The term "scalawag" refers to Southern whites who supported Reconstruction in the years after the Civil War, and *Scalawag*, the magazine, covers the politics and culture of the New South in long-form articles that resemble those in *The Atlantic*. *Scalawag* publishes two new articles a week in its free online newsletter, "This Week in the South." In addition, the editors curate and link to what they consider the most interesting stories on the South published in sources as varied as *Rolling Stone* and *Politico*. Revenue comes from subscriptions to the magazine and a variety of fund-raising efforts. While *Scalawag* pays its freelancers for the photography, poetry, and articles that run in the magazine, the regular staff receives only a small monthly stipend or hourly wages as of 2017. *Scalawag's strategic priority*: moving beyond start-up mode and gaining firm financial grounding.

The Strategic Digital Media Entrepreneur, First Edition. Penelope Muse Abernathy and JoAnn Sciarrino.
© 2019 John Wiley & Sons, Inc. Published 2019 by John Wiley & Sons, Inc.
Companion website: www.wiley.com/go/abernathy/StrategicDigitalMediaEntrepreneur

The *News Reporter* was founded in 1896 and is located in rural eastern North Carolina in the community of Whiteville. In 1953, the *News Reporter* became one of the smallest papers ever to receive the prestigious Pulitzer Public Service Medal for its courageous reporting on the Ku Klux Klan's infiltration of local police and fire departments. The *News Reporter*, with a print circulation of 10,000, serves readers and advertisers in one of the poorest counties in the state. While the paper was an early digital pioneer and has an active website and social media presence, print revenues associated with the twice-weekly newspaper have declined significantly in recent years, prompting concern about the long-term viability of the company. The editor of the paper is the third generation in his family to lead the paper. He is hoping his youngest daughter, who is in college majoring in journalism, will return home and assume the mantle for the fourth generation. The *News Reporter's strategic priority*: establishing a five-year business plan that allows the newspaper to remain family-owned and family-operated.

The *Pilot* was founded in 1920 and is located in Southern Pines, an affluent retirement and resort community in the Sandhills region of central North Carolina. Like the *News Reporter*, the *Pilot*, which has a print circulation of 12,000 readers, is family-owned and family-operated. The publisher estimates that Southern Pines retailers draw customers from five surrounding counties. Anticipating that income from the twice-weekly newspaper would decline, the publisher began diversifying, purchasing other assets, and starting new products in the mid-2000s. By 2017, the *Pilot* also published three city magazines (distributed in major metropolitan areas of the state) and two telephone directories published in adjacent counties. It also owned and operated a digital ad agency, as well as a local bookstore. The rear entrance to Fort Bragg, one of the largest military bases in the country, is adjacent to the city limits of Southern Pines. As a result, the area has attracted a sizeable number of young residents in recent years, with officers stationed at the base purchasing homes in the area. In an attempt to better serve these new residents, in 2016 the *Pilot* began publishing an online email newsletter, "created by millennials for millennials." The content is similar to *theSkimm*, but locally oriented. The publisher realizes he must come up with more digital products and services to reach these new residents, many of whom are not interested in reading a print newspaper published twice a week. The *Pilot's strategic priority*: selecting the next digital project.

The characteristics of the audiences of each of these four media enterprises vary dramatically. The audience for *theSkimm*, for instance, is much younger and more technologically savvy than that of the *News Reporter*. Similarly, the resources available to each of them vary significantly. After years of living frugally, *theSkimm* has just received a significant cash infusion while *Scalawag* still couldn't afford to pay its permanent staff a regular salary in 2017.

How do the leaders of each of these media enterprises use the limited resources and assets that they possess to best advantage so that they meet the expectations of their customers and maximize their return on investment? In this chapter, we will develop a digital strategy map to help media entrepreneurs—those leading small start-ups, as well as large legacy enterprises—align their company's unique value proposition with their available resources as well as the media environment in which they operate. This will help managers of these four small media enterprises prioritize investments in key assets and capabilities that ultimately drive transformation and profitability.

Among the questions we'll consider:

- What is the type of media environment in which a digital enterprise operates?
- What are the key resources and assets that a company has available to meet the expectations of its current and future customers?

- What is the framework for aligning the media environment with a company's key resources?
- What are the pathways to digital transformation?
- How do you determine where to place your bets to ensure profitability of the entire enterprise?

Understanding the Different Media Environments

Digital strategies are built on a company's promise to deliver unique value to its customers, in ways that differentiate it from competitors. In Chapters 6–9, we explored how to segment customers based on their wants and needs, identify the most promising and profitable customers, enhance relationships with them, and choose beneficial partners. Now let's consider the dynamics of the media culture or environment in which an enterprise operates and interacts with the various consumers of its products and services.

Sociologists David Altheide and Robert Snow observed that media cultures form or "coalesce" around various content formats. The culture is determined by how an audience chooses to interact with the content provided by the medium. Their two influential books, *Media Logic* and *Media Worlds in the Postjournalism Era*, were written prior to the digital era. However, their observation seems as relevant today as then, especially given the interactivity, immediacy, and interconnectedness of Internet-enabled communication.

Altheide and Snow referred to media "cultures." However, the term "culture" carries various meanings in various disciplines of study. Therefore, to avoid confusion in this chapter, we'll be referring to *media environments*. Specifically, we'll want to know the degree of involvement of an audience—or a customer segment—with a specific medium's content and format.

In an attempt to understand the various ways people interacted with social media, Forrester® Research has developed a schematic "technographics ladder" that segments consumers of social media content based on their behavior. At the top end of the ladder are the people who are the most actively involved with social media. This includes people who create and upload blogs, articles, and video (the *creators*), or post ratings and make comments on the content others create (the *critics*). In the middle of the ladder are the *collectors*, who actively save and share content and links, and will vote or "like" certain postings, as well as *joiners*, who maintain a social media profile but only infrequently post comments or share material. At the lower end are *spectators* and *inactives*. Spectators read blogs and ratings, and watch video or listen to podcasts, but don't actively comment, share content, or create any postings. Inactives might have joined in the past, but no longer interact with social media.

A similar sorting technique can be used by any medium—from newspapers to magazines and television shows—to determine the dominant media environment in which they operate. Is a majority of the audience actively involved and interacting with the content they are consuming—creating and posting comments and actively saving and sharing material? If so, this is what we will refer to as a *dynamic media environment*. In such an environment, customers want to be active participants in conversations with each other *and* they want to interact with the content they consume. Stated another way, they place a high premium on interactivity and connectedness. By providing many opportunities to interact and connect, a media enterprise creates a unique value proposition that engenders customer loyalty and attachment to the medium.

At the opposite end of the spectrum are the customers who consume content, but don't expect to actively interact with it. They watch, read, or listen to the content, and may even share it on occasion. They can be *very* loyal readers, listeners, and viewers, who place a high value on the news, information, or entertainment provided by a media enterprise. However, they have no expectation of carrying on a robust, ongoing conversation with others or with the media enterprise. This is what we will refer to as a *passive media environment*. Generationally, millennials (born between 1980 and 2000) and gen Xers (born prior to 1980) are more likely to expect and demand active involvement than baby boomers (born between 1945 and 1965). However, this can vary considerably by geographic market, or by the characteristics of certain types of communities built around shared interests, affiliations, or backgrounds. For example, those in university communities or wired urban centers may expect and demand more involvement, regardless of age. Similarly, subscribers to conservative blogs may be more likely to join an online forum to critique the opinion of others, or add their own views.

Using the schematic in Figure 10.1, we can see that *Scalawag* and *theSkimm* operate in the most dynamic environments. Millennial women, the target audience for *theSkimm*, actively engage with the content, as well as the various products (Skimm the Vote) and services (Daily Skimm calendar app) that the online enterprise develops. Similarly, *Scalawag* is aimed at an audience that cares about the New South and the social justice issues it confronts—from drug abuse in Appalachia to political shenanigans in state legislatures. Both audiences expect and want to be involved in advancing the conversation—online and offline.

The Whiteville *News Reporter* is on the opposite end of the spectrum. It serves a geographic community with an older audience that does not necessarily expect or demand a lot of interactivity or involvement with the paper or its website. The newspaper's subscribers rely on the paper's Twitter feeds and Facebook posts to inform them of major news. Although they may share links with others, they are not inclined to interact with the online content posted by the *News Reporter*.

The *Pilot* is somewhere in between the two extremes, and is encountering a much more dynamic media environment. The Southern Pines and Pinehurst retirement and resort community is more affluent than Whiteville. Many of the retirees in the community have served as executives in major corporations or at high levels in state or national governments. They are often active Facebook users and are comfortable expressing their opinions online and in letters to the editor. The demographics in the community have begun changing in recent years as the families of young military officers stationed at nearby Fort Bragg have moved into the area. Like the readers of *Scalawag* and *theSkimm*, these younger subscribers want and expect to be digitally connected to their peers, as well as to the content that they consume. The free twice-weekly online newsletter, *Sway*, launched by the *Pilot* in 2016, was designed to reach these young families in a way that the newspaper and glossy monthly print magazine, *Pinestraw*, didn't. Much to the surprise of the *Pilot*, a sizeable portion of the early subscribers were retiree baby boomers who liked the conversational, breezy prose of *Sway*.

Figure 10.1 From passive to dynamic: the media environments for four digital enterprises.

As the *Pilot* example shows, digital technology can change the dynamics rather quickly in a community, especially given the swift adoption of smartphones, which has made it possible to stay connected even in the most out-of-the-way places. Understanding the degree of involvement expected and demanded by an audience is the first step in priorizing digital investment. The next step is to identify which resources your company possesses that can be used in your strategic transformation efforts.

Identifying the Key Resources Available to Your Company

A balance sheet lists a company's tangible and intangible assets in a manner that makes accounting sense. But it does not begin to account for all the resources that a typical media company can use to transform its business models. Perhaps the best way to begin identifying those resources is to ask: What key resources support our value propositions, customer relationships, and revenue streams?

Key resources include:

- capabilities your company possesses that have a significant value to current customers and prospects;
- relationships with suppliers, vendors, competitors, and employees, as well as established and potential partnerships with other firms;
- the various channels for reaching and engaging with current customers and prospects.

In fact, the *most important resources* or *assets* are likely to be intangible ones—your company's *capabilities*. For example, *theSkimm* began with only $60,000 in seed money. However, early on, it identified an intangible and very valuable asset—its capability of producing engaging and conversational online content for millennial women. It leveraged that capability, along with its digital marketing expertise, to rapidly build an audience of 3.5 million subscribers in 18 months.

In *The Essential Advantage*, management consultants Paul Leinwand and Cesare Mainardi define capabilities as:

> the interconnected people, knowledge, tools and processes that establishes a company's "right to win'" in a business or industry. The "right to win" is a clear path to sustained profitability, higher market share, or both, supported by [a company's] critical set of capabilities.

To identify the scope and scale of your company's capabilities, ask these questions:

- What is the unique value proposition that we currently deliver?
- What capabilities currently support that?
- Given the way consumer tastes and expectations are changing, what capabilities do we need in the future to continue delivering a unique value proposition?

A recent survey by the consulting group Strategy& found that two-thirds of 2,400 senior executives believed their company did not have the capabilities to create value, or win against a competitor. "It's much harder to build capabilities than to leverage what you already do exceptionally well," say Leinwand and Mainardi. Therefore, they recommend identifying three to six "first-in-class interlocking capabilities" and then building a strategy for growth of revenue and profits around harnessing those resources, doing what your company does better than anyone else. This is in contrast to traditional strategies

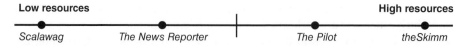

Figure 10.2 From low to high: the resources available to four digital enterprises.

that often focus on responses to competitive threats or seizing market opportunities, without first considering whether a company has the resources to prevail.

As with the media environment, the "resources" available to a company (including its tangible and intangible assets) can be ranked from high to low (Figure 10.2). Due to an infusion of $8 million in venture capital in 2017, *theSkimm* ranks high on available financial resources, and has developed significant intangible assets—including digital capabilities around the creation, marketing, and distribution of its engaging products and services. *Scalawag*, in contrast, has many fewer financial resources to tap at the moment. However, it has attracted an affluent and engaged audience, and produces and curates quality content on social justice issues that it may be able to leverage to attract more resources—from nonprofit foundations or other sponsors.

The *Pilot* has aggressively diversified its revenue and profits, and today the newspaper is one of many products in the company's portfolio. Along the way, it has developed significant capabilities. On the content side, it has created and distributed print and online lifestyle magazines and telephone directories for other markets, a subscriber-based digital newsletter, and short videos. On the marketing side, it has launched an in-house digital agency providing a variety of marketing services for local businesses.

The *News Reporter* is in a much less affluent market and much more dependent financially on the profitability of its newspaper than is the *Pilot*. However, the newspaper has moved quickly to attempt to transform itself—creating special online "pages" for its readers, publishing a twice-yearly lifestyle magazine, maintaining an active social media presence, and launching a small in-house digital marketing agency.

As these four examples show, when you consider your company's capabilities as resources that can be strategically deployed to transform your business model, even cash-strapped enterprises are wealthier than they realize.

Developing a Digital Strategy Map and Framework

Let's now create a grid that overlays the media environment in which an enterprise operates with the available resources that can be used to strategically transform a business. There are four resulting quadrants in Figure 10.3.

The horizontal axis in Figure 10.3 represents the resources, ranked from high to low. Available resources include tangible assets, as well as processes, activities, and capabilities that a company can leverage. The vertical axis measures the degree of dynamic involvement by the audience with a medium and the products and services it produces. Dynamic audiences are more oriented toward being active creators of content, conversationalists, and critics. Passive audiences are more oriented toward being spectators. Let's see how this might be used by the four media enterprises to plot their current position in Figure 10.4.

The *News Reporter* is in Quadrant One (low resources, passive media environment). This is the most challenging quadrant on the map, but it is not without opportunity to move forward with digitization. The *News Reporter*'s digital initiatives have included: limited products and services, including the creation of "Sports of All Sorts" and the lifestyle

Figure 10.3 Environment and resources: putting it together.

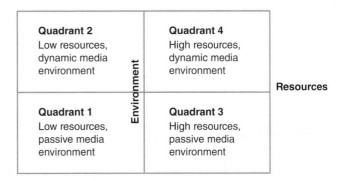

Quadrant 2
Low resources, dynamic media environment

Quadrant 4
High resources, dynamic media environment

Environment

Resources

Quadrant 1
Low resources, passive media environment

Quadrant 3
High resources, passive media environment

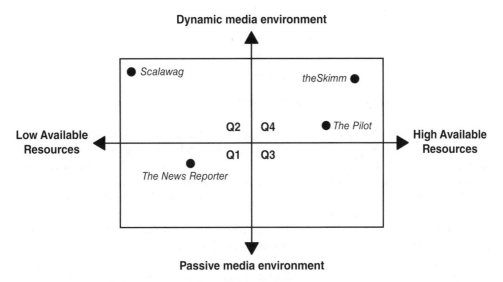

Dynamic media environment

● *Scalawag*

theSkimm ●

Q2 | Q4

● *The Pilot*

Low Available Resources

High Available Resources

Q1 | Q3

●
The News Reporter

Passive media environment

Figure 10.4 Map of digital transformation for four media enterprises.

section "POP" (both are digital products aimed at building engagement with a younger audience); marketing and distribution efforts (its use of social media to market its content and the establishment of an in-house digital marketing agency); and limited efforts at digitizing its supply chain (contracting with a digital service to design websites for its advertisers).

Scalawag is in Quadrant Two (low resources, dynamic media environment). *Scalawag*, the print magazine, is supported through revenue from subscriptions and nonprofit funds. *Scalawag*'s digital initiatives are limited to the creation of one product (a free weekly email newsletter) and the marketing and distribution of this newsletter. However, it has a very engaged audience that it might be able to leverage for fund-raising efforts.

theSkimm is in Quadrant Four (high resources, dynamic media environment), operating in a dynamic media culture with significant available resources, as a result of receiving venture capital funding of $16 million over five years. *theSkimm* began life in 2012 in Quadrant Two (low resources, dynamic media environment), but rapidly built its engaged millennial audience to 3.5 million subscribers in 18 months with a carefully curated collection of articles in its daily digital newsletter that was viewed as "accessible" by its target audience. *theSkimm*'s platform has now expanded to include not only the *Daily Skimm*, but also Skimm Ahead, Skimm the Vote, and Skimm Guides, which include Snapchat

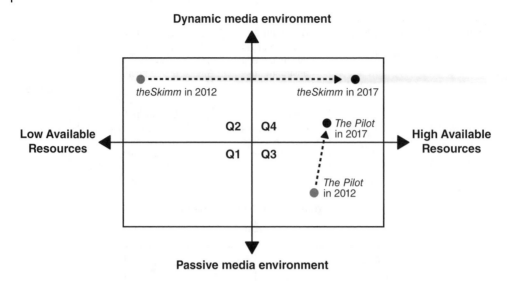

Figure 10.5 Moving across the grid: the transformation of *theSkimm* and the *Pilot*.

recommendations, a brief on the Panama Papers, and an update on what the Kardashians are doing. *theSkimm* implemented a grassroots approach to growing the audience rapidly and has about 13,000 "Skimm'bassadors" spreading the word. Skimm'bassadors get rewards such as tote bags and other swag for telling their friends to sign up and read. *theSkimm*'s digital efforts to date include development of products and services, as well as marketing and distribution efforts.

The *Pilot* is also in Quadrant Four (high resources, relatively dynamic media audience). The *Pilot* has a diversified portfolio of products and services. (It also owns and operates a brick-and-mortar retail outlet—a book store.) Its website has more than a million visitors a month. Recent digital initiatives include: products and services (revamping the newspaper website in 2010 to provide blogging tools, multimedia, and user-generated content and launching *Sway* in 2016); supply chain (outsourcing its printing operations); and marketing and distribution (launching an in-house digital marketing agency in 2016).

It is worth noting that two of the four enterprises moved from one quadrant to another between 2012 and 2017 (Figure 10.5). *theSkimm* began life in Quadrant Two (dynamic audience, low resources), in the same place where *Scalawag* is currently located. The *Pilot* was in Quadrant Three (high resources, passive audience) in 2012, having focused primarily on diversifying its portfolio of print products. Both companies were able to move into a more attractive quadrant by being very strategic in using all available resources and being very disciplined about how they prioritized their digital efforts. This suggests that this strategy framework can also be used as a *Digital Transformation Map*, that guides and prioritizes digital investment strategies for each of the four media companies.

Digital Transformation Pathways and Strategies

There are four strategies that all media companies—regardless of size and scale—can employ to digitally transform their business models. They can create digital products and services, develop digital marketing and distribution capabilities, digitize their business processes and supply chains, and disrupt the ecosystem with a digital innovation. Here's how these four strategies have been used by our four small media enterprises.

- *Products and services*: This is the first digital strategy employed by most media enterprises, including both start-ups (such as *theSkimm* and *Scalawag*) and legacy enterprises (such as the *Pilot* and *News Reporter*). Print newspapers typically begin this effort by digitizing content that has been created for their newspaper or magazine and placing it on a web platform. While this initial step is important, it does not reflect the totality of the digital transformation of products and services. The product or service must also be adapted to account for an audience's consumption habits, considering how the audience is most likely to access the material (e.g., on a website or through a mobile app), and the various ways in which customers will use and share the content. Also, most media enterprises begin by digitizing all their content, without differentiating between their most valuable and least digital assets. By not prioritizing the most valuable franchises, they expend resources (time, attention, effort) on digitizing content that creates very little value to consumers.
- *Marketing and distribution*: Half of 1,500 companies surveyed in 2017 by McKinsey & Company had made efforts to digitize their distribution and marketing. This made strategic sense, according to McKinsey, "given the extraordinary impact digitization has already had on customer interactions and the power of digital tools to target marketing investments." This level of digital media transformation for media companies most commonly deals with issues around pricing, promotion, and distribution. All four news outlets—*theSkimm*, *Scalawag*, the *Pilot*, and the *News Reporter*—use digital tools to promote their products and services to subscribers and potential subscribers. This includes their use of social media and the repackaging of previously published content for free online distribution. Since *Scalawag* is nonprofit, all of its digital marketing and distribution efforts are aimed at increasing the number of subscribers to its print magazine. However, many of the marketing and distribution efforts of the other three outlets focus on advertisers. Subscribers to the *Daily Skimm* receive the newsletter for free, but *theSkimm* delivers its mobile-optimized email in such a way that it can provide very specific targeted information to its advertisers, garnering higher advertising rates per thousand than similar online news publications. Minute targeting is less important to the *Pilot* and *News Reporter*. Both of them have focused on creating in-house digital marketing agencies that provide advertisers with a variety of online services, ranging from SEO (search engine optimization) to website design.
- *Business processes and supply chains*: This next level of digitization involves reducing, streamlining, or eliminating low value-added costs. The McKinsey study found that digitization of the business processes and supply chains had a significant impact on profits. Yet only 2% of companies surveyed by McKinsey reported that this was a primary focus of their digital transformation efforts. Many newspapers and magazines, such as the *Pilot* and *Scalawag*, have outsourced their printing and/or distribution processes. But most efforts to digitize the supply chains in media companies have not progressed beyond these two processes. News outlets usually begin their journey by digitizing their products and services, as well as their marketing and distribution efforts. Many have not yet focused on aligning the digitization of all business processes and supply chains with the products and services they are producing or with their marketing and distribution efforts.
- *Ecosystem disruption:* This involves the creation and marketing of a *new* digital platform, product, or service that revolutionizes the way customers interact with a medium.

The result is the creation of a new space that is distinct from the existing contested space. The disruptive digital innovation creates new benefits and services for customers, while simultaneously reducing costs. The biggest return on investment, according to the McKinsey study, goes "to those that initiate digital disruptions. Fast-followers can also reap significant payouts." But, in general, an eco-system disruption can only be attempted by a media company after the other levels of the digital transformation and integration have been fully achieved.

In deciding which of the four digital transformation strategies to prioritize, media enterprises need to consider how to best utilize their available resources (most especially intangible ones, such as their capabilities). Among the questions to ask: How are you going to build the necessary capabilities for each strategy? In what order will you do it? What changes will this require you to make to your business structure or your portfolio of products and services?

Here's how each of four media enterprises could use the *Digital Transformation Map* to guide future investments and priorities.

Quadrant One: Low Resources, Passive Media Culture

Digital Transformation Priority: Digitizing High Value Products and Services

Media firms in this quadrant, such as the *News Reporter*, are challenged by both their available resources, as well as the environment in which they operate. This requires strategic discipline. Leaders of these companies should focus *first* on identifying and prioritizing the digitization of the products and services that support their unique value proposition. To successfully leverage limited resources, these media organizations should study how current and potential customers prefer to receive and interact with their products and services, and then design their digital products and services to meet their customer expectations and needs. This may involve breaking the media organization's mass audience into many smaller, micro-segments, and designing digital products that are substantially different from the legacy product. For example, research has shown that readers of the *News Reporter* place a high value on its coverage of local sports. Usage of the paper's website spikes on the day of the week when it publishes "Sports of All Sorts." One possible next step would be the development of a weekly subscription sports newsletter that could also be ad- or sponsor-supported.

Quadrant Two: Low Resources, Dynamic Media Environment

Digital Transformation Focus: Products and Services, as well as Marketing and Distribution Efforts

Media firms in this quadrant, like *Scalawag*, are challenged by available resources, but are advantaged by the engagement and involvement of their audience. Their focus should be on enhancing high-value features or services, without significantly increasing the cost base. These could involve both online and offline products and services that serve a dual marketing purpose. For example, the nonprofit *Texas Tribune*, founded in 2009, produces and distributes long-form online articles about Texas politics, government, and social issues, as well as reams of data about various legislative bills. It serves a very engaged audience similar to that of *Scalawag*. To raise awareness, the *Tribune* held forums around the state in 2010, interviewing legislators and politicos about important issues confronting the state. By 2014, those forums had become must-attend events, and the *Tribune* received significant revenues from the fees charged to corporations that sponsored the events. By 2017, the *Tribune* has gained funding from nonprofit foundations and for-profit corporations, subscribers and from a variety of products and services.

Quadrant Three: High Resources, Passive Media Environment

Digital Transformation Focus: Products and Services, Marketing and Distribution Efforts, as well as Business Processes and Supply Chain

Media organizations in this quadrant should be following rapid prototyping to continue to innovate and introduce products and services, or marketing and distribution efforts, that add value for either subscribers or advertisers. Additionally, they should be reducing, streamlining, or eliminating costs through improvements in business processes and their supply chains. The *Pilot* was in this quadrant in 2006. Over the next decade, it greatly expanded its products and services, developed new marketing capabilities, and outsourced all its printing. It continually invested in the development of new products and services that engaged both the retirees in the market, as well its young military families. As a result, it moved into Quadrant Four.

Quadrant Four: High Resources, Dynamic Media Environment

Digital Transformation Focus: Products and Services; Price, Promotion, and Distribution; Business Processes and Supply Chain; Creation of New Ecosystems

Media firms in this quadrant should be well on the way to fully digitizing their products and services, their marketing and distribution efforts, as well as their business processes (including their supply chain). They may then be able to invest their resources in identifying an uncontested space (not currently occupied by a competitor) and proceed to create new platforms, products, or services that attract customers to that space. *theSkimm* could conceivably create such an ecosystem disruption with its new video products.

Building a Profitable and Sustainable Business Model

Think of a strategy statement as having two parts. The first part articulates and canonizes what a company *will do*—the goals it will pursue and how it will accomplish those goals. The second part is unspoken, but just as powerful. It exposes, through omission, what a company *will not do*.

The above strategy framework prioritizes digital investment based on available resources and the dynamics of the media environments, however, it does not preclude the possibility of constantly reassessing your priorities or adjusting strategy. As discussed in Chapter 4, in order to keep pace with changes that are occurring in the marketplace, businesses need to have a strategy for transforming their business model at an average annual rate of 6%. That is why leaders of media enterprises need to be constantly evaluating both their cost and revenue structures.

In a 2017 study, McKinsey & Company surveyed executives at more than 1,500 companies, including 86 media enterprises, to gauge the impact of technology on their business model and bottom line. The media, retail, and high-tech sectors had been the most aggressive in adopting and integrating digital technology into their business processes. Executives in those industries estimated that at least 50% of their business processes were "digitized." However, even they concluded there was still much more they needed to do to transform their business models. Executives told McKinsey that the most immediate financial impact of digital technology was often a decrease of both revenue and profit. However, "bold, tightly integrated digital strategies" improved profitability.

Driving profitability begins with the elimination of costs associated with products, services, processes, and functions that add little value. Yale professor Richard Foster identified three types of cost reductions in *Creative Destruction: Why Companies that Are Built to Last Underperform the Market.* Incremental cost reductions are just that, the sort of adjustments that companies make each year, based on projected revenue. Significant reductions of 10% or more often involve the elimination of a product or service. Transformative change of a business model, he said, occurs only when a company succeeds in cutting expenses by 50% or more. That is why he argued that CEOs of established firms confronted by a disruptive innovation—such as the *Pilot* and *News Reporter*—must attempt to shed costs associated with the legacy technology (print) as quickly as possible. Funds freed up from shedding legacy costs should be invested in building customer value with the new technology (digital).

In *The Essential Advantage*, authors Leinwand and Mainardi detail a four-step process for calculating costs and then aggressively eliminating the expenses that do not contribute directly to a company's value proposition. The process begins with itemizing and categorizing all costs on four dimensions:

- *Lights-on expenses*: The bare minimum an enterprise needs to stay in business. This includes the cost of facilities, as well as other operational expenses. Estimated to be 10% of total costs.
- *Table stakes*: This is what an enterprise needs to maintain its current position in its market. It includes marketing and production costs. Estimated to be 20–30% of total costs.
- *Capabilities-driven costs*: Costs that support an enterprise's unique value proposition and allow it to "play to win." This, the authors estimated, is 20–30%, and "usually deserves more."
- *Everything else*: This includes whole functions, such as logistics and distribution. Estimated to be as much as 50%.

Only *capabilities-driven costs* differentiate your business, the authors argue, and ultimately drive profitability. Therefore, every other type of cost should be scrutinized. Can the product, business unit or function be sold, outsourced, streamlined, or shuttered? Every dollar a company can save by trimming costs in these three categories—*lights-on expenses*, *table stakes*, and *everything else*—frees up resources for developing capabilities that drive value and profitability for the company.

After calculating the cost of the entire enterprise, as well as each function or capability within the enterprise, media enterprises then need to match the costs with the revenue from each of the digital transformation strategies. There are a number of ways to measure profitability: at the product, project, or customer levels. In general, the profitability of digital products and services can be measured at both the product level (with marketing and distribution costs allocated) or at the customer level. (Chapter 8 explains how to calculate *Customer Lifetime Value* for each customer segment.) The profitability of digital transformation efforts involving marketing and distribution, or those concerned with business processes and supply chains, can be measured at the project level.

Ultimately, the profitability of any digital transformation strategy is captured over time in a company's EBIT (earnings before interest and taxes), which was discussed in detail in

Chapter 2. The 2017 McKinsey study found that "current levels of digitization have already taken out, on average, up to six points of annual revenue and 4.5 points of growth in EBIT. And there's more pressure ahead, our research suggests, as digital penetration deepens."

However, the McKinsey research indicated that

> the more aggressively companies respond to the digitization of their industries—up to and including initiating digital disruption—the better the effect on their projected revenue and profit growth...[B]old, tightly integrated digital strategies will be the biggest differentiator between companies that win and companies that don't...and the biggest payouts will go to those that initiate digital disruptions. Fast-followers with operational excellence won't be far behind.

Four Small Companies at a Strategic Crossroads

Leaders at each of the four small media enterprises in this chapter—*theSkimm*, *Scalawag*, the *News Reporter*, and the *Pilot*—are at an inflexion point in 2017. They have limited resources, so they must make difficult decisions about where to invest, prioritizing only a few of the most promising projects. They must be disciplined and focused in implementing their strategies. They must also be rigorous in assessing whether their investments have a positive return, pulling the plug when necessary.

theSkimm and the *Pilot* have the most resources to invest, and they operate in dynamic media environments. Both have been successful in recent years in transforming their business model. Their primary strategic challenge is prioritizing their investment spending so they achieve maximum return. In contrast, leaders of *Scalawag* and the *News Reporter* have little room for error. The three-year-old nonprofit *Scalawag* is still trying to gain a toehold in the market. It has few resources, but engaged subscribers. Its founders are passionate and committed to the cause—social justice—but they would also like to draw a regular salary. The *News Reporter* was an early digital pioneer and has continued to innovate. The century-old, Pulitzer-Prize-winning community paper has created digital products and services that are popular with its audience and offered its local advertisers a variety of digital services. But its revenues have declined significantly in recent years. The paper is located in one of North Carolina's poorest counties. "We know there are a lot of quality of life issues here...that will affect our future," said Les High, editor of the paper. "And if we don't cover them, no one else will." High is the third generation of his family to work at the paper. The decisions that he makes in 2017 may well determine whether a fourth generation owns the paper.

Exercise: Charting a Strategic Path

Let's revisit the major strategic issues facing each of these four enterprises and consider these questions about how to prioritize investment:

theSkimm's strategic priority: Deciding how best to invest the new round of capital for the greatest ROI.

- Can five-year-old *theSkimm* use $8 million in venture capital to disrupt the ecosystem?
- Or should it focus on continuing to grow subscribers to the *Daily Skimm* through video?

Scalawag's strategic priority: Moving beyond start-up mode and gaining firm financial grounding.

- Can this nonprofit digital magazine follow the example of the successful *Texas Tribune* and produce events?
- Or should it emulate *theSkimm* and create another digital newsletter for nonsubscribers?

The Pilot's strategic priority: Selecting the next digital project.

- The company owns and operates three city magazines, a bookstore, a digital ad agency, and the newspaper. Where should the company invest next—creating a digital publication for non-subscribers, for example, or developing its video products and services?

The News Reporter's strategic priority: Establishing a five-year strategic plan that allows the newspaper to remain family-owned and operated.

- Should the *News Reporter* develop digital newsletters for nonsubscribers, similar to *Sway?* If not, what other digital products and services should it develop for its readers and advertisers?

Summary

In this chapter, we developed a digital strategy map that leaders of media enterprises can use to prioritize their investments and projects. Every entrepreneur needs to consider the unique characteristics of their market and their business operations when developing digital strategies.

Some enterprises have significant resources, other have limited resources. Resources include not just the assets listed on a balance sheet, but also a company's capabilities. We defined *capabilities* as the interconnection of people, knowledge, tools, and processes that contribute to a company's value proposition and give it a competitive advantage. Similarly, some media enterprises operate in rich, dynamic environments. Their customers like to be engaged in creating content and connecting with it. Other media firms have customers who prefer to be passive spectators.

With the strategy map we sought to match the dynamics of the media environment with the amount and type of resources that leaders of media enterprises can use to transform their business. We identified four quadrants and four pathways to digital business transformation. Each quadrant is ranked according to the amount of resources available to the media enterprises (ranked from high to low) and the type of environment (ranked from dynamic to passive). Each of the quadrants has a strategic priority for investment. The four pathways to business model transformation are:(1) creating digital products and services; (2) developing digital marketing and distribution capabilities; (3) digitizing business processes and supply chains; and (4) disrupting the ecosystem through innovation.

In order to free up dollars for investment, companies must be diligent about constantly re-evaluating their cost structures. Recent studies have shown that digital technology initially depresses earnings for most companies. However, companies that aggressively pursue integrated digital strategies are most likely to survive and thrive in the years ahead.

Part III

Leadership in a Time of Change

Most of the time, if you're honest with yourself, you know that your vision of the future is just your best estimate at the moment: The practice of leadership requires the capacity to keep asking basic questions of yourself and of the people in your organizations and community. The assumptions that hold you also constrain you from seeing any other points of view.

(Ronald Heifetz and Marty Linsky, *Leadership on the Line: Staying Alive through the Dangers of Leading*)

The Strategic Digital Media Entrepreneur, First Edition. Penelope Muse Abernathy and JoAnn Sciarrino.
© 2019 John Wiley & Sons, Inc. Published 2019 by John Wiley & Sons, Inc.
Companion website: www.wiley.com/go/abernathy/StrategicDigitalMediaEntrepreneur

11

Entrepreneurial Leadership and Culture

The appointment in 2002 of Mathias Döpfner as CEO of Axel Springer was met with skepticism within the half-century-old German publishing company. Promoted from the newspaper division, where he had served as editor of *Die Welt*, 39-year-old Döpfner had been preceded by a revolving door of executives, each with a new vision for the company. Employees braced for the announcement of yet another "strategy."

Hinrich Springer and his son Axel, a reporter and editor, had established Axel Springer in 1946 as a printing company, based in Hamburg. Over the next decade, the company grew by either starting or buying newspapers and magazines, including *Bild*, a tabloid newspaper with an emphasis on crime and sex, and *Die Welt*, the more respectable broadsheet that became the flagship of the enterprise. With tensions mounting between East and West, the company moved its headquarters to West Berlin in 1959 and situated its new building right on the demarcation line. In the 1960s, it towered above the Berlin Wall, serving as a "symbol of freedom," according to the founders. Over the next four decades, the company went public and grew to have both a print and broadcast presence in over 20 countries in Europe and Asia.

Döpfner's appointment at the beginning of the new millennium was controversial with both employees and stockholders, many of whom questioned whether his educational background in music and theater had prepared him to lead the company at a time when the publishing industry was just beginning to feel the economic effects of the Internet. Should the company hunker down, defending, and investing in its legacy media, or should it plunge headfirst into an uncertain digital future? Döpfner didn't hesitate to choose the latter option, laying out a unifying company-wide strategy and goal. Axel Springer, he announced, would become the premier digital media company in Europe.

Yet, despite several acquisitions and partnerships, by 2006 only 1% of the company's revenues came from digital assets. In that year, Germany's antitrust agency rejected Axel Springer's bid to purchase the country's largest television broadcaster. This caused Döpfner to reevaluate his digital strategy. Instead of focusing on acquisitions of legacy broadcast media, he declared that the company would instead focus on organic growth and acquisitions of late-stage digital start-ups. He challenged the employees of the company to produce half of revenue and earnings from digital by 2016.

It seemed like a moonshot at the time. However, a mere decade later, the goal had been reached—and surpassed. It was accomplished in two separate stages—with the first beginning in 2006, and the second in 2012. The transformation of Axel Springer from disrupted legacy print company to disrupting digital pioneer is instructive for both start-ups and traditional media companies. It is a story of leadership—on many levels—during a time of tremendous disruptive change in the industry.

The Strategic Digital Media Entrepreneur, First Edition. Penelope Muse Abernathy and JoAnn Sciarrino.
© 2019 John Wiley & Sons, Inc. Published 2019 by John Wiley & Sons, Inc.
Companion website: www.wiley.com/go/abernathy/StrategicDigitalMediaEntrepreneur

The economics confronting today's media companies require both a new organizational structure and a new leadership style. A media company's core competencies in the digital age—content creation, new revenue development, and technological competitiveness—must align with its organizational structure. Leaders must have the ability to "zoom in and zoom out," as Microsoft founder Bill Gates describes it. They must be *both* outward-looking, constantly surveying the competitive landscape, *and* inwardly focused, identifying real and imagined internal obstacles to change. They must be disruptive, but also realistic in their aspirations; flexible, yet focused on achieving bottom-line results; collaborative, yet decisive. In this chapter, we explore the competing demands and priorities within media organizations and the core skills needed by the leaders of those enterprises.

Among the questions we'll consider:

- What is organizational culture and why is it so important?
- What types of structures and cultures exist in organizations?
- What types of organizational structure and leadership are needed in the Media 2.0 environment?
- What is the role of teams in this new environment?
- What qualities make for successful leaders?

Why Is Organizational Culture So Important?

Culture eats strategy for breakfast.

In his 1985 book entitled *Organizational Culture and Leadership*, Massachusetts Institute of Technology professor Edgar Schein noted, "[c]ulture determines and limits strategy." Over the years, his observation morphed into a more memorable statement—"culture eats strategy for breakfast"—which has been variously attributed to author Peter Drucker (perhaps apocryphally) and Mark Fields, the President of the Ford Motor Company, as well as to a host of other executives and consultants.

In 2008, Clark Gilbert, a former Harvard Business School professor, became CEO of Deseret Management Corporation, which is owned by the Mormon Church. Gilbert's assignment was to reposition the *Deseret News*, the oldest continuously published daily paper in Utah, for the digital era. Looking back on his five-year tenure in 2013, he remarked in an interview for the book, *Saving Community Journalism*,

> There is a joke I tell on myself. I tell my former colleagues [at Harvard] that it's a lot easier to lay out a strategy on a PowerPoint slide than it is to do it in real life. I vastly underestimated the amount of cultural work that would be needed...I now believe that a good strategy is, at best, only 49% of the solution.

While the new economics of media requires transformational change, many firms underestimate the power of culture and only focus on strategy. As Gilbert's statement suggests, if the culture and capabilities of an organization are not aligned and integrated, the strategy will ultimately fail. A recent study by McKinsey & Company suggests only around one quarter of all transformations are successful.

Why is it so difficult for an organization to transform itself? Economists, psychologists, and sociologists often use the term *path dependence* to describe the behavior of organizations, such as Axel Springer prior to 2006 or the *Deseret News* prior to Gilbert's arrival. The decisions companies make are determined by knowledge of how they solved similar problems in the past and the values employees share. Therefore, when confronted with a challenge, they apply the same strategies and values used in the past to address the present-day issue. They literally stay on the same path, even if that path is leading them over the cliff.

Culture consists of the collective values, beliefs, and principles of an organization's members. Organizational culture can affect the way people and groups interact with each other, with clients, and with stakeholders. Schein identified three levels of an organization's culture: (1) visible *artifacts and symbols*; (2) well-articulated and *espoused values*; and (3) shared (often subconscious) *assumptions* and values. Leaders need to understand the factors that determine behaviors and responses in each level in order to affect transformational change. Schein's organizational model is often represented by concentric circles as in Figure 11.1.

Artifacts and symbols are in the outer circle. These are the visible elements of a company's culture that can be recognized by those both inside and outside the organization. This includes everything from the architecture of a company's headquarters to its logos and the dress code of its employees. Leaders can attempt to alter a company's culture by changing its symbols. In 2007, the *New York Times* moved out of its Art Deco style

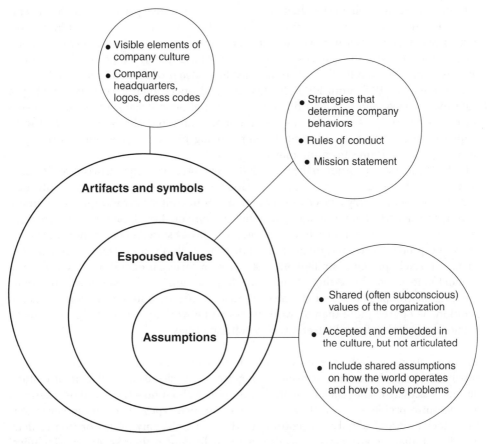

Source: Adapted from Schein, (2013).

Figure 11.1 The three components of Edgar Schein's organizational model.

building off Times Square into a contemporary skyscraper, designed by architect Renzo Piano, across from the Port Authority Terminal, a major transportation hub in the city. The open internal spaces and the transparent glass partitions between offices and floors of the new building were intended to suggest the integration of the print and digital components of the *Times*. Similarly, after making several acquisitions of US-based digital publishing properties, Axel Springer announced in 2016 it was establishing a second "headquarters" in New York City to signify it was "a major media investor" in the country.

Leaders can also attempt to alter the next level—the well-articulated and *espoused values* of an organization. These are the rules of conduct, the mission statement, and the strategies that have determined the outward and inward behaviors of a company. Organizations that "have taken leadership positions in their industries…typically have done so by narrowing their business focus," according to Michael Treacy and Fred Wiersema, authors of *The Discipline of Market Leaders*. They identified three *value disciplines* that most companies focus on—operational excellence, customer intimacy, and product innovation. They concluded that market leaders tended to excel at only one of the value disciplines, while simply meeting industry standards with the other two. The mission statements and strategies tend to reflect the value disciplines a company has chosen to emphasize.

Companies, such as FedEx Express and Walmart, that value operational excellence deliver an extremely reliable product or service, at competitive prices and high convenience. Organizations, such as the Ritz-Carlton and Nordstrom, that succeed in consistently providing customer intimacy use data and stress operational flexibility to respond quickly and precisely to their customers' needs. Those that value product innovation, such as Apple, aim to offer their customers leading-edge products and services. From its establishment in 1997 until 2011, Netflix pursued operational excellence, building a state-of-the-art system that distributed the content of other organizations to a targeted set of customers. As streaming has become more common, Netflix has flipped from emphasizing its distribution system to emphasizing product innovation—creating its own original television shows and movies.

In the Media 1.0 era—prior to the year 2000—news organizations such as Axel Springer achieved market leadership by valuing operational excellence. They were vertically integrated, controlling every aspect of production—from content creation to distribution. Profitability depended on leveraging the efficiency and quality of their various processes and systems. They were typically very siloed, with profit statements for individual divisions and product lines and distinctive cultures in each division. Döpfner indicated a change in Axel Springer's strategy in 2006—from a focus on operational excellence to product innovation—by setting an audacious financial goal, and then immediately reorganizing the company to eliminate the cultural silos that separated print from digital. In addition, he offered more than 50 workshops and networking events designed to teach employees digital skills and introduce new cultural values.

The inner circle of Schein's cultural model—the shared (often subconscious) values of an organization—is always the most difficult to change. These values are not immediately apparent, even to those who are insiders. They are accepted and embedded in the culture, but not articulated. They include shared assumptions about how the world operates and how to solve problems when they arise. There are two types of threats organizations face—technical and adaptive—according to Harvard University professor Ron Heifetz, who has studied how organizations deal with challenges to their strategies. Technical challenges can be solved with current skills, as well as an institutional knowledge of how others solved similar problems. An exogenous, disruptive threat, however, requires adaptive behavior. Old behaviors, skills and values need to be unlearned, before new behaviors can be adopted. "Without learning new ways—changing attitudes, values, and behaviors—people cannot make the adaptive leap necessary to thrive in the new environment," says Heifetz.

In other words, the "DNA" of an organization needs to change. "Adaptive change forces people to question and perhaps redefine aspects of their identity; it also challenges their sense of competence," wrote Heifetz in *Leadership on the Line: Staying Alive through the Dangers of Leading.* "No wonder people resist."

Research by numerous organizational and business scholars has shown that a transformational shift in culture occurs in stages, some overlapping. The first stage involves articulating new values and identifying a guiding coalition of innovative and entrepreneurial employees who understand the business imperative and can easily adapt to the changed environments. These new values and skill sets must be reinforced and supported with new organizational structures, as well as new institutionalized systems of measuring success. Throughout the entire process, it is imperative to periodically step back, reassess strategic direction, and then reinvigorate the cultural transformation.

After establishing a new direction for Axel Springer in 2006, Döpfner reinforced the imperative to change the culture by articulating two new values that would be important to the company's future success. First, cannibalization of current products and services was acceptable, if it had a long-term benefit. Second, entrepreneurial and innovative ideas and employees were welcome. Finally, in place of the old silos, he reorganized the company into three new business segments or divisions, all focused on digital growth: classified advertising, marketing (i.e., serving advertising clients), and paid content.

At the midpoint, in 2012, he made another unorthodox move. He bought three of his top executives one-way tickets to Silicon Valley. Their assignment was to build relationships and learn from the tech giants. These three executives spent six months touring tech start-ups and giants, such as Google and Facebook, asking a lot of questions, and devising new ways to solve the challenges that Axel Springer faced. In 2013, they hosted a management retreat in Silicon Valley for 70 of the company's top executives, sharing what they had learned. Additionally, Döpfner established a rotating six-week Visiting Fellows program in Silicon Valley for Axel Springer employees. As Döpfner realized from the beginning, no matter how well thought-out a strategy may be, transformative change does not occur unless the company develops a new strand of DNA that aligns cultural values with the skill set of the employees.

What Are the Types of Structure and Culture Found in Organizations?

Strategy, culture, *and* structure: all three need to be aligned if there is to be true organizational transformation. A 1978 business classic—"Organizational Strategy, Structure and Process," published in the *Academy of Management Review*—identified three types of strategic organizational structures and three fundamental problems, or challenges, an organization encounters. According to the authors, how a company responds and adapts its strategies to respond to those three strategic challenges depends on its structure and the established processes for dealing with problem-solving that are already in place.

The three types of environmental challenges that confront organizations are: entrepreneurial, engineering, and administrative. Entrepreneurial challenges involve a strategic commitment by an organization to create and launch a new product or service.

Engineering challenges require companies to make a technological and financial commitment to producing and distributing the new product. Administrative challenges involve the formulation and implementation of processes and procedures that will allow the organization not only to produce a specific product, but to continue to evolve and innovate. In order to successfully bring a new product to market—or respond to a competitive threat—an organization must have in place a structure that allows its employees to solve each of these three interrelated and complex challenges.

As a company moves through the various stages of growth—from start-up to the mature phase—the culture changes, from one of risk-taking to one of defensiveness. The structure also tends to change. Start-ups typically assume a structure that encourages prospecting and innovating. Market leaders are typically defenders.

Prospectors create and maintain an environment that encourages continual identification and exploitation of new products and market opportunities. Prospector organizations are in a continuous and fluid state of developing or introducing new products or services. Because the prospector organization is so adept at managing and adapting to change, it often gains market share during periods of disruption. Needless to say, prospectors have a proclivity for living with higher risk than other organizations. Such organizations tend to approach engineering and administrative problems with a great deal of flexibility, not wanting to commit to a single technology and seeking decentralized processes that encourage collaboration. Prospector organizations are usually led by marketing and/or research and development experts, and thrive in high growth or volatile markets. On the downside, prospector organizations often have a breadth of product offerings and struggle with low profit margins. Additionally, they may fail to focus on the most promising markets.

Defenders strive for a stable and predictable environment. These are often market leaders, who approach the launch of new products cautiously. They often create a very narrow product line that is produced and distributed to a potential market and invest significantly in a core technology that is very cost-efficient, but not flexible. The goal of a defender is to anticipate moves by competitors and prevent them from contesting and encroaching on its domain. Defenders often are successful in stable, low-growth industries, however, they tend to be very insular and miss major industry developments or shifts in customer preferences and trends. Organizational structure and processes are focused on the core technology and efficient administration. Therefore, they have little capacity and skill to identify and exploit new market opportunities. In the Media 1.0 era, most legacy media organizations were defenders.

Analyzers attempt to implement a strategy that is a hybrid of the prospector and defender organizations. They seek to exploit market opportunities and launch new products and services, while also maintaining and defending the profitable "cash cows." This is a very difficult balance to maintain, as analyzer organizations must pick and choose opportunities wisely. If existing capabilities can be leveraged to support new opportunities, analyzer organizations can achieve higher profit margins than either defenders or prospectors. However, an analyzer organization must constantly balance stability and flexibility, or risk being neither efficient nor effective.

It is very difficult—if not impossible—for an organization to transition from defender to prospector, without first adopting an analyzer structure. When he announced his digital strategy in 2006, Döpfner sought to achieve a delicate balance between old and new, legacy and start-up, print and digital revenue in Axel Springer. By reorganizing the company into three business segments or divisions—classified advertising, marketing, and paid content—he was able to preserve the "identity" of specific legacy products (such as

Bild and *Die Welt*), while also restructuring the company so it could take advantage of new digital opportunities. Such a restructuring had two strategic advantages. It encouraged the legacy print media products to focus on future revenue growth opportunities (primarily in digital), instead of defending their current market position, which was eroding. Additionally, it allowed executives in the company to more easily target potential digital acquisitions and partnerships that would support revenue growth in one of the three business segments.

Finally, a word of caution about the strategic choices that leaders make on organizational strategy and structure. There is a fourth type of organization—the *reactor*—which is classified as "a strategic failure" in the article cited above ("Organizational Strategy, Structure and Process") because "inconsistencies exist among its strategy, technology, structure and process." Reactor organizations typically evolve from one of the other three types of organizations—prospector, defender, and analyzer. In reactor organizations, leadership has not clearly articulated the organization's strategy, nor has it aligned strategy with structure. Reactors cannot exist for long in a competitive environment and risk becoming road kill.

What Organizational Structure and Leadership do Media Companies Need in the 2.0 Era?

In the Media 1.0 world, successful media organizations typically had a culture that valued operational excellence and a strategic organizational structure designed to defend its profitable market position. The business divisions within large companies were typically organized into product divisions that were vertically integrated—with content creation, packaging, marketing, production, and distribution housed within the division.

In the Media 2.0 era, successful media companies will have a culture that values innovation and a strategic organizational structure designed to encourage prospecting. The primary strategic focus will be that of delivering to the audience a unique value proposition that differentiates one company's content from another. This suggests that the core competencies of a successful media organization will be: creation of engaging content, cultivation of new revenue sources, and savvy use of technology to connect with customers regardless of where they are. Therefore, the most important leadership roles in the media company will be *Chief Content Officer*, *Chief Revenue Officer*, and *Chief Technology Officer*. But these will be very different roles from those of the Media 1.0 era. These roles will be cross-functional, interrelated, and very customer-focused. Additionally, all three will have a highly developed sense of how content, revenue, and technology work together to develop new and sustainable business models.

- *Chief Content Officer*: Whether editor of a newspaper or director of a movie, the Chief Content Officer will be responsible not only for producing quality content, but also for understanding how to engage an audience—both retaining and building the loyalty of current customers, as well as attracting new viewers, visitors, and readers. This will require a sophisticated understanding of audience analytics and marketing techniques, as well as knowledge of how to use technology most effectively to tell compelling stories in multiple ways on multiple platforms—including online forums and offline, in-person events.
- *Chief Revenue Officer*: This important role in the triumvirate expands from that of selling space or time to selling solutions to both advertisers and consumers of the content

produced by a media company. This most likely will require a total rethinking of the advertising sales function so that media companies begin offering a range of marketing services typically offered by ad agencies. Additionally, as digital business models evolve, Chief Revenue Officers will need to understand how to sell content directly to consumers. Therefore, like the Chief Content Officer, the Chief Revenue Officer will need to be very proficient with audience data analysis and have a nuanced understanding of how to use technology to reach current and new consumers wherever and whenever.

- *Chief Technology Officer*: In contrast to the past when the Chief Technology Officer was primarily responsible for keeping the content-creation and distribution systems updated and running efficiently, this new role is outwardly focused, with the aim of providing a unique customer experience—for a company's advertisers, as well as its viewers, visitors, and readers. This means that the Chief Technology Officer must have a nuanced and in-depth understanding of how consumers interact with content and design systems that lead to greater customer engagement and, ultimately, loyalty.

Whether consciously or not, in 2012, Döpfner acknowledged the importance of these three roles in Axel Springer's future digital success when he chose three executives to spend six months in Silicon Valley, learning everything they could. He chose the editor of *Bild* (Chief Content Officer), the CMO of Axel Springer (Chief Revenue Officer), and the founder of Ideolo, a digital price comparison platform (Chief Technology Officer). Their vision for Axel Springer, presented to other executives at the 2013 retreat, acknowledged how interrelated content, revenue, and technology were in the Media 2.0 environment. The core competencies were no longer focused on operational excellence but on innovative ways to connect and engage Axel Springer's customers.

What Is the Best Way to Use Teams?

When a company is faced with a difficult decision, invariably someone suggests, "let's form a team." Teams are not a solution to every organizational problem, according to longtime management consultant Jon Katzenbach, co-author of *The Wisdom of Teams*. Wrongly used, teams can waste time and disrupt performance. However, Katzenbach hastens to add, his research has shown that real teams outperform individuals acting alone or other types of working groups, especially when there is a need to solve a problem that requires multiple skills, perspectives, and experiences.

In uncertain, fast-paced times, leaders of media enterprises need to rely on cross-functional skill sets and multiple viewpoints when making strategic decisions. Therefore, knowing when and how to use a team-based approach to decision-making is critical. Katzenbach distinguishes between three types of functional organizational units—the working group, the real team, and the high-performance team. Most organizational units labeled "teams" are, in fact, what Katzenbach calls working groups, or potential teams. Working groups share information, best practices, and perspectives. Working groups can be quite effective, depending on how they are used and tasked. For example, the three executives that Döpfner sent to Silicon Valley for six months formed a very effective working group. Their assignment: learn everything they could about the digital future and then share it with their colleagues.

In contrast to working groups, real teams have a charter—usually from senior management—that defines an overarching purpose and specific performance goals. Leadership responsibilities on a team are shared (instead of having one designated leader). All members are actively involved in problem-solving, and each member of the team assumes both individual and mutual accountability for delivering a collective work product.

Real teams consist of only a few people—no more than five to seven members, with specific skills, perspectives, and experience. While there is often a good deal of focus on putting together a team with cross-functional skills and knowledge, less attention is paid to the perspectives each team member brings. Just as organizations tend to respond to a strategic challenge or opportunity in one of three ways—either as a prospector, defender, or analyzer—people within an organization often bring similar mindsets to problem-solving. Having a mixture of strategic perspectives on a team is very useful for both start-up media enterprises trying to get to the next level, as well as for legacy media organizations trying to embrace a digital future. Prospectors are adept at finding and exploiting opportunities. Defenders are intent on protecting the overarching mission and values of the company. Analyzers look for ways to minimize risk and maximize profit, and often play a key role in resolving the different approaches of the defenders and prospectors.

In addition, the personalities of the different team members can affect the pace at which members arrive at decisions and the quality of their recommendations. Recent research by Deloitte Consulting identified four types of personalities that are usually present on most teams: pioneers, drivers, guardians, and integrators. Team performance can be significantly improved by understanding how each personality interacts and adjusting the mix of team members, based on what needs to be accomplished. Pioneers and drivers, for example, tend to be very focused on problem-solving, prefer brisk and to-the-point discussion and want to make clear connections between what is being discussed and the presenting problem. On the other hand, integrators and guardians like to focus on getting to know other team members and seeking the perspectives of all stakeholders (including those not on the team). Depending on the problem that needs to be solved and the deadline imposed, the mix of team members can be adjusted based on personality.

Teams are typically best used by media enterprises either to make a specific recommendation—such as suggest a new strategy—or to make or create a new product or service. In addition, recent research by McKinsey and Company also found that cross-functional teams can be very effective in responding to a major company crisis—such as hacking, product defects, hostile takeovers by activist shareholders, and competitive thrusts by new entrants in the market. Significant (and meaningful) performance challenges can energize teams, but Katzenbach notes that high-performance teams are very rare. As distinguished from other teams, members of high-performance teams have an unusually high commitment to one another's performance, as well as to the team's.

Although high-performance teams are rare, Katzenbach urges leaders to encourage the sorts of behavior and values in an organization that nurture team development since interactions and performance at this most basic of levels have the potential to change the DNA of an entire organization. High-performance organizations tend to produce high-performance teams. He identifies these traits that are found in both high-performance companies and teams.

- Breakthrough performance goals aimed at delivering superior results to employees, customers, and shareholders.
- Clear, challenging aspirations in the charter or statement of purpose (i.e., the vision, mission, or strategy statement).
- Committed and focused leadership with an unrelenting dedication to communication, measurement, and experimentation.

- An energized, skilled workforce dedicated to productivity and learning.
- A nurturing of core competencies and skills that give an organization a competitive advantage.
- Open communications and knowledge-sharing at all levels.

What Qualities Make for Successful Leaders?

Especially in recent years, there have been numerous articles in both the scholarly and popular press about the differences between managers and leaders. Often management has gotten a bad rap. Who wants to be a bureaucrat, keeping the trains on time, when you can aspire to be a coach leading your team to victory? Harvard University professor John Kotter was among the first scholars to make a distinction. "Management is a set of processes that keeps an organization running...planning, budgeting, staffing, measuring performance, and problem-solving when results do not go to plan." Leadership, he says, "is always about change," not about mobilizing people to do what they've always done. It's about "aligning people to the vision, about buy-in and communication, motivation and inspiration." In *Leading Change*, he lays out an eight-step plan for accomplishing just that, which begins with creating a "sense of urgency" about the need to change and establishing a guiding coalition of other leaders within the organization to help you lead the change.

Other scholars have pointed out that even during periods of fast-paced change, leadership and management must exist in tandem in high-performance organizations. John Gosling, a professor at the University of Exeter Business School, argues that "a leader needs to inspire employees" to change and achieve goals, while also "thinking of new ways of reaching" goals. In this view, good leaders know how to adapt the principles of management—planning, measuring, and problem-solving—to the challenges the organization faces.

But, how exactly do managers become leaders? In a 2012 article for *Harvard Business Review*, Michael Watkins, professor at the International Institute of Management Development, laid out seven seismic shifts that managers—or leaders of a function—must navigate in others to become leader of an organization (Table 11.1).

A recent study by the executive search firm Russell Reynolds Associates speaks to the yin-and-yang tensions that drive success in the C-suite, and in organizations these executives lead. Effective leaders, the study found, demonstrate a complex mix of abilities and

Table 11.1 Shifting from a manager to a leader.

Specialist to generalist	Aim to understand a wider range of business tools for your organization
Analyst to integrator	Start using cross-functional knowledge to solve problems
Tactician to strategist	Zoom in and out on details
Bricklayer to architect	Learn how to align strategy, structure and operating processes
Problem-solver to agenda-setter	Define key challenges and opportunities
Warrior to diplomat	Influence internal and external stakeholders
Supporting crew to star	Inspire others with your behavior and communications

Source: Adapted from Watkins, (2012).

traits, many of which would seem to be contradictory. For example, during times of fast-paced change, leaders must pursue disruptive strategies, but also be mindful of how fast their organizations are capable of changing. Here is the mix of skills that make for successful C-suite executives, according to Russell Reynolds:

- *Disruptive and pragmatic*: Leaders challenge the status quo and make the case for fundamental change, yet also act as an organizational filter during times of volatility. They understand the practical limits of how much change an organization can absorb.
- *Risk-taking and reluctant*: Leaders thrive in ambiguity and adapt nimbly and quickly. Yet, they also exercise caution in taking risks by discerning and anticipating threats on the horizons.
- *Heroic and vulnerable*: Leaders know their own strengths and display perseverance in the face of challenges. But they are also aware of their own limitations. In other words, they know what they don't know.
- *Galvanizing and connecting*: Leaders inspire trust through charisma, influence, and drive, yet also let others take the spotlight. They empower others to create strong networks within and beyond the organization.

A separate study by Russell Reynolds found that executives who successfully led their organizations through a digital transformation tended to have five traits that distinguished them from other executives. They were innovative and always challenging traditional thinking; disruptive and willing to take calculated risks; bold and decisive; socially adept and could adapt their messages to communicate with different audiences; and finally, they were determined, optimistic, and achievement-oriented.

According to *strategy + business*, the consulting arm of PwC, the most iconic enterprises—from Apple and Amazon to Starbucks—"are exceptionally coherent. They put forth a clear winning value proposition, backed up by distinctive capabilities, and apply this mix of strategy and execution to everything they do." If a company cannot align strategy and execution, "the thousands of decisions made each day by people at every level," then it risks operating at cross-purposes. Yet, in a recent global survey by PwC, less than 10% of business executives rate their company's top leaders as being skilled and effective at both strategy creation and execution. PwC identified 10 characteristics of executives who successfully matched overarching strategic goals with day-to-day implementation at all levels of the organization (Table 11.2).

The 1993 book, *The Wisdom of Teams*, identified five qualities of a successful leader that seem as relevant today as then—whether you are leading a start-up, or attempting, like Döpfner, to fearlessly lead a legacy media organization into an uncertain digital future. First, "leaders clarify purpose and goals." That's self-explanatory, but never easy in uncertain times. Second, "leaders build commitment and self-confidence." Good leaders understand that what motivates an accountant is probably different from what motivates the marketing specialist. Each need to understand how their work contributes to helping the company succeed. Third, "leaders strengthen a team's collective skills." A leader knows his or her weaknesses and strives to build a team in which the individual members have complementary strengths and skills. Fourth, "leaders remove obstacles." That means they're forward-thinkers, always anticipating what lies around the curve. And finally, "leaders create opportunities for others"—not themselves. Smart leaders, though, understand that in performing this seemingly selfless act, they inspire loyalty and devotion from their followers.

Table 11.2 Ten principles of executive success.

1) Aim high	Set ambitious goals for your strategy and execution. Formulate a clear message for why these goals are important.
2) Build on your strengths	Take stock of your strongest capabilities. Where do you excel over your competitors? Analyze what you do best.
3) Be flexible	Cultivate your ability to switch between strategy and execution, zoning in on details and out on strategy.
4) Shore up employee engagement	Explain to your workers why their jobs – and your company – are important.
5) Match structures to strategy	Organize internal structures so they correspond to your overall strategy.
6) Break down barriers	Focus on outcomes, not functions. Encourage collaboration across your organization.
7) Embrace digital	Look for ways to create new digital experiences for your customers.
8) Keep it simple	Be as simple as possible without sacrificing core capabilities and processes.
9) Manage your value chain	Use leading technology to align analytics and processes across your value chain.
10) Seek collective mastery	Seek open, fluid and constant communication across levels.

Exercise: Axel Springer: The Path to Transformation

In retrospect, the successful transformation of Axel Springer from publisher to digital innovator and entrepreneur almost seems easy and pre-ordained. However, when Döpfner laid out his initial vision in 2002—making Axel Springer the premier digital media organization in Europe—he had very few followers. In the first four years of his tenure, the company made only tentative forays into digital, continuing primarily to invest in and acquire legacy media products or companies. A decision by the German government in 2006 to deny Axel Springer's petition to purchase the country's largest television network forced a moment of reckoning on Döpfner and the company. It created, what Harvard Professor John Kotter calls, "a sense of urgency." There was no way to reach the 2016 goal without adjusting strategy.

The new strategy focused on organic growth, as well as investments in late-stage digital companies, many of which had no direct relationship to publishing. The objective of these acquisitions was to learn as much as possible about the technology and then apply the knowledge to the publishing company. In his 2006 reorganization, Döpfner hoped to avoid the perception that there would be winners—the digital enterprises—and losers—the legacy publications and divisions. So he reorganized the company into three business segments, each with specific targets—classified advertising, marketing, and paid content. All three segments had both print and digital components, and were built around the three core competencies of the company: creating quality journalism that would attract subscribers (paid content), knowing how to both attract and reach the audiences that advertisers coveted (marketing), and finding a way to stem the erosion of print-classified revenue (technology).

From the beginning, Axel Springer led the way in both implementing a business model for charging digital subscribers for content *and* developing the technology to give other publishers the ability to charge digital subscribers. Axel Springer's digital distribution platform, iKiosk, released in 2011, is now used by most major magazine and newspaper publishers in the world.

While the first stage was about repositioning the company as a digital enterprise, the second stage, launched in 2012, focused on expanding the company's already significant digital footprint by building, acquiring, or partnering with other companies. The focus was on learning and then integrating the new approach into the company, creating a culture of continuous innovation. Zanox, a digital marketing company, as well as Uber and Airbnb, are among the start-up companies that Axel Springer has either invested in or purchased. In addition, Axel Springer significantly expanded its geographic footprint, purchasing in 2015 and 2016 the US online publishers, Business Insider and eMarketer.

As a self-appointed spokesman for other international publishers, Döpfner also began raising competitive and regulatory questions about the scale and resources of "frenemies," tech giants such as Google and Facebook, who were rapidly become fierce competitors for advertisers and viewers. Simultaneously, Axel Springer began developing technological products—such as the news aggregation site Upday, launched in 2015 to counter the competitive threat of the tech giants.

By 2016, digital revenue accounted for almost two-thirds of Axel Springer's total revenue. In contrast, between 2006 and 2016, many other leading publishers had failed to nudge their digital revenues above 20%, and still others filed for bankruptcy. However, given the continuing decline of print advertising and circulation revenue, Döpfner felt the need to begin a third stage of reinvention, focusing on countering competition from existing rivals, including tech giants such as Facebook and Google, and from start-ups that were still operating just below the visible horizon. He had two objectives: continuing to protect his market leading position in Germany, while finding new ways to grow and transform the company internationally and digitally. Looking back on Döpfner's tenure, consider these questions:

- Döpfner faced tremendous skepticism in the beginning. How did he convince others to follow him in 2006, and again in 2012?
- Successful leaders are adaptive to their environment. Consider all the ways that Döpfner could both directly and indirectly influence the culture and values of Axel Springer.
- What were the keys to Axel Springer's successful transformation?
- What internal and external factors prevented other leading global publishing organizations from achieving a similar evolution?
- What are the applicable lessons for leaders of start-up organizations?
- What's next for Döpfner and for Axel Springer?

Summary

As many executives have observed, creating a new strategy is easy compared to the challenges of implementing it successfully. Leaders of both start-ups and legacy media companies must be able to motivate others to set out on unchartered seas. In order to successfully navigate turbulent waters and make it to the new destination, leaders need to be mindful of both the prevailing culture and the organizational structure of the company.

There are typically three levels of culture in every organization. The first two levels are visible and can be directly influenced by the leadership. This includes *artifacts and symbols*, such as the architecture of a company's headquarters and its dress codes, and the *espoused values*, such as those articulated in a company's mission statement and rules of conduct. In the inner circle are the unspoken values and behaviors of an organization. These are most likely to derail any strategy. Faced with a disruptive threat, organizations need to unlearn behaviors, values, and skills before new ones can be learned. That is why many leaders link the announcement of new strategies with a reorganization of a company's structure since this becomes a powerful symbol that change is occurring, and the ship is sailing.

Classic business literature identifies three types of strategic structures in most companies: *prospectors*, *defenders*, and *analyzers*. Depending on the strategic focus of a company, it responds differently to these three challenges: an entrepreneurial response results in the creation of a new product or service, an engineering response in the development of processes that support the new offering, and an administrative response in the establishment of systems that allow the company to continue innovating. Prior to the spread of the Internet, most media companies were defenders of their market leading positions. In the digital era, they need to become prospectors and analyzers.

The team or working group is the most basic organizational unit in a company. Real teams outperform individuals or any other type of working group in an organization. Media enterprises can effectively use teams to recommend changes in a company's strategy, develop new products and services, and respond to crises. Management and development of teams is as much science as it is art, and requires a mix of skills, perspectives, and experiences. High-performance teams are very rare. High-performance companies and teams share many of the same traits—including a clearly defined vision and a collaborative, energized workforce.

Founders of start-ups, as well as executives in established media companies, must be both managers and leaders. Managers plan, measure, and evaluate current performance. Leadership is about the future and motiving others in an organization to follow a new path. Leaders demonstrate a mix of traits, some of them contradictory. They must be decisive and confident about the future, but also adaptive when confronted with new opportunities and unforeseen circumstances. Leaders of successful digital transformations tend to be innovative, bold in their vision, and socially confident and optimistic (but realistic) about the future.

12

What the Future Holds

We began our journey in 1450 in what is today the German city of Mainz. After years of experimentation, an inventor in his early fifties had finally discovered how to combine four separate processes and print a bound copy of a Bible that was of equal, if not superior, quality to those laboriously produced by monastic scribes. His innovation would revolutionize communication, making possible the rapid dissemination of ideas that spawned political, economic, and social movements. Yet, Johannes Gutenberg lived and died in relative anonymity, oblivious to the far-reaching consequences his invention would have on world history, or even the nascent publishing business.

Flash forward more than 550 years. On our journey through the intervening years, we have met entrepreneurs from around the globe, those in small start-ups, as well as those in media empires. In the previous chapter, we circled back to Germany, this time to the city of Berlin where the CEO of Axel Springer, Mathias Dopfner, had made significant progress transforming a twentieth-century European publisher of newspapers and magazines into a twenty-first-century global digital enterprise. Like all the entrepreneurs in this book, he is attempting to peer into the future and anticipate how digital technology will revolutionize his company's business model.

Streaming videos and e-books are just two digital products that seemed like remote futuristic possibilities in the mid-1990s, as the practice of sending emails was just beginning to take hold. But within a decade, consumer habits had shifted dramatically. The music and publishing industries were the first to be tossed about by the "gales of creative destruction." The very term *creative destruction* embodies both threat (destruction of old business models) and opportunity (creation of new ones). In 2015, two of the world's largest companies in terms of market valuation—Google and Facebook—had not existed two decades previously.

We are at the very beginning of another revolutionary era in communication. Like Gutenberg five centuries ago, we are largely ignorant of the changes in store for the media industry and society. Nevertheless, successful entrepreneurs acknowledge that the business models that underpinned their enterprises for centuries have changed dramatically, and then fix their gaze on the potential unleashed by digital technology. In this book, we've laid out a new business model for media entrepreneurs, one that acknowledges the new business and economic realities. Those who succeed in this new environment will be disciplined and focused, reevaluating their strategies often, but also collaborative and agile, able to adjust course quickly if necessary.

The Strategic Digital Media Entrepreneur, First Edition. Penelope Muse Abernathy and JoAnn Sciarrino.
© 2019 John Wiley & Sons, Inc. Published 2019 by John Wiley & Sons, Inc.
Companion website: www.wiley.com/go/abernathy/StrategicDigitalMediaEntrepreneur

What We Know So Far

There is much that we don't know about what lies ahead. However, much has already come into focus. Before tackling the unknown, let's consider what we have learned so far about the strategic business imperatives for media enterprises in the current environment.

The Customer Will Be the Ultimate Driver of Profitability and Sustainability

Entrepreneurs of all media organizations—including those purely journalistic—need to understand and appreciate how, when, and where customers interact with the products and services an enterprise creates, packages, markets, and distributes. Based on a decade of surveying thousands of firms, the consulting firm, PwC, found that companies focused on enhancing the customer experience consistently reported stronger earnings. Your strategy statement is a promise that you will deliver unique value to your customers. That is why we devoted three chapters to identifying the needs and wants of your current and potential audience, segmenting customers based on their desires, and understanding how best to reach them and enhance relationships with them. Companies that are focused on customer behavior, wants, needs, emotions, and motivations are able to adapt quickly to changes in the ecosystem and anticipate disruptions. "Digital is a behavior, not an audience," as Tom Rosenstiel, executive director of the American Press Institute, likes to stress. While his message is intended for news organizations, it speaks to all media organizations—advertising agencies, as well as entertainment firms.

The Winners Will Be Those Companies with a Tightly Integrated Digital Strategy

Digital capabilities are intangible assets that differentiate your company from others. Capabilities should inform strategy, and your company's strategy should recognize the imperative of digitally transforming every business process—both the external, customer-focused ones, as well as the internal ones that streamline and enhance operations. Digital technology has only begun to penetrate most companies, according to a 2017 study by McKinsey & Company. While media companies have been among the most aggressive in adopting the new technology, there is still much more to be done and the faster the better. According to the McKinsey study, companies that aggressively incorporated digital technology into their strategies had the biggest increase in overall profitability.

Content Is Still King

Digital content needs to meet the changing needs and preferences of consumers. Content in the digital space is being created not only by media enterprises, but also by their customers. Customer-generated content can be more valuable than what is created by the media enterprise since it provides insight into the involvement and engagement of customers. On the other hand, content created by a media enterprise for a specific, targeted audience has the potential to sell at a premium. Technology giants, such as Amazon and Netflix, are increasingly moving into the media space and they are creating content, both to attract more users and subscribers, as well as strengthen their relationship with current customers. These trends require a new mind-set for leaders of technology companies. For example, even though Facebook continued to insist throughout 2016 that it was "not a media company," it began hiring online moderators to assess whether its user-generated content was violent or potentially harmful and should be removed from the site.

How You Bundle Products and Services Can Set You Apart from Your Competitors

This is true whether you are a large cable provider considering *à la carte* pricing of select television channels, or a newspaper publisher partnering with other news outlets to offer your subscribers access to a shared digital platform. Bundling is also important to the digital business models of B2B enterprises, such as the large advertising holding companies that can offer their clients a suite of services—from programmatic buying and data analytics to the creation of native content. Whether B2B or B2C, bundling requires a keen understanding of customer wants, needs, and motivations.

Business Basics Are as Important as Ever

There are numerous ways to measure product, customer, and project profitability. But the bottom line—the profitability of the overall enterprise—remains the ultimate measure of the financial health of an enterprise. Hedge fund managers push leaders of publicly traded companies to increase year-over-year earnings. Venture capitalists are being more frugal, denying a second round of funding to digital start-ups that are not on the path to sustainability. Successful entrepreneurs will know how to link long-term digital strategies to short-term financial results. They will have a nuanced understanding of how each process, product, and service affects the long-term profitability of their company.

Change Is Accelerating

The average lifespan of companies on the S&P 500 today is 16 years—down from 50 years in 1970. This means successful companies will have a strategy in place to completely transform their business models over the same period of time. Start-ups must gain financial traction and reach scale quickly. Established companies must shed costs associated with legacy technologies, even as they attempt to diversify their revenue and income streams. Leaders of both start-ups and established companies must follow the technology and their customers, if they hope to also follow the money.

Scale Matters, Even for Small Enterprises

Scale relates to the size of the potential market. It determines whether an enterprise can segment its audience and offer advertisers access to specific targets at a premium price. Start-ups must move beyond the early adopters of their technology and attract mainstream users. Community newspapers must make attempts to reverse print circulation declines and connect digitally with as large an audience as possible in their geographic markets, so they can offer local advertisers the ability to target specific segments, such as parents or sports fans, with their messages. Also, small community newspapers can compete against the large-scale tech giants—Google and Facebook—by offering their advertisers digital services (such as search engine marketing and website design) that allow small businesses in their area to reach and target a wider audience beyond that of the newspaper.

Local Tastes and Habits Remain Important, Even on the Global Stage

Alibaba, not Amazon, dominates the e-commerce market in China, and WeChat, developed by Tencent, is the most popular mobile instant messaging app. Movies made in Bollywood attract a larger audience in many countries in Asia than those made in Hollywood. That's why it is important—no matter the size of a company—that media entrepreneurs know their audience exceedingly well. In Chapter 10, we provided a digital map that aligns the media environment in which an organization operates with the assets and capabilities it has available to transform its business.

Organizational Culture and Leadership Make the Difference

Executives need to nurture digital leaders at all levels of their organizations, who have the skills and capabilities to make discerning choices every day. They need to establish a culture with a common mindset about the importance of the customer and the customer experience. They need to lead by example, as Dopfner did at Axel Springer. As the 2017 PwC survey concluded, employees need to be "conversant in disciplines outside their own." In most companies, "the skills gap is significant, and closing it will require senior leaders to commit to widespread training…to harness technology."

Increasingly, whether considering entertainment companies or news outlets, the economics of the media business tends to be driving companies toward one of two poles—small and niche, or large in scale and scope. Those media enterprises that survive and thrive—whether traditional existing businesses or start-ups—will be constantly asking: If we succeed, how will we look to our customers? What must my employees learn to provide a unique and valued customer experience? What will this mean for our shareholders?

The Current State of Business

Since 2000, creative destruction has swept across the media landscape, decimating the business models of some media enterprises, while leaving others relatively unscathed, at least for now. In Chapter 4, author and consultant Richard Foster pointed out there are two tipping points that determine whether an existing media enterprise will survive an assault by a disruptive technology. These two inflexions also determine whether a start-up will achieve scale and long-term sustainability. The first occurs when customer behavior changes. That is why both existing and start-up enterprises need to constantly monitor the behavior of current and potential customer targets. The second tipping point occurs when the economics begin to work in favor of the disrupter. This typically occurs when the start-up reaches scale in terms of the size of the audience it attracts to its new product or service. At that point, the disrupter can cut prices and drive the existing enterprise into bankruptcy. Alternatively, it can raise prices and demand a premium for its services.

Here's a snapshot of how the main industries are faring roughly a quarter of a century after the Internet attacked and disrupted their business models.

The News Industry

Arguably the newspaper industry has been hardest hit—at least in the United States and European countries. In only a couple of decades, the Internet—and the new tech giants it spawned, from search to social media—has destroyed the business model that supported print newspapers for almost two centuries. That model, which relied on print advertising dollars for as much as 90% of total revenue, peaked in 2000 in the United States. A mere decade later, newspaper advertising dollars, adjusted for inflation, had fallen below 1950 levels, the year it was first tracked. Over the past decade, newspaper publishers and owners scrambled to cut costs as revenues nose-dived, and to create new digital products for their advertisers and readers. But digital advertising sells for mere cents on the dollar compared to the price of print advertising. Complicating matters, most newspapers were late charging subscriptions or fees to the consumers of their digital content.

By 2011, more people were getting their news online than from print newspapers, according to the Pew Research Center. Despite numerous efforts to attract local business to new digital platforms, most newspapers in the United States—from the *New York Times* (profiled in Chapter 5) to the very small Whiteville *News Reporter* (profiled in Chapter 10)—have continued to experience year-over-year ad revenue declines. That is because under the pre-digital newspaper business model, advertisers were paying, *not* for the content that the newspaper produced and distributed, but instead for access to the newspapers' readers. As readers migrated to the Internet, where they could often get their news free, advertisers followed. Because of both their reach and targeting abilities, Google, Facebook, and Amazon are much more attractive advertising and marketing options for local businesses, even in very small communities. As a result, these tech giants have made significant inroads into small and mid-sized markets, where newspapers often receive less than 5% of the available digital dollars.

This upheaval has led to consolidation in a shrinking industry. In 2014, there were 138 fewer daily papers and more than 500 fewer weeklies in the United States than in 2004, according to a 2016 report by the University of North Carolina, "The Rise of a New Media Baron and the Emerging Threat of News Deserts." During that decade, more than a third of the country's 8,000 newspapers—most of them serving small communities—changed ownership, some sold two or more times. Many of the papers were bought by large investment entities—private equity, hedge, and pension funds—during bankruptcy proceedings in the wake of the 2008 recession. Unlike the newspaper owners of the twentieth century, these new owners lack journalism expertise and a sense of civic mission to the communities that their newspapers served, and therefore focus almost exclusively on financial performance.

Extensive research in the academy, government, and the profession has found that newspapers in the United States have historically helped set the agenda for debate on important policy issues, encouraged regional economic growth, and fostered a sense of geographic community. For that reason, economists have classified the content produced and distributed by newspapers as a *public good* since it has positive spillovers for society at large. This generates expectations of social responsibility for media companies that create news content and (increasingly) for social media platforms that distribute content. In *Democracy's Detectives*, Stanford University economist James Hamilton attempted to quantify the economic impact of investigative pieces on topics such as heroin treatments, hog farms, and the trucking industry. The stories, he argues, saved lives (as a result of the policy changes they inspired) and resulted in an overall improvement in the quality of lives of citizens in those communities. As a result, they had both an economic and a social benefit.

A 2011 Federal Communication Commission (FCC) report, *The Information Needs of Communities*, took note both of the economic peril confronting local news organizations, and of the vitally important role newspapers had historically played in informing citizens in a democracy, especially at the grassroots level. It noted that, by some estimates, US newspapers produce as much as 85% of the "news that feeds democracy." Newspapers have been especially important in covering local news that occurs outside the major metro areas, where regional television stations are located, according to the FCC.

Because the FCC has no regulatory authority over newspapers, its 2011 report could only document the issue and suggest indirect ways that the vital news function could be supported during this period of creative destruction. The report recommended that local cable news channels consider ways they might fill some of the news void and it called for more support for nonprofit ventures. Several hundred nonprofit news organizations have been established since 2004 in the United States. However, most focus on producing international, national, or state news, instead of local news. Additionally, a report by the Knight Foundation in 2015 found that of 20 nonprofit news organizations surveyed, only a handful were on solid financial footing. The average nonprofit news outlet relied on support from philanthropic organizations to cover more than 60% of operating expenses.

Both start-up digital news outlets and long-time newspaper publishers are struggling to develop sustainable business models. Start-ups of news organizations covering local news—versus the national outlets like *theSkimm* or BuzzFeed, which received venture funding,—are primarily dependent on philanthropic largesse and subscribers, while publishers of many newspapers still rely on print advertising and print subscriptions to pay the bills. Both need new business models, focused on connecting with a younger generation and tapping new sources of digital dollars. Additionally, this transition—with the fate of local news hanging in the balance—has already surfaced a number of antitrust and taxation issues that will be determined by decisions made by government agencies and courts over the next decade. Among the issues: Should owners of regional television stations be allowed to purchase newspapers in the same city? Should newspapers be allowed to form an alliance to negotiate with Google and Facebook? Can tax policies encourage more entrepreneurship in existing and start-up news organizations?

The Business-to-Business Information and Data Providers

The large B2B information providers, such as Bloomberg and Reed Elsevier, have fared much better than the news organizations. In fact, they may be the most advantageously positioned of all media sectors. In the latter part of the twentieth century, when large corporations integrated technology into their day-to-day business processes, the B2B media enterprises that supplied these companies with data and information followed suit and converted to digital delivery of their content. Therefore, they, unlike newspapers, were able to quickly shed legacy print and distribution costs, which were significant. Additionally, the information and data they provided could be sold at a premium direct to the corporation. As a result, they have managed to continue to achieve profit margins roughly commensurate with pre-digital levels. With digital technology fully integrated into all their strategies, future success for B2B enterprises—whether information providers or advertising agencies—depends on whether they can create and provide their clients with a unique bundle of products and services that they need and want, in the manner in which they wish to receive and utilize it. As all professions and corporations become more and more data-driven in their business decisions, the B2B media enterprises are expected to provide not only the data, but also the data analytics. That means they must understand the best way to integrate digital capabilities into the user experience, and they need to continuously look for ways to disrupt their own business models, to prevent others from doing so.

The Business-to-Consumer Media Conglomerates

A reckoning is awaiting the large conglomerates that formed in the latter half of the twentieth century. Many of these conglomerates are publicly traded, but, as we discussed in Chapter 3, the majority of the shares are held by investment firms, including hedge and pension fund managers. These institutional investors push these companies to increase year-over-year earnings. However, most of the revenue and income for these conglomerates come from mature or declining industries, such as broadcast or cable. So often executives must make tough choices. Should they milk the "cash cow," or take funds generated by the "cash cow" and invest in a "problem child," in the hopes of making it a "star" (on the BCG matrix, discussed in Chapter 6).

Meanwhile, industry trends and customer behavior are working to undermine the long-term financial underpinnings of the "cash cow." Cord-cutting has continued to erode viewership of both broadcast and cable networks, as audiences increasingly prefer streaming and *à la carte* options. Smaller audiences result in less advertising revenue. If audiences are spending more time online than watching television, ad dollars will shift to the new medium. In 2017, more dollars went to online advertising outlets than to television in the United States—a pivotal tipping point. Therefore, television networks can expect to experience continued erosion of traditional advertising revenue in the years ahead. As for the large book publishers and movie studios, their consumers have more choices online and offline than ever before. This puts a premium on understanding the wants and demands of ever narrower segments of audiences and then figuring how to best reach those customers through digital marketing and distribution channels. In the meantime, they remain dependent on the blockbuster hits to pay the bills.

These two dynamics—pressure from investors and a rapidly shifting media landscape—have led to a constant reshuffling of the deck through mergers, acquisitions, and divestitures. Divisions within these conglomerates are spun off from the parent company. News Corp and Gannett, for example, separated their newspaper divisions from the other faster-growing broadcast and film assets, in 2013 and 2015, respectively. The newspaper companies retained the parent company's name while the other divisions were given a new corporate name—21st Century Fox and Tegna—perhaps in an attempt to suggest a break with past business practices. Once spun off, these new enterprises often merge with or acquire other companies. Time Warner Cable spun off from Time Warner in 2009, then merged with Charter Communications and Bright House Networks under the Spectrum name in 2017. Other large cable providers, such as Comcast, subsume content providers, such as NBC Universal, under their brand name. Smaller niche cable networks—such as Discovery—acquire other networks—Scripps Network Interactive—in an attempt to attract advertisers and marketers who want to target a specific customer segment. The game of musical chairs will most likely increase as the media conglomerates look to prop up the revenue from mature businesses, while simultaneously seeking to acquire the next "digital" star that will help them transform their business models.

The Technology Companies

Even the technology companies face issues and some degree of economic uncertainty as smartphone growth, which has propelled online advertising, slows. Also, as more audiences embrace digital viewing, regulatory questions loom around the future of net neutrality in the United States, and whether telecommunications and cable operators should be allowed to charge more for delivery of data-intensive streaming content. As a result, many US tech giants have looked abroad for growth. But in some of the largest international markets, such as China and India, the tech giants often find it difficult to win market share from already established local companies. This is especially true when local companies are protected by the government through regulations that limit foreign ownership to minority stakes, or require onerous licensing procedures. The tech giants—Amazon, Apple, Microsoft, Google, and Facebook—are also confronting regulatory and antitrust scrutiny in Europe concerning the scale and scope of their empires, and questions about whether their strategies and tactics prevent the entry of new competitors.

Additionally, as they become more similar to media companies by offering content and unfettered access to information, the executives of the tech companies are confronting the same issues that traditional media companies have confronted in the past. In the wake of the 2016 US presidential elections, for example, Facebook faced criticism for the way it selected articles for its news feeds, even though CEO Mark Zuckerberg has consistently maintained that Facebook is a "technology company, not a media company." There have been similar issues of editorial judgment raised over videos that have surfaced on social media, portraying or inciting violence (including deaths, kidnapping, torture, and suicide). As they seek to increase their market share in countries outside the United States, the tech giants also routinely confront issues over censorship and privacy. Should they, for example, acquiesce when a foreign government demands censorship of content or access to sites outside the country? Under pressure from the Chinese government, which was attempting to block access to certain foreign sites and services, Apple agreed to remove the *New York Times* news app from its App Store in China in 2016. Then, in July 2017, it removed several VPN (virtual private network) services, which Chinese residents used to get around government censorship of sites such as the *New York Times*. Decisions such as the ones Apple made in China, and the ones Facebook made about monitoring and removing offensive material, are often based on both business strategic objectives, as well as a company's spoken and unspoken values. China is a very important market for Apple because of its size and projections of growth in the mobile market. So, Apple pushed aside concerns about censorship and agreed to remove the apps, rather than risk its position in the market.

Strategic decision-making often involves making ethical and value-based choices. Several of the companies highlighted in this book have made ethical decisions that have come back to haunt them. This includes the controversy surrounding the NFL's dismissive response to numerous studies that documented permanent brain damage suffered by players who had suffered repeated concussions on the playing field. Similarly, in the summer of 2016, in the months leading up to the US presidential election, Fox News, the powerhouse cable network owned by 21st Century Fox, confronted allegations that it had made a series of payouts over more than a decade to cover up allegations of sexual harassment by its CEO and a highly-rated commentator. Both were forced to resign, and primetime ratings for the network suffered.

A study by EY (formerly Ernst and Young) asked 1,470 executives of international companies this question: "What is the main purpose of your corporation: maximizing shareholder return, bringing value to customers, creating value for employees or creating value for stakeholders (including society and the environment)?" Most US executives—41%—chose bringing value to customers, while a majority of Chinese executives—67%—chose creating value for stakeholders. Regardless of whether a company prioritizes customer and stakeholder value, both can be destroyed by bad strategic decisions. In a digital and globally connected era, executives are routinely confronted with strategic decisions that require ethical or value-based judgment calls. Quite apart from the disruption to business models caused by the adoption of the Internet, questionable ethical decisions can impact the bottom line, customer relationships, a media company's reputation, and its long-term sustainability. This is true for start-ups and multinational corporations, or technology companies and newspapers.

So You Want to Be a Successful Entrepreneur?

Perhaps enticed by visions of creating the next Google or Facebook, entrepreneurs form approximately 600,000 new businesses each year in the United States, according to the Small Business Administration. At least half will fail within five years, and, at most, only a third will make it to the ten-year mark, according to a survey by the US Department of Labor Statistics, which counts all businesses that have employees, even if they are not making a profit. Other surveys, which consider the profitability of a firm, place the ten-year failure rate much higher—between 75% and 95%. How do you beat such daunting odds? Recent research has focused on several key steps that entrepreneurs should take at the very beginning that can increase the odds of long-term success.

First, Do Your Homework on the Market

The success rate is almost double for start-ups that have a business plan, according to a small business survey conducted by Wells Fargo. As discussed in Chapter 5, a key component of any business plan is a thorough industry and competitive analysis. This will map out all competitors, describing how long they've existed, their performance, and their customer profile. It will also offer insights into the size of the market, as well as the customer wants, needs, emotions, and motivations (discussed in Chapter 6). The market intelligence firm, CB Insights, conducted 101 post-mortem essays written by founders of start-ups that failed. Forty-two percent of the founders cited the lack of a market need for their product or service as the number one reason their company failed.

In interviews with the *Harvard Business Review*, two venture capitalists weighed in on the importance of having a thorough understanding of your market. "It's all about the market," said Sonja Hoel Perkins, Managing Director of Menlo Ventures.

> I always look at the market first. Market is not how to sell a can of Coke or a car on TV. It's more strategic than that. It includes evaluating market growth, market size, competition and customer adoption rates...We funded a deal once because we really liked the CEO; he's a really great CEO. Unfortunately the company wasn't a great company because it didn't have a large enough market.

Robert Simon, then director at the venture firm Alta Partners, added, "Under the heading of market, we have customer pain. How much pain does the customer feel and how much will the customer pay to solve it? We get to market size by estimating how many customers feel the pain."

Test Your Plan and Be Willing to Change It

Roughly half of all start-ups do not have a business plan, with specified financial and growth targets, based on market and customer insights gained from research and competitive analysis. As a result, they enter the market without any sort of reliable benchmarks that can indicate whether they are on the right path, in the long term. Approximately 80% of start-ups will make it through the first year, but will slowly fail over the next four years, dragging out the inevitable. According to the research done by CB Insights, 29% of start-up entrepreneurs who failed said they shuttered their company because it ran out of cash.

That is why many consultants and venture capital funders are now advocating that companies learn how to "fail fast" so they can adjust their business plans and strategies. Using this approach, entrepreneurs adopt the mindset of drug manufacturers who test many potential products before successfully bringing one to market. Steve Blank, professor at Stanford Business School, advocates launching a lean start-up, testing hypotheses early and frequently, assuming you will fail several times before finding the right approach. Blank recommends analyzing such key strategic components as those discussed in Chapters 5–10: value propositions, customer relationships and segments, channels for reaching customers, and the resources you will deploy. After you've articulated your hypothesis, it's time to talk to as many customers as possible about the product or service you plan to bring to market. If customer feedback reveals your business hypotheses are wrong, you need revise them or pivot to new ones. (Chapter 7 discussed human-centered design techniques and methods for mapping the customer journey.)

In an article for the *Harvard Business Review*, "Beating the Odds When You Launch a New Venture," Clark Gilbert and Matthew Eyring, wrote:

> At the start of a new venture the only thing you can know about your initial strategy is that it's probably part right and part wrong. One of our colleagues conducted a study of the Inc 500 entrepreneurs and found the most successful ventures had redirected their strategy at least five times before they hit a solid growth trajectory.

Make It Legal

Many entrepreneurs wait to legally register their company, opening themselves up to a range of liabilities, including claims that they stole an idea. Registration is relatively inexpensive and can be done with or without a lawyer. Consultants recommend registration as an initial step, even if you plan to leave your company dormant for the first year or so. Professors Tanya Marcum and Eden Blair at Indiana University's Kelley School of Business note that entrepreneurs often undervalue the legal implications of their early decisions because they lack the time and knowledge to make deliberative and reflective decisions. They recommend getting a legal advisor, and incorporating, if entrepreneurs can answer yes to any of the following decisions:

- Is this an idea about a product or service?
- Have others have been contacted about joining the venture?
- Has a business name has been created?
- Have there been discussions about designing a prototype?
- Will financing be sought?

Choose People Wisely

The choice of co-founders and first hires can determine the initial success of a venture, especially during the early lean years. Most start-ups have more than one founder, even though there is usually a single person primarily responsible for coming up with the idea and putting together the initial team. Steve Hogan, head of Tech-Rx, which helps turn around failing tech companies, says that companies with only one founder are most likely to fail. Therefore, he advocates choosing at least one other co-founding partner. As we discussed in Chapter 11, there are really three legs—content, technology, and marketing—to a successful media strategy. Failure of any of the legs and the stool collapses. Therefore, co-founders and/or first hires should be chosen based on their knowledge and skills in one of these three areas.

Harvard Business School professor Noam Wasserman found that a relational team—one consisting of friends and family—is common among start-ups because it's easy to form and members have a high initial level of trust in one another. However, the long-term disadvantages of a relational team can often outweigh its early benefits. Relational teams tend to be too homogeneous in their problem-solving and often avoid addressing contentious issues. His research suggests that teams composed of past co-workers are the most stable as the venture progresses. Wasserman also found that it was essential to define the roles and rewards of start-up employees. All start-ups need a clear decision-making process. Many start out as consensus-based and evolve to be more hierarchical. When negotiating the initial equity split with co-founders, consider each founder's past and current contributions to the venture, as well as the expected future contributions.

Research Your Investors and Consider All Options

According to research conducted by Babson College, over half of shuttered businesses failed because of lack of profits or financial funding. One of the biggest issues is under-capitalization in the early years. As we discussed in the Chapter 3, most start-ups are initially reliant on friends, family, and loans. In an interview with the *Wall Street Journal*, Toby Haas, professor at the University of California at Berkeley, described this as "boot-strapping your company [by]…not drawing a salary and depleting whatever savings you have." That is why it is critical that entrepreneurs have a well-thought-out business plan and use the lean start-up model (advocated by Stanford professor Steve Blank) in order to preserve capital in the early years.

Companies without venture backing tend to fail more often in the first four years than venture-backed companies, because they don't have the money to continue operating if the business model fails, according to Harvard Business School professor Shikhar Ghosh. In contrast, most venture-backed companies failed between the fourth and eighth years, when investors stopped injecting capital into the business. But the reality is, *very few companies* ever qualify for venture funding. Of the 600,000 start-ups in the United States, only 300 or so will receive significant venture funding in any given year. That means 99.95% of start-ups will not receive funding. Bloomberg examined 890 US start-ups founded between 2009 and 2015 that had received at least $20 million in venture and other equity funding. They found that 93% of the founders were male, and California was the most popular place for entrepreneurs to set up shop. Some 57% of the companies that got venture funding were later acquired by larger companies. Venture capitalists say that their due diligence process is the same for a $1 million deal as a $10 million deal, according to a 2017 article in *Fortune* magazine. In general, though, the largest venture investors target companies with the potential to generate revenue in excess of $100 million, or even $500 million, in three to five years.

There are both advantages and disadvantages to venture funding. Research by John Mullins, professor at the London Business School, found that the vast majority of successful entrepreneurs never take any venture capital. He noted two major drawbacks to venture funding in the early years. First, serving the interest of venture investors distracted start-up founders from engaging with customers. Second, the term sheets and shareholder agreements often substantially reduced the co-founders' stake in the company. By building your start-up to a level where your potential is evident, you are more likely to attract the interest of venture funds. This allows you to research and choose the right venture firm, negotiate better terms, and keep more control. Among the questions you should ask when researching potential venture investors: Does your proposal meet the firm's criteria in terms of industry, stage, and geography? Does the fund have money to invest? How big is the fund? Does the fund have the manpower to do your deal? Does the firm have technical and business skills? Be sure to do reference checks.

In the end, venture capital often gives entrepreneurs the potential to fail—or succeed—spectacularly. In 2017, there were 105 "unicorns" (start-up companies worth more than $1 billion) in the United States. The two unicorns with the most funding were Uber, with $15 billion raised, and Airbnb, with $4.4 billion. California had the highest number of unicorns—62—followed by New York with 15. The other ten states where unicorns were located had five or less.

If you are convinced you have the next Google or Facebook, and need to seek venture funding, there is some good news. The number and the size of venture funds are increasing. In 2016, US-based venture firms raised 30 funds totaling at least $500 million each, according to Dow Jones Venture Source. This is up from 17 funds in 2015, and is the most in a year since 2000, when there were 54.

What We Still Don't know

L.A. Noire, a video game released in 2011, caught the attention of several media and literary critics. The game featured a plot and visual esthetics reminiscent of the film noirs of the 1940s and 1950s. A new digital motion technology captured the facial expressions of the actors from numerous angles, rendering them almost lifelike. The plot featured twists and turns that could result in hundreds of endings. Essentially users of the game created their own plots. *L.A. Noire* became the first video game to be shown at the Tribeca Film Festival. Literary critics commented on the ingenious plot and wondered if the game might presage a new direction for fictionalized novels, as well as movies, in the twenty-first century. As one critic put it, the novel has followed its current form for almost three centuries, and is overdue for a major disruptive innovation. Digital technology now offers the prospect of taking the words on the iPad screen and giving users an entirely new experience. Might this be the dawn of a new age for the novel?

In 2017, Mary Meeker, longtime Internet analyst with Kleiner Perkins Caufield and Byers, spent a considerable portion of her annual report (a collection of 355 slides) discussing interactive gaming. She noted how immersive gaming tools were being used by organizations, ranging from the military to professional sports teams, to improve performance. She also noted the number of CEOs—including Elon Musk and Mark Zuckerberg—who credit video games with sparking their interest in both digital technology and innovation. Could interactive gaming be preparing "society for the ongoing rise of human-computer interaction?" she asked.

In the twentieth century, the various mediums were defined by the content they produced and the manner in which they were distributed. The experience of reading a book was not the same as viewing a film, or playing a video game. As the digital features of the various mediums become more and more similar, it is worth considering Meeker's question as we peer into the immediate future and contemplate all the various digital technologies that have the potential to enrich our customers' experiences and their interactions with us.

The Internet of Things (IoT) connects us constantly to our devices and lets us communicate with them. Drones give us the ability to view our lives from many angles. Augmented reality (AR) has already taken hold on Snap and Facebook's Instagram. AR and virtual reality (VR) have the potential to transform our experiences with movies, television programs, digital books, and interactive games—as well as, potentially, the news and information we receive.

Our distribution technology can be transformed with 3D printing. Artificial intelligence (AI) and robotics can transform our business and design processes. And, don't forget blockchain, the tracking system for the first digital currency, Bitcoin. "The technology likely to have the greatest impact on the next few decades has arrived. And it's not social media. It's not big data. It's not robotics. It's not even AI," according to strategy consultant and author Don Tapscott. "You'll be surprised to learn that it's the underlying technology of digital currencies. It's called the blockchain." Technologists foresee that blockchain will disrupt industries ranging from real estate to banking, and can improve everything from electronic voting to management of patient health care information. Is it so far-fetched to assume it might also significantly affect the creation, packaging, and distribution of content produced by media enterprises?

Technology consultants emphatically believe we've only begun to glimpse the future and our digital potential. The key to effecting digital transformation within a business, say the PwC consultants who conduct an annual Digital IQ survey of industry, is to have a "dedicated in-house team with a systematic approach to determining which...technologies [are] critical to evolving the business and which will ultimately end up as distractions." They recommend that companies

> start by identifying a tangible business goal that addresses a problem that cannot be solved with existing technology...and then develop the talent, digital innovation capabilities, and user experience to solve it. These three areas are...all equally important; choosing to focus on just one or two won't be enough.

In a 2015 article for *Foreign Affairs*, Klaus Schwab, founder and executive chairman of the World Economic Forum, the annual gathering of global business and political leaders in Davos, Switzerland, wrote:

> We stand on the brink of a technological revolution that will fundamentally alter the way we live, work, and relate to one another. In its scale, scope, and complexity, the transformation will be unlike anything humankind has experienced before.... Now a Fourth Industrial Revolution is building on the Third, the digital revolution that has been occurring since the middle of the last century. It is characterized by a fusion of technologies that is blurring the lines between the physical, digital, and biological spheres...When compared with previous industrial revolutions, the Fourth is evolving at an exponential rather than a linear pace. Moreover, it is disrupting almost every industry in every country...The possibilities of billions of people connected by mobile devices, with unprecedented processing power, storage capacity, and access to knowledge, are unlimited. And these possibilities will be multiplied by emerging technology breakthroughs in fields such as artificial

intelligence, robotics, the Internet of Things, autonomous vehicles, 3-D printing, nanotechnology, biotechnology, materials science, energy storage, and quantum computing.

As current and future media entrepreneurs contemplate how they should respond to the challenges and opportunities confronting them, take a moment to travel back in time. Imagine purchasing a Gutenberg Bible in 1455 and holding that exquisite creation in your hands. Before then, could you have imagined that a hand-operated wooden press—a rather ugly piece of equipment—could produce a rendering as rich as that of the artisan scribes?

Over the past five centuries, media enterprises have brought stories to life through the printed and spoken word, over airwaves, and on celluloid and vinyl. Now, at the start of a new millennium, a new medium—digital technology—has the power to transform the art of story-telling once again. Flash forward another five, or ten, years into the future. What is the story you want your shareholders, employees, and, most of all, your customers to be telling about you?

How to Use the Complementary Instructional Website

How you approach a book such as this will depend on whether you are a student or an instructor. In either case, you'll undoubtedly want to know more about certain topics. Therefore, we've created two websites with online and interactive material that will complement and expand upon what is bound together in this print copy.

On the instructor's website, www.wiley.com/go/abernathy/StrategicDigitalMedia Entrepreneur, you'll find lesson plans for each chapter, PowerPoint presentations that summarize the main points and can be used in a classroom, potential assignments related to the case studies or exercises in each chapter, updates to the case studies, and suggested supplemental readings.

On the student and professional website, www.cislm.org/digitalstrategy, you'll find essays and interviews with innovators and entrepreneurs in for-profit and nonprofit media enterprises who are attempting to develop sustainable digital business models, as well as prognosticators who are anticipating "the next big thing." They'll share insights they've gained and lessons learned so you don't have to reinvent the wheel. There will also be podcasts, videos and webinars that explain the concepts in the book. For example, short instructional videos explain how to calculate the financial value of a media enterprise, or how to map a customer's journey from awareness of your media offering to purchase and re-purchase. This book is part of a broader initiative, the Center for Innovation and Sustainability in Local Media, funded by a grant from the Knight Foundation. Therefore, you are also encouraged to explore the broad range of resources housed on the Center's site, www.cislm.org, including material provided by our faculty and research colleagues at the School of Media and Journalism at the University of North Carolina at Chapel Hill.

As both an innovator and entrepreneur, you'll encounter exciting possibilities and challenging obstacles. The journey ahead is unpredictable. You need a strategic framework for making short-term and long-term decisions. Our websites will offer opportunities for you to give us feedback that we can share with others as they, too, set out on an adventure of discovery in the digital age.

The Strategic Digital Media Entrepreneur, First Edition. Penelope Muse Abernathy and JoAnn Sciarrino.
© 2019 John Wiley & Sons, Inc. Published 2019 by John Wiley & Sons, Inc.
Companion website: www.wiley.com/go/abernathy/StrategicDigitalMediaEntrepreneur

References

References are listed by chapter (1–12) and by subject matter (e.g. "History of Communication Innovation" or "Book Industry"), in the order in which they are cited in each chapter. References for the case studies included in each chapter are listed separately at the end of each chapter listing (e.g. Case Study: Facebook).

Chapter 1 From Gutenberg to Zuckerberg

History of Communication Innovation

Man, John. *Gutenberg: How One Man Remade the World with Words*. New York: John Wiley & Sons, 2002.

The Gutenberg Museum Mainz. http://www.gutenberg-museum.de/index.php?id=29&L=1. (accessed August 17, 2017).

Eisenstein, Elizabeth. *The Print Revolution in Early Modern Europe*. Cambridge: Cambridge University Press, 2005.

Moran, James. *Printing Presses: History and Development from the 15th Century to Modern Times*. Berkeley: University of California Press, 1973.

Suarez S.F., Michael F. Suarez and H. W. Woudhuysen. *The Book: A Global History*. Oxford: Oxford University Press, 2013.

Wheen, Andrew. *Dot Dash to Dot.Com: How Modern Telecommunications Evolved from the Telegraph to the Internet*. New York: Springer Praxis, 2010.

Baldwin, Neil. *Edison: Inventing the Century*. Chicago: University of Chicago Press, 2001.

Dixon, Wheeler, and Gwendolyn Foster. *A Short History of Film*. New Brunswick, NJ: Rutgers University Press, 2008.

Abramson, Albert. *The History of Television: 1942 to 2000*. Jefferson, NC: McFarland & Company, 2003.

Jurgensen, John. "How Many TV Shows Can Your Brain Handle?" *Wall Street Journal*, June 12, 2015.

Isaacson, Walter. *The Innovators: How a Group of Hackers, Geniuses and Geeks Created the Digital Revolution*. New York: Simon & Schuster, 2014.

Schwab, Klaus. "The Fourth Industrial Revolution: What It Means and How to Respond." *Foreign Affairs*, December 12, 2015. https://www.foreignaffairs.com/articles/2015-12-12/fourth-industrial-revolution.

Drucker, Peter F. *Innovation and Entrepreneurship: Practice and Principle*. Oxford: Elsevier, 1985.

The Strategic Digital Media Entrepreneur, First Edition. Penelope Muse Abernathy and JoAnn Sciarrino.
© 2019 John Wiley & Sons, Inc. Published 2019 by John Wiley & Sons, Inc.
Companion website: www.wiley.com/go/abernathy/StrategicDigitalMediaEntrepreneur

Innovation and Entrepreneurship Research

Christensen, Clayton M., Michael E. Raynor, and Rory McDonald. "What Is Disruptive Innovation?" *Harvard Business Review* 93, no. 12 (December 2015): 44–53.

Christensen, Clayton M. *The Innovator's Dilemma: When New Technologies Cause Great Firms to Fail.* Boston: Harvard Business School Press, 1997.

Christensen, Clayton M., and Michael E. Raynor. *The Innovator's Solution: Creating and Sustaining New Growth.* Boston: Harvard Business School Press, 2003.

Lepore, Jill. "The Disruption Machine: What the Gospel of Innovation Gets Wrong." *New Yorker,* June 23, 2014. http://www.newyorker.com/magazine/2014/06/23/the-disruption-machine

Dyer, Jeffrey H., Hal Gregersen, and Clayton M. Christensen. "The Innovator's DNA." *Harvard Business Review* 87, no. 12 (December 2009): 60–67.

Dyer, Jeff, Hal Gregersen, and Clayton M. Christensen. *The Innovator's DNA: Mastering the Five Skills of Disruptive Innovators.* Boston: Harvard Business Review Press, 2011.

Allen, James. "The Surprising Truth Behind the Myth of the Lone Entrepreneur." *The Experts* (blog), *Wall Street Journal,* May 6, 2016. https://blogs.wsj.com/experts/2016/05/06/the-surprising-truth-behind-the-myth-of-the-lone-entrepreneur/

Picken, Joseph C. "From Founder to CEO: An Entrepreneur's Roadmap." *Business Horizons* 60, no. 1 (January–February 2017). https://doi.org/10.1016/j.bushor.2016.09.004

Hamm, John. "Why Entrepreneurs Don't Scale." *Harvard Business Review* 80, no. 12 (December 2002): 110–115.

Case Study: Facebook

Moss, Caroline. "Mark Zuckerberg: 'We Just Cared More.'" *Business Insider*, February 4, 2014. http://www.businessinsider.com/open-letter-from-mark-zuckerberg-2014-2

Hjelmgaard, Kim. "Mark Zuckerberg Reflects on Facebook at 10." *USA Today*, February 4, 2014. https://www.usatoday.com/story/tech/2014/02/04/facebook-10-years-zuckerberg-message/5198787/

Pepitone, Julianne and Stacy Cowley. "Facebook's First Big Investor, Peter Thiel, Cashes Out." *CNNMoney*, August 20, 2012. http://money.cnn.com/2012/08/20/technology/facebook-peter-thiel/index.html

Manjoo, Farhad. "The Great Tech War of 2012." *Fast Company*, October 17, 2011. https://www.fastcompany.com/1784824/great-tech-war-2012

Kirkpatrick, David. *The Facebook Effect*. New York: Simon & Schuster, 2011.

Williams, Jed. *Facebook's Historic IPO: BIA Kelsey's Take*. BIA Kelsey Advisory #12-03. Chantilly, VA: BIA/Kelsey, February 10, 2012.

Williams, Jed. "The Morning After... What We Really Learned from Facebook's Earnings Call." *BIA/Kelsey* (blog), July 27, 2017. http://blog.biakelsey.com/index.php/2012/07/27/the-morning-after-what-we-really-learned-from-facebooks-earnings-call/

Bothun, Deborah, and Emmanuelle Rivet. "Facebook's Carolyn Everson on Connecting at Scale." *strategy+business*, June 7, 2016. https://www.strategy-business.com/article/Facebooks-Carolyn-Everson-on-Connecting-at-Scale?gko=20eb8&utm_source=itw&utm_medium=20160825&utm_campaign=resp

Facebook, Inc., Annual Report (Form 10-K), (February 3, 2017). https://www.sec.gov/Archives/edgar/data/1326801/000132680117000007/fb-12312016x10k.htm

Chapter 2 The Story Behind the Numbers

Understanding Financial Statements

Taparia, Jay. *Understanding Financial Statements: A Journalist's Guide*. Oak Park, IL: Marion Street Press, 2003.

Harvard Business Review. *Finance Basics: Decode the Jargon, Navigate Key Statements, Gauge Performance*. 20 Minute Manager Series. Boston: Harvard Business Review Press, 2014. See esp. "Navigating the Three Major Financial Statements."

U.S. Securities and Exchange Commission. "Beginner's Guide to financial Statements." *Investor Publications*. Last modified February 5, 2007. https://www.sec.gov/reportspubs/investor-publications/investorpubsbegfinstmtguidehtm.html

QuickMBA. "The Four Financial Statements." http://www.quickmba.com/accounting/fin/statements/ (accessed August 19, 2017).

Ittelson, Thomas R. *Financial Statements: A Step-by-Step Guide to Understanding and Creating Financial Statements*. Revised and expanded edition. Franklin Lakes: Career Press, 2009.

News Corp, Annual Report (Form 10-K), (August 13, 2015). https://www.sec.gov/Archives/edgar/data/1564708/000119312515288946/d55323d10k.htm

News Corp, Annual Report (Form 10-K), (August 12, 2016). https://www.sec.gov/Archives/edgar/data/1564708/000119312516679975/d210462d10k.htm

Bertelsmann. "Financial Reports." https://www.bertelsmann.com/investor-relations/financial-publications/financial-reports/ (accessed August 19, 2017).

New York Times Company. *2015 Annual Report*. February 24, 2016. http://s1.q4cdn.com/156149269/files/doc_financials/annual/2015/Bookmarked-2015-Annual-Report.pdf

Szalai, George. "News Corp. Unveils Post-Split Logo Based on Rupert Murdoch's Handwriting." *Hollywood Reporter*, May 28, 2013. http://www.hollywoodreporter.com/news/news-corp-post-split-logo-559126

Friedman, Jon. "Can the New News Corp. Overcome the Old Skeptics?" *Motley Fool*, July 26, 2013. https://www.fool.com/investing/general/2013/07/26/can-the-new-news-corp-overcome-the-old-skeptics.aspx

Schumpeter, Joseph A. *Capitalism, Socialism and Democracy*. New York: Harper & Row, 1950.

The Book Industry

Greco, Albert N., Jim Milliot, and Robert M. Wharton. *The Book Publishing Industry*. Third Edition. New York: Routledge, 2014.

Rivera, Edward. *Book Publishing in the US*. IBIS World Industry Report 51113. IBIS World, Inc., 2017.

Rich, Motoko. "Math of Publishing Meets the E-Book." *New York Times*, February 28, 2010.

Hughes, Evan. "Book Publishers Scramble to Rewrite Their Future." *Wired*, March 19, 2013. https://www.wired.com/2013/03/publishing-industry-next-chapter/

"Burying the Hachette: Amazon Plays Tough with Publishers over E-Book Prices." *Economist*, May 31, 2014. https://www.economist.com/news/business/21603036-amazon-plays-tough-publishers-over-e-book-prices-burying-hachette

Bluestone, Marisa. "U.S. Publishing Industry's Annual Survey Reveals $28 Billion in Revenue in 2014." *Association of American Publishers*, June 10, 2015. http://publishers.org/news/us-publishing-industry%E2%80%99s-annual-survey-reveals-28-billion-revenue-2014

Friedman, Jane. "The State of the Publishing Industry in 5 Charts." *Jane Friedman* (blog), September 24, 2015. https://www.janefriedman.com/the-state-of-the-publishing-industry-in-5-charts/

Maryles, Daisy. "The Year in Bestsellers: 2015." *Publisher's Weekly*, January 8, 2016. https://www.publishersweekly.com/pw/by-topic/industry-news/bookselling/article/69108-the-year-in-bestsellers.html

"Many Thought the Tablet Would Kill the Ereader. Why It Didn't Happen: Ereader Usage Still Growing, Especially Among Older Americans." *eMarketer*, February 29, 2016. http://www.emarketer.com/Article/Many-Thought-Tablet-Would-Kill-Ereader-Why-Didnt-Happen/1013638?ecid=NL1001#sthash.pVe6Ju1m.dpuf

McIlroy, Thad. "What the Big 5's Financial Reports Reveal About the State of Traditional Book Publishing" *BookBusiness*, August 5, 2016. http://www.bookbusinessmag.com/post/big-5-financial-reports-reveal-state-traditional-book-publishing/

Sherer, John. Director, UNC Press, in discussion with author on economics of book publishing, February 17, 2017.

HarperCollins Publishers. "Company Profile." http://corporate.harpercollins.com/about-us/company-profile (accessed August 19, 2017).

HarperCollins Publishers. "HarperCollins Worldwide." http://corporate.harpercollins.com/publishing-divisions (accessed August 19, 2017).

Bertelsmann. "Bertelsmann at a Glance." https://www.bertelsmann.com/investor-relations/bertelsmann-at-a-glance/ (accessed August 19, 2017).

Bertelsmann. "Penguin Random House." https://www.bertelsmann.com/divisions/penguin-random-house/#st-1 (accessed August 19, 2017).

Case Studies: HarperCollins and News Corporation

Trachtenberg, Jeffrey. "Will Harper Lee's New Book Shift Focus to Reading?" By Paul Vigna. *Moneybeat* video, 3:43. February 4, 2015. http://www.wsj.com/video/will-harper-lee-new-book-shift-focus-to-reading/6CE4E99B-28C3-43ED-8FBC-8C46D5495FFA.html

Kovaleski, Serge F., and Alexandra Alter. "Harper Lee's 'Go Set a Watchman' May Have Been Found Earlier Than Thought." *New York Times*, July 2, 2015. https://www.nytimes.com/2015/07/03/books/harper-lee-go-set-a-watchman-may-have-been-found-earlier-than-thought.html

Trachtenberg, Jeffrey A. "HarperCollins Has a Lot Riding on Harper Lee's 'Go Set a Watchman.'" *Wall Street Journal*, July 9, 2015.

Lynch, John. "Harper Lee's 'Go Set a Watchman' Sells a Record-Breaking 1.1 Million Copies." *Business Insider*, July 15, 2015. http://www.businessinsider.com/go-set-a-watchman-sold-more-than-11-million-copies-2015-7

Matthew, Jennie. "Reactions to Harper Lee's New Novel Are 'Charitable at Best, Scathing at Worst.'" *Business Insider*, July 15, 2015. http://www.businessinsider.com/afp-harper-lee-book-flies-out-of-stores-to-mixed-reviews-2015-7#ixzz3gXPjZ9sx

Giraldi, William. "Harper Lee's 'Go Set a Watchman' Should Not Have Been Published." *New Republic*, July 16, 2015. https://newrepublic.com/article/122318/harper-lees-go-set-watchman-should-not-have-been-published

Nocera, Joe. "The Harper Lee 'Go Set a Watchman' Fraud." *New York Times*, July 24, 2015. https://www.nytimes.com/2015/07/25/opinion/joe-nocera-the-watchman-fraud.html?_r=0

Grimes, William. "Harper Lee, Author of 'To Kill a Mockingbird,' Dies at 89." *New York Times*, February 19, 2016. https://www.nytimes.com/2016/02/20/arts/harper-lee-dies.html?_r=0

Amazon. "Amazon Best Sellers of 2015." https://www.amazon.com/gp/bestsellers/2015/ books/ref=zg_bsar_cal_ye (accessed August 19, 2017).

Alpert, Lukas I. "News Corp Swings to Profit on Book, Real Estate Growth." *Wall Street Journal*, August 8, 2016.

De Pratto, Giuditta, and Jean Paul Simon. *Digital Media Worlds: The New Economy of Media*. New York: Palgrave Macmillan, 2014.

Chapter 3 What Is a Company Worth?

Calculating Financial Valuations and Return on Investment

Foster, Richard, and Sarah Kaplan. *Creative Destruction: Why Companies That Are Built to Last Underperform the Market—And How to Successfully Transform Them*. New York: Doubleday, 2001.

Knight, Joe. *Business Valuation*. HBR Tools. Boston: Harvard Business School Publishing, 2016.

News Corp, Annual Report (Form 10-K), (August 12, 2016). https://www.sec.gov/Archives/ edgar/data/1564708/000119312516679975/d210462d10k.htm

Aguilar, Luis A. "Institutional Investors: Power and Responsibility." April 19, 2013. Transcript. J. Mack Robinson College of Business, Georgia State University. https://www. sec.gov/news/speech/2013-spch041913laahtm

NASDAQ. "Home Page." Information on CBS, Comcast, et al. http://www.nasdaq.com/ (accessed March 3, 2017).

Noam, Eli M. *Media Ownership and Concentration in America*. Oxford: Oxford University Press, 2009.

Hardymon, G. Felda, Josh Lerner, and Ann Leamon. "Best Practices: Decision Making Among Venture Capital Firms." *Harvard Business School Background Note* 804-176. Boston: Harvard Business School Publishing, 2007.

Lee, Aileen. "Welcome to the Unicorn Club: Learning from Billion-Dollar Startups." *TechCrunch*, November 2, 2013. https://techcrunch.com/2013/11/02/welcome-to-the-unicorn-club/

Frier, Sarah, and Eric Newcomer. "The Fuzzy, Insane Math That's Creating So Many Billion-Dollar Tech Companies." *Bloomberg*, March 17, 2015.

Rao, Leena. "The Most Expensive Sake that Jack Ma Ever Made." *Fortune*, September 25, 2013. http://fortune.com/2015/09/25/yahoo-alibaba-investment-jack-ma/

Ramana Nanda, cited in Blanding, Michael. "Amazon Web Services Changed the Way VCs Fund Start-Ups." *Working Knowledge: Business Research for Business Leaders* (blog), Harvard Business School, May 10, 2017. http://hbswk.hbs.edu/item/amazon-web-services-changed-the-way-vcs-fund-startups?cid=spmailing-15064584-WK%20Newsletter%2005-10-2017%20(1)%20A-May%2010,%202017

Nanda, Ramana, Sampsa Samila, and Olav Sorenson. "The Persistent Effect of Initial Success: Evidence from Venture Capital." Harvard Business School Working Paper, No. 17-065, January 2017.

U.S. Securities and Exchange Commission. "Initial Public Offerings, Why Individuals Have Difficulty Getting Shares." *Fast Answers*. Last modified November 24, 1999. https://www. sec.gov/fast-answers/answersipodiffhtm.html

Fruhan, William E., Jr. "The Hedge Fund Industry." *Harvard Business School Background Note 208-126*. Boston, Harvard Business School Publishing, 2010.

Tan, Andrea, and Benjamin Robertson, "Why Investors are Fretting Over Dual-Class Shares." *Bloomberg*, July 10, 2017. https://www.bloomberg.com/news/articles/2017-07-10/why-investors-are-fretting-over-dual-class-shares-quicktake-q-a

Nicholas, Blair, and Brandon Marsh. "One Share, No Vote: Dual Class Structures Are a Recipe for Executive Entrenchment, Fiduciary Misconduct, and Erosion of Shareholder Rights." *The Advocate for Institutional Investors* (Summer 2017): 1–5. https://www.blbglaw.com/news/publications/data/00210/_res/id=File1/AdvSummer2017_Nicholas_Marsh.pdf

Mitchell, Greg. "McClatchy Buys Knight Ridder, But Will Sell 12 Papers." *USA Today*, March 13, 2006.

Posen, Robert. "If Private Equity Sized Up Your Business." *Harvard Business Review* 85, no. 11 (November 2007): 78–87.

MarketWatch. "Home Page." Information on Facebook, Google, News Corp., and Twitter. http://www.marketwatch.com/ (accessed March 6, 2017).

Knight, Joe. *Return on Investment (ROI)*. HBR Tools. Boston: Harvard Business School Publishing, 2015.

Google. "Finance." Information on Apple, Facebook, CBS, Netflix, Disney, et al. https://www.google.com/finance?ei=XgqnWenmCoaGmAHs54PwBA (accessed on March 6, 2017).

MarketWatch. "Stocks." Information on Apple, Facebook, CBS, Netflix, Disney, et al. http://www.marketwatch.com/investing/stocks (accessed on March 6, 2017).

Case Study: Snap

Chafkin, Max, and Sarah Frier. "How SnapChat Built a Business by Confusing Olds." *Bloomberg Businessweek*, March 3, 2016. https://www.bloomberg.com/features/2016-how-snapchat-built-a-business/

Frier, Sarah, and Alex Barinka. "Can Snapchat's Culture of Secrecy Survive an IPO?" *Bloomberg*, January 17, 2017. https://www.bloomberg.com/news/features/2017-01-17/can-snapchat-s-culture-of-secrecy-survive-an-ipo

McLaughlin, Tim. "Fidelity, T. Rowe Price Poised for Gains on Snap IPO." *Reuters*, February 24, 2017. http://www.reuters.com/article/us-snap-ipo-funds-idUSKBN16323B

Morris, Betsy, and Georgia Wells. "Where is Evan Spiegel? Snap Inc's Founder Is Elusive, Secretive, and Soon to Be Very Rich." *Wall Street Journal*, February 27, 2017. https://www.wsj.com/articles/snap-ipo-a-22-billion-test-for-the-unsocial-social-network-and-its-elusive-founder-1488235747

"Snap IPO: Five Things Critics Are Saying." *Wall Street Journal* video, 3:08. February 28, 2017. http://www.wsj.com/video/snap-ipo-five-things-critics-are-saying/9D2B8019-7B19-4D22-BD2F-F0C558731947.html

"eMarketer Releases New Snapchat Usage Numbers: Growth Driven by People Ages 45 to 54." *eMarketer*, February 28, 2017. https://www.emarketer.com/Article/eMarketer-Releases-New-Snapchat-Usage-Numbers/1015324#sthash.d0OP6OGO.dpuf

Driebusch, Corrie, and Maureen Farrell. "Snapchat Parent Snap Valued at $24 Billion After IPO Pricing." *Wall Street Journal*, March 1, 2017. https://www.wsj.com/articles/snapchat-parent-snap-prices-ipo-above-projected-range-1488400583

De la Merced, Michael. "Snap Prices I.P.O. at $17 a Share, Valuing Company at $24 Billion." *New York Times*, March 1, 2017. https://www.nytimes.com/2017/03/01/business/dealbook/snap-ipo-snapchat.html?mcubz=0

Solomon, Steven Davidoff. "In Snap's I.P.O., Evidence of Banker's Strategy." *New York Times*, March 1, 2017. https://www.nytimes.com/2017/03/01/business/dealbook/in-snaps-ipo-evidence-of-bankers-strategy.html?mcubz=0

Kats, Rimma. "How Snapchat Stacks Up." *eMarketer*, March 2, 2017. https://www.emarketer.com/Article/How-Snapchat-Stacks-Up/1015353?ecid=NL1001#sthash.KWVb51g1.dpuf

Stewart, James B. "How a Money-Losing Snap Could Be Worth So Much." *New York Times*, March 2, 2017. https://www.nytimes.com/2017/03/02/business/snap-ipo-valuation.html

Brown, Eliot. "Snapchat Investors Found Their Golden Goose in a Field of Turkeys." *Wall Street Journal*, March 3, 2017. https://www.wsj.com/articles/snapchat-investors-found-their-golden-goose-in-a-field-of-turkeys-1488537002

Wells, Georgia. "Snapchat Parent Posts Disappointing User Growth; Stock Plunges." *Wall Street Journal*, May 10, 2017. https://www.wsj.com/articles/snapchat-posts-2-2-billion-loss-in-first-quarterly-report-stock-plunges-1494446940?mod=djemalertNEWS

Alexander, Gary. "Snap Has Further to Fall: Worrying User Trends in Focus." *Seeking Alpha*, August 3, 2017. https://seekingalpha.com/article/4094325-snap-fall-worrying-user-trends-focus

Kesarios, George. "Why Snap is Not Worth More Than $7.4-Per-Share." *Seeking Alpha*, August 3, 2017. https://seekingalpha.com/article/4094453-snap-worth-7_4-per-share

Kats, Rimma. "Instagram, Snapchat Duel for Millennial Attention: New Study Finds Similar Reach and Usage." *eMarketer*, August 10, 2017. https://www.emarketer.com/Article/Instagram-Snapchat-Duel-Millennial-Attention/1016316?ecid=NL1001

Google. "Finance: Snap Inc." https://www.google.com/finance?q=NYSE%3ASNAP&ei=JsGMWfmZFJO1mAGy_Z7QCw (accessed March 6, 2017).

MarketWatch. "Snap Inc." http://www.marketwatch.com/investing/stock/snap (accessed March 6, 2017).

Chapter 4 The Transformed Competitive Landscape

Growth Strategies and Disruption of Business Models

Taparia, Jay. *Understanding Financial Statements: A Journalist's Guide*. Oak Park, IL: Marion Street Press, 2003.

Foster, Richard, and Sarah Kaplan. *Creative Destruction: Why Companies That Are Built to Last Underperform the Market—And How to Successfully Transform Them*. New York: Doubleday, 2001.

Knee, Jonathan A., Bruce C. Greenwald, and Ava Seave. *The Curse of the Mogul: What's Wrong with the World's Leading Media Companies*. New York: Penguin Group, 2009.

Zook, Chris, and James Allen, Bain & Company Consultants. "Growth Outside the Core." *Harvard Business Review* 81, no. 12 (December 2003): 66–73. https://hbr.org/2003/12/growth-outside-the-core

Bort, Julie. "Cisco's John Chambers: What I Look for Before We Buy a Startup." *Business Insider*, July 23, 2014. http://www.businessinsider.com/cisco-john-chambers-acquisition-strategy-2014-7

Foster, Richard. *Innovation: The Attacker's Advantage*. New York: Summit Books, 1986.

Schumpeter, Joseph A. *Capitalism, Socialism and Democracy*. New York: Harper & Row, 1950.

Abernathy, Penelope, and Richard Foster. "The News Landscape in 2014: Transformed or Diminished? (Formulating a Game Plan for Survival in the Digital Era)." Paper presented at the Yale University Conference on Information, the Law and Society, November 12, 2009.

Moore, Geoffrey, *Crossing the Chasm: Marketing and Selling High-Tech Products to Mainstream Customers*. New York: HarperBusiness, 1991.

Christensen, Clay M. *The Innovator's Dilemma: When New Technologies Cause Great Firms to Fail*. Boston: Harvard Business School Press, 1997.

Hoskins, Colin. *Media Economics: Applying Economics to New and Traditional Media*. Thousand Oaks, CA: Sage Publications, 2004.

Doyle, Gillian. *Understanding Media Economics*. Second edition. London: Sage, 2013.

Porter, Michael. *Competitive Strategy: Creating and Sustaining Superior Performance*. With a new Introduction. New York: Free Press, 1998.

Shaw, Donald. *The Rise and Fall of American Mass Media: Roles of Technology and Leadership*. Bloomington: Indiana University Press, 1991.

Eisenmann, Thomas R. "Black Swans and Big Trends Can Ruin Anyone's Internet Prediction." *Working Knowledge: Business Research for Business Leaders* (blog), Harvard Business School, August 15, 2016. http://hbswk.hbs.edu/item/black-swans-and-big-trends-can-ruin-anyone-s-internet-predictions

Noam, Eli. *Media Ownership and Concentration in America*. Oxford: Oxford University Press, 2009.

Drucker, Peter F. "The Discipline of Innovation." *Harvard Business Review* 80, no. 8 (August 2002): 95–103.

Case Study: Viacom

La Monica, Paul R., and David Ellis. "Shakeup at the Top at Struggling Viacom: Media Giant Taps Board Member to Succeed MTV Pioneer Freston as President and CEO." *CNNMoney*, September 5, 2006. http://money.cnn.com/2006/09/05/news/newsmakers/viacom_freston/index.htm

Grove, Lloyd. "Sumner's Discontent." *Condé Nast Portfolio*, February 9, 2009.

California Cable & Telecommunications Association. "History of Cable." https://www.calcable.org/learn/history-of-cable/ (accessed August 20, 2017).

Cable Center. "The Cable History Project." http://cablecenter.org/cable-history/108-the-cable-history-project-overview.html (accessed August 20, 2017).

Keach, Hagey. "The Relationship that Helped Sumner Redstone Build Viacom Now Adds to its Problems." *Wall Street Journal*, April 11, 2016. https://www.wsj.com/articles/the-relationship-that-helped-sumner-redstone-build-viacom-now-adds-to-its-problems-1460409571

Steel, Emily. "At Viacom, Now Comes the Hard Part." *New York Times*, August 16, 2016. https://www.nytimes.com/2016/08/20/business/media/viacom-sumner-redstone-philippe-dauman.html?mcubz=0

Steel, Emily. "Inside the Battle for Sumner Redstone's $40 Billion Empire." *New York Times*, December 12, 2016. https://www.nytimes.com/interactive/2016/business/media/sumner-redstone-saga.html?_r=0

Favaro, Ken. "Has Your Strategy's Shelf Life Expired?" *s+b blogs*, March 4, 2016. https://www.strategy-business.com/blog/Has-Your-Strategys-Shelf-Life-Expired?gko=d2304

Price, Brian. "Former Viacom CEO Tom Freston Speaks Out on Company's 'Serious Errors.'" *CNBC*, June 15, 2016. http://www.cnbc.com/2016/06/15/former-viacom-ceo-tom-freston-speaks-out-on-companys-serious-errors.html

Shaw, Lucas, and Alex Sherman. "Viacom Names Bakish CEO Following End of Talks to Merge with CBS." *Bloomberg*, December 12, 2016. https://www.bloomberg.com/news/articles/2016-12-12/viacom-drops-on-report-shari-redstone-withdraws-cbs-proposal

James, Meg. "Viacom's New CEO Unveils Updated Strategy as Earnings Fall." *Los Angeles Times*, February 7, 2017. http://www.latimes.com/business/hollywood/la-fi-ct-viacom-earnings-paramount-20170209-story.html

Case Study: Yahoo!

Thomas, Daniel. "Yahoo—Where Did It All Go Wrong?" *BBC News*, January 7, 2016. www.bbc.com/news/technology-35243407

Desjardins, Jeff. "One Chart That Explains the Rise and Fall of Yahoo." *Business Insider*, August 1, 2016. http://www.businessinsider.com/one-chart-that-explains-the-rise-and-fall-of-yahoo-2016-8?IR=T

McGee, Suzanne. "Yahoo's Marissa Mayer is a Reminder That CEO Is Still Elusive for Women." *The Guardian*, July 28, 2016. https://www.theguardian.com/technology/us-money-blog/2016/jul/28/yahoo-marissa-mayer-female-ceo-women

Chafkin, Max. "Yahoo's Marissa Mayer on Selling a Company While Trying to Turn It Around." *Bloomberg Businessweek*, August 4, 2016. https://www.bloomberg.com/features/2016-marissa-mayer-interview-issue/

Carlson, Nicholas. "Yahoo Could Have Bought Facebook for 2% of Today's Valuation." *Business Insider*, January 3, 2011. http://www.businessinsider.com/facebook-is-selling-just-4-of-the-company-for-2x-as-much-as-yahoo-could-have-paid-to-buy-the-whole-thing-2011-1

Wells, Nick, and Mark Fahey. "How Yahoo's 1 Billion Account Breach Stacks Up with the Biggest Hacks Ever." *CNBC*, December 20, 2016. https://www.cnbc.com/2016/12/15/how-yahoos-1-billion-account-breach-stacks-up-with-biggest-hacks-ever.html

Alesci, Cristina, Seth Fiegerman, and Charles Riley. "Verizon is Buying Yahoo for $4.8 Billion." *CNN Tech*, July 25, 2016. http://money.cnn.com/2016/07/25/technology/yahoo-verizon-deal-sale/index.html

Swisher, Kara. "Marissa Mayer Will Not Be Part of the New AOL-Yahoo Combined Company Called Oath." *Recode*, April 3, 2017. https://www.recode.net/2017/4/3/15167998/marissa-mayer-out-tim-armstrong-new-aol-yahoo-company-oath?mod=djemCMOToday

Sullivan, Danny. "Yahoo Directory Closes, Five Days Early." *Search Engine Land*, December 27, 2014. http://searchengineland.com/yahoo-directory-closes-211784.

LaFrance, Adrienne. "Yahoo's Demise Is a Death Knell for Digital News Orgs." *Atlantic*, April 20, 2017. https://www.theatlantic.com/technology/archive/2017/04/yahoos-demise-is-a-death-knell-for-digital-news-orgs/523692/

Chapter 5 A Strategy for Dealing with the New Business Imperatives

Developing a Digital Strategy Framework for Media Enterprises

Rosenstiel, Tom. "Newspaper Journalism in the Digital Era of Distraction." Presentation given at the 129th Annual Meeting of Inland Press Association, Chicago, IL, October 20,

2014. http://www.inlandpress.org/stories/download-presentations-from-inlands-129th-annual-meeting-oct-19-21,1011

Noam, Eli. *Media Ownership and Concentration in America*. Oxford: Oxford University Press, 2009.

Bothun, Deborah, and Art Kleiner. "The Next Pop Star Just Might Be a Robot." *strategy+business*, April 26, 2017. https://www.strategy-business.com/article/The-Next-Pop-Superstar-Just-Might-Be-a-Robot

Bradley, Chris, and Clayton O'Toole. "An Incumbent's Guide to Digital Disruption." *McKinsey Quarterly*, May 2016. http://www.mckinsey.com/business-functions/strategy-and-corporate-finance/our-insights/an-incumbents-guide-to-digital-disruption

Harvard Business Review. *Creating Business Plans: Gather Your Resources, Describe the Opportunity, Get Buy-In*. 20 Minute Manager Series. Boston: Harvard Business Review Press, 2014.

Nanda, Ramana, Sampsa Samila, and Olav Sorenson. "The Persistent Effect of Initial Success: Evidence from Venture Capital." Harvard Business School Working Paper, No. 17-065, January 2017.

Harvard Business School. *Strategy: Create and Implement the Best Strategy for Your Business*. Harvard Business Essentials Series. Boston: Harvard Business School Press, 2005. See esp. chap. 1, "SWOT Analysis 1," and chap. 2, "SWOT Analysis 2."

Harvard Business Review. *SWOT Analysis*. HBR Tools. Boston: Harvard Business School Publishing, 2015.

Strategy&, cited in De Souza, Ivan, Richard Kauffeld, and David van Oss. "10 Principles of Strategy Through Execution." *strategy + business*, February 13, 2017. https://www.strategy-business.com/article/10-Principles-of-Strategy-through-Execution

Osterwalder, Alex, and Yves Pigneur. *Business Model Generation: A Handbook for Visionaries, Game Changers, and Challengers*. Hoboken, NJ: John Wiley & Sons, 2010.

Robert Kaplan and David Norton *The Strategy-Focused Organization*. Boston: Harvard Business Review Press, 2000.

Robert Simons *Seven Strategy Questions*. Boston: Harvard Business School Publishing, 2010.

Hamel, Gary, and C. K. Prahalad. *Competing for the Future*. Boston: Harvard Business School Press, 1995.

Case Study: *New York Times* and Bloomberg

Alpert, Lukas I. "Twitter Teams Up with Bloomberg for Streaming News." *Wall Street Journal*, April 30, 2017. https://www.wsj.com/articles/twitter-teams-up-with-bloomberg-for-streaming-news-1493600580?mod=djemCMOToday&mg=prod/accounts-wsj

Moses, Lucia. "Facebook Faces Increased Publisher Resistance to Instant Articles." *Digiday*, April 11, 2017. https://digiday.com/media/facebook-faces-increased-publisher-resistance-instant-articles/

MarketLine. *The New York Times Company: Company Profile*. MarketLine, 2016.

MarketLine. *Bloomberg L.P.: Company Profile*. MarketLine, 2016.

Bloomberg. "About Bloomberg." https://www.bloomberg.com/company/bloomberg-facts/ (accessed April 10, 2017).

Thomson Reuters. "About Us: Company History." https://www.thomsonreuters.com/en/about-us/company-history.html (accessed April 8, 2017).

Loomis, Carol J. "Bloomberg's Money Machine." *Fortune*, April 5, 2007. http://archive.fortune.com/magazines/fortune/fortune_archive/2007/04/16/8404302/index.htm

S&P Global. "Who We Are." https://www.spglobal.com/who-we-are/our-company/our-history (accessed April 8, 2017).

Bodine, Paul. *Make It New: Essays in the History of American Business*. Lincoln, NE: iUniverse, 2004.

Bennett, James. "The Bloomberg Way." *Atlantic*, November 2012. https://www.theatlantic.com/magazine/archive/2012/11/the-bloomberg-way/309136/

Knee, Jonathan, and Miklos Sarvary. "Bloomberg LP: More Than a Box?" *Columbia CaseWorks* 140308. New York: Columbia CaseWorks, 2014.

Christensen, Clayton M., Richard G. Hamermesh, and Jeremy Dann. "Bloomberg L.P." *Harvard Business School Case* 399-081. Boston: Harvard Business School Publishing, 1999.

Abernathy, Penelope Muse. "A Nonprofit Model for The New York Times." Paper presented at the Duke Conference on Nonprofit Media, May 4-5, 2009.

Case Study: Huffington Post

Braiker, Brian. "Inside Lydia Polgreen's Mission to Make HuffPo a Must-Read." *Digiday*, April 4, 2017. https://digiday.com/media/inside-lydia-polgreens-mission-make-huffpo-must-read/

Sarno, David. "A Brief History of the Huffington Post." *Los Angeles Times*, February 7, 2011. http://articles.latimes.com/2011/feb/07/business/la-fi-huffington-post-timeline-20110207

Eisenmann, Thomas R., Toby E. Stuart, and David Kiron. "The Huffington Post." *Harvard Business School Case 810-086*. Boston: Harvard Business School Publishing, 2010.

"AOL to Buy Huffington Post in $315m Media Merger." *BBC News*, February 7, 2011. http://www.bbc.com/news/business-12379623

Wilson, Bill. "Huffington Post Founder Arianna Huffington to Step Down." *BBC News*, August 11, 2016. http://www.bbc.com/news/business-37047416

Andrews, Suzanna. "Arianna Calling." *Vanity Fair*, December 2005. https://www.vanityfair.com/news/2005/12/huffington200512

Segal, David, "Arianna Huffington's Improbable, Insatiable Content Machine." *New York Times Magazine*, June 30, 2015. https://www.nytimes.com/2015/07/05/magazine/arianna-huffingtons-improbable-insatiable-content-machine.html?mcubz=0

Chapter 6 Defining a Unique Value Proposition

Identifying and Developing Unique Value Propositions

Kaplan, Robert S., and David P. Norton. "Transforming the Balanced Scorecard from Performance Measurement to Strategic Management: Part I." *Accounting Horizons* 15, no. 1 (March 2001): 87–104.

Clarke, Irvine. "Emerging Value Propositions for M-Commerce." *Journal of Business Strategies* 25, no. 2 (Fall 2008): 41–57.

Osterwalder, Alexander, Yves Pigneur, Gregory Bernarda, and Alan Smith. *Value Proposition Design: How to Create Products and Services Customers Want*. Hoboken, NJ: John Wiley & Sons, 2014.

Osterwalder, Alexander, Yves Pigneur, and Christopher L. Tucci. "Clarifying Business Models: Origins, Present, and Future of the Concept." *Communications of the Association for Information Systems* 16 (July 2005): 1–25.

Wernerfelt, Birger. "A Resource-Based View of the Firm." *Strategic Management Journal* 5, no. 2 (April/June 1984): 171–180.

Henderson, Bruce D. *The Experience Curve – Reviewed: IV. The Growth Share Matrix or the Product Portfolio*. Boston: Boston Consulting Group, 1973. https://www.bcg.com/documents/file13904.pdf

Vernon, Raymond. "International Investment and International Trade in the Product Cycle." *Quarterly Journal of Economics* 80, no. 2 (May 1966): 190–207.

Moore, Geoffrey. *Crossing the Chasm: Marketing and Selling High Tech Products to Mainstream Customers*. New York: HarperBusiness, 1991.

Ballantyne, David, and Richard Varey. "Creating Value-In-Use Through Marketing Interaction: The Exchange Logic of Relating, Communicating and Knowing." *Marketing Theory* 6, no. 3 (2006): 335–348.

Hair, Joseph, Mary Wolfinbarger Celsi, David J. Ortinau, and Robert Bush. *Essentials of Marketing Research*. Third edition. New York: McGraw-Hill, 2013.

Hinterhuber, Andreas. "Towards Value-Based Pricing—An Integrative Framework for Decision Making." *Industrial Marketing Management* 33, no. 8 (November 2004): 765–778.

Hinterhuber, Andreas. "Customer Value-Based Pricing Strategies: Why Companies Resist." *Journal of Business Strategy* 29, no. 4 (2008): 41–50.

Nagle, Thomas, John Hogan, and Joseph Zale. *The Strategy and Tactics of Pricing*. London: Routledge, 2014.

Hoskins, Colin, Stuart McFadyen, and Adam Finn. *Media Economics Applying Economics to New and Traditional Media*. Thousand Oaks, CA: Sage Publications, 2004.

Bakos, Yannis, and Erik Brynjolfsson. "Bundling Information Goods: Pricing, Profits, and Efficiency." *Management Science* 45, no. 12 (December 1999): 1613–1630.

Flanders, Jefferson. CEO of MindEdge and Circulation Director of *Harvard Business Review* in 2001, in discussion with author on the pricing strategy for the *Harvard Business Review*, February 28, 2017.

Fetscherin, Marc, and Gerhard Knolmayer. "Business models for content delivery: an empirical analysis of the newspaper and magazine industry." *International Journal on Media Management* 6, no. 1/2 (2004): 4–11.

Christensen, Clayton M. *The Innovator's Dilemma: When New Technologies Cause Great Firms To Fail*. Boston: Harvard Business School Press, 1997.

Yang, Mengchieh Jacie, and Hsiang Iris Chyi. "Competing with Whom? Where? and Why (Not)? An Empirical Study of U.S. Online Newspapers' Competition Dynamics." *Journal of Media Business Studies* 8, no. 4 (2011): 59–74.

Case Study: Netflix

Seijts, Jana, and Paul Bigus. "Netflix: The Public Relations Box Office Flop," *Harvard Business School Case W12-918*, April 2012.

Wasserman, Todd. "Netflix Loses 800,000 Customers in a Quarter." *Mashable*, October 24, 2011. http://mashable.com/2011/10/24/netflix-loses-800000-customers-in-quarter/

Sandoval, Greg. "Netflix's Lost Year: The Inside Story of the Price-Hike Train Wreck." *CNET News*, July 11, 2012. http://www.cnet.com/news/netflixs-lost-year-the-inside-story-of-the-price-hike-train-wreck/

Van Duyn, Aline. "DVD Rentals Pass Their Screen Test." *Financial Times*, October 4, 2005. https://www.ft.com/content/577fbf0c-342f-11da-adae-00000e2511c8.html?ft_site=falcon&desktop=true#axzz4qbrVVuZT

Shih, Willy C., Stephen P. Kaufman, and David Spinola. "Netflix." *Harvard Business School Case 607-138*, May 2007. (Revised April 2009.)

O'Brien, Chris. "My Conversation with Netflix CEO Reed Hastings." *Business Insider*, May 9, 2016. http://www.businessinsider.com/my-conversation-with-netflix-ceo-reed-hastings-2016-5

Netflix. "Netflix's Annual Revenue From 2002 To 2016 (In Million U.S. Dollars)." https://www.statista.com/statistics/272545/annual-revenue-of-netflix/ (accessed August 18, 2017).

Castillo, Michelle. "Amazon Is 'Awfully Scary' Says Netflix CEO Reed Hastings." *CNBC*, May 31, 2017. http://www.cnbc.com/2017/05/31/netflix-ceo-reed-hastings-amazon-is-awfully-scary.html

Abkowitz, Alyssa. "How Netflix Got Started." *Fortune Magazine*, January 28, 2009. http://archive.fortune.com/2009/01/27/news/newsmakers/hastings_netflix.fortune/index.htm

Snider, Mike. "Netflix Ditches Qwikster Plan." *USA Today*, October 10, 2011. Retrieved from http://usatoday30.usatoday.com/MONEY/usaedition/2011-10-11-Netflix-axes-Quikster_ST_U.htm

Chatterjee, Sayan, Wayne Barry, and Alexander Hopkins. "Netflix Inc.: Proving the Skeptics Wrong." Harvard Business School Case W16-763, November 2016.

Ramachandran, Shalini and Bowdeya Tweh. "Netflix's Subscriber Growth Slows at Home and Abroad." *Wall Street Journal*, April 17, 2017.

Favaro, Ken. "Lessons from the Strategy Crisis at Netflix." *s+b blogs*, September 6, 2016. https://www.strategy-business.com/blog/Lessons-from-the-Strategy-Crisis-at-Netflix?gko=1f1e1

Scholer, Kristen. "Where Netflix Shares Are Headed After Its Stock Split." *Wall Street Journal*, July 15, 2017. https://blogs.wsj.com/moneybeat/2015/07/15/where-netflix-shares-are-headed-after-its-stock-split/

MarketWatch. "Netflix Inc." http://www.marketwatch.com/investing/stock/nflx (accessed August 11, 2017).

Olson, Annika, and Eddie Yoon. "Netflix Will Rebound Faster Than You Think." *Harvard Business Review*, January 26, 2012. https://hbr.org/2012/01/netflix-will-rebound-faster-th

Chatterjee, Sayan, Wayne Berry, and Alexander Hopkins. "Netflix Inc.: The Second Act - Moving into Streaming." Harvard Business School Case W16-761. Boston: Harvard Business School Publishing, 2016.

"Reed Hastings Revealed." Bloomberg Game Changers video, 25:15. Aired May 24, 2011. http://www.tv.com/web/bloomberg-game-changers-how-influential-leaders-changed-the-world/watch/netflixs-reed-hastings-revealed-bloomberg-game-changers-1468493/

Frick, Walter. "How Can Companies Compete with Amazon? Netflix Has the Answer." *Harvard Business Review*, June 19, 2017. https://hbr.org/2017/06/how-can-companies-compete-with-amazon-netflix-has-the-answer

Copeland, Michael V. "Reed Hastings: Leader of the Pack." *Fortune*, November 18, 2010. http://fortune.com/2010/11/18/reed-hastings-leader-of-the-pack/

Ahmed, Tufayel. "Netflix Ratings Revealed? These Are the Top 25 Original Streaming Shows of 2016." *Newsweek*, January 15, 2017. http://www.newsweek.com/netflix-ratings-revealed-these-are-top-25-original-streaming-shows-2016-538877

Hufford, Austen. "Netflix Surprises with Big Subscriber Gains, Shares Soar." *Wall Street Journal*, July 17, 2017. https://www.wsj.com/articles/netflix-rises-on-strong-subscriber-growth-1500324661?mod=e2tw&mod=djemCMOToday

O'Reilly, Lara. "CMO Today: Netflix Acquires Millarworld; CBS Embraces Digital; FX Launches Ad-Free Upgrade." *Wall Street Journal*, August 8, 2017. https://www.wsj.com/articles/cmo-today-netflix-acquires-millarworld-cbs-embraces-digital-fx-launches-ad-free-upgrade-1502193834

Chapter 7 Understanding Customer Relationships in a Digital World

Segmenting Customers Based on Wants, Needs and Motivations

Crawford, John E. "Cutting the Cord—A Marketing Case: An Examination of Changing TV Viewership." *Atlantic Marketing Journal* 5, no. 2 (2016): 137–150. http://digitalcommons.kennesaw.edu/amj/vol5/iss2/11/

Dibb, Sally, and Lyndon Simkin. "Targeting, Segments and Positioning." *International Journal of Retail & Distribution Management* 19, no. 3 (1991): 4–10.

Nijssen, Edwin, and Ruud Frambach. "Delivering Customer Value: Executing Marketing Strategy." In *Creating Customer Value Through Strategic Marketing Planning*, 111–130. Boston: Kluwer Academic Publishers, 2001.

Smith, Wendell R. "Product Differentiation and Market Segmentation as Alternative Marketing Strategies." *Journal of Marketing* 21, no. 1 (July 1956): 3–8.

Canhoto, Ana Isabel, Moira Clark, and Paul Fennemore. "Emerging Segmentation Practices in the Age of the Social Customer." *Journal of Strategic Marketing* 21, no. 5 (August 2013): 413–428.

Beane, T., and D. Ennis. "Market Segmentation: A Review." *European Journal of Marketing* 21, no. 5 (1987): 20–42.

Kotler, Philip, and Gary Armstrong. *Principles of Marketing*. Tenth edition. Upper Saddle River, NJ: Prentice Hall, 2004.

Assael, Henry. "Segmenting Markets by Group Purchasing Behavior: An Application of the AID Technique." *Journal of Marketing Research* 7, no.2 (May 1970): 153–158.

Lin, Chin-Feng. "Segmenting Customer Brand Preference: Demographic or Psychographic." *Journal of Product & Brand Management* 11, no. 4 (2002): 249–268.

Füller, Johann, and Kurt Matzler. "Customer Delight and Market Segmentation: An Application of the Three-Factor Theory of Customer Satisfaction on Life Style Groups." *Tourism Management* 29, no. 1 (February 2008): 116–126.

Magin, Vera. *Competition in Marketing: Two Essays on the Impact of Information on Managerial Decisions and on Spatial Product Differentiation*. Wiesbaden: Deutscher Universitäts-Verlag, 2006.

Kobrak, Harry. "How to Avoid Five Common Mistakes in Market Segmentation." *Advertising Age*,February20,2012.http://adage.com/article/cmo-strategy/avoid-common-mistakes-market-segmentation/232796/

Chasser, Ezra. "The Dangers of Over-Segmenting." *Sore Thumb Marketing* (blog), February 11, 2013. http://sorethumbmarketing.com/2013/02/11/the-dangers-of-over-segmenting/

Crompton, John. "Selecting Target Markets – A Key to Effective Marketing." *Journal of Park and Recreation Administration* 1 (January 1983): 7–26.

Sharma, Arun, and Douglas M. Lambert. "Segmentation of Markets Based on Customer Service." *International Journal of Physical Distribution & Logistics Management* 20, no. 7 (1990): 19–27.

Kotler, Philip. *Marketing Management: Analysis, Planning, Implementation, and Control*. Tenth edition. Englewood Cliffs, NJ: Prentice Hall, 1999.

Rogers, Stuart C. *Marketing Strategies, Tactics, and Techniques: A Handbook for Practitioners*. Westport, CT: Quorum Books, 2001.

Porter, Michael. "How Competitive Forces Shape Strategy." *Harvard Business Review* 57, no. 2 (March/April 1979): 137–145.

Dibb, Sally, and Lyndon Simkin. *Market Segmentation Success: Making It Happen!* New York: Routledge, 2008.

Lee, Jang Hee, and Sang Chan Park. "Intelligent Profitable Customers Segmentation System Based on Business Intelligence Tools." *Expert Systems with Applications* 29, no. 1 (July 2005): 145–152.

Homburg, Christian, Mathias Droll, and Dirk Totzek. "Customer Prioritization: Does It Pay Off, and How Should It Be Implemented?" *Journal of Marketing* 72, no. 5 (September 2008): 110–130.

Berman, Saul J., and Lynn Kesterson-Townes. "Connecting with the Digital Customer of the Future." *Strategy& Leadership* 40, no. 6 (2012): 29–35.

Ghodeswar, Bhimrao M. "Building Brand Identity in Competitive Markets: A Conceptual Model." *Journal of Product & Brand Management* 17, no. 1 (2008): 4–12.

Lavidge, Robert J., and Gary A. Steiner. "A Model for Predictive Measurements of Advertising Effectiveness." *Journal of Marketing* 25, no. 6 (1961): 59–62.

Rogers, Everett. *Diffusion of Innovations.* New York: Free Press, 2003.

Reitsma, Reineke. "The Data Digest: Twitter and Social Technographics." *Forrester* (blog), January 22, 2010. https://go.forrester.com/blogs/10-01-22-the_data_digest_twitter_and_social_technographics/

Chambers, John C., Satinder K. Mullick, and Donald D. Smith. "How to Choose the Right Forecasting Technique." *Harvard Business Review* 49, no. 4 (July/August 1971): 45–70.

Cantamessa, Marco, and Francesca Montagna. "The Dynamics of Innovation." In *Management of Innovation and Product Development*, 53–79. London: Springer, 2016.

Maloney, Chris. "The Secret to Accelerating Diffusion of Innovation: The 16% Rule Explained." *Innovate or Die* (blog), May 10, 2010. http://innovateordie.com.au/2010/05/10/the-secret-to-accelerating-diffusion-of-innovation-the-16-rule-explained/

Gladwell, Malcolm. *The Tipping Point: How Little Things Can Make a Big Difference.* Boston: Little, Brown, 2000.

Schawbel, Dan. "Geoffrey Moore: Why Crossing the Chasm in Still Relevant." *Forbes*, December 17, 2013. http://www.forbes.com/sites/danschawbel/2013/12/17/geoffrey-moore-why-crossing-the-chasm-is-still-relevant/

May, Matthew. "How to Cross the Tech Chasm." Matthew E May & Associates (blog), May 9, 2014. https://matthewemay.com/how-to-cross-the-tech-chasm/

Osterwalder, Alexander, and Yves Pigneur. *Business Model Generation: A Handbook for Visionaries, Game Changers, and Challengers.* New York: John Wiley & Sons, 2013.

American Customer Satisfaction Index. "Benchmarks by Industry." http://www.theacsi.org/index.php?option=com_content&view=article&id=148&Itemid=213 (accessed August 24, 2017).

Evans, Dave. *Social Media Marketing: The Next Generation of Business Engagement.* Indianapolis, IN: Wiley Publishing, Inc., 2010.

Zaichkowsky, Judith Lynne. "Measuring the Involvement Construct." *Journal of Consumer Research* 12, no. 3 (December 1985): 341–352.

Gambetti, Rossella, and Guendalina Graffigna. "The Concept of Engagement." *International Journal of Market Research* 52, no. 6 (2010): 801–826.

Klinger, Eric. *Structure and Functions of Fantasy.* New York: Wiley, 1971.

Holbrook, Morris B., and Elizabeth C. Hirschman. "The Experiential Aspects of Consumption: Consumer Fantasies, Feelings and Fun." *Journal of Consumer Research* 9, no. 3 (September 1982): 132–140.

Csikszentmihalyi, Mihaly. *Finding Flow: The Psychology of Engagement with Everyday Life.* New York: Basic Books, 1997.

Calder, Bobby, and Malthouse, Edward. "Managing Media and Advertising Change with Integrated Marketing." *Journal of Advertising Research* 45, no. 4 (2005): 356–361.

Aitken, Robert, Brendan Gray, and Robert Lawson. "Advertising Effectiveness from a Consumer Perspective." *International Journal of Advertising* 27, no. 2 (2008): 279–297.

Hennig-Thurau, Thorsten, Edward C. Malthouse, Christian Friege, Sonja Gensler, Lara Lobschat, Arvind Rangaswamy, and Bernd Skiera. "The Impact of New Media on Customer Relationships." *Journal of Service Research* 13, no. 3 (2010): 311–330.

"How Marketers Are Measuring Customer Engagement." *eMarketer*, January 26, 2016. http://www.emarketer.com/Article/How-Marketers-Measuring-Customer-Engagement/1013525

Reichheld, Frederick, and Thomas Teal. *The Loyalty Effect: The Hidden Force Behind Growth, Profits, and Lasting Value.* Boston: Harvard Business School Press, 1996.

Satmetrix. *U.S. Consumer 2017: Net Promoter Benchmarks at a Glance.* Research completed January/February 2017. https://info.satmetrix.com/hubfs/Infographic/satmetrix-infographic-2017-b2c-nps-benchmarks-glance-061217.pdf?t=1500528018120

Reichheld, Fred. *The Ultimate Question: Driving Good Profits and True Growth.* Boston: Harvard Business School Press, 2006.

Meola, Andrew. "Traditional Pay-TV May Be Doomed." *Business Insider*, February 22, 2016. http://www.businessinsider.com/sling-tv-cant-help-dish-network-stop-subscriber-bleed-2016-2

Case Study: Sling

Snider, Mike. "Sling TV Streaming-Video Service Open for Business." *USA Today*, February 9, 2015. http://www.usatoday.com/story/tech/personal/2015/02/09/sling-tv-official-launch/23110535

Farrell, Mike. "Dish Unveils Sling TV." *Multichannel News*, January 5, 2015. http://www.multichannel.com/news/technology/dish-unveils-sling-tv/386592

Perez, Sarah. "Cord Cutting Service Sling TV Gets Its First Broadcast Channel with Addition of ABC." *TechCrunch*, February 19, 2016. http://techcrunch.com/2016/02/19/cord-cutting-service-sling-tv-gets-its-first-broadcast-channel-with-addition-of-abc/

Welch, Chris. "Sling TV Reportedly Has Over 600,000 Subscribers." *Verge*, February 19, 2016. http://www.theverge.com/2016/2/19/11067532/sling-tv-600000-subscribers-dish

Levy, Adam. "Sling TV Is Cannibalizing DISH Network." *Motley Fool*, February 29, 2016. http://www.fool.com/investing/general/2016/02/29/sling-tv-is-cannibalizing-dish-network.aspx

Crimson Hexagon. *US Consumer Trends Report: Analyzing Social Media to Uncover Emerging Trends in Health, Entertainment, Technology and Transportation.* http://pages.crimsonhexagon.com/rs/284-XQB-702/images/US-Trends-Full-Report.pdf?mkt_tok=eyJpIjoiWkdabE5XSmpPVEU0WXpOaiIsInQiOiI0VkdOXC9KT0c5SEhHaz FHRUZFeHBwd2xJa1wvMHExb0E2QUo0eE95aUV4TTRjYnFta3BRYnhINGF5NzJrQ 3dxd3dOMVFBMTkrQ2JucGJ6QXMyTWJTRWtuU2l (accessed August 24, 2017).

3Cinteractive. *2017 Mobile Loyalty Report: How Brands Are Bridging the Technology Gap to Meet Consumer Demand for Loyalty Programs.* 3Cinteractive, 2017. http://go.3cinteractive.com/l/13622/2017-04-13/338s6s

Sgarro, Victoria, and Laura Nichols. "Infographic: What Cable Can Learn from Cord Cutters." *MediaShift*, March 29, 2017. http://mediashift.org/2017/03/infographic-cable-can-learn-cord-cutters/

Ramachandran, Shalini. "Dish Chairman Ergen to Add CEO Title." *Wall Street Journal*, February 23, 2015. https://www.wsj.com/articles/dish-chairman-ergen-to-add-ceo-title-1424689501

Ramachandran, Shalini, Laura Stevens, and Ryan Knutson. "Amazon and Dish Network: A Match in the Making?" *Wall Street Journal*, July 6, 2017. https://www.wsj.com/articles/amazon-dish-and-a-shared-vision-of-a-wireless-internet-of-things-1499333403

O'Reilly, Lara. "CMO Today: TV Upfronts Kick Off; Cord-Cutting Accelerates; Hack Attack Dangers." *Wall Street Journal*, May 15, 2017. https://www.wsj.com/articles/cmo-today-tv-upfronts-kick-off-cord-cutting-accelerates-hack-attack-dangers-1494848610

Ramachandran, Shalini. "As Stream Services Amp Up, Not All TV Channels Make the Cut." *Wall Street Journal*, May 14, 2017. https://www.wsj.com/articles/as-streaming-services-amp-up-not-all-tv-channels-make-the-cut-1494766801

Hufford, Austen. "Dish Network Loses More Subscribers in Third Quarter." *Wall Street Journal*, November 9, 2016. https://www.wsj.com/articles/dish-network-loses-more-subscribers-in-third-quarter-1478694569

Ramachandran, Shalini. "Sling TV Targets Cord-Cutters with New Ad Campaign." *Wall Street Journal*, August 30, 2016. https://www.wsj.com/articles/sling-tv-targets-cord-cutters-with-new-ad-campaign-1472562002

Steele, Anne. "Dish Network Tops Profit Views, Loses Subscribers." *Wall Street Journal*, July 21, 2016. https://www.wsj.com/articles/dish-network-tops-profit-views-loses-subscribers-1469097197

Ramachandran, Shalini, and Imani Moise. "Dish Network CEO Sees Pickup in Wireless Deal-Making." *Wall Street Journal*, February 22, 2017. https://www.wsj.com/articles/dish-network-swings-to-profit-1487765040

Bisson, Guy. "The Entertainment-Brand Power List." *Ampere Analysis*, March 23, 2016. https://www.ampereanalysis.com/blog/69edaa74-4b88-40cb-aa7e-555c9e8a6979

FierceCable. "Number of Sling TV Subscribers in the United States from March 2015 to June 2017 (in Thousands)." https://www.statista.com/statistics/539242/sling-tv-subscribers/ (accessed July 10, 2017).

Tadena, Nathalie. "AdWatch: Dish Spot Likens Traditional TV Providers to Childhood Bullies." *Wall Street Journal*, July 20, 2015. https://blogs.wsj.com/cmo/2015/07/20/adwatch-dish-spot-likens-traditional-tv-providers-to-childhood-bullies/

Beilfuss, Lisa. "Dish Expands Streaming Service Sling with International Programming." *Wall Street Journal*, April 3, 2015. https://www.wsj.com/articles/dish-expands-streaming-service-sling-with-international-programming-1428078187

Ramachandran, Shalini. "Dish's Charlie Ergen Says Sling TV Will Cannibalize Business." *Wall Street Journal*, March 25, 2015. https://blogs.wsj.com/cmo/2015/03/25/dishs-charlie-ergen-says-sling-tv-will-cannibalize-business/

"Ergen Talks Sling." *Cablefax*, March 26, 2015. http://www.cablefax.com/distribution/ergen-talks-sling

Zook, Chris, and James Allen. *Profit from the Core: A Return to Growth in Turbulent Times.* Boston: Harvard Business Press, 2010.

Chapter 8 Reaching Current and New Customers

Identifying Channels and Best Practices

Skjøtt-Larsen, Tage, Philip B. Schary, Juliana H. Mikkola, and Herbert Kotzab. *Managing the Global Supply Chain*. Third edition. Copenhagen: Copenhagen Business School Press, 2007.

Kotler, Philip, and Gary Armstrong. *Principles of Marketing*. Sixteenth edition. Harlow: Pearson Education, 2016.

BizFilings. "Distribution Methods Affect Bottom Line" https://www.bizfilings.com/toolkit/research-topics/marketing/distribution-methods-affect-bottom-line (accessed August 26, 2017).

Bolton, Ruth N., and Crina O. Tarasi. "Managing Customer Relationships." In *Review of Marketing Research*, edited by Naresh K. Malhotra, vol. 3, 3–38. Armonk, NY: M.E. Sharpe, 2007.

Galetto, Molly. "What is Customer Acquisition?" *NGDATA*, June 9, 2017. http://www.ngdata.com/what-is-customer-acquisition/

Thomas, Jacquelyn S., Werner Reinartz, and V. Kumar. "Getting the Most Out of All Your Customers." *Harvard Business Review* 82, no. 7/8 (July/August 2004): 116–123.

Rajagopal. *Darwinian Fitness in the Global Marketplace*. New York: Palgrave Macmillan, 2012.

Rajagopal. *Systems Thinking and Process Dynamics for Marketing Systems: Technologies and Applications for Decision Management*. Hershey, PA: Business Science Reference, 2012.

Borle, Sharad, Siddharth S. Singh, and Dipak C. Jain. "Customer Lifetime Value Measurement." *Management Science* 54, no. 1 (January 2008): 100–112.

Gupta, Sunil, Dominique Hanssens, Bruce Hardie, William Kahn, V. Kumar, Nathaniel Lin, Nalini Ravishanker, and S. Sriram. "Modeling Customer Lifetime Value." *Journal of Service Research* 9, no. 2 (2006): 139–155.

Kim, Su-Yeon, Tae-Soo Jung, Eui-Ho Suh, and Hyun-Seok Hwang. "Customer Segmentation and Strategy Development Based on Customer Lifetime Value: A Case Study." *Expert Systems with Applications* 31, no. 1 (July 2006): 101–107.

Rust, Roland T., Valarie A. Zeithaml, and Katherine N. Lemon. *Driving Customer Equity: How Customer Lifetime Value Is Reshaping Corporate Strategy*. New York: The Free Press, 2000.

McCalley, Russell W. *Marketing Channel Management: People, Products, Programs, and Markets*. Westport, CT: Praeger, 1996.

Villanueva, Julian, Shijin Yoo, and Dominique M. Hanssens. "The Impact of Marketing-Induced Versus Word-of-Mouth Customer Acquisition on Customer Equity Growth." *Journal of Marketing Research* 45, no. 1 (February 2008): 48–59.

Meeker, Mary. "Internet Trends 2017." Presentation given at Code Conference, Rancho Palos Verdes, CA, May 31, 2017. http://www.kpcb.com/internet-trends

Konrad, Alex. "Here Is Mary Meeker's Internet Trends Report for 2017." *Forbes*, May 31, 2017. https://www.forbes.com/sites/alexkonrad/2017/05/31/mary-meeker-internet-trends-for-2017/

"US Adults Spend 5.5 Hours with Video Content Each Day." *eMarketer*, April 16, 2015. http://www.emarketer.com/Article/US-Adults-Spend-55-Hours-with-Video-Content-Each-Day/1012362

McKinsey & Company. *Global Media Report 2015*. McKinsey & Company Global Media and Entertainment Practice, September 2015. https://www.mckinsey.com/~/media/

McKinsey/dotcom/client_service/Media%20and%20Entertainment/PDFs/McKinsey%20Global%20Report%202015_UK_October_2015.ashx

Pew Research Center. "State of the News Media 2015." April 29, 2015. http://assets.pewresearch.org/wp-content/uploads/sites/13/2017/05/30142603/state-of-the-news-media-report-2015-final.pdf

"Connected Devices Become Key to Content Consumption." *eMarketer*, February 17, 2012. http://www.emarketer.com/Article/Connected-Devices-Become-Key-Content-Consumption/1008849

Baumgartner, Jeff. "Half of Viewers Under 32 Won't Pay for TV by 2025." *Multichannel News*, October 8, 2015. http://www.multichannel.com/news/content/50-viewers-under-32-won-t-pay-tv-2025/394391

Moens, Marie-Francine, Juanzi Li, and Tat-Seng Chua. "Mining User Generated Content and Its Applications." In *Mining User Generated Content*, edited by Marie-Francine Moens, Juanzi Li, and Tat-Seng Chua, 3–18. Boca Raton, FL: CRC Press, 2014.

Nakamura, Reid. "NFL Star Travis Kelce Gets Reality Dating Show on E!" *TheWrap*, January 28, 2016. http://www.thewrap.com/nfl-star-travis-kelce-gets-reality-dating-show-on-e/

Malthouse, Edward C., Bobby J. Calder, Su Jung Kim, and Mark Vandenbosch. "Evidence that User-Generated Content that Produces Engagement Increases Purchase Behaviours." *Journal of Marketing Management* 32, no. 5–6 (2016): 427–444.

MacLeod, Ishbel. "Infographic: What Happens in a YouTube Minute?" *The Drum*, July 28, 2014. http://www.thedrum.com/stuff/2014/07/28/infographic-what-happens-youtube-minute

Dodez, Aaron. "User-Generated Video Content is Drowning Out Brands: But There's Hope." *tubularinsights*, May 7, 2015. http://tubularinsights.com/user-generated-content-brand-videos/

Cisco. "Cisco Visual Networking Index: Forecast and Methodology, 2014–2019." White Paper. Cisco, May 27, 2015. http://s2.q4cdn.com/230918913/files/doc_downloads/report_2014/white_paper_c11-481360.pdf

Raddon, Rich. "YouTube: The Power of the Global Everything Network." *Adweek*, May 18, 2015. http://www.adweek.com/socialtimes/rich-raddon-zefr-youtube-global-everything-network/620398

Walker, Rob. "Can SoundCloud be the Facebook of Music?" *Bloomberg Businessweek*, July 10, 2015. http://www.bloomberg.com/news/features/2015-07-10/can-soundcloud-be-the-facebook-of-music-

Wattpad. "About." https://www.wattpad.com/about/ (accessed August 26, 2017).

Colhoun, Damaris. "Should We Be Monetizing User-Generated Content?" *Columbia Journalism Review*, March 8, 2016. http://www.cjr.org/analysis/should_we_be_monetizing_user_generated_content.php

Stray, Jonathan. "Drawing Out the Audience: Inside BBC's User-Generated Content Hub." *NiemanLab*, May 5, 2010. http://www.niemanlab.org/2010/05/drawing-out-the-audience-inside-bbc%E2%80%99s-user-generated-content-hub/

Harsh, Anurag. "The Internet is Changing the Way We Do Business." *LinkedIn*, April 20, 2016. https://www.linkedin.com/pulse/digital-revolution-how-internet-changing-way-we-do-business-harsh

Satell, Greg. "Why the Digital Revolution Is Really Just Getting Started." *Forbes*, April 5, 2014. https://www.forbes.com/sites/gregsatell/2014/04/05/why-the-digital-revolution-is-really-just-getting-started/#41dda4aa3a72

Schifrin, Matt. "Why Alibaba's Long Tail Makes Amazon's Look Like a Bobcat's." *Forbes*, May 8, 2014. https://www.forbes.com/sites/schifrin/2014/05/08/why-alibabas-long-tail-makes-amazons-look-like-a-bobcats/#4cff7c7a7a20

Enright, Allison. "E-commerce and Higher Operational Costs Put Pressure on Retail Chains to Change." *Internet Retailer*, January 16, 2014. https://www.digitalcommerce360.com/2014/01/16/e-commerce-and-operational-costs-put-pressure-retail-chains/

Peterson, Tim. "Digital to Overtake TV Ad Spending in Two Years, Says Forrester." *Advertising Age*, November 4, 2014. http://adage.com/article/media/digital-overtake-tv-ad-spending-years-forrester/295694/

Sweney, Mark. "Marketing Gloom Deepens as Companies Cut Ad Spend on Traditional Media." *Guardian*, January 19, 2012. http://www.theguardian.com/media/2012/jan/19/marketing-gloom-ad-spend-media

Tadena, Nathalie. "Four of Top Five Advertisers Cut Traditional Ad Spending in First Half—Kantar." *Wall Street Journal*, September 16, 2014. https://blogs.wsj.com/cmo/2014/09/16/four-of-top-five-advertisers-cut-traditional-ad-spending-in-first-half-kantar/

Edmonds, Rick. "Classified Ad Revenue Down 70 Percent in 10 Years, with One Bright Spot." *Poynter*, February 1, 2010. http://www.poynter.org/2010/classified-ad-revenue-down-70-percent-in-10-years-with-one-bright-spot/100565/

Lobello, Carmel. "Craigslist Took Nearly $1 Billion a Year Away from Dying Newspapers." *The Week*, August 15, 2013. http://theweek.com/articles/461056/craigslist-took-nearly-1-billion-year-away-from-dying-newspapers

Agrawal, AJ. "How Top Marketplace Startups Built Their Businesses on the Cheap." *Inc.*, November 22, 2015. https://www.inc.com/aj-agrawal/how-top-marketplace-startups-built-their-businesses-on-the-cheap.html

Ingram, Mathew. "Airbnb, Coursera, and Uber: The Rise of the Disruption Economy." *Bloomberg Businessweek*, October 25, 2012. http://www.bloomberg.com/news/articles/2012-10-25/airbnb-coursera-and-uber-the-rise-of-the-disruption-economy

Cooper, James. "Ad Industry Needs to Get Used to Low Growth Being 'the New Normal,' Martin Sorrell Says." *Adweek*, April 18, 2016. http://www.adweek.com/news/advertising-branding/ad-industry-needs-get-used-low-growth-being-new-normal-martin-sorrell-says-170898

O'Neil-Hart, Celie, and Howard Blumenstein. "The Latest Video Trends: Where Your Audience Is Watching." *Think with Google*, April 2016. https://www.thinkwithgoogle.com/consumer-insights/video-trends-where-audience-watching/

Meeker, Mary. "Internet Trends 2014." Presentation given at Code Conference, Rancho Palos Verdes, CA, May 28, 2014. http://www.kpcb.com/blog/2014-internet-trends.

Berman, Saul J. "Digital Transformation: Opportunities to Create New Business Models." *Strategy& Leadership* 40, no. 2 (2012): 16–24.

Berman, Saul J., Bill Battino, Louisa Shipnuck, and Andreas Neus. "The End of Advertising as We Know It." In *Television Goes Digital*, edited by Darcy Gerbarg, 29–55. New York: Springer, 2009.

Guynn, Jessica. "Facebook Shares Surge on Strong Mobile Ad Growth." *USA Today*, April 27, 2016. http://www.usatoday.com/story/tech/news/2016/04/27/facebook-first-quarter-earnings-beat/83568522/

Kendall, Tim. "New Promoted Pin Options to Help You Reach Your Goals." *Pinterest Business* (blog), May 18, 2015. https://business.pinterest.com/en/blog/new-promoted-pin-options-help-you-reach-your-goals

Cohen, David. "Facebook Adds Video Creative to Carousel Ads." *Adweek*, October 23, 2015. http://www.adweek.com/digital/video-creative-carousel-ads/

Buhr, Sarah. "Former Hulu CEO Jason Killar's Vessel Launches to the Public." *Tech Crunch*, March 24, 2015. http://techcrunch.com/2015/03/24/former-hulu-ceo-jason-kilars-vessel-launches-to-the-public/

Sloane, Garrett. "Has Google Perfected the Retail Search Ad with Its Local Inventory Offering?" *Adweek*, March 19, 2015. http://www.adweek.com/news/technology/has-google-perfected-retail- search-ad-its-local-inventory-offering-163567

Halzack, Sarah. "Why the Social Media 'Buy Button' Is Still There, Even Though Most Never Use It." *Washington Post*, January 14, 2016. https://www.washingtonpost.com/news/business/wp/2016/01/14/why-the-social-media-buy-button-is-still-there-even-though-most-never-use-it/

Hasso Plattner Institute of Design at Stanford University. "About." https://dschool.stanford.edu/about/ (accessed August 26, 2017).

Cohen, Reuven. "Design Thinking: A Unified Framework for Innovation." *Forbes*, March 31, 2014. https://www.forbes.com/sites/reuvencohen/2014/03/31/design-thinking-a-unified-framework-for-innovation/#345923c08c11

Brown, Tim. "Design Thinking." *Harvard Business Review* 86, no. 6 (June 2008): 84–92.

Malhotra, Naresh K., ed. *Review of Marketing Research*. Vol. 10. Bingley: Emerald Group Publishing Limited, 2013.

Hu, Elise. "How Human-Centered Design Thinking Can Transform Community Media." *Knight Foundation* (blog), February 11, 2013. https://www.knightfoundation.org/articles/how-human-centered-design-thinking-can-transform-community-media

Saffer, Dan. *Designing for Interaction: Creating Smart Applications and Clever Devices*. Berkeley, CA: New Riders, 2007.

Boag, Paul. "All You Need to Know About Customer Journey Mapping." *Smashing Magazine*, January 15, 2015. https://www.smashingmagazine.com/2015/01/all-about-customer-journey-mapping/

Boag, Paul. "Customer Journey Mapping—The Secret to Digital Transformation." *Boagworld*, April 29, 2014. https://boagworld.com/usability/customer-journey-mapping/

Court, David, Dave Elzinga, Susan Mulder, and Ole Vetvik. "The Customer Decision Journey." *McKinsey Quarterly*, June 2009. http://www.mckinsey.com/business-functions/marketing-and-sales/our-insights/the-consumer-decision-journey

Edelman, David C., and Marc Singer. "Competing on Customer Journeys." *Harvard Business Review*, November 2015. https://hbr.org/2015/11/competing-on-customer-journeys

Freier, Anne. "More Fans Use Mobile Devices to Access Live Sports Content, but There's Room for Growth." *Business of Apps*, May 11, 2015. http://www.businessofapps.com/more-fans-use-mobile-devices-to-access-live-sports-content-but-theres-room-for-growth/

Svensson, Göran. "Vulnerability Scenarios in Marketing Channels." *Supply Chain Management: An International Journal* 7, no. 5 (December 2002): 322–333.

Banyte, J., R. Gudonaviciene, and D. Grubys. "Changes in Marketing Channels Formation." *Engineering Economics* 22, no. 3 (2011): 319–329.

Rosenbloom, Bert. *Marketing Channels*. Mason, OH: South-Western College Publishers, 2011.

Anderson, James C., James A. Narus, and Wouter van Rossum. "Customer Value Propositions in Business Markets." *Harvard Business Review* 84, no. 3 (March 2006): 90–99.

Barber, Felix, and Rainer Strack. "The Surprising Economics of a 'People Business.'" *Harvard Business Review* 83, no. 6 (June 2005): 80–90.

Bendapudi, Neeli, and Venkat Bendapudi. "Creating the Living Brand." *Harvard Business Review* 83, no. 5 (May 2005): 124–132.

Mascarenhas, Oswald A., Ram Kesavan, and Michael Bernacchi. "Customer Value-Chain Involvement for Co-Creating Customer Delight." *Journal of Consumer Marketing* 21, no. 7 (December 2004): 486–496.

Mascarenhas, Oswald A., Ram Kesavan, and Michael Bernacchi. "Lasting Customer Loyalty: A Total Customer Experience Approach." *Journal of Consumer Marketing* 23, no. 7 (December 2006): 397–405.

Shaw, Colin, and Ivens, John. *Building Great Customer Experiences*. New York: Palgrave Macmillan, 2002.

Sciarrino, JoAnn, and Prudente John. "She's Just Not That into You: The Mediating Impact of Brand Attachment on Digital Interactions." *Journal of Digital & Social Media Marketing* 4, no. 2 (Summer 2016): 157–169.

Thomson, Matthew, Deborah J. MacInnis, and C. Whan Park. "The Ties That Bind: Measuring the Strength of Consumers' Emotional Attachments to Brands." *Journal of Consumer Psychology* 15, no. 1 (2005): 77–91.

Battaglio, Stephen, and Paresh Dave. "NFL Chooses Twitter as a Streaming Partner for 'Thursday Night Football.'" *Los Angeles Times*, April 5, 2016. http://www.latimes.com/entertainment/envelope/cotown/la-et-ct-twitter-nfl-streaming-20160405-story.html

Case Study: NFL

Thompson, Derek. "How Superstar Economics Is Killing the NFL's Ratings." *Atlantic*, January 10, 2017. https://www.theatlantic.com/business/archive/2017/01/nfl-ratings/512624/

Chmielewski, Dawn C. "NFL Amps Up Its Digital Media, Launching a Fantasy Football Effort." *Los Angeles Times*, July 30, 2013. http://www.latimes.com/entertainment/envelope/cotown/la-fi-ct-nfl-digital-20130730-story.html

Lefton, Terry. "NFL Network Touts Its Never-Ending Season in Super Bowl Ad." *Street & Smith's Sports Business Journal*, January 26, 2009. http://m.sportsbusinessdaily.com/Journal/Issues/2009/01/20090126/Marketingsponsorship/NFL-Network-Touts-Its-Never-Ending-Season-In-Super-Bowl-Ad.aspx

Neisser, Drew. "Want a Branding Challenge? Try Marketing an NFL Team." *Fast Company*, July 23, 2012. http://www.fastcompany.com/1843230/want-branding-challenge-try-marketing-nfl-team

Badenhausen, Kurt. "The NFL Signs TV Deal Worth $27 Billion." *Forbes*, December 14, 2011. http://www.forbes.com/sites/kurtbadenhausen/2011/12/14/the-nfl-signs-tv-deals-worth-26-billion/

Futterman, Matthew, S. Schechner, and S. Vranica. "NFL: The League That Runs TV." *Wall Street Journal*, December 15, 2011. http://www.wsj.com/articles/SB10001424052970204026804577098774037075832

Abboud, Leila, and Elaine He. "Soccer Is Losing Its Grip on TV." *Bloomberg Gadfly*, January 16, 2017. https://www.bloomberg.com/gadfly/articles/2017-01-16/football-is-losing-its-grip-on-tv

"Fans Explain the NFL's Ratings Decline." *SI.com*. https://www.si.com/mmqb/2016/10/27/nfl-ratings-decline-football-fans-explain-viewership (accessed August 26, 2017).

"For the First Time, More Than Half of Americans Will Watch Streaming TV." *eMarketer*, February 3, 2016. https://www.emarketer.com/Article/First-Time-More-Than-Half-of-Americans-Will-Watch-Streaming-TV/1013543

Frankel, Daniel. "Sling TV Ended Q1 with 1.3M Subscribers, Dish Is Reportedly Telling Wall Street." *FierceCable*, April 28, 2017. http://www.fiercecable.com/online-video/sling-tv-ended-q1-1-3m-subs-dish-reportedly-telling-wall-street

Heath, Alex. "Twitter Lost Its Marquee Video Deal with the NFL to Amazon." *Business Insider*, April 4, 2017. http://www.businessinsider.com/amazon-beats-twitter-to-stream-nfl-thursday-night-football-with-50-million-bid-2017-4

McAlone, Nathan. "The NFL Season Is Over—But Its Ratings Problem Might Be Just Starting." *Business Insider*, February 6, 2017. http://www.businessinsider.com/nfl-ratings-down-for-2016-and-might-continue-to-slump-2017-2

McAlone, Nathan. "This Chart Shows How More and More Commercials Are Being Jammed into NFL Games." *Business Insider*, January 11, 2017. http://www.businessinsider.com/how-many-ads-are-in-nfl-games-chart-2017-1

McFarlane, Greg. "How the NFL Makes Money." *Investopedia*, June 25, 2015. http://www.investopedia.com/articles/personal-finance/062515/how-nfl-makes-money.asp

Reyes, Lorenzo. "NFL Exec Acknowledges Ratings Decline Goes beyond Interest in Election." *USA Today*, November 10, 2016. https://www.usatoday.com/story/sports/nfl/2016/11/10/declining-ratings-presidential-debates-commercials/93592374/

Sandomir, Richard. "As Olympic Viewership Falls, NBC Thinks of the Bigger Picture." *New York Times*, August 10, 2016. https://www.nytimes.com/2016/08/11/sports/olympics/tv-ratings-for-olympics-on-nbc-down-20-percent-from-london-games.html

Pallotta, Frank, and Brian Stelter. "Super Bowl 50 Audience Is Third Largest in TV History." *CNNMoney*, February 8, 2016. http://money.cnn.com/2016/02/08/media/super-bowl-50-ratings/index.html

Sports Media Watch. "The NFL TV Ratings Page." http://www.sportsmediawatch.com/nfl-tv-ratings-viewership-nbc-cbs-fox-espn-nfln-regular-season-playoffs/ (accessed August 26, 2017).

Thompson, Derek. "Which Sports Have the Whitest/Richest/Oldest Fans?" *Atlantic*, February 10, 2014. https://www.theatlantic.com/business/archive/2014/02/which-sports-have-the-whitest-richest-oldest-fans/283626/

Wagner, Kurt. "How the NFL Juggles the Future of Streaming, the Decline of TV, and Billions of Dollars." *Recode*, May 1, 2017. https://www.recode.net/2017/5/1/15386694/nfl-live-stream-amazon-prime-thursday-night-football-ratings

Groke, Nick. "Why the NFL's TV Ratings Crashed in 2016. And How They Might Rebound." *Denver Post*, December 4, 2016. http://www.denverpost.com/2016/12/04/nfl-tv-ratings-crashed-2016/

Battaglio, Stephen. "YouTube Now Bigger than TV among Advertisers' Target Audience." *Los Angeles Times*, May 5, 2016. http://www.latimes.com/entertainment/envelope/cotown/la-et-ct-you-tube-ad-spending-20160506-snap-story.html

Chapter 9 Competing in a Networked World

Contested Boundaries and Media Competition

Gray, Steve. "Mass Media Bubble Bursts, Leaving News Publishers Vulnerable." *INMA*, July 1, 2013. https://www.inma.org/blogs/disruptive-innovation/post.cfm/mass-media-bubble-bursts-leaving-news-publishers-vulnerable

Klinck, Stephen. "What Real AdMen Think of Mad Men." *Esquire*, April 4, 2013. https://www.esquire.com/entertainment/tv/a21451/mad-men-admen/

Gray, Steve. "End of Mass Media Era Means End of Mass-Media Business Model." *INMA*, July 2, 2013. http://www.inma.org/blogs/disruptive-innovation/post.cfm/end-of-mass-media-era-means-end-of-mass-media-business-model

Gray, Steve. "News is No Longer Enough to Support a Geography-Based Media Business Model." *INMA*, July 3, 2013. http://www.inma.org/blogs/disruptive-innovation/post.cfm/news-is-no-longer-enough-to-support-a-geography-based-media-business-model

Morris Communications, cited in Gray, Steve. "Transforming Our Business Models: How Local Media Companies Can Survive and Thrive." Presentation given at the Southern Newspaper Press Association Conference, Chapel Hill, NC, May 15, 2015.

Cassidy, John. "Me Media: How Hanging Out on the Internet Became Big Business." *New Yorker* 82, no. 13 (May 2006): 50–59.

Cvijikj, I., E. Spiegler, and F. Michahelles. "Evaluation Framework for Social Media Brand Presence." *Social Network Analysis and Mining* 3, no. 4 (January 2013): 1325–1349.

Pew Research Center. "State of the News Media 2015." April 29, 2015. http://assets. pewresearch.org/wp-content/uploads/sites/13/2017/05/30142603/state-of-the-news-media-report-2015-final.pdf

Alphabet. "Alphabet Investor Relations." https://abc.xyz/investor/ (accessed August 26, 2017).

Bond, Shannon. "Google and Facebook Build Digital Ad Duopoly." *Financial Times*, March 14, 2017. https://www.ft.com/content/30c81d12-08c8-11e7-97d1-5e720a26771b

Heath, Alex. "Facebook and Google Completely Dominate the Digital Ad Industry." *Business Insider*, April 26, 2017. http://www.businessinsider.com/facebook-and-google-dominate-ad-industry-with-a-combined-99-of-growth-2017-4

Helft, Miguel, and Tanzina Vega. "Retargeting Ads Follow Surfers to Other Sites." *New York Times*, August 29, 2010. https://www.nytimes.com/2010/08/30/technology/30adstalk.html

Ingram, Mathew. "Google and Facebook Account for Nearly All Growth in Digital Ads." *Fortune*, April 26, 2017. http://fortune.com/2017/04/26/google-facebook-digital-ads/

Ingram, Mathew. "Here's How Google and Facebook Have Taken Over the Digital Ad Industry." *Fortune*, January 4, 2017. http://fortune.com/2017/01/04/google-facebook-ad-industry/

"Facebook Reports Second Quarter 2017 Results." *PR Newswire*, July 26, 2017. http://www.prnewswire.com/news-releases/facebook-reports-second-quarter-2017-results-300494811.html

"Google, Facebook Increase Their Grip on Digital Ad Market." *eMarketer*, March 14, 2017. https://www.emarketer.com/Article/Google-Facebook-Increase-Their-Grip-on-Digital-Ad-Market/1015417.

Lee, Kai-Fu. "The Real Threat of Artificial Intelligence." *New York Times*, June 24, 2017. https://www.nytimes.com/2017/06/24/opinion/sunday/artificial-intelligence-economic-inequality.html

DeFleur, Melvin L., and Sandra J. Ball-Rokeach. *Theories of Mass Communication*. Fifth edition. New York: Longman, 1989.

Pauwels, Luc, and Patricia Hellriegel. "Strategic and Tactical Uses of Internet Design and Infrastructure: The Case of YouTube." *Journal of Visual Literacy* 28, no. 1 (March 2009): 51–69.

Kim, Yong-Chan, and Joo-Young Jung. "SNS Dependency and Interpersonal Storytelling: An Extension of Media System Dependency Theory." *New Media & Society* 19, no. 9 (September 2017): 1458–1475.

Ha, Louisa, Kisung Yoon, and Xiaoqun Zhang. "Consumption and Dependency of Social Network Sites as a News Medium: A Comparison Between College Students and General Population." *Journal of Communication and Media Research* 5, no. 1 (April 2013): 1–14.

Winkler, Rolfe. "As Google Builds Out Own Content, Some Advertisers Feel Pushed Aside." *Wall Street Journal*, August 18, 2014. http://www.wsj.com/articles/googles-richer-content-worries-some-advertisers-1408391392

Young, Alexa. *Frenemies*. New York: HarperCollins, 2008.

Blanding, Michael. "Why Apple and Amazon Choose to Be 'Frenemies.'" *Forbes*, August 3, 2015. https://www.forbes.com/sites/hbsworkingknowledge/2015/08/03/why-apple-and-amazon-choose-to-be-frenemies/#2e5432403483

Weir, Kirsten. "Fickle Friends: How to Deal with Frenemies." *Scientific American*, May 1, 2011. http://www.scientificamerican.com/article/fickle-friends/

Adner, Ron, Jianqing Chen, and Feng Zhu. "Frenemies in Platform Markets: The Case of Apple's iPad vs. Amazon's Kindle." Harvard Business School Working Paper 15–087. Boston: Harvard Business School Publishing, 2015.

Pew Research Center. "Digital News Fact Sheet." August 7, 2017. http://www.journalism.org/fact-sheet/digital-news/

"US Ad Spending: The eMarketer Forecast for 2017." *eMarketer Report*, March 15, 2017. https://www.emarketer.com/Report/US-Ad-Spending-eMarketer-Forecast-2017/2001998

Wattles, Jackie. "Facebook Hits One Billion Users in a Single Day." *CNNMoney*, August 28, 2015. http://money.cnn.com/2015/08/27/technology/facebook-one-billion-users-single-day/

LaFrance, Adrienne. "Facebook is Eating the Internet." *Atlantic*, April 29, 2015. http://www.theatlantic.com/technology/archive/2015/04/facebook-is-eating-the-internet/391766/

Mitchell, Amy, Jeffrey Gottfried, and Katerina Eva Matsa. "Facebook Top Source for Political News among Millennials." Pew Research Center (blog), June 1, 2015. http://www.journalism.org/2015/06/01/facebook-top-source-for-political-news-among-millennials/

New York Times Company. "Q1 2017 Earnings Conference Call." Transcript by Seeking Alpha. May 3, 2017. https://seekingalpha.com/article/4070320-new-york-times-nyt-ceo-mark-thompson-q1-2017-results-earnings-call-transcript

"Mobile Will Influence $1.4 Trillion in Offline Sales By 2021." *Forrester Research*, February 17, 2017. https://www.forrester.com/Mobile+Will+Influence+14+Trillion+In+Offline+Sales+By+2021/-/E-PRE9694

Bothun, Deborah, and Christopher A. H. Vollmer. "2016 Entertainment & Media Industry Trends." *Strategy&*, 2016. https://www.strategyand.pwc.com/trends/2016-entertainment-media-industry-trends

Ferriss, Timothy. *The 4-Hour Workweek: Escape 9-5, Live Anywhere, and Join the New Rich.* First revised edition. New York: Crown Publishers, 2009.

Rowling, J. K., and Mary GrandPré. *Harry Potter and the Sorcerer's Stone.* First American edition. New York: A.A. Levine Books, 1998.

Pulizzi, Joe. "How to Build Your Audience with Media Partnerships." *Content Marketing Institute* (blog), July 13, 2015. http://contentmarketinginstitute.com/content-inc/blog/media-partners/

Ellsberg, Michael. "The Tim Ferriss Effect: Lessons from My Successful Book Launch." *Forbes*, January 11, 2012. https://www.forbes.com/sites/michaelellsberg/2012/01/11/the-tim-ferriss-effect/#149e32d0363e

Holiday, Ryan. "How Tim Ferriss Became the 'Oprah of Audio'—Behind the Podcast with 70M-Plus Downloads." *Observer*, May 3, 2016. http://observer.com/2016/05/how-tim-ferriss-became-the-oprah-of-audio-behind-the-podcast-with-60m-downloads/

Hochman, Jonathan. "The Cost of Pay-Per-Click (PPC) Advertising—Trends and Analysis." *Hochman Consultants* (blog), November 24, 2015. https://www.hochmanconsultants.com/cost-of-ppc- advertising/

"Clustering." *Economist*, August 24, 2009. http://www.economist.com/node/14292202

Porter, Michael E. "Clusters and the New Economics of Competition." Harvard Business Review 76, no. 6 (November/December 1998): 77–90.

Emerson, Richard M. "Power-Dependence Relations." *American Sociological Review* 27, no. 1 (February 1962): 31–41.

Emerson, Richard M. "Social Exchange Theory." *Annual Review of Sociology* 2 (1976): 335–362.

Benner, Katie, and Emily Steel. "Virtual Reality Lures Media Companies to a New Frontier." *New York Times*, April 19, 2016. https://www.nytimes.com/2016/04/20/technology/virtual-reality-lures-media-companies-to-a-new-frontier.html?mcubz=3&_r=0

Hardy, Brian, Bob Hudson, and Eileen Waddington. *Assessing Strategic Partnership: The Partnership Assessment Tool*. London: Strategic Partnering Taskforce, 2003.

Berman, Saul J., Bill Battino, and Karen Feldman. "New Business Models for Emerging Media and Entertainment Revenue Opportunities." *Strategy& Leadership* 39, no. 3 (May 2011): 44–53.

Peek, Donna. "Evaluating and Selecting a Strategic Partner." *Kauffman Entrepreneurs* (blog), December 1, 2006. http://www.entrepreneurship.org/resource-center/evaluating-and-selecting-a-strategic-partner.aspx

Homans, George Caspar. *Social Behavior: Its Elementary Forms*. New York: Harcourt, Brace & World, 1961.

Jakob, Doreen. "Media Clusters: Spatial Agglomeration and Content Capabilities Edited by Charlie Karlsson and Robert G. Picard." *Journal of Regional Science* 52, no. 5 (December 2012): 888–889.

Case Study: *Sesame Street*

Malik Ducard, cited in Folkenflik, David. "Beyond 'Sesame Street': A New Sesame Studios Channel on YouTube." NPR, May 6, 2016. http://www.npr.org/2016/05/06/476913166/beyond-sesame-street-a-new-sesame-studios-channel-on-youtube

IBM. "Sesame Workshop and IBM Watson Team Up to Advance Early Childhood Education." April 27, 2016. https://www-03.ibm.com/press/us/en/pressrelease/49585.wss

Gorenstein, Colin. "Christina Hendricks Is 'Mad' about Technology in Her 'Sesame Street' Appearance." *Salon*, May 19, 2015. http://www.salon.com/2015/05/19/christina_hendricks_is_mad_about_technology_in_her_sesame_street_appearance/

Chapter 10 Investing in Key Assets and Capabilities

Identifying Assets and Prioritizing Investments

Altheide, David, and Robert Snow. *Media Logic*. Sage Library of Social Research 89. Beverly Hills, California: Sage Publications, 1979.

Altheide, D., and Snow. *Media Worlds in the Postjournalism Era*. Communication and Social Order. New York: Aldine de Gruyter, 1991.

Forrester Research. "The Social Technographics® Ladder." Forrester Research, Inc., 2017.

Leinwand, Paul, and Cesare Mainardi. *The Essential Advantage: How to Win with a Capabilities-Driven Strategy*. Boston: Harvard Business Review Press, 2011.

Curran, Chris, and Tom Puthiyamadam. "Winning with Digital Confidence." *strategy+business*, May 22, 2017. https://www.strategy-business.com/article/Winning-with-Digital-Confidence?gko=37c1d&utm_source=itw&utm_medium=20170530&utm_campaign=respB

Christensen, Clayton M., Taddy Hall, Karen Dillon, and David S. Duncan. *Competing Against Luck: The Story of Innovation and Customer Choice.* New York: HarperBusiness, 2016.

Bughin, Jacques, Laura LaBerge, and Anette Mellbye. "The Case for Digital Reinvention." *McKinsey Quarterly*, February 2017. http://www.mckinsey.com/business-functions/digital-mckinsey/our-insights/the-case-for-digital-reinvention

Foster, Richard, and Sarah Kaplan. *Creative Destruction: Why Companies that Are Built to Last Underperform the Market—And How to Successfully Transform Them.* New York: Doubleday, 2001.

Case Study: *theSkimm, Scalawag, Pilot* and *News Reporter*

High, Les. Editor of the Whiteville (NC) *News Reporter*, in discussion with authors, April 2017–August 2017.

Walker-Wells, Evan. Co-founder and publisher of *Scalawag* (Durham, NC), in discussion with authors, April 2017–August 2017.

Woronoff, David. Publisher of the *Pilot* (Southern Pines, NC), in discussion with authors, April 2017–August 2017.

theSkimm. "Who are theSkimms?" http://www.theskimm.com/about (accessed 10 April 2017).

Chafkin, Max. "How theSkimm Became a Must-Read for Millennials." *Bloomberg Businessweek*, November 2, 2016. https://www.bloomberg.com/news/articles/2016-11-02/how-the-skimm-became-a-must-read-for-millennials

Fortt, Jon. "Legacy of the Lemonade Stand: The Skimm's Founders Talk Creativity, Work Ethic and Sexism." *CNBC*, July 13, 2017. https://www.cnbc.com/2017/07/13/legacy-of-the-lemonade-stand-the-skimms-founders-talk-creativity-work-ethic-and-sexism.html

Cox, Ana Marie. "The Founders of theSkimm Think They're a Gateway Drug to the News." *New York Times Magazine*, April 26, 2017. https://www.nytimes.com/2017/04/26/magazine/the-founders-of-theskimm-think-theyre-a-gateway-drug-to-the-news.html?_r=0

Ha, Anthony. "The New York Times Invests in theSkimm." *TechCrunch*, September 26, 2017. https://techcrunch.com/2016/09/26/nyt-backs-theskimm/

Shontell, Alyson. "How 2 Roommates Got Shot Down by Hundreds of Startup Investors and Racked Up Credit-Card Debt—But Built a Newspaper Empire Anyway." *Business Insider*, April 21, 2017. http://www.businessinsider.com/how-carly-zakin-danielle-weisberg-founded-theskimm-podcast-interview-2017-4

Scalawag Magazine. "About Us." https://www.scalawagmagazine.org/about/ (accessed April 12, 2017).

Vitiello, Chris. "New Magazine 'Scalawag' Aims to Tell the South's Untold Stories." *Indy Week*, December 2, 2015. https://www.indyweek.com/indyweek/new-magazine-scalawag-aims-to-tell-the-souths-untold-stories/Content?oid=4922066

Walker-Wells, Evan. "Interview with Evan Walker-Wells." By Yemi Adewuyi. *Scalawag Magazine*, podcast audio, November 2, 2016. http://ajf.org/evan-walker-wells-scalawag-magazine/

Abernathy, Penelope Muse. "Chasing the Community Newspaper Rainbow: The *Whiteville News Reporter* and the Digital Age." Case Consortium @ Columbia CSJ-14-0055.0. New York: Columbia Center for Teaching and Learning, 2014.

Woronoff, David. "Launching a Digital Ad Agency." UNC Center for Innovation and Sustainability in Local Media YouTube video, 2:55. February 7, 2017. https://www.youtube.com/watch?v=r2BygQIJSNI

Nagy, John. "Seeking New Relationships: The Sway Can Be Our Way." *Pilot*, November 19, 2016. http://www.thepilot.com/opinion/seeking-new-relationships-the-sway-can-be-our-way/article_83732fb0-adc5-11e6-99a5-a79206c5dc47.html

Chapter 11 Entrepreneurial Leadership and Culture

Organizational Culture, Structure, and Leadership

Abernathy, Penelope M. *Saving Community Journalism: The Path to Profitability*. Chapel Hill, NC: University of North Carolina Press, 2014.

Katzenbach, Jon, and Paul Leinwand. *Culture Eats Strategy for Breakfast: Webinar. Strategy&*, March 31, 2015. https://www.strategyand.pwc.com/media/file/Katzenbach-Center_Webinar_Culture-Eats-Strategy-for-Breakfast.pdf

Schein, Edgar. *Organizational Culture and Leadership*. Fourth Edition. San Francisco: Jossey-Bass, 2010.

Treacy, Michael, and Fred Wiersema. *The Discipline of Market Leaders: Choose Your Customers, Narrow Your Focus, Dominate Your Market*. Reading, MA: Addison-Wesley Publishing Company, 1995.

Treacy, Michael, and Fred Wiersema. "Customer Intimacy and Other Value Disciplines." *Harvard Business Review* 71, no. 1 (January/February 1993): 84–93.

Giang, Vivian. "The Woman Who Created Netflix's Enviable Company Culture." *Fast Company*, February 2, 2016. http://www.fastcompany.com/3056187/the-future-of-work/the-woman-who-created-netflixs-enviable-company-culture

Heifetz, Ronald A., and Marty Linsky. *Leadership on the Line: Staying Alive through the Dangers of Leading*. Boston: Harvard Business School Press, 2002.

Miles, Raymond E., and Charles C. Snow. *Organizational Strategy, Structure, and Process*. New York: McGraw-Hill, 1978.

Gray, Steve. "Transforming Our Business Models: How Local Media Companies Can Survive and Thrive." Presentation at the Southern Newspaper Press Association Conference, Chapel Hill, NC, May 15, 2015.

Tushman, Michael L., and Charles O'Reilly, III. "The Ambidextrous Organizations: Managing Evolutionary and Revolutionary Change." *California Management Review* 38, no. 4 (Summer 1996): 8–30.

Jacquemont, David, Dana Maor, and Angelika Reich. (2015, April). "How to Beat the Transformation Odds." *McKinsey & Company*, April 2015. http://www.mckinsey.com/business-functions/organization/our-insights/how-to-beat-the-transformation-odds

Ravasi, Davide, and Majken Schultz. "Responding to Organizational Identity Threats: Exploring the Role of Organizational Culture." *Academy of Management Journal* 49, no. 3 (June 2006): 433–458.

Katzenbach, Jon R., and Douglas Smith. *The Wisdom of Teams: Creating the High-Performance Organization*. Boston: Harvard Business School Press, 1993.

Vickberg, Suzanne M. Johnson, and Kim Christfort. "Pioneers, Drivers, Integrators and Guardians." *Harvard Business Review*, March–April 2017. https://hbr.org/2017/03/the-new-science-of-team-chemistry#pioneers-drivers-integrators-and-guardians

Schaubroeck, Ruben, Felicita Holztejn Tarczewski, and Rob Theunissen. "Making Collaboration Across Functions a Reality." *McKinsey Quarterly*, March 2016. http://www.

mckinsey.com/business-functions/organization/our-insights/making-collaboration-across-functions-a-reality

Kotter, John. *Leading Change*. Boston: Harvard Business School Press, 1996.

Aiken, Carolyn B., and Scott P. Keller. "The CEO's Role in Leading Transformation." *McKinsey & Company*, February 2007. http://www.mckinsey.com/business-functions/organization/our-insights/the-ceos-role-in-leading-transformation

John Gosling, cited in Ratcliffe, Rebecca. "What's the Difference between Leadership and Management?" *Guardian*, July 29, 2013. https://www.theguardian.com/careers/difference-between-leadership-management

Watkins, Michael. "How Managers Become Leaders." *Harvard Business Review* 90, no. 6 (June 2012): 64–72.

Murphy, Clarke, and Tomas Charmorro-Premuzic. "C-suite Potential: Why the Best Executives Don't Play to Their Strengths." *Forbes*, March 27, 2017. https://www.forbes.com/sites/tomaspremuzic/2017/03/27/c-suite-potential-why-the-best-executives-dont-play-to-their-strengths/#6e003ee061cc

Russell Reynolds Associates. "Productive Disruptors: Five Characteristics that Differentiate Transformational Leaders." August 12, 2015. http://www.russellreynolds.com/insights/thought-leadership/productive-disruptors-five-characteristics-that-differentiate-transformational-leaders

Schwieters, Norbert, and Bob Moritz. "10 Principles for Leading the Next Industrial Revolution." *strategy+business*, March 23, 2017. https://www.strategy-business.com/article/10-Principles-for-Leading-the-Next-Industrial-Revolution?gko=f73d3&utm_source=itw&utm_medium=20170328&utm_campaign=resp

Case Study: Axel Springer

Pfanner, Eric. "European Newspapers find Creative Ways to Thrive in the Digital Age." *New York Times*, March 29, 2009. http://www.nytimes.com/2009/03/30/business/media/30paper.html

Eddy, Melissa. "Axel Springer's New Focus on Digital Draws Cries of Betrayal." *New York Times*, August 6, 2013. http://www.nytimes.com/2013/08/07/business/media/axel-springers-new-focus-on-digital-draws-cries-of-betrayal.html

Smale, Alison. "In Germany, Strong Words over Google's Power." *New York Times*, April 16, 2014. https://www.nytimes.com/2014/04/17/business/international/in-germany-strong-words-over-googles-power.html

Döpfner, Mathias. "Keynote Address by Mathias Döpfner, CEO of Axel Springer SE." *Deutsche Welle Global Media Forum* YouTube video, 32:43. Posted July 16, 2014. https://www.youtube.com/watch?v=NO2vJtpIQ3k

Pein, Corey. "Mathias Döpfner, Digital Counterrevolutionary." *Columbia Journalism Review*, November 20, 2014. http://archives.cjr.org/behind_the_news/mathias_dopfner_digital_counte.php

Somaiya, Ravi, and Nicola Clark. "Axel Springer to Acquire Controlling Stake in Business Insider." *New York Times*, September 29, 2015. https://www.nytimes.com/2015/09/30/business/media/axel-springer-to-acquire-controlling-stake-in-business-insider.html

Ingram, Mathew. "Who Is Axel Springer?" *Fortune*, October 1, 2015. http://fortune.com/2015/10/01/who-is-axel-springer/

Jervell, Ellen Emmerentze. "Axel Springer Sets Lofty Goals in U.S." *Wall Street Journal*, May 11, 2016. https://www.wsj.com/articles/axel-springer-looks-to-u-s-for-digital-growth-1462973407

Clark, Nicola. "An Old Media Empire, Axel Springer Reboots for the Digital Age." *New York Times*, December 20, 2015. https://www.nytimes.com/2015/12/21/business/media/an-old-media-empireaxel-springer-reboots-for-the-digital-age.html?_r=0

Burgelman, Robert A., Robert Siegel, and Ryan Kissick. "Axel Springer in 2016: From Transformation to Acceleration?" Case. No. E610. Stanford: Stanford Business School, 2016.

Axel Springer. "Official Website." http://www.axelspringer.de/en/ (accessed May 10, 2017).

Bloomberg. "Mathias Dopfner." https://www.bloomberg.com/profiles/people/3171011-mathias-dopfner (accessed August 24, 2017).

Chapter 12 What the Future Holds

State of the Media and the Future of Media

Bughin, Jacques, Laura LaBerge, and Anette Mellbye. "The Case for Digital Reinvention." *McKinsey Quarterly*, February 2017. http://www.mckinsey.com/business-functions/digital-mckinsey/our-insights/the-case-for-digital-reinvention?cid=reinventing-eml-alt-mkq-mck-oth-1703

Lederer, Chris, and Megan Brownlow. "A World of Differences." *strategy+business*, June 7, 2016. https://www.strategy-business.com/article/A-World-of-Differences?gko=895c8

Curran, Chris, and Tom Puthiyamadam. "Winning with Digital Confidence." *strategy+business*, May 22, 2017. https://www.strategy-business.com/article/Winning-with-Digital-Confidence?gko=37c1d&utm_source=itw&utm_medium=20170530&utm_campaign=respB

Rosenstiel, Tom. "Newspaper Journalism in the Digital Era of Distraction." Presentation given at the 129th Annual Meeting of Inland Press Association, Chicago, IL, October 20, 2014. http://www.inlandpress.org/stories/download-presentations-from-inlands-129th-annual-meeting-oct-19-21,1011

Pew Research Center. "Previous State of the News Media Reports." http://www.journalism.org/2017/06/01/archived-state-of-the-news-media-reports/. See esp. reports for 2013-2016 (accessed August 26, 2017).

Pew Research Center. "State of the News Media." http://www.pewresearch.org/topics/state-of-the-news-media/. (accessed August 26, 2017).

Jones, Alex. *Losing the News: The Future of the News That Feeds Democracy*. Oxford: Oxford University Press, 2009.

Hamilton, James T. *Democracy's Detectives: The Economics of Investigative Journalism*. Cambridge, MA: Harvard University Press, 2016.

Abernathy, Penelope Muse. *The Rise of a New Media Baron and the Emerging Threat of News Deserts*. Chapel Hill, NC: Center for Innovation and Sustainability in Local Media, University of North Carolina at Chapel Hill/University of North Carolina at Chapel Hill School of Media and Journalism, 2016. http://newspaperownership.com/newspaper-ownership-report/

Waldman, Steven, and the Working Group on Information Needs of Communities. *The Information Needs of Communities: The Changing Media Landscape in a Broadband Age*. Washington, DC: Federal Communications Commission, 2011. https://transition.fcc.gov/osp/inc-report/The_Information_Needs_of_Communities.pdf

Knight Foundation, cited in Frier, Sarah, and Aki Ito. "How Fake News Blew Up into a Political Crisis for Facebook." *Bloomberg*, November 22, 2016. https://www.bloomberg.com/news/articles/2016-11-22/how-fake-news-blew-up-into-a-political-crisis-for-facebook

Deighton, John, and Leora Kornfeld. "Amazon, Apple, Facebook and Google." Harvard Business School Case 513-060. Boston: Harvard Business School Publishing, 2013.

Taplin, Jonathan. "Is it Time to Break Up Google?" *New York Times*, April 22, 2017. https://www.nytimes.com/2017/04/22/opinion/sunday/is-it-time-to-break-up-google.html?mcubz=0

Taplin, Jonathan. "Can the Tech Giants be Stopped?" *Wall Street Journal*, July 14, 2017. https://www.wsj.com/articles/can-the-tech-giants-be-stopped-1500057243

EY Beacon Institute. *How Can Purpose Reveal a Path Through Disruption? Mapping the Journey from Rhetoric to Reality*. EYGM Limited, 2017.

Schielsel Seth. "Video Games: A 1947 Mystery that Matters Now." *New York Times*, May 16, 2011. http://www.nytimes.com/2011/05/17/arts/video-games/la-noire-by-rockstar-games-review.html

Meeker, Mary. "Internet Trends 2017." Presentation given at Code Conference, Rancho Palos Verdes, CA, May 31, 2017. http://www.kpcb.com/internet-trends

Kurweil, Ray. *The Singularity is Near: When Humans Transcend Biology*. New York: Viking Press, 2005.

Satell, Greg. "3 Reasons to Believe the Singularity is Near." *Forbes*, June 3, 2016. https://www.forbes.com/sites/gregsatell/2016/06/03/3-reasons-to-believe-the-singularity-is-near/#1ec159777b39

Kelly, Kevin. *The Inevitable: Understanding the 12 Technological Forces That Will Shape Our Future*. New York: Viking Press, 2016.

Rao, Anand. "A Strategist's Guide to Artificial Intelligence." *strategy+business*, May 10, 2017. https://www.strategy-business.com/article/A-Strategists-Guide-to-Artificial-Intelligence?gko=0abb5

Tapscott, Don. "How the Blockchain Is Changing Money and Business." Filmed June 2016. TED video, 18:49. https://www.ted.com/talks/don_tapscott_how_the_blockchain_is_changing_money_and_business/transcript

Schwab, Klaus. "The Fourth Industrial Revolution: What It Means and How to Respond." *Foreign Affairs*, December 12, 2015. https://www.foreignaffairs.com/articles/2015-12-12/fourth-industrial-revolution

The Dynamics of Start-Ups

CB Insights, cited in Gage, Deborah. "The Venture Capital Secret: 3 Out of 4 Start-ups Fail." *Wall Street Journal*, September 20, 2012. https://www.wsj.com/articles/SB10000872396390443720204578004980476429190.

Roberts, Michael J., and Lauren Barley. "How Venture Capitalists Evaluate Potential Venture Opportunities." Harvard Business School Case 805-019. Boston: Harvard Business School Publishing, 2004.

Griffith, Erin. "Why Start-ups Fail According to their Founders." *Fortune*, September 25, 2014. http://fortune.com/2014/09/25/why-startups-fail-according-to-their-founders/.

Blank, Steve. "Why the Lean Start-up Changes Everything." *Harvard Business Review* 91, no. 5 (May 2013): 63–72.

Gilbert, Clark G., and Matthew J. Eyring. "Beating the Odds When You Launch a New Venture." *Harvard Business Review* 88, no. 5 (May 2010): 92–98.

Mullins, John. "VC Funding Can be Bad for Your Start-up." *Harvard Business Review*, August 4, 2014. https://hbr.org/2014/08/vc-funding-can-be-bad-for-your-start-up.

Forrest, Conner. "The Dark Side of Venture Capital: Five Things Startups Need to Know." *TechRepublic*, March 10, 2014. http://www.techrepublic.com/article/the-dark-side-of-venture-capital-five-things-startups-need-to-know/.

Marcum, Tanya, and Eden Blair. "Entrepreneurial Decisions and Legal Issues in Early Venture Stages: Advice that Shouldn't Be Ignored." *Business Horizons* 54, no. 2 (March–April 2011): 143–152.

Wasserman, Noam. "Assembling the Startup Team." Harvard Business School Background Note 812–122. Boston: Harvard Business School Publishing, 2012.

Dow Jones Venture Source, as cited in Kelley, Donna, Slavica Slinger, and Mike Herrington. *Global Entrepreneurship Monitor: 2015/16 report.* Global Entrepreneurship Research Association, 2016. Published in Association with Babson College. http://gemconsortium.org/report/49480.

Professor Shikhar Ghosh, cited in Nobel, Carmen. "Why Companies Fail and How Their Founders Can Bounce Back." *Working Knowledge: Business Research for Business Leaders* (blog), Harvard Business School, March 7, 2011. http://hbswk.hbs.edu/item/why-companies-failand-how-their-founders-can-bounce-back.

Meisler, Laurie, Mira Rojanasakul, and Jeremy Scott Diamond. "Who Gets Venture Capital Funding?" *Bloomberg*, May 25, 2016. https://www.bloomberg.com/graphics/2016-who-gets-vc-funding/.

Toby Haas, cited in Brown, Eliot. "In Silicon Valley, the Big Venture Funds Keep Getting Bigger." *Wall Street Journal*, July 25, 2017. https://www.wsj.com/articles/in-silicon-valley-the-big-venture-funds-keep-getting-bigger-1501002000.

Index

Page numbers appearing in italics refer to figures. Page numbers appearing in bold refer to tables.

The Strategic Digital Media Entrepreneur, First Edition. Penelope Muse Abernathy and JoAnn Sciarrino.
© 2019 John Wiley & Sons, Inc. Published 2019 by John Wiley & Sons, Inc.
Companion website: www.wiley.com/go/abernathy/StrategicDigitalMediaEntrepreneur